INVESTIGATIVE REPORTING

from premise to publication

BIG STORY · BUILDING THE BIG STORY ·

Marcy Burstiner

HUMBOLDT STATE UNIVERSITY

HOLCOMB HATHAWAY, PUBLISHERS

Scottsdale, Arizona 85250

Library of Congress Cataloging-in-Publication Data

Burstiner, Marcy.
   Investigative reporting from premise to publication : building the big
story / Marcy Burstiner.
       p. cm.
   ISBN 978-1-890871-91-8
1. Investigative reporting.   I. Title.
   PN4781.B785 2009
   070.4'3—dc22

                                                        2009016585

This book is dedicated . . .

to the memory of my mother, Selma Zitron,
who encouraged me to ask questions and seek answers;

to my little girl, who always asks why;

to my husband, for his constant belief in my abilities;

and to my students in JMC 326, who teach me.

Holcomb Hathaway, Publishers, Inc.
6207 North Cattletrack Rd.
Scottsdale, Arizona 85250
480-991-7881
www.hh-pub.com

10 9 8 7 6 5 4 3 2 1

ISBN 978-1-890871-91-8

Printed in the United States of America.

C O N T E N T S

4

REQUESTING PUBLIC RECORDS   63

5

THE GAME PLAN   81

PART II   Gathering Information   117

6

THE INTERVIEW PROCESS   119

7

ANALYZING THE BIG STORY   153

8

DOCUMENTING THE STORY   175

12

LEGAL AND ETHICAL CONSIDERATIONS   267

13

ADVANCED REPORTING METHODS   291

14

PITCHING THE STORY   317

APPENDICES   331

A   Sample Investigative Stories   332

B   The Game Plan Checklist   367

C   An Excel Cheat Sheet   370

Please note: The author and publisher have made every effort to provide current website addresses in this book. However, because web addresses change constantly, it is inevitable that some of the URLs listed here will change following publication of this book.

"NOW THAT'S A STORY SOMEONE SHOULD DO . . . "

The term "investigative reporter" scares some people. It worries people who think the reporter will put them in a hot seat and blame them for something terrible. Sometimes it also frightens other reporters, to whom the term may imply a covert and cold-hearted reporter who will stop at nothing to get a story. What I discovered was that any reporter can do investigative reporting.

Although in college I was the editor of my campus newspaper, I decided I would not be a journalist upon graduation. I didn't think I had the thick skin I assumed all reporters needed. When I subsequently went to work for Ralph Nader, I realized that I *did* want to be a reporter, but after hearing famed investigative reporter Seymour Hersh speak about investigating the CIA, layer by layer, I decided that I wasn't an *investigative* reporter. It was decades later, after reporting for daily newspapers, a weekly newspaper and an online publication, and after editing a business magazine, that I learned I. F. Stone, one of the great investigative journalists of the 20th century, never considered himself an investigative reporter at all. Only when I joined Investigative Reporters and Editors, Inc. (IRE) and saw all the great reporting done on smaller topics — local governments, school systems, congressional campaign finance — did I realize I'd been doing investigative reporting all along. Like Stone, I was just doing what I thought I needed to be done: I simply asked the questions that needed to be asked. Shouldn't every reporter do that?

So, what, if anything, sets "investigative reporters" apart from those who don't carry that label? One fundamental characteristic distinguishes reporters such as Seymour Hersh and I. F. Stone: they are methodical. They start with a question or a set of questions, and they ask it again and again and read through every relevant document they can find, until their questions have been answered.

I think most aspiring reporters have questions in their heads they know are worth investigating. But they may push them aside, because they don't know how to go about getting those questions answered and because they lack a system for carrying out an investigation over a long period of time. Too often among a group of reporters someone makes the comment, "That's a story someone should do" — but doesn't follow through.

It is my belief that any good investigative reporter must follow what I. F. Stone practiced: You take a question that few people seem to be asking, one that cannot be answered without considerable reporting and analysis, and methodically get the question answered.

Investigative Reporting from Premise to Publication shows reporters how to apply a methodical approach to their stories. It teaches skills that will get their questions answered and stories written. This book explains how to conduct an investigation in an organized manner that allows for careful analysis, prevents stories from breaking down and leads to publication.

THE INVESTIGATIVE STORY

This book looks at investigative or "big project" journalism, a term often used for a story or a series of stories that takes time to report and requires substantial space in a publication. Although methodology and organization are useful tools for all good reporting, they are essential in investigative reporting — in both the information-gathering and the story writing process. These stories often require a number of components: interviews with many different people, document discovery, data analysis, connections between complicated patterns and explanation of confusing contradictions. Readers will learn how to do all of these steps by carrying out one big story in the process of using this text.

This book focuses on the big story because when it is done right, the big story commands attention and spurs action. Consider that in 1905, it was an investigation by the Chicago Tribune into deaths and injuries at college football games that led to the creation of the Inter-Collegiate Athletic Association, which evolved into the NCAA.[1] And that in 1971, it was Associated Press reporter Jean Heller who exposed a 40-year study conducted by the U.S. Public Health Service on black men in Tuskeegee, Ala., in which doctors withheld penicillin from syphilis patients. After the story's publication, the government launched an investigation, and the surviving patients sued and won from the government a $10 million settlement.[2] And it was an investigation into the treatment of injured U. S. soldiers at Walter Reed Army Medical Center by Washington Post reporters Dana Priest and Anne Hull in 2007 that forced the army to pour resources into programs geared to helping returning vets.

Between 2006 and 2008 I gave several seminars to students at college journalism conferences in California. Whenever my focus was on investigative journalism, students packed the session, and many of them asked me for information they could take back to their student newspapers. Young journalists are eager to do investigative reporting, if only someone will show them how.

HOW THIS BOOK IS ORGANIZED

Investigative Reporting from Premise to Publication is organized in three parts that parallel the investigative process. The first part discusses how to find stories, plan an investigation, decide on multimedia content and do preliminary research. The second part covers the information-gathering process, including doing interviews and finding documents and data. The third part concentrates on the writing process and on more advanced reporting techniques: how to outline the story, how to find a narrative thread, how to use computer-assisted reporting, how to avoid legal and ethical problems and how to pitch an investigative project to an editor.

Within the parts, most chapters introduce and explain an individual step in the process of carrying out an investigative project. This step-by-step approach is what I call the Game Plan, and it includes the following:

- Develop a story premise (Chapter 3)
- Gather the data (Chapters 6, 8 and 9)
- Analyze the information gathered (Chapters 6, 8 and 9)
- Outline the story (Chapter 10)
- Draft the story (Chapter 11)
- Verify the information (Chapters 11 and 12)
- Publish the story (Chapters 11 and 14)

This plan presumes that the reader has little experience with investigative reporting. He or she may be coming straight out of a beginning reporting class, or may have worked professionally but only on deadline reporting, reactive news stories or light features. Investigative reporting is a step beyond beginning reporting. It requires a high level of critical thinking, patience, persistence and long-term focus, qualities that are emphasized throughout the book.

Chapter-end exercises will help readers put ideas into practice and develop investigative reporting abilities. Each chapter also asks readers to complete the next steps of "The Big Story Project," a series of tasks designed to guide the readers' own investigations. The process will work for both team projects and solo projects.

Throughout the book I have included examples of published stories and tips from investigative reporters from news organizations across the country. I believe that readers will benefit from hearing the voices of their peers, so the text also includes examples of successful investigative journalism by students from campuses across the country.

Investigative Reporting from Premise to Publication includes references to the abundant tools and information available on the Internet. Of course, because new ones emerge all the time, the suggestions found here are just examples. Readers will find others (and perhaps better ones!) as they work. My goal is to show how to incorporate ever-changing technology into the information-gathering and analyzing processes and how to use new tools to tell and present stories in new ways.

This book also demonstrates the benefits of using a spreadsheet program in information gathering and during analysis. Spreadsheets are one of the most useful and basic tools an investigative reporter relies on. My examples and walk-throughs use Microsoft Excel, but the information applies to other spreadsheet programs, as well. For those who don't feel comfortable working with a spreadsheet program, the book is designed in such a way that spreadsheet use can be eliminated from the project.

The book ends with several helpful appendices. Appendix A includes complete sample stories based on successful investigations, including eight conducted by journalism students from across the country. Appendix B provides a Game Plan Checklist for quick reference. Appendix C presents a short primer on the basic functions of Excel for readers who are new to the program.

An instructor's manual and PowerPoint presentation are available to instructors who adopt this book. In addition a student Web site has been created at **http://BigStory.hh-pub.com**. Refer your students to page xv, "To the Student," for information about the web site and other book features.

HOW TO USE THIS BOOK

I like cookbooks. I like nothing better than to spend a lazy day at my stove, tossing ingredients from my refrigerator, little by little, into a big pot, and tasting the stew as the flavors simmer and blend throughout the day. I almost never follow a recipe to the teaspoon. Instead, I imagine the final creation and set that as my goal. Then I consider the ingredients, the proportions and the method of preparation as general guidelines. They help me decide what to throw into the pot and the steps I will need to take in order to produce the result I envision. I use cookbooks in the way I hope this book will be used: as a guidebook that will demonstrate how to build something creative, useful and significant.

To help readers build their own creative, useful and significant projects, the book encourages readers to come up with their own story ideas. It demonstrates ways to find stories, but does not dictate what story to do. It presents an overall strategy that will be useful regardless whether the investigation looks at the educational system, sports organizations, the environment, government or corporate shenanigans, police conduct or some other topic.

This book's step-by-step approach teaches not only how to find an investigative story idea and how to do investigative reporting, but what to do with the resulting information. There is little point in spending time on a story that doesn't get published. Not all investigative stories result in action, but one thing is certain — an unpublished investigation won't spur reader action or political change.

Too often, published investigative stories are poorly organized, tedious to read, or both. In trying to make sense of the various points and data, reporters sometimes sacrifice clarity and readability, even though these qualities are as essential in good journalism as accuracy and balance. This book shows reporters how to keep stories on track and how to produce results that will interest and enlighten an audience.

THE TIME IS RIGHT

 n the last day of 2008, New York Times editorial writer Maura Casey warned: "If the power of journalism is measured by its ability to spark anxiety in government officials, it's hard to imagine a more relaxing time to hold public office." Her editorial discussed the death of two local newspapers in Connecticut: The Herald of New Britain and The Bristol Press. The owner of those dailies also had its 13 weekly papers on the sales block; it would shut those down as well, if a buyer didn't emerge. Casey worries that the death of some local newspapers and cuts at others will put the watchdog function served by journalism at risk. Without it, corruption will thrive.[3]

All around the country, news organizations — television and radio included — have slashed staffs, laying off reporters and editors and offering buyouts to others. With these gloomy reports, it would seem to be a bad time to go into journalism and into a type of journalism that requires such dedication as investigative reporting. But the need for quality reporting does not disappear. Regardless of whether citizens learn about problems in the pages of a newspaper delivered to their driveway, from articles they collect as RSS feeds on their computer or as video they stream, they still need to be informed about the problems around them and they still need help in understanding an increasingly complex world. In terms of journalism education, that simply means that reporters must learn how to gear their reporting for new media.

What about the need for investigative reporting in particular? In 2006, George Washington University Professor Mark Feldstein argued that investigative reporting goes through cycles: At some points in our history, journalists produce story after story, digging up and exposing political and economic wrongdoings. At other times, it seems that the investigative reporter is part of a very small and lonely group. Feldstein argues that this ebb and flow is natural, and that a "more docile journalism" tends to prevail unless political, economic and social turmoil intersects with the emergence of new technologies and journalistic competition supported by a tolerant legal climate.[4]

If you look at what is happening around us, you will see that we are facing the very conditions that Feldstein says produce the greatest supply of and demand for investigative reporting. It is indeed a time when political, economic, and social challenges intersect with technological change and increased competition. The Internet gives journalists all kinds of new tools to help them gather information, analyze it in new ways and distribute their stories to both wider and more targeted audiences than was possible before. At the same time, the Internet offers an unprecedented choice of content and is thus causing intense competition for readers and viewers. In order to gain attention, news organizations will have to produce and publish information that is creative, original and relevant to people's lives.

This book is intended to nurture the investigative journalist inside every beginning reporter. It demonstrates that investigative reporting is not a mysterious process; instead, it is a systematic method for satisfying a reporter's natural curiosity in a way that results in a publishable story or series of stories that matters. With this book, I hope to enable budding reporters to realize their potential.

ACKNOWLEDGMENTS

I began this book as a method for teaching investigative reporting that involved a five-stage interviewing process. It evolved into much more only with the tremendous help of journalists throughout the country. In particular, I relied on information compiled by Investigative Reporters & Editors, Inc., the National Institute for Computer Assisted Reporting, the Reporter's Committee for the Freedom of the Press, the National First Amendment Coalition, the Sunlight Foundation, the Poynter Institute, the Dart Center for Journalism and Trauma, and the Student Press Law Center.

Journalists to whom I give special thanks include Eden Laiken, Dawn MacKeen, Bob Butler, Myron Levin, Mindy McAdams, Scott Reeder, Eric Nalder, Howard Rosenberg, Geanne Rosenberg, Bruce Shapiro, David Dietz, Joe Demma, Sarah Cohen, Maud Beelman, Suzanne McBride, David Donald, J. David McSwane, Mary Shanklin, Ziva Branstetter, Frank LoMonte, Charles Davis, Jacqueline McLean, Pat Simms, Asra Nomani, Gary Craig, Julie Schmit, Hank Sims, George Papajohn, Morton Mintz, Matt Waite, Douglas Pardue, Barbara Feinman Todd, Christine Young, Tisha Thompson, Oliver Symonds and Thadeus Greenson.

My sincere thanks to the following reviewers, who read earlier versions of this book and offered their constructive suggestions to help me improve it: Matthew Baker, The University of Utah; Mary Alice Basconi, East Tennessee State University; Fred Bayles, Boston University; Jeff Boone, Angelo State University; Don Corrigan, Webster University; Yvonne Daley, San Francisco State University; Stephen Doig, Arizona State University; Allison Barlow Hess, Weber State University; Barry Hollander, The University of Georgia; Rachele Kanigel, San Francisco State University; Maria Marron, Central Michigan University; Hugh J. Martin, University of Georgia; Rachel Mersey, University of Minnesota; Louise F. Montgomery, University of Arkansas; James Mueller, University of North Texas; David Poulson, Michigan State University; Bob Rawitch, Winner & Associates; Michael Sweeney, Utah State University; Frank Thayer, New Mexico State University; and Chris Warden, Troy University.

I want to thank Lauren Miller and Colette Kelly of Holcomb Hathaway, Publishers, for encouraging me and supporting me at every step in the process. Finally, thank you to Mark Larson at Humboldt State University for his belief in me when, in 2004, he assigned to me my first class on investigative reporting, though I was a journalist and not a teacher at the time.

Notes

1. Judith Serrin and William Serrin. *Muckracking!: The Journalism that Changed America.* New Press, 2002, p. 203.
2. Ibid., pp. 63–65.
3. Maura Casey. "When the Watchdogs Don't Bark." *The New York Times,* Dec. 30, 2008.
4. Mark Feldstein. "A Muckraking Model Investigative Reporting Cycles in American History." *The Harvard International Journal of Press/Politics, 11* (2) 2006, pp. 105–120.

Here is a little information about the book, to get you started.

Building a Story

Each chapter in this book ends with exercises and a feature called "The Big Story Project." The exercises help you apply and review chapter content, while The Big Story Project, in Steps 1–13, will help you initiate and follow through on an investigative story of your own. The Big Story Project steps are intended to be followed in order, though you or your instructor may modify steps or add more steps, according to the needs of your class. Using The Big Story Steps, you should be able to build your own investigative story, from premise to publication.

Appendices

The text includes three practical appendices:

- **Appendix A, "Sample Investigative Stories,"** includes nine previously published stories. Eight of these stories were written by students, proving that excellent investigative reporting can be done from the very beginning of your career. As you read through the text itself, you will come across cross-references to these stories, and reading the full text of each story will allow you to see how each example works within the larger piece.

- **Appendix B, "The Game Plan Checklist,"** will help keep you on track and ensure that you have been thorough in preparing your story. While you may develop your own plan of action over time, this checklist will provide a starting foundation for your investigation.

- **Appendix C, "An Excel Cheat Sheet,"** offers a quick rundown of how to make the spreadsheet program work efficiently for your reporting and writing needs. It reviews basic formatting and formulas and will help you move beyond simply entering text into cells. I focus on Microsoft's Excel because it is the most widely used such program, but other spreadsheets will also work. Open source programs such as OpenOffice's Calc are very close in format, and most of the cheat sheet information also applies to such programs.

Student Web Site

We've created a Web site to accompany *Investigative Reporting from Premise to Publication* to provide additional resources for your investigative stories. On the site, you'll find all of the book's WWW sites, for easy linking, as well as additional online resources. The student site also includes Steps 1–13 of "The Big Story Project." Finally, you may access many of the book's checklists and other art, including the spreadsheets and data used in Chapter 10, for your reference and practice.

You'll find the site at **http://BigStory.hh-pub.com**.

Getting Started

P A R T   O N E

1

Introduction

CHAPTER PREVIEW In this chapter, you will find answers to the following questions: What is investigative reporting, and how does it differ from other types of news coverage? What qualities make a reporter investigative? How has the Internet presented investigative reporters with new challenges while giving them exciting new opportunities to gather information, find sources and tell the story?

1

C H A P T E R

WHAT IS INVESTIGATIVE REPORTING?

L ouise Kiernan, a Pulitzer Prize-winning editor for the Chicago Tribune, once wrote that when people would ask her whether she was an investigative reporter, she never knew how to answer. "Categorizing journalism is in part why many investigative stories are dull, feature stories can be superficial, and explanatory stories explain so little," she wrote. "For complicated stories we need to combine all three."[1]

In the 1930s, a young reporter for the San Francisco News named John Steinbeck went to migrant camps in California to cover the immigration of people driven out of Oklahoma when dust storms ruined their farms. He documented massive starvation and desperation. He is now known as one of our nation's greatest novelists, but at the time he was an investigative reporter.[2]

In 1972, two beat reporters at the Washington Post broke a series of stories that would become known as Watergate. Bob Woodward, a young reporter on the Metro desk, was assigned a fairly routine court story. You didn't need to be an investigative reporter to smell something fishy about five well-dressed men caught breaking into the Democratic National Committee headquarters with electronic equipment and $2,300 in cash, especially after one identified himself as ex-CIA.[3] But the reporting on the story by Woodward and his colleague Carl Bernstein would lead to the resignation of President Richard Nixon and spur a generation of young journalists to follow in their footsteps as investigative reporters.

In 2007, after the University of Washington complained to police about convicted sex offenders living near the campus, the state relocated 13 of them. That prompted University of Oregon student Whitney Malkin to wonder about the people living near her school. In 2007, she checked a state database of sex offenders and found five of them living in one building one block from campus. She found 20 more living in the area. Why so many? Because, she discovered, Oregon law prohibited sex offenders from living near schools, playgrounds and day-care centers. That made many areas in the state off-limits to them. But they were free to live near universities. The story she wrote, published in the Register-Guard newspaper, was a great example of investigative reporting. She started with a question: How many sex offenders live near my campus? The answer she found identified an immediate problem in her local area and exposed a larger issue: The failure of state law to adequately address a threat to the safety of a vulnerable segment of the population. You can read her story in full, in Appendix A.1 of this book.[4]

So what is investigative reporting? You might think that it entails working on one story for months and months at a time. Or that it requires you to squeeze information from people who don't want to give it. You might think that to be considered investigative reporting your story must lead to the resignation of a politician, the arrest of a crook, the passage of a new law or the winning of the Pulitzer Prize. There is the image of someone who pours through stacks of secret documents to uncover political corruption and financial mismanagement. In movies, the investigative reporter holds conversations in a hushed voice over the phone and meets with a whistle-blower in a dark underground garage. But most investigative reporters don't fit the movie image. Many carry no special title at all. Many newspapers, magazines, television stations, Internet publications and radio stations do investigative reporting even though they have no "investigative reporters" or "investigative team" on staff.

Investigative Reporters and Editors, Inc., an organization of some 900 journalists and journalism educators, defines *investigative reporting* as "the reporting, through one's own initiative and work product, of matters of importance to readers, viewers or listeners. In many cases, the subjects of the reporting wish the matters under scrutiny to remain undisclosed." To win an award in IRE's annual contest, a submission must "uncover facts that someone or some agency may have tried to keep from public scrutiny."[5]

But not everyone believes that investigative reporting requires uncovering secrets. Five-time Pulitzer Prize-winner Jonathan Neumann once argued that 90 percent of all major investigations are done on stories that are already known. He reasoned that you can't keep secret something that affects people, because surely the people affected would know it is happening to them. "If [the stories] weren't known, they couldn't be very good stories. They wouldn't affect anyone," he said.[6]

Often it is the wider ramifications, the seriousness of an action, or the failure to act that is secret and needs to be uncovered. One or two people might know that they are being harmed, for example, but they don't know that they are two of hundreds. Or hundreds might know that they are drinking polluted water, but they don't know that drinking the water will give them cancer.

Other times it is something that many people know but haven't been able to document or prove. What is secret that needs to be uncovered are the documents and proof, what we call *the smoking gun*. As an example, consider stories that New York newspapers do from time to time that uncover organized crime connections in the construction industry. The Mafia has a long history of involvement in the construction industry in New York. But those connections are difficult to document, and stories that seek to document and prove the criminal connections are valid investigative stories.

For the purpose of this book, we will define *investigative journalism* as the reporting of important stories that start with a question and involve systematically gathering and analyzing information until that question is answered. In getting those answers, investigative reporters expose a problem, explain the reasons for it and propose ways to solve the problem or rectify the situation.

CHARACTERISTICS OF INVESTIGATIVE STORIES

You will find investigative stories in odd places. In a 2004 feature in the food section of the San Francisco Chronicle, Carol Ness told how markets sold fish labeled "organic" even though no government in the country or world had an organic certification to cover fish, as many did for vegetables and land animals.[7]

You will find investigative stories in nonprofit publications and the blogging world. But regardless of whether a story is on the food or sports pages, on the front page of the New York Times, inside Cosmopolitan magazine or Reader's Digest, or on our local TV news show, investigative stories share certain characteristics.

They go beyond the basic facts

Investigative stories often attempt to explain complex problems and issues. An investigative take on seemingly routine stories, such as a verdict in a criminal trial or passage of a new law, will acknowledge the many sides to a story and show how people are "for" in some ways and "against" in others. An investigative story aims to explain, rather than avoid, paradoxes.

To get a full understanding of a situation, an investigative reporter recognizes the need for a variety of sources. The investigative reporter will think about all the different types of people who would have knowledge about a particular subject: those with expertise, those involved in an issue, people affected by the problem, policy makers and money controllers.

They are analytical

Investigative stories give depth and perspective to problems and issues. They explore a problem's scope and its origin and evolution. They look at patterns and connections, and they make comparisons by looking at the same problem in other places. Let's say there's an outbreak of E. coli at a local restaurant. The daily news publications report on the outbreak and its causes and what is being done about it. An investigative story might also look at how many outbreaks occurred over the past five years. It might explore the similarities in the conditions under which they occurred and find out the chain of events that led to the problem.

They need to be uncovered

Investigative stories often focus on problems that are largely hidden or ignored. The problems aren't one-time occurrences, and there is no press conference to cover them or big announcement made about them, at least not until the investigative reporter brings them to light.

They take time

Investigative reporting isn't quick and it isn't easy. While some investigative stories take longer to do than others, no investigative story can be done on an afternoon deadline. If the subject is complicated, the information is buried, and it is difficult to find knowledgeable people, the story will take time. Some investigative stories can be done in a couple of days, others take months or years, added to bit-by-bit as the reporter covers other stories and other beats.

When former Los Angeles Times investigative journalist Myron Levin spoke to an undergraduate journalism class, a student asked him what story in his career he enjoyed working on the most. The question stumped him because in retrospect, every story he did seemed painful. Like many investigative reporters, Levin often found himself compelled to do an investigation. But doing the story was a long process.[8] In 2007, he completed a year-long investigation into U-Haul International, a company that supplies rental trucks and trailers that people use to move their goods across the country. In 2007, it culminated in a series Levin co-authored with Alan Miller that found the company's practices increased the risk of road accidents, and when accidents happened, the company invariably blamed the customer. Levin said that he feels the need to work on issues that are underreported, not ones that will get the biggest headlines.[9]

They explore big issues

Investigative stories often highlight systemic problems: corruption, wrongdoing, inequity, health hazards, fraud, or misuse of public money. The story Carol Ness did on organic fish in 2004 wasn't just about the misleading sales practice of one or a few markets. The larger issue was weak laws and an inadequate organic food certification and labeling system. Investigative stories also address the effect of these problems on ordinary people. In September 2003, San Francisco Chronicle sports reporters Mark Fainaru-Wada and Lance Williams learned about a raid on a little-known company called BALCO and on the home of the trainer of baseball legend Barry Bonds. When they tried to get more information, they discovered that two grand jury investigations were probing possible steroid use in baseball. Their subsequent investigations put in doubt a decade's worth of sports stats and baseball records.[10] Perhaps more important, cheating in the big leagues filters down to college and high school sports. Does society want to send the message to young people that to be the next Barry Bonds they need to take performance-enhancing drugs?

They aim to spur action or change

In February 2007, Dana Priest and Anne Hull were national security correspondents for the Washington Post when they wrote:

> Behind the door of Army Spec. Jeremy Duncan's room, part of the wall is torn and hangs in the air, weighted down with black mold. When the wounded combat engineer stands in his shower and looks up, he can see the bathtub on the floor above through a rotted hole. The entire building, constructed between the world wars, often smells like greasy carry-out. Signs of neglect are everywhere: mouse droppings, belly-up cockroaches, stained carpets, cheap mattresses.[11]

Their series of stories exposed the terrible conditions at Walter Reed Army Medical Center, which housed and treated thousands of wounded and ill soldiers returning from the Iraq War, and mistreatment and neglect of military veterans in general. It led to the firing of the secretary of the army, the resignation of the Army's surgeon general, a reorganization of the U.S. Army's entire top leadership, and a massive improvement in the way the nation treats our wounded soldiers.

An investigative story goes beyond the identification of a problem to an exploration of its repercussions and possible solutions. It aims to remedy a bad situation or prevent it from happening in the future. What will it take to solve the problem? Why haven't those steps been taken until now? For many reporters, that's the whole point of being a journalist.

David Dietz, a senior writer for Bloomberg Markets Magazine wrote that investigative reporting rattles windows; it wakes up the sleepy citizen and policy maker. "This kind of reporting takes time, demands the resilience of a prize-fighter and likely won't give you a good night's sleep," he wrote. "But it gets answers and makes change. And it's what we're here for."[12]

WHO IS AN INVESTIGATIVE REPORTER?

In media organizations, fewer and fewer people hold the title of investigative reporter. These are the reporters who spend their days poring through documents looking for political or corporate corruption or malfeasance. They court whistle-blowers and spend months or a year on a single story.

But many other reporters practice investigative reporting even as they cover their regular beats for newsweeklies, local papers, TV stations or radio news. They might uncover mismanagement in a local police department or shady dealings between real estate developers and government officials. They might look into complaints by parents about dangerous toys or suspicions by teachers who don't believe that high school dropout rates are as low as the school district reports.

Any reporter, regardless of job title, beat covered, or type of news organization, can and should be an investigative reporter. You don't need a thicker skin. You don't need to like drawing information from reluctant sources. You don't need to be the type of person who likes to spend all weekend going through boxes of tedious papers. You just need to be the type of person who asks questions that aren't being asked about problems that are ignored and who follows through until those questions get answered. However, successful investigative reporters share some common traits.

Investigative reporters are truth seekers

The rules of basic journalism require accuracy and balance. Investigative reporters don't stop there. They weigh facts and opinions against a sense of fairness, justice and common sense. The law allows a certain level of arsenic in the drinking water. But is it making people sick and should that be permitted? A jury of 12 people convicted someone of murder. But what if the man is really innocent? What drives investigative reporters is the fear that if they don't uncover the truth and publish it, no one will ever know the truth.

In 2006, that fear drove Christine Young, a reporter on the Times-Herald newspaper in upstate New York, to revisit a story she found herself connected to 20 years earlier as a journalism student in New York City.

Back then, she met a Salvation Army worker while trying to do a story on runaways who end up as prostitutes. The worker told her about a young woman known as "Blue Eyes." Months later, Blue Eyes, whose real name was Michael-anne Hall, was murdered, her head bashed in and her body mutilated. Police arrested and charged LeBrew Jones, a security guard at the site where Hall's body was found. Young told the police that the Salvation Army worker had seen Blue Eyes the night before the body was found, information that should have put him in the clear. Soon after, Young left the city for a job in New England, and Jones was convicted of second-degree murder.

Two decades later, Young found Jones serving time in a prison just 12 miles from where she now worked. His conviction still bothered her; she knew he hadn't done it. She convinced her editor at The Times Herald Record to let her investigate Jones' case. The information she uncovered convinced the New York City district attorney's office to reopen the case. In September 2008, the mother of Michaelanne Hall made a public plea for Jones to be released. The opening online page of Young's multimedia story is shown in Exhibit 1.1.[13]

WWW.

Christine Young's Story
http://thr-investigations.com/lebrewjones

Christine Young incorporates audio, video, interactive maps and other multimedia elements to tell the story of a man convicted of a murder she is convinced he never did.

EXHIBIT 1.1

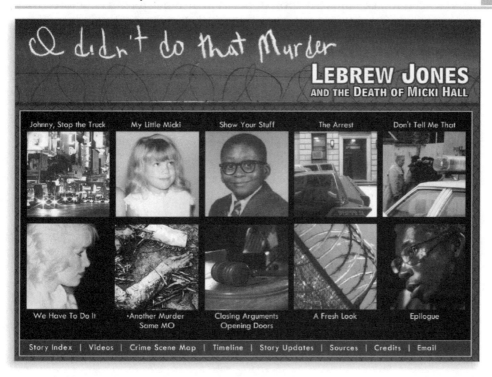

Investigative reporters are curious

Some reporters are diligent but not curious. In being diligent, they prepare for a story by doing all the necessary background research to know what questions to ask and make sure they touch on all the key points in each story. But they aren't curious to know more than what is necessary to file a story. Investigative reporters tend to be sincerely interested in the topics they cover. For curious reporters, every answer they get leads to more questions. Curious reporters don't just ask questions, they question the answers.

When someone says that a project will cost taxpayers money, investigative reporters want to know exactly how much it will cost them and what it will do. When a politician speaks of a win-win situation, they want to know who will lose. I once interviewed a Silicon Valley power broker, a lawyer whose list of corporate clients was a Who's Who of great technology companies. He boasted that he grew up in a middle-class neighborhood in New York, and that despite his success, he didn't live an ostentatious lifestyle. He drove an aging car, his son went to public school and he owned only one house. My next question was: What's the square footage of your house? He paused, then burst out laughing, because while I hadn't caught him in a lie, he realized that I had exposed the hypocrisy behind his statement: He lived in a mansion.

Investigative reporters don't wait for news to come to them. Instead they often feel compelled to go after stories that aren't announced. Rather than simply collect facts and opinions, investigative reporters ask questions that other reporters fail to ask, and they look in places that other reporters ignore. They don't accept that problems just happen. Very little happens in this world without a person or a group of people making a decision or a set of decisions that ultimately led to the problem. So when there is a problem, the investigative reporter wants to know why it happened and who is responsible.

Investigative reporters are persistent

People often don't want to answer hard questions. Sometimes, to answer your question they must search through files and people are simply too busy. When you ask questions no one has thought to ask before, some people will find you irritating and tell you that you ask the wrong questions. Sometimes they will insist that there is no story. They will think you waste their valuable time. Investigative reporters don't go away just because someone is too busy to answer the question. When they find one person won't provide the information they seek, they look for others who will. A good investigative reporter is stubborn, patient and persistent.

Investigative reporters are scientists

Both investigative reporters and scientists must be methodical. Scientists start out with a hypothesis and then go about gathering and analyzing information systematically. They know that collecting information is the process, not the goal; they gather information to discover or prove something. That's true too for investigative reporters. These reporters don't high-five each other for getting an interview with a key person for a story. They continue collecting information until they feel satisfied that their research yields the information that helps them prove something is happening or at least makes a convincing case that something is wrong.

Investigative reporters are storytellers

One more characteristic separates investigative reporters from other reporters: It's the ability to turn a complicated set of disjointed information into a compelling story. The investigative reporter doesn't just see data. While a spreadsheet filled with names and numbers might get some investigative reporters excited — it is not the names and numbers alone that excite them. In those lists they see the people affected and the problem taking shape. And they understand how to paint a picture in words to communicate that excitement to readers. In journalism, we say that a reporter who can get a story done is someone who can *execute*. In investigative reporting, the ability to execute includes spotting a problem worth investigating and having the persistence needed to gather and analyze the information as well as turning it into a finished story that's compelling to read. Investigative reporters don't just spot problems, they spot stories that need to be told and they figure out how to tell those stories.

INVESTIGATIVE REPORTING IS THRIVING

Y ou can do important investigative journalism regardless of the medium in which you work. Newspapers may seem to be dying. But that just means that that particular format for journalism will change. More will be written online. You may still be a writer for the Seattle Times or Baltimore Sun, but most, if not all, of your readers may read your stories over the Internet.

You will find investigative journalism on television, in magazines, on Internet sites and in business publications. And investigative reporters publish in blogs and books as well. Nonprofit organizations like the Center for Public Integrity, the Center for Investigative Reporting and ProPublica launch their own projects and work with other media outlets to get them broadcast or published. And finally, in cross-media partnerships, reporters from various venues — magazines, television stations, newspapers, radio stations, online publications and other online sites — work together and jointly publish a story in multiple formats.

To get a good idea of the number of stories and the scope of investigative journalism that happens every day, check out the Extra! Extra! section at the home page of Investigative Reporters and Editors (IRE). There you can find links to the latest stories printed or broadcast. You don't need to be a member of IRE to access that portion of the site.

Extra! Extra!
http://ire.org/
extraextra

| EXHIBIT 1.2 | Investigative reporting across the media. |

IN NEWSPAPERS	IN THE STUDENT PRESS
▪ In December 2007, Gary Craig from the Democrat and Chronicle in Rochester, N.Y., investigated how young children in foster care were often prescribed psycho-tropic drugs.[14] ▪ Also in 2007, Kevin Craver of the 40,000-circulation Northwest Herald in Crystal Lake, Ill., investigated claims that a local company had dumped carcinogenic chemicals causing high cancer rates in the area.[15] ▪ Sports reporter Brent Schrotenboer of The San Diego Union-Tribune pored through tax records in 2007 to show how the college football bowl system is a big money-making machine run by people who are richly compensated.[16]	▪ In 2007, Allison Riggio and Hunter Clauss, students at Columbia College in Chicago, examined nepotism in the city government and found that four of the 12 Chicago aldermen up for re-election hired relatives on their publicly funded staffs, at a cost to taxpayers of $400,000 a year.[20] ▪ In December 2007, University of Oregon student Whitney Malkin showed how laws preventing sex offenders from living near schools, playgrounds or day-care centers were resulting in clusters of them living near college campuses.[21]

ON TELEVISION	IN MAGAZINES AND NEWSWEEKLIES
▪ In 2006 in San Francisco, Anna Werner of KPIX-TV looked into a planned spraying of pesticides to eradicate the Asian Apple Moth and found that it was poorly planned, unneces-sary and would likely be ineffective and possibly harmful.[17] ▪ In November 2007, Paul Aker of WBNS in Columbus, Ohio, looked at two years' worth of 911 calls to find that the time it took dispatchers to respond to emergencies exceeded national standards.[18] ▪ In Phoenix in 2008, reporter Josh Bernstein of KNXV-TV examined tire inspection records at the local school district to find that children were going to school on buses that sat atop tires so old and worn they posed a safety hazard.[19]	▪ By analyzing records from the Florida Department of State in 2007, Jacksonville Business Journal reporter Mark Szakonyi was able to show that big money backed a grassroots campaign to limit develop-ment in the state and was turning it into the most expensive referendum in U.S. history.[22] ▪ In Mother Jones magazine in 2007, Jennifer Gonnerman found a psychiatric facility that routinely punished autistic, mentally retarded and emotionally troubled teenagers with electric shock treatment.[23]

Exhibit 1.2 contains some examples of what various news organizations have managed to do. Note that some tiny media outlets manage to carry out large-scale investigations.

Investigative reporting in the Internet world

In 1906, Upton Sinclair published "The Jungle," a tale of the harrows of the meatpacking industry. The book was a best seller, and the public outcry over it was so loud that it led to massive government reforms. But would it have had so great an effect in present times? In the 21st century, the book would have to compete against television shows, radio, MP3 players, text messaging on cell phones, video games, social networking sites and RSS feeds. Today, readers are immersed in so much media, can investigative journalism still grab readers, hold their attention and get them to act?

The answer is yes. With the Internet you can reach so many more readers and viewers than with traditional formats only. Not only can interested readers find you through search engines, Google alerts, news aggregators, chat boards and RSS feeds, but with e-mail, stories get transmitted from person to person and organization to organization. The Internet gives writers and reporters at small publications the power of distribution that in the past only journalists at the largest publications once had. It gives stories a staying power they never had. Readers no longer have only one chance to read a story on the day it is published. Now, they might hear about a story a week or two weeks after publication, and it is usually still available on the Internet for them to read; it hasn't disappeared into the landfill. Despite the competition for attention, readers still hunger for information that is relevant, interesting and that helps them understand the increasingly complicated world in which they live.

The Internet presents incredible opportunities for investigative journalists in information analysis, information sourcing, and the ability to tell a story in an interesting way. With e-mail, investigative reporters can file Freedom of Information requests for documents and data on a daily basis. With data management programs such as Excel and data mining programs such as Django, they can obtain and sift through thousands of lines of information to find patterns, trends and anomalies they never could before. With specialized search engines, access to chat boards and social networking sites, they can find obscure sources in obscure places. Stories that once might have stayed hidden in the dark basements of corporations and government bureaucracies might now come to light. Mapping programs allow reporters to see how problems affect different groups of people. The Internet presents journalists with new techniques, such as the ability to involve readers in an investigation to unearth problems and gather data.

In presentation, the Internet may present challenges to investigative reporters used to more linear writing formats of newspapers, magazines and books. However, it presents great opportunities to tell a compelling story in an engaging way through audio, video, interactive mapping, charts, graphs, photos, illustrations and animation.

Journalism that can zero in on important topics and stories that tell readers something they didn't know in a reader-friendly way will rise above the sea of superficial and super-specialized content that is so much of the Web. The use of the Internet in your reporting will be discussed in more detail in later chapters.

Investigative reporting can make a career thrive

Investigative reporting can elevate your standing and the reputation of your newsroom. Washington, D.C., television reporter Tisha Thompson credits her career rise to her ability to create data-based investigative broadcast stories. She points to a story she did on unsafe bridges, in which she plotted on a map the inspection reports for bridges in her region, that landed her a job in Baltimore. She was able to make her next move to a station in Washington, D.C., after she did a story that predicted which neighborhoods would be hit hard by foreclosures, based on federal home mortgage data.[24]

Scott Matthews, director of programming for the special investigations unit for CNN, said investigative stories help stations enhance their brand. "A lot of the time we are all covering the same stuff," he said. "The SIU [special investigation unit] gives viewers a clear alternative. People really want answers. They want someone to hold their governments and leaders accountable."

In surveys and focus groups viewers repeatedly stress certain themes that they want covered on a deeper level, such as how the government spends taxpayer money, and doing those stories well helps give CNN a competitive edge, he said. "We try to provide viewers with a smart aggressive look at the things that are affecting their lives."

Yvette Miley, a news director with WTVJ in South Florida, said investigative pieces can boost a reporter's standing as well: "As a reporter and journalist, you have to think of your own brand."[25]

CONCLUSION

In the movies, the investigative reporter pores through secret documents and meets with the whistle-blower in a dark underground garage. But most investigative reporters don't fit the movie image. Instead, today's investigative reporters are journalists who spot problems and ask questions, and then go about getting those questions answered in order to bring the problems to light. They are persistent, curious truth seekers who do methodical research and tell compelling stories that aim to spur change. There are countless problems that people need to know about and stories waiting to be told. The next chapter will look at how to find them.

EXERCISE

1. Go to the Web site for the journalism organization Investigative Reporters and Editors at www.ire.org/extraextra. Pick one investigative story that is spotlighted on that page. What was the focus of the story? What are some ways the reporters might have seemingly "stumbled onto" that story? Is there a way the story could apply to your town?

1.1 On paper or computer, make a list of the last five books you read for pleasure and the magazines you read or documentaries or fact-based dramas you chose to see in the theater or on television in the past year.

1.2 Out of this list, which topics seem to interest you enough that you would seek out a diverse range of materials about it? In other words, what do you naturally want to find out more about on an ongoing basis?

1.3 Narrow down one of those wide subject areas to a topic to investigate that you could picture as a documentary or series of articles that could spur positive change.

NOTES

1. Louise Kiernan. "Writing complicated stories." *Essay in Telling True Stories: A Non-fiction Writer's Guide.* Edited by Mark Kramer and Wendy Call. Plume, 2007.

2. Judith Serrin and William Serrin. *Muckraking! The Journalism That Changed America.* The New Press, 2002, pp. 9–11.

3. Carl Bernstein and Bob Woodward. *All the President's Men.* Simon and Schuster, 1974, pp. 1–18.

4. Whitney Malkin. "No room for sex offenders: Campus housing may be one of few areas available for convicts." *The Register-Guard,* Dec. 2, 2007. See full story in Appendix A.1.

5. See the Web site of Investigative Reporters & Editors at http://ire.org.

6. Margaret Jones Patterson and Robert Russell. *Behind the Lines: Case Studies in Investigative Reporting.* Columbia University Press, 1986, p. 18.

7. Carol Ness. "Organic label muddies the waters." *The San Francisco Chronicle,* April 28, 2004, p. F1.

8. Myron Levin. Comments made to Humboldt State University class on investigative reporting, April 6, 2006, and e-mail correspondence February 23, 2009.

9. See the story by Myron Levin and Alan Miller, "Driving with rented risks: U-Haul International is the nation's largest provider of rental trailers; A Times investigation finds the company's practices raise the risk of accidents on the road." *Los Angeles Times,* June 24, 2007.

10. Columbia Journalism Review interview with Mark Fainaru-Wada by Susan Q. Stranahan at www.cjr.org/the_water_cooler/mark_fainaruwada_on_the_sports.php?page=all.

11. Dana Priest and Anne Hull. "Soldiers face neglect, frustration at Army's top medical facility." *Washington Post,* Feb. 18, 2007, p. A01.

12. David Dietz. E-mail correspondence, Nov. 1, 2006.

13. Christine Young. "I didn't do that murder: LeBrew Jones and the death of Micki Hall." *The Times Herald Record* at http://thr-investigations.com/lebrewjones.

14. Gary Craig. "Potent pills: More foster kids getting mood-altering drugs." *Democrat and Chronicle,* Dec. 9, 2007, p. 18. See the story at http://www.democratandchronicle.com/apps/pbcs.dll/article?AID=/20071209/NEWS01/71206023.

15. Kevin Craver. "Did chemical exposure cause cancers for McCullom Lake residents?" *Northwest Herald,* Dec. 19, 2007. See the story at http://www.nwherald.com/articles/2007/12/19/mccullom_lake_lawsuits/doc47620d4a12812648217171.txt.

16. Brent Schrotenboer. "Bowling for dollars: Despite cries for a playoff system to legitimize the national-championship picture, organizers pad their pockets while 64 teams go . . ." *The San Diego Union-Tribune,* Dec. 12, 2007. You can find the story at http://www.signonsandiego.com/sports/college_football/20071212-9999-1s12bowls.html.

17. Anna Werner. "CBS 5 investigates: Is the Apple Moth really a risk? CBS5.com, April 16, 2008. See http://www.10tv.com/?story=sites/10tv/content/pool/200711/925181893.html.

18. Paul Aker. "County's 911 calls not always sending help quickly." WBNS Columbus. Aired Nov. 28, 2007. You can find the story at http://www.wbns.com/live/contentbe/EPIC_shim.php?story=sites/10tv/content/pool/200711/925181893.html.

19. Josh Bernstein. "School buses with old worn tires transporting children." KNXV-TV Phoenix. Aired May 22, 2008. You can view the story at http://www.abc15.com/content/news/investigators/story.aspx?content_id=11dbdbf2-5330-4608-9494-89e0198fbbe1.

20. Allison Riggio and Hunter Clauss. "Public payroll, family affairs: Aldermen keep it relative." *Beachwood Reporter,* April 12, 2007. The story is reprinted in Appendix A.7.

21. Whitney Malkin. "No room for sex offenders: Campus housing may be one of few areas available for convicts." *The Register-Guard,* Dec. 2, 2007. See full story in Appendix A.1.

22. Mark Szakonyi. "Hometown democracy debate proving costly." *Jacksonville Business Journal,* Dec. 7, 2007.

23. Jennifer Gonnerman. "School of shock." *Mother Jones,* Aug. 20, 2007.

24. Tisha Thompson. E-mail correspondence, Dec. 15, 2008.

25. Matthews and Miley both spoke at a workshop entitled "How investigations build your reputation" at the IRE National Convention in Miami in June 2008.

Finding the Story

CHAPTER PREVIEW Where do investigative reporters find stories, and how can you train yourself to spot them wherever you are? Investigative projects often start from a small kernel of an idea. You can get ideas for these stories by observing people and events that occur around you. Stories may also come out of gossip tips, but you need to listen for them and follow up on them. Investigative reporters scan the briefs, spot the unasked questions in daily newspaper stories and zero in on mundane references in press releases and government documents. They look for problems that might be more widespread than reported and connections between seemingly unrelated events.

2

C H A P T E R

HOW TO FIND STORY IDEAS

Y ou don't typically "stumble over" investigative stories. You have to look for them and recognize them when you see them. Potential stories are all around you. The television series "The Naked City," which ran from 1958 to 1963, ended each episode with this memorable quote: "There are 8 million stories in the naked city. This has been one of them."[1] That became and remains the mantra for journalists throughout the country. Journalists understand that if there are eight million people in New York City, there are eight million stories worth telling. That means that if there are 6.6 billion people in the world today, there are 6.6 billion stories. But that doesn't mean they are easy to spot.

Indiana University Professor Annie Lang, who has studied media psychology, theorized that while people are information processors, we can't process all the information that comes to us. Instead we tend to process, analyze and keep only the information that pertains most closely to our personal goals or the information that is new or different.[2] She applied her theory to how we process what we see on television, but the theory can be applied to how reporters find stories, as well. With stories all around us, we tend to notice first what is obviously new and different. After that, we notice the stories that will help us meet our personal goals — meeting the daily or weekly deadline; pleasing our editor so we get promoted, getting a front page story; or getting a story before the competition does. An investigative story might not meet either of those two categories. It might involve an ongoing problem that isn't new or different. And doing the story might not please an editor who prefers quantity over quality. So you must train yourself to look for stories that are important even if they aren't new and that you know will earn your news organization long-term prestige — even if your editor doesn't jump for joy when you propose them.

So much information comes into your brain that you tend to ignore much of it. To find investigative stories you have to train yourself to focus on things that other people and other reporters ignore.

Authors Judith Bolch and Kay Miller once wrote that an investigative reporter must be able to "hook a story idea as it glides by in conversation."[3] Reporters find investigative stories in idle gossip, serious issues in news briefs, and patterns out of seemingly random tidbits of information. When someone gives them a tip, they follow up on it. And they read everything that crosses their desk from a tedious press release, to minutes from a local government meeting, testimony from a U.S. Senate hearing or an 80-page public agency report.

Exhibit 2.1 provides a quick reference to use when you start looking for your own stories.

Begin with a small idea

Big stories often begin as small ideas. A U.S. census statistic on the number of children in a county living in poverty could lead to a story about children going

Story idea search list.   **EXHIBIT 2.1**

- **Begin with a small idea.** Look at small bits of information like stats, findings and facts.

- **Follow up on tips.** When someone lets you know that a problem or issue may be occurring, go check it out.

- **Pay attention to gossip.** There may be truth behind rumors and a story in what people are complaining about to each other.

- **Be observant in everyday situations.** Keep your eyes and ears open as you go about your daily activities.

- **Scan the briefs.** Check out the smallest stories in the newspaper, online or during a broadcast.

- **Spot the widespread problem in the daily story.** When a problem occurs, find out if it has happened before or will happen again.

- **Find the interesting in the mundane.** Read everything that comes across your desk.

- **Replicate an investigation done elsewhere.** What happens in another city or state may very well be going on in your own community.

- **Read the fine print and footnotes.** The least emphasized parts of documents or reports may have the biggest stories.

- **Look for similarities in seemingly unrelated events.** A pattern may appear once you connect the dots.

- **Work back from a problem to its cause.** What was the unreported event that rippled out to the reported consequences?

hungry. A traffic accident that results in a pedestrian getting injured could lead to an examination of dangerous intersections and how stop signs are distributed around town. In a county report on crime you might notice that an inordinate number of Native Americans seem to get arrested. That leads you to compare statistics on the jail and county population, and you discover that the percentage of Native Americans in the jail is five times greater than in the larger population. Barbara Ehrenreich's undercover investigation of minimum-wage employment that led to her 2005 best-selling book, "Nickel and Dimed," started during a conversation over a high-priced lunch when she wondered aloud how anyone could manage to live on a minimum-wage salary.[4]

A general rule of thumb is: If it is wrong or someone is hurt by it, if you think you can prove that it is happening, and if you can show a way to resolve it or at least lessen the harm, then you should do the story.

Follow up on tips

When I wrote about the stock market for an online financial publication, a financial analyst told me he'd heard that a company I covered was having problems with a particular project. Moreover, it had previously boasted about the project to get people to buy its stock. If true, the company faced an embarrassing failure. I called the company's public relations representative, and he assured me that the project was an insignificant part of the company's overall plan and wasn't important to its future. I might have stopped there, as the company contradicted my tipster and that likely meant my source was misinformed. But earlier in this book we saw how investigative reporters are naturally suspicious. I trusted my source and I didn't trust the company spokesman. Because he was so adamant about the insignificance of the project, I speculated that the project was so significant that the company couldn't acknowledge the problems with it. My gut told me to follow the story.

On the Internet I poked through corporate records and found a PowerPoint presentation shown to investors at an annual shareholders meeting held just three months earlier. It listed the project I was interested in as the company's "Priority #1." So either the company had changed its overall strategy drastically in just three months, or it had lied to its investors or lied to me.

I then pored through past press releases and news stories written over the past few years to find financial activity related to the technology at the heart of the project and found a series of corporate acquisitions that amounted to several hundred million dollars' worth of investment in it. Finally, I conducted research on competing companies and found at least one that had already been successful where the company I was researching had apparently failed, and another, much smaller company, that was well on its way to successful production of the product. By following up on the original tip, I was able to publish a story on the failure of the company's project in time for a presentation its chief executive made to shareholders and potential investors at a prestigious financial conference.[5] The history of investigative reporting is filled with examples of persistent reporters who followed through on a tip.

In another example, in 1962, Washington Post reporter Morton Mintz followed up on a tip that a doctor in the Food and Drug Administration had refused to approve a drug for use inside the United States prescribed to women elsewhere for morning sickness. It turned out that the drug, thalidomide, had been shown to cause birth defects; when some women took it they gave birth to children who had severe limb malformities. As a result of the story, Congress passed laws that changed the way drugs could be tested and marketed in this country. After subsequent congressional hearings, drugmakers had to prove drugs were safe and effective before they could sell them in this country. See Box 2.1 for more on the investigative story by Morton Mintz.

Pay attention to gossip

A common mistake many reporters make is that they ignore problems people complain about because the problems are not new. But some of the best stories come from refusing to ignore an ongoing problem that other people accept as a fact of life. You need to pay attention to the things people gossip and complain about, and to do that you need to be in a place where you can hear it. That means that you have to get out of your newsroom or home and into places where you will interact with different kinds of people. It helps to keep

What can happen when you follow a tip BOX 2.1

MORTON MINTZ ON BREAKING THE STORY OF THE THALIDOMIDE BABIES[6]

"The thalidomide story changed my life—changed it profoundly [. . .] It's why I won my first journalism prizes. It's why I came to devote much of the last 40 plus years to reporting on corporate crime and grave misconduct, particularly in the drug, tobacco, and automobile industries.

"The effects on me were the least of it. For example, the story dealt a lasting blow to a notion, widely if foolishly held, that science and technology always or nearly always produce benign results.

"The lead, from the Washington Post of Sunday, July 15, 1962, sums it up: 'This is the story of how the skepticism and stubbornness of a government physician prevented what could have been an appalling American tragedy, the birth of hundreds or indeed thousands of armless and legless children.'

"[. . .] In September 1960, the U.S. licensee of the German investor and manufacturer of thalidomide —a sedative or tranquilizer, depending on dosage—applied for FDA approval to sell it in the United States. Not until April 1962 did it become widely known that in numerous other countries, the mothers of several thousand thalidomide children (who were born without limbs due to the drug) had taken the drug during the first trimester of pregnancy. I interviewed Dr. Kelsey three months later.

"I finished the story—2400 words—at around 2 a.m. on Saturday, July 14th. Several hours later, my wife, Anita, and I and our three children left by car for Cape Cod. My spies told me afterward that the Managing Editor thought the piece was too long, but the News Editor had said, 'I can get it in.' He did.

"Seventeen days later, a Senate subcommittee led by Hubert Humphrey held an FDA oversight hearing at which it came out that in a promotional stunt, the licensee, the William S. Merrell Co., had contrived to give away 2.5 million so-called 'experimental' thalidomide pills to physicians, causing 10 American infants to be born with seal-like flippers rather than arms and legs.

"Sy Fishbein, an assistant city editor, had assigned me to interview Dr. Kelsey after a colleague, the late Bernard Nossiter, passed on a tip that she had kept thalidomide off the market. I learned subsequently that Sy picked me because he wanted an interviewer with a capacity for outrage; I had that, famously or infamously, along with zero expertise about the FDA or medicines.

"The tip came from an aide to Estes Kefauver, who had been fighting a long, losing battle to drastically strengthen the Food, Drug, and Cosmetic Act of 1938. Building on findings in investigative hearings by his Senate Antitrust Subcommittee, he proposed amendments to require a manufacturer to provide the FDA with substantial scientific evidence—well-controlled clinical studies—showing that a medicine was not only safe, but also effective in its intended use. The amendments also proposed mechanisms to prevent the price-gouging that was rampant even then.

"Only a few weeks before my story ran, his Senate foes, mostly Republican friends of the pharmaceutical industry, gutted the amendments. They did this in a secret meeting he'd known nothing about.

"The story transformed Capitol Hill. Suddenly, Congress became a tiger, rushing to toughen the drug law by passing what came to be called the Kefauver–Harris Amendments of 1962."

Reprinted with permission of the author.

the earphones out of your ears while you are in line at the supermarket or while paying a traffic ticket at the courthouse so that you can hear what people chat about various topics. If the opportunity is right, engage in spontaneous conversations with strangers.

Maintain contact with the different types of people you meet who might be in a position to hear or see interesting things. Listen to local talk radio shows on which people air their opinions and complaints. Read letters to the editor in your local paper. On those talk shows and in those letters you can find the problems reporters often ignore.

Tap into gossip through local blogs and online comments and chats. What are people angry about? What frustrates or frightens them? Those are the questions at the heart of all good stories. A blog post turned Thadeus Greenson, a reporter for the Times-Standard newspaper in Eureka, Calif., onto a story in 2008. He was investigating the strange case of a small-town police chief who had been arrested on suspicion of raping his spouse. Greenson suspected that the chief may have been guilty of other things as well. On a local blog, he noticed that in one comment about the scandal, the author made a passing reference to an Internet post that sought former officers from the town's police department to join in a class-action lawsuit against the city. He found the ad and tracked down its author, who told him that at least four officers had filed complaints with the city about improprieties by the chief, but the city had failed to act. Greenson then filed a public records act request with the city and found that eight officers hired while the chief was in charge were fired after less than a year of service. Greenson said he scans the blogs and the comments section of his own publication's Web site every morning looking for story leads.[7]

Thadeus Greenson's Story

www.times-standard.com/localnews/ci_10554028

Be observant in everyday situations

You might notice something that leads you to believe that a problem exists. Suppose you injure yourself and go to the local emergency room where you wait a long time to see a doctor. You ask yourself a series of questions: Is this wait typical here? Is it the industry norm? Is this hospital understaffed? Does it operate with insufficient funds? Does it mismanage its funds? Does it fail to give people proper treatment in time? Is the wait the same at other hospitals in the area?

In 2004, the San Francisco Chronicle ran a series of stories by reporters Reynolds Holding and Erin McCormick about disproportionately high rates of infant mortality in some areas of California. McCormick later wrote that the project began when she found herself listening to the breathing of her newborn baby. She began to wonder how many babies die and whether some babies are more likely to die than others.[8]

In fall 2006, a Humboldt State University student named Oliver Symonds noticed an expired inspection certificate in an elevator he rode on his way to class. He wondered how often the elevators were inspected. He wondered how many

Erin McCormick's Story

www.sfgate.com/cgi-bin/article.cgi?f=/c/a/2004/10/03/MNINFANTMOMAP.DTL

elevators were on campus. And he wondered whether elevators that weren't inspected frequently broke down more often. When he sought answers to those questions, he discovered that the problem worried students who are disabled, faculty and staff who depended on those elevators to get around a campus nick-named "Hills and Stairs University."[9] See Appendix A.2 for the story.

Scan the briefs

Chicago Tribune Assistant Managing Editor for Projects George Papajohn said that when you run dry on ideas for investigations look for the smallest stories in the newspaper and look for anything that doesn't add up or smells funny.[10] News-papers and online news sites cover so much news on such a global scale and at such a fast, constant pace that many stories get briefed that might warrant a more serious look. Often the briefs cover the who, what, where and when, but not the why or the how. For example, a news brief might give the following information:

> A company called Marin Ceramic announced it was recalling sets of ceramic pitch-ers and cups because of concerns of lead in the glaze. The recall was a result of a routine FDA test. The company asked consumers to return the products within 30 days for a full refund.

Recall announcements are a great example of what you can find in a news brief. Often the brief is just a rewritten press release. Rarely does a reporter or news organization follow it up. But such a brief raises all kinds of questions to the investigative eye. Why are consumers permitted just 30 days to get a refund if the product sold to them was deemed unsafe? How often are these routine inspections done, and what's the chance that other lead-tainted products are still on the market? Where did the glaze come from, and do other companies use it in their products that are still on the market? Was the recall voluntary, and if not, are other companies caught marketing similar products with lead been allowed to let their products stay on the market?

Recall announcements are just one type of news brief you can look for. You can look in police stories for possible problems in how your community spends crime-fighting resources or in how police treat people and crimes in different neighborhoods. Accident stories might give you hints that there are problems with infrastructure — streets aren't getting repaired or needed signs aren't get-ting put up or replaced. A notice of a workshop for CPR training might get you wondering what percentage of elementary schoolteachers are trained in CPR and what kind of procedures and training the schools have for medical emergencies involving young children. A brief about a new administrator hired at a university might get you wondering what happened to the last guy in the post. That might make you wonder how many other administrators have left or been fired, wheth-er the university has a difficult time retaining managers and whether that reflects a failure in top management. And a notice about a meeting of a local agency that provides poor people with affordable housing might get you wondering about how poor you need to be to qualify and whether there is a waiting list.

Spot the widespread problem in the daily story

USA Today reporter Julie Schmit said that whenever she reads about one incident she suspects that it isn't the first and only time that ever happened. And if it was one in a series of such incidences, then how could the problem be allowed to happen? In other words, she wonders about the systems and processes that failed to prevent the problem from happening. Consider a story she did on airline safety. Her investigation began when she read a story about a commuter airplane crash; the story mentioned that the pilot had been fired from a previous job at another airline. Schmit wondered how it was possible that an airline would hire a pilot to fly its planes after another airline had fired him. And she wondered if that was the first time that had happened. In trying to answer those questions, she discovered a commuter airline industry that was growing too fast, a dearth of qualified pilots and inconsistent and often inadequate training of new pilots. "If you read something and it makes your eyebrows go up," Schmit said, "chances are there is a good story."[11]

Find the interesting in the mundane

You might find investigative story ideas in the myriad of reports or studies that few people bother to read. Lazy reporters push aside the piles of information dumped on them, while investigative reporters tend to scan everything that passes over their desks for nuggets that suggest a problem that is going largely unnoticed.

Julie Schmit's Story
www.usatoday.com/
money/industries/
food/2007-10-09-fda-
import-safety_N.htm

When in 2006, the U.S. Food and Drug Administration released a report on an outbreak of *E. coli* bacteria on spinach, most reporters read the executive summary and wrote a daily story on that. Schmit, at USA Today, carefully read the full report and found information no one else reported, which led to a series of investigative stories on where our food comes from and how inadequately it gets inspected.[12]

Laura Paskus, an environmental reporter at the Santa Fe Reporter, says that every day she reads the "god-awful boring press releases" that federal and state agencies send out when they issue permits, hold hearings or announce that they will accept public comments on proposed changes to rules and regulations. "Often, there are good stories buried in those press releases, and I'm enough of a nerd to find them when other reporters just report the basic facts or ignore the announcements altogether."

As an example, other reporters might ignore a press release for a state hearing concerning a permit request for a landfill site. But it could lead to a good story. Paskus says "I can look at what town the landfill is planned for, check how many other landfills there are, look at the town's demographics — and then perhaps find an environmental justice story. A few isolated stories here and there do end up pointing towards trends."[13]

Replicate an investigation done elsewhere

Greed, laziness and incompetence are universal traits. Since governments and businesses often copy what other agencies and businesses do elsewhere, corruption and malfeasance may carry over from one community or state to another. What one investigative reporter uncovers in her community you may also find in yours. As mentioned in Chapter 1, the Extra! Extra! section of the IRE.org Web site is an ongoing listing of recent stories by journalists across the country and across media. Some stories may not specifically apply to your area. For example, in the "Taken for a Ride" investigation done by the Miami Herald in 2008, reporter Larry Lebowitz found that for six years Dade County had been misspending sales tax money that was supposed to go to massive improvements in mass transit.[14] But your city or state probably has a sales tax, and you may discover problems with oversight in spending those sales tax revenues.

You can replicate the investigation by doing a search in the electronic archives of your state or local newspapers for voter-approved bond measures and sales tax increases. What did the voters approve the money for? What did the government promise them? Now request the financial statements from the agency in charge that show how the money was actually spent and what projects are funded by the money.

Or consider a story that Orlando Sentinel reporters Dan Tracy and Mary Shanklin published in March 2008. They asked for the records of vehicle use for government business for some 90 local government agencies. They found that even as government officials talked about their efforts to make their governments environmentally friendly, they drove gas-guzzling cars and trucks.[15] You might find a similar problem if you request those types of records for your state or locality. You could do an investigation on college campuses as well. Not only can you find out what government-owned cars faculty, staff and administrators drive but where they take them and for what purpose. Are they energy efficient, or has the school chosen luxury over economy and the environment?

Read the fine print and footnotes

When some people need a plumber, they go to the phone book and look for the guy with the least conspicuous listing. He's so good, they think, he doesn't need a big ad. You might look for potential stories the same way. Look for the least-advertised item on the city council agenda, for example, one that seems not very important. Examine the agenda for a routine city council meeting for the town of Orinda, Calif., in Exhibit 2.2. It includes a number of mundane items including the dedication of an amateur radio station at City Hall, the payment of city

EXHIBIT 2.2   Agenda for a routine city council meeting for the town of Orinda, Calif.

CITY COUNCIL
AGENDA
June 3, 2008
7:00 P.M. – REGULAR MEETING
7:00 P.M. – REGULAR SESSION - LIBRARY AUDITORIUM
A. CALL TO ORDER / ROLL CALL:
B. PLEDGE OF ALLEGIANCE
C. CLOSED SESSION REPORT
D. ADOPTION OF AGENDA
The City Council may take action on any item listed on the agenda.
E. ITEMS FOR THE GOOD OF THE CITY
Dedication of City Hall Amateur Radio Station to the City of Orinda from the Orinda Rotary Club
Endowment Fund
F. PUBLIC FORUM
The Public Forum provides an opportunity for members of the public to speak on any item within
the jurisdiction of the Council that is not on the agenda.
G. CONSENT CALENDAR
Consent Calendar items are considered to be routine by the City Council and will be enacted by one
motion. By approval of the Consent Calendar the staff recommendation will be adopted. There will
be no separate discussion on these items unless a Councilmember or a member of the public
requests removal of an item from the Consent Calendar.
G-1 Approval of regular warrants #29944 - #30190, payroll checks #4341 - #4390 and payroll
vouchers #36167 - #36236 Recommendation: Approve list of warrants through May 27, 2008.
G-2 City Council Minutes:
(a) May 20, 2008 Recommendation: Approve.
G-3 Authorization of City Sponsorship of Fourth of July Events and Official Closure of Roads for
Parade Route Adopt Resolution 33-08, Sponsorship of Fourth of July Events and Official Closure of
Roads for Parade Route
G-4 Appointment of City of Orinda Alternate Representative to the Contra Costa
County Library Commission Recommendation: Appointment of N. Earl Austin as the City
Alternate Representative to the Contra Costa County Library Commission.
G-5 Review of Final Plans and Specifications for the Community Center Roof and Authorization to
Solicit Bids Recommendation: Staff recommends that the City Council review and approve the final
plans for the replacement of the Community Center roof and authorize staff to advertise for bid.
H. PUBLIC HEARINGS
H-1 Public He
Public Works   G-5 Review of Final Plans and Specifications for the Community Center
Department R   Roof and Authorization to Solicit Bids Recommendation: Staff
the proposed n   recommends that the City Council review and approve the final plans for
I. POLICY M   the replacement of the Community Center roof and authorize staff to
I-1 Status Upd   advertise for bid.
Recommendat
informational
I-2 Adoption
State Video Franchise Holders Recommendation: Waive the full reading of the text of the ordinance
and Adopt Ordinance No. 08-05 titled: An Ordinance Amending the Orinda Municipal Code to
Address State Video Franchise Holders.
J. CITY MANAGER'S REPORT
K. CITY COUNCIL REPORTS
Councilmembers' announcements or brief reports on his/her activities.
L. MATTERS INITIATED
Consideration of matters a Councilmember wishes to initiate for placement on a future Council
agenda.
N. ADJOURNMENT

warrants and payroll checks, the planning for July 4th events, a public hearing on raising development fees, and an update on a project to improve streets and sidewalks. Then there is item G-5: a discussion of the plans to replace the community center roof and the bidding of contracts for it. It is written as a standard line item, but this might be worth investigating. It could be a big, unnecessary project that ends up being a waste of taxpayers' money. The bidding could be rigged in such a way as to favor contractors who helped the council members get elected or who have contributed to their re-election campaigns.

Look for similarities in seemingly unrelated events

Douglas Pardue, the special assignments editor for The Post and Courier in Charleston, S.C., began to notice that whenever firefighters responded to house fires in rural areas, the house was almost always too far gone to save by the time the firefighters arrived. He wondered whether this had to do with the fact that rural fires are generally fought by volunteer fire departments. His investigation exposed a nationwide crisis: Volunteer fire departments across the country were underfunded and undertrained, and often the firefighters were not sufficiently fit for the work. More volunteer firefighters died on duty from heart attacks and in traffic accidents than they did fighting fires.[16]

A comparison of unrelated accusations of police brutality might reveal problems with a system of oversight at the police department. Unrelated firings on your college campus might reveal change in policy direction from the top of the administration that no one publicized. And a close look at a spate of unrelated real estate purchases in a blighted neighborhood might reveal undisclosed plans by a government agency to offer development incentives.

Work back from a problem to its cause

After doctors at the University of Southern California School of Medicine found damaged lungs inside children who lived in highly polluted Southern California cities, Riverside Press-Enterprise Project Editor Cathy Armstrong asked how her county could have allowed so many warehouses to be built when they bring in high-polluting diesel trucks. Working backward, she and reporter David Danelski found that the county and the consultants who studied the environmental impacts of the proposed projects failed to adequately address potential problems, as required by state law.[17]

FINDING INVESTIGATIVE STORIES ON YOUR CAMPUS

Once you start thinking about ways to find stories, you will come up with one idea after another. The following discussion presents possible ideas to get you started on your campus.

College clubs. The student government on just about every college campus across the nation collects fees from students to finance clubs and activities. Get a list of the clubs and the amount of money allocated for each. Then track down the club's expense reports for the previous year. What was the money supposed to be used for? What was it actually used for? See if you can figure out which clubs spend the most money for the fewest members. See if you can find clubs that seem to serve no beneficial purpose. Perhaps the student government has allocated $5,000 for the Talk Like a Pirate Club, when the Soroptomist Club, which helps elderly ladies and children who are disabled, received $1,000 less than it requested.

Faculty sabbaticals. Many colleges and universities allow professors to take off a semester or a year from time to time fully paid for scholarship purposes. Many work on books or serve as visiting scholars overseas. Others sit home and watch football. Request a list of all sabbaticals granted over the past five years and track down the professors to see if they can produce evidence of what they did with their time off. Consider too, that at public universities these sabbaticals are likely paid for with taxpayer subsidies. You can also investigate which sabbatical requests got turned down.

Food quality. Find out who supplies the food served in your college's cafeterias. Then track down individual food items through the supplier to the point of origin. Does the meat come from big meat processors? How much of the food is frozen or canned versus fresh? How much is imported from outside the country? What kinds of health training must the cafeteria workers go through? What are the minimal standards the college must meet before it can serve any food item in the cafeteria? Compare what you find to similar data from other colleges in your state and in other states.

Energy conservation. Find an energy consultant, or auditor, to accompany you on a tour through your campus to determine how energy efficient your school is.

Building safety. Talk to home inspectors — the people home buyers hire to give a home the once-over before going into escrow — about what problems to look for in any basic building inspection. Using that information, inspect the buildings on your campus to see how safe they are. Find out how often buildings on your campus are inspected and when the last inspection occurred. Get a list of deferred maintenance projects on your campus and see what kinds of building repairs the college has put off because of tight funds.

Emergency preparedness. In 2008, some of my students noticed that the doors to the "mass casualty unit" van, permanently parked on campus in case of a catastrophe, were open. When they peeked inside, they found the van empty. They began wondering if all the disaster response vehicles on the campus were similarly empty. They discovered that the school wasn't adequately prepared for an emergency. So the question you need to ask is this: Where does all the money go that your college spends on emergency response, and is your college as prepared for a disaster as it says it is?

CONCLUSION

You can hit on a good investigative idea in any of a number of ways. Train yourself to spot potential stories. Once you spot one, ask yourself a series of questions and seek out the answers. Remember, investigative reporters are systematic.

Here's how that might happen: You hear a concern, read a story, get a tip or spot a problem. It sparks your interest. You ask yourself a series of questions about the ramifications and scope of the problem. You do preliminary research to see if your questions are off base or on target. You follow up with a plan of action. If you train your mind this way and keep your eyes and ears open, other reporters will wonder how you seem to "stumble over" investigative story ideas all the time. The next chapter will explore that plan of action.

EXERCISES

1. Find a story in a local newspaper about a problem in the community. How might it be part of a wider trend? See if the news story asked the following questions:
   a. Why did it happen?
   b. What would have prevented it from happening?
   c. Were there other instances of similar problems?
   d. Is there a government agency or laws in place to prevent it from happening or to punish those responsible? If so, are they being enforced?

2. Try to come up with an idea for an investigation based on the story you read in Exercise 1. What will you investigate? What do you think you might find?

3. Scan the news briefs in your local paper. See if you can take each one and turn what was a reactive story into an idea for a proactive investigation. What issue or issues do you see that you could look into? How would you take a proactive approach to reporting the story?

4. Pick one day out of your week to visit different places around town. Try to find an investigative story out of what you notice in the course of the day. Keep your eyes and ears open for something that might cause people problems, for complaints people have, for accidents waiting to happen, for anything that might cause a danger to public health and safety or that might lead to violations of equality and justice. What is it that sparked your curiosity? What problem do you suspect might be happening? How might you investigate it further?

2.1   Beginning with the narrow topic you selected in Chapter 1, select one problem to look into. What major questions come to mind that need to be answered? What might be the challenges involved in carrying out these investigations? Why might this story be important?

2.2   If you will be doing the investigation as a group project, then as a group compare the story ideas and pick one to work on.

2.3   See if you can synthesize the story idea down to a statement of 30 words or less that summarizes what you hope or expect to find.

2.4   Start your preliminary research by doing a basic online search of your topic.

    a. Try to find blogs in which people discuss issues events or issues related to your topic.

    b. Try to find academic studies that examine your topic.

    c. Using a news search engine, try to find news stories related to your topic.

NOTES

1. See the Internet Movie Database online at http://www.imdb.com/title/tt0051297.

2. Annie Lang. "The limited capacity model of mediated message processing." *Journal of Communication* 50 (Dec. 2000): 46–70.

3. Judith Bolch and Kay Miller. *Investigative and In-Depth Reporting.* Hastings House, 1978.

4. Barbara Ehrenreich. *Nickel and Dimed: On (Not) Getting By in America.* Henry Holt, 2001.

5. Marcy Burstiner. "Montgomery Tech Conference: National Semi CEO gives LAN program intensive care." TheStreet.com, Feb. 3, 1999. You can read the story at http://www.thestreet.com/tech/semis/713213.html.

6. Morton Mintz. "Morton Mintz on the collapse of congressional oversight." Remarks made to a gathering of Nieman Fellows in Washington, D.C., in May 2005. Reprinted on the Nieman Foundation's Nieman Watchdog site, www.niemanwatchdog.org.

7. Thadeus Greenson. "Former BLPD officers consider suing the city." *The Times-Standard,* Sept. 25, 2008. And e-mail correspondence with Greenson, Nov. 17, 2008.

8. Erin McCormick. "Mapping project logs decade of mortality for poorest residents, polluted areas." *IRE Journal* (Sept./Oct. 2005).

9. Oliver Symonds. "Running on borrowed time: HSU elevators operating on expired permits." *The Lumberjack,* Sept. 6, 2006, p. 5.

10. George Papajohn. Comments made at a workshop on "Bulletproofing the investigation." IRE national convention, Miami. June 2008.

11. Julie Schmit. Interview, Sept. 25, 2007.

12. Ibid.

13. Laura Paskus. E-mail correspondence, Sept. 2007.

14. Larry Lebowitz. "Taken for a ride." *The Miami Herald,* June 8, 2008.

15. Mary Shanklin and Dan Tracy. "Orlando-area agencies shun hybrid vehicles." *Orlando Sentinel,* March 10, 2008.

16. Doug Pardue. E-mail correspondence, Dec. 12, 2008.

17. David Danelski. "Dirty deals: In reshaping economy, county eases way for diesel truck pollution. *IRE Journal* (Sept./Oct. 2003), p. 18.

Setting Up the Investigation

CHAPTER PREVIEW Investigative reporting is a process of discovery. But the more you already know when you talk to people, the more information you will likely get from your interviews. Thorough background research gives you a starting point for your investigation by showing you what has already been written on the topic and by suggesting people to interview and questions to ask. You can get background information by searching news databases, using Internet search engines, going through government and corporate records and by using social networking sites on the Web. Sometimes the investigation works best as team reporting, allowing multiple reporters to contribute their unique talents to the story. No matter what shape your story will take, it is crucial that you take the time to prepare for your investigation.

3

SETTING THE COURSE FOR RESEARCH: THE STORY PREMISE

I n 1497, Portuguese explorer Vasco de Gama sailed around southern Africa looking for a sea route to India. He found it 10 months later and returned not only with spices but the discovery that citrus fruits prevent scurvy. His trip was a success, but when he set off, he didn't know what he would find, how long it would take to get there or how difficult the voyage would be.

When you investigate a story you explore for information. You won't know what you will find, how long it will take or how hard your journey will be. You start with just a piece of information and a question. That first piece might be a campaign donation made from a businessperson to a politician. Or it could be the firing of a university administrator. It might be a surprising statistic or an anecdotal comment that something doesn't seem right. To turn the statistic or tip into a story is a process of exploration. But before you set out, you need to prepare for the voyage.

You need to have an idea of what you want. You need to take your story idea and turn it into a *premise*. That's a short statement that describes what you expect to find. It is a guess. Over the course of your investigation, you will seek information that shows that you guessed right or that proves it wrong. Keep your premise as focused as possible. "I'm planning on doing a story about how inept the city government is," is too broad and too vague. Instead, a focused and more workable premise is:

> "I'm going to investigate whether car accidents are going up because the city takes too long to repair potholes."

Think of your premise as a very short version of a story. It needs the who, what, where and when. Note that the example premise contains these elements. Start with a question that can't be answered without significant reporting and when answered would tell readers something they didn't know. The most interesting stories start from questions that have to do with people.

Now identify what you already know about the story topic and think about what you need to learn. In Appendix A.3 is a story published in the North Coast Journal in May 2008 that investigated the suicide of a man in a county jail in northern California. The story came out of an investigative reporting class project at Humboldt State University in California. The premise was that the man was mentally ill and his incarceration and death may be a reflection of the failure of the state and county to care for people who are mentally ill. Exhibit 3.1 shows some of the initial thoughts that the students began with.

Out of the list in 3.1, you can start drawing up a rough plan for getting information. Exhibit 3.2 shows the list of information the Humboldt students decided they needed to focus on for their preliminary research on jail suicides.

What we know and don't know about the jail suicide.   **EXHIBIT 3.1**

WHAT WE KNOW	WHAT THAT MIGHT MEAN
A man died in the county jail.	The death could have been prevented.
He reportedly killed himself.	He was mentally ill.
He was Native American.	This could be a case of discriminatory treatment.

WHAT WE DON'T KNOW	WHY WE NEED TO FIND OUT
Was it really suicide?	It could be a case of criminal neglect or official misconduct.
Was he mentally ill?	He might have needed treatment he didn't get or needed to be in a hospital.
Is someone responsible?	Solutions will be hard to push for if we can't name a culprit responsible.
Was it significant that he was Native American?	Perhaps the county discriminates against Native Americans or fails to take into account cultural factors.
His criminal background.	Maybe he didn't belong in jail.
Jail procedures.	Either they weren't followed or they were inadequate.
Number of suicides in the jail.	There could be a pattern of neglect or abuse.
How the death could have been prevented.	Steps could be taken in the future to prevent suicides.

A plan of action.   **EXHIBIT 3.2**

1. Get data
   - Statistics from the county on inmate population and death
   - Statistics from the U.S. Department of Justice on deaths in jails and demographics of inmate populations
   - Statistics on suicides among Native Americans
   - Statistics on the number of people in the jail who are mentally ill

2. Get documents
   - Standard jail protocol
   - Protocol for treating people in the jail who are mentally ill
   - Case files and other court records concerning the case
   - Medical and psychological evaluations and records, if possible
   - Birth and death certificates
   - Autopsy report
   - School records

3. Conduct initial interviews
   - Probation officer
   - Jail guard
   - Expert on mental health and jails
   - Victims of crimes he was charged with
   - Someone from Atascadero State Hospital
   - Someone from county mental health department
   - District attorney
   - Public defender
   - Judge

A PRELIMINARY RESEARCH PLAN

 nce you have a rough idea of what you will need, begin your preliminary research. In your preliminary research, look for the following:

1. A list of names and contact information of people to interview
2. The initial questions you need to ask these people in the interviews
3. The basic terminology that you will need in order to understand their answers
4. Initial data and suggestions for data you might need to track down
5. Possible subtopics that may come up or are worth exploring
6. Information you don't need to pursue right now

Good background research will also give you a sense of what areas have already been well covered by other reporters and other publications; what information you likely won't need; and what data will be off-limits or nearly impossible to get.

The people

In 2004, Newsday reporter Dawn MacKeen was one of a team of reporters who investigated the treatment of elderly people in assisted living centers. She said her investigation required "old-fashioned reporting" whereby one person leads to another who leads to another.[1]

It is difficult to find the first person in the string; he won't just come to you. You will likely find your initial sources by reading through all kinds of documents — old news stories, press releases, court records, government reports, meeting agendas — anything that you can get your hands on that seems relevant to the problem you are interested in.

Down the road, you will want a diverse range of human sources in your story, which will be discussed more in Chapter 6. During your preliminary research you must keep your eyes open for these people. They may be cited in news stories or referred to in court records or government documents and include:

- People affected by the problem, such as residents, students, patients, workers, consumers or parents.
- People who regulate or monitor the problem. They might work for government or police agencies, or industry and watchdog organizations.
- People responsible for the problem, such as businesspeople or people employed by corporations, or nonprofit or governmental organizations including charities, hospitals or educational institutions.
- People who are independent and knowledgeable about the problem, such as psychologists or sociologists, scientists or financial or legal experts.

The questions

Once you identify the people you need to talk to, you must figure out what questions you need to ask them. Background research will help you identify the important issues that you can focus your questions around. The more you already know when you go into an interview, the better the information that you take from it will be. Sources don't expect reporters to be experts, but they do expect them to be familiar with the topic, the main players involved in it and the main events that shaped it.

The terminology

You should brief yourself on basic terminology. We live in a world in which most people speak at least two languages. Their first language is the one they use in their everyday life — it could be English or Spanish or Tagalog. But almost everyone speaks a second "language," and that might be computerese, legalese, or the jargons of finance, science, engineering or medicine. While you don't want your finished story to be filled with legal or technical language, if the people you will need to interview speak that language, you need to understand it. You will find that people will be more willing to be interviewed when you can demonstrate knowledge about the topic. A variety of Internet resources are available to give you a crash course in terminology. Exhibit 3.3 has a sampling of them.

The data

Just as one person leads to another, one number often leads to others. You might find that because of cuts to the state budget, the local school board will cut school budgets by 10 percent across the board, and that will include the free lunch program. This presents a number of questions: Will the school cut 10

A sample of free online dictionaries to help you translate "foreign" languages.   **EXHIBIT 3.3**

LANGUAGE YOU NEED TRANSLATED	ONLINE DICTIONARY	SOURCE
Architecture	http://architecture.about.com/library/bl-glossary.htm	About.com
Engineering	www.engnetglobal.com	EngNet Engineering Network
Law and Finance	www.thefreedictionary.com	Farlex Inc.
Math and Science	www.scienceworld.wolfram.com	Wolfram Research.com
Medical	www.medlineplus.gov	The U.S. National Library of Medicine
Technology	www.techdictionary.com	The Online Computer Dictionary

percent off the food budget for the lunch program, so that each child gets a meal that costs 10 percent less, or will 10 percent fewer children be given lunch? Meanwhile, what's the rate of applications? Are fewer children expected to apply, or will there be 10 percent more applications? Are food prices rising? If food prices are expected to rise 10 percent, *and* 10 percent more children are expected to apply for free lunches *and* the school plans to cut the current budget by 10 percent, does that mean that the cuts actually work out to 30 percent? These and similar types of questions on the data are vital to an investigative story.

Look carefully for any and all data in the material you read in your preliminary research. You can find numbers in the same places you find the names of people to interview. Use the numbers as a starting point. If you discover that one in four children in your area live below the poverty line, which is already at a low level, you might decide to investigate the possibility that children in your community go hungry. If you discover that 17 percent of the county jail's inmate population is Native American when Native Americans account for only 8 percent of the county's overall population, you might investigate the relationship between police and Native American tribes in your area.

The subtopics

Only if you know the different subtopics that exist within your broader topic can you focus your investigation around the issues that you deem most pressing. In a story about cuts to school lunch programs, for instance, you will interview a number of people, each of whom will know a lot about a little area within the broad topic of school lunches: how food gets purchased and supplied, nutrition needs, food safety concerns, government regulations, children's eating habits, community standards and expectations and so on. You need to know what subtopics may come up and which ones will most benefit your story. This also helps you to get the right information from the right source by showing the source that you are knowledgeable. You don't want to line up an interview with someone knowledgeable about federal government regulations and start out with questions about local community standards and expectations.

The tangents

It is also important at this early stage to start to get a sense of what you don't need. Editors don't want you to waste time. So focus on what's relevant. You can expand your examination later if the evidence you gather suggests different questions to ask. Jot down interesting information, data and people that don't seem particularly relevant, and set them aside in a special folder that you can call "tangents." Doing so could prove useful later when you or a source connect dots and this information proves to be part of an important thread. If you toss it or misplace it now and it later turns out to be relevant, you will waste time redoing research.

THE BASICS OF BACKGROUND RESEARCH

Background research may be done in many ways. What sources you turn to will depend on the topic you choose to investigate. Some topics lend themselves well to Internet research, while for others you will find little information online. Try to be as thorough as possible in your search without wasting time following endlessly from one hyperlink to another online or chasing after reports and news records that yield little information.

Although you want to focus your research, you don't want to rule out too much information at this point. Look for general information about a topic, person or organization. Look for people who have some type of relationship with the topic, person or organization. The sources you need to turn to will depend on the topic you wish to research. But it is important to understand how to tailor your research to the needs of your particular investigation.

If you think of the background research as the starting point for a journey, you know you will need a map and directions that will get you to your destination. So you will want to talk to the relevant people and sift through databases that can provide you with those directions. For example, for an investigation of school lunches, you may learn through reading news stories and scholarly and government reports that you should start with the school board and local PTA, that you will want to talk to someone at the U.S. Department of Education, that food suppliers might play a role and that there have been some lawsuits over lunch programs. You find a study by a food economist who could be a good source and who mentions historical trends. And you find an article in an education trade paper that suggests a correlation between nutrition and a child's ability to learn. Together, those form an initial route for you to follow.

Keep the news angle in mind

Many times investigative stories involve ongoing problems. So when you scan news or government or corporate reports look for news angles — recent or proposed changes in regulations, new developments in the planning stage, changes in strategy or business practices, even new hires or fires of important people related to the problem you are interested in. Political elections always present opportunities for looking at ongoing problems if one or more candidates address the problem or one related to it. If you find a news angle to peg your investigation on, you will find it easier to sell your story proposal to your editor or producer.

Think narrow to broad

Just as your story began with a small fact, your research should start small. If you start broad and then work your way in, you will likely overwhelm yourself and find yourself wasting time chasing after too many tangents. If you are interested in a person, search first for just that person. Then search for information about an organization the person worked with and by the position that he or she held. If you are interested in a company, you search first for information about the company, then information about the sector of business the company operates in. If you are interested in an issue, look locally, then regionally, then at problems statewide, then nationally. Use multiple searches and multiple approaches.

Once you find a few stories that have information relevant to your investigation, you will want to read the stories, highlight issues they raise and redo your search using the new and relevant terms you have found. Also scan the stories for experts previous reporters talked to and then search for other articles those experts might have written or are cited in. Note any news angles you could build your investigation around.

**Alternative Press
News Center**

www.altpress.org

Understand that there isn't any one completely thorough news database. Some search only the top newspapers and magazines. Some miss Web publications and advocacy publications entirely. You may need to use different search engines to find specialized sources. For example, to search advocacy publications, you need to search the Alternative Press Center's index.

A search of multiple news databases during background research for the Humboldt State project on a jail suicide failed to yield an excellent 20-story package on jail deaths done in 2004 by a Kentucky newspaper. However, such a package was the result of a search of IRE's story archives, available only to IRE members, as you can see in Exhibit 3.4.

Nor did a search of multiple news databases yield an 11-story package on Humboldt County suicides done in 2003 by a relatively new daily newspaper in

---

EXHIBIT 3.4   IRE membership gives you access to stories the major news databases miss.

Copyright © 2009, Investigative Reporters and Editors, Inc.

A screen shot of the search engine available at AlterNet.   **EXHIBIT 3.5**

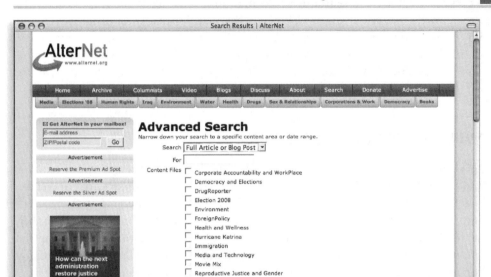

the region. To find it you needed to search the newspaper's own story archives. And news databases failed to turn up Silja J.A. Talvi, an editor at an alternative magazine called In These Times, who has written extensively on the subject of our penal system and the problems of mental health and women and minorities in prison. Students found her through an online resource called Alternet.org, a Web publication shown in Exhibit 3.5 that generates its own content and republishes articles printed in small, independent media outlets.

AlterNet
www.alternet.org

Keep the background information organized

In your preliminary search, keep track of the information you gather and where you gather it. It's a good idea to start logging all your information into a spreadsheet file with columns for the information source, the date of the article, where you found it, possible news angles or subtopics it suggests, any new possible sources identified, and any other information nuggets you cull from it. Entering information into a spreadsheet program allows you to organize it into a database. We will talk more about using your spreadsheet notes later on in this book. Next to the Internet, a spreadsheet program is the number one tool of investigative reporters. The earlier you learn how to use it, and the more proficient you become with it, the better an investigative reporter you will be.

I discuss Excel specifically in this text. But other spreadsheets also function as databases; they can search for information according to different criteria. In other words, as with a database, you can ask many spreadsheet programs to find you information that meets certain specifications within a massive amount of data. If you haven't used a spreadsheet program or you are rusty, you will find an Excel primer in Appendix C of this book. A number of free tutorials also are on the Internet.

WHERE TO START LOOKING

J ust as there is no one way to do background research, there is no one place to find the information you seek. The resources discussed next are good starting points, but new databases and other sources emerge all the time and others fall into disuse. I intend for the following to serve as examples only. And remember, while the Internet can be a powerful tool, sometimes you just have to pick up the phone and talk to someone. The following resources are excellent tools, especially for background research, but they can't be your entire investigation.

News databases and archives

A good place to start is with the news itself. You should look up the articles or broadcasts that your own news organization and competing news organizations have done on the topic. Then check a host of other news sources — weekly and monthly magazines; national (and international if appropriate) newspapers; industry, trade and specialized publications; advocacy publications; and press releases. One common way of doing this is through a news database such as LexisNexis, which most college students have free access to through their college or university library. If you are unfamiliar with checking news databases, sit down with the reference librarian at your college or university.

Exhibit 3.6 shows LexisNexis, which allows you to search not only print publications but broadcast transcripts, blogs and online publications as well. It will also organize a search by subtopics, geography or people around whom the articles focus.

You'll get different information from different databases, so it is useful to plug the same or slightly altered terms into different databases. Make sure you understand how the database works: what types of publications it searches, how far back it goes and whether it offers full text of articles it finds or simply citations.

Don't limit yourself to newspapers or general interest publications. Information is plentiful, but it is spread over daily newspaper articles, magazine features, trade and industry publications, and academic papers in scholarly journals and books. You want to do at least a quick scan for relevant source material in all those categories.

Searches using LexisNexis.   **EXHIBIT 3.6**

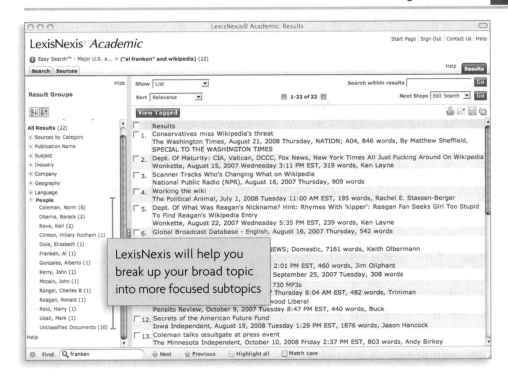

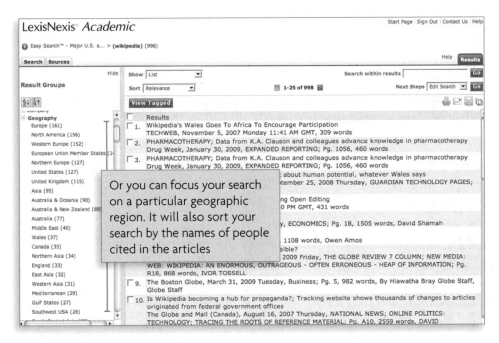

Wikipedia

I list Wikipedia next not due to order of importance, but because it tends to be the first place students and many professional journalists turn to when they want to find information about an unfamiliar subject or they want to refresh their knowledge about a topic. It is a terrific *starting point*. The information in its entries will help you to formulate the questions you need to ask. But when you use Wikipedia, consider all the "facts" in it as information you might get from someone you don't completely trust. You'd double-check anything he or she told you before using it in an article for publication.

Wikipedia
www.wikipedia.org

Perhaps more useful than the rundown Wikipedia gives you is its list of citations at the bottom of each article, which indicates where the information supposedly came from. Those citations can lead you to good sources. Say you wanted to look into the safety of elevators on your campus. As you can see in Exhibit 3.7, the end of Wikipedia's entry on elevators contains a link to the Timeline of the Elevator. That's published online by the Virtual Elevator Museum, which is published by Elevator World magazine, which also publishes a state-by-state directory of elevator industry professionals, including consultants.

Be warned, however, that using Wikipedia as anything *but* a starting point is dangerous. Some news organizations found that out the hard way by reprint-

---

EXHIBIT 3.7   The final portion of Wikipedia's "elevator" entry.

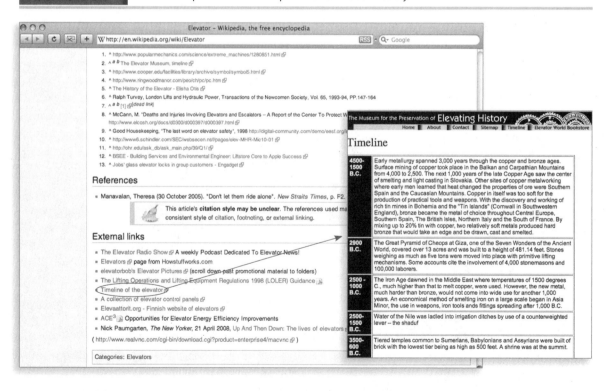

ing information that turned out to be untrue. In March 2007, the comedian and actor Sinbad called news organizations to inform them that he was not, in fact, dead, as his entry on Wikipedia had announced.[2] And an online tracking tool called Wikiscanner has found that thousands of changes and deletions made to entries on politicians and companies are changed by representatives of the politicians and companies.[3] It even traced back edits to an entry about writer, comedian and politician Al Franken to Fox News Network. They had changed information regarding statements Franken made on the radio show Fresh Air about his book "Lies and the Lying Liars Who Tell Them: A Fair and Balanced Look at the Right," which was a tongue-in-cheek attack on the Fox News Network.[4] As you can see, because of its continuing lack of credibility, journalists who cite Wikipedia as a source look foolish.

Other people's stories

It is helpful to think of the whole journalism establishment as one big collaborative effort to educate and inform the public. Why start gathering information from scratch when someone else has already gathered it? The best journalism builds on knowledge that is already out there. Journalists grab sources other reporters have found and follow up on questions other reporters have asked but failed to get answered.

When you find articles in your background news searches, look for the names of people who might help you in your project. Note too, the types of people the reporters on those stories sought out — you can try finding experts, policy makers and activists in similar positions closer to the subject of your story or geographically closer to home. Note what questions those reporters asked to see if you should ask similar questions.

Also, look for terms that apply to your subject. These articles may explain them for you or can give you a primer on words you need to look up.

Internet search engines

Most people have a rudimentary knowledge about search engines, and most use only the main engines at Google or Yahoo! But Google provides a long list of specialized search engines. You can find experts on a topic through Google Scholar. Google Blog Search is a great way to find people involved in particular activities like sports or hobbies, and people who work for various corporations or nonprofit organizations or are members of associations. For finding background on legislation or publicly available federal records, you may use Google's U.S. Government search engine.

Many people don't realize that other search engines, such as Alta Vista and Hotbot, typically produce different results. You may seek preliminary information through specialized search engines as well. Let's say someone suggests to

Google's Other Searches
http://scholar.google.com
http://blogsearch.google.com
www.google.com/unclesam

Specialized Search Engines
Science: www.scirus.com
Scholarly: http://infomine.ucr.edu

you that there is a problem with doctors who inappropriately recommend magnetic resonance imaging scans. You want to know more about MRIs. You could try Google or you could try searching on a site called Scirus, which searches through scientific sites and filters out nonscientific material. Or you can go to InfoMine to use a search engine created by university librarians for scholarly research. There you can search by subtopics such as business and economics or biological, agricultural and medical sciences.

Understanding how search engines work and searching for information in different ways, even within the same search engine, are important investigative skills; when you reword the phrases you search for, often you will get a different list of possibly useful links.

First determine what you want or need to find. Write that down on a piece of paper as a reminder. Once you focus on the topic that interests you, jot down different terms that are unique to it. The library at the University of California at Berkeley, which has a great online tutorial on using Internet search engines, suggests you try acronyms, distinctive names and abbreviations. It also suggests thinking about societies, organizations and groups that work on the issue that you are interested in and searching their sites for other links they find useful, as well as discussion groups, articles they cite or journals they publish.

Search Engine Tutorial
www.lib.berkeley.edu/TeachingLib/Guides/Internet/FindInfo.html

Each time you hit on a link that seems useful, refocus on the question you started your investigation with. Ask yourself:

- How relevant is this information to my topic?
- What questions does it answer?
- Does it provide a name of someone or suggest someone who might be worthwhile tracking down for more information?
- Does it raise interesting, relevant and important issues worth exploring?

Jot down the relevant information you find, the names and titles of the people worth tracking down and the interesting and important issues worth exploring. You will turn that into your initial To Do list. Over the course of your investigation, you will add tasks to that list and cross them off as you get them done. This process will help you stay focused, which is important even in the preliminary research stage. Without focus, you can get so wrapped up in searching for more and more relevant information that you never get to your main purpose — thorough reporting and analysis in order to publish your own, original content.

I will go into more detail about finding and analyzing relevant data from Web-based sources in Chapter 8.

Academic search engines

Most college and university libraries provide students access to databases such as ProQuest or Academic Search Elite. These allow you to search not only newspapers and magazines but also what's known as peer-reviewed journals —

publications that print articles only after they have been reviewed by a panel of reputable scholars in the field. And you can download full text copies of many of these articles.

A growing community of scholars are frustrated by the peer review process. They say it is time-consuming and acts as a barrier to free sharing of information. They publish their research electronically on what is known as the Open Archives Initiative — university, hosted sites that are accessible to the public through various specialized search engines. Some search engines focus on psychological papers, others on physics, economics, information science, social sciences and so on. For an example of how this kind of search would work, let's return to the topic of jail suicides. If you go to a search engine called BASE (for Bielefeld Academic Search Engine) and plug in the terms "suicide" and "jail," you get a list of more than 50 articles. One example citation is provided in Exhibit 3.8.[5]

The citation in Exhibit 3.8 includes useful information: two possible sources for interviews and a contact e-mail address, the idea that there are accepted protocols to follow (you could check to see if your local jail follows those protocols) and key words for follow up searches. The article promises you useful data.

Open Archive Search Providers

www.openarchives. org/service/ listproviders.html

Search engine results from www.base-search.net.   **EXHIBIT 3.8**

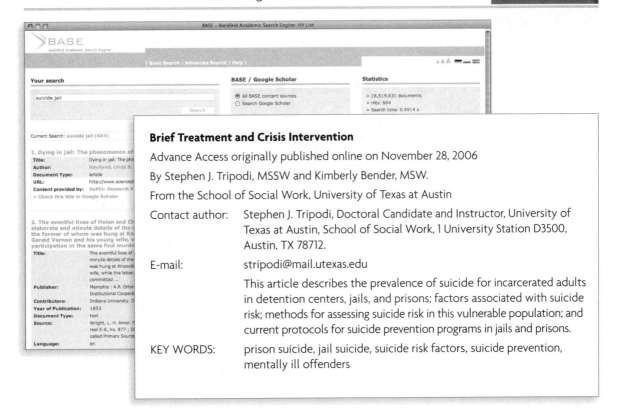

Brief Treatment and Crisis Intervention

Advance Access originally published online on November 28, 2006

By Stephen J. Tripodi, MSSW and Kimberly Bender, MSW.

From the School of Social Work, University of Texas at Austin

Contact author: Stephen J. Tripodi, Doctoral Candidate and Instructor, University of Texas at Austin, School of Social Work, 1 University Station D3500, Austin, TX 78712.

E-mail: stripodi@mail.utexas.edu

This article describes the prevalence of suicide for incarcerated adults in detention centers, jails, and prisons; factors associated with suicide risk; methods for assessing suicide risk in this vulnerable population; and current protocols for suicide prevention programs in jails and prisons.

KEY WORDS: prison suicide, jail suicide, suicide risk factors, suicide prevention, mentally ill offenders

Government records

Later in your investigation you will do more in-depth Internet searching to find documents and data, but you can do some basic, preliminary research with government records. You could start by plugging an individual's name in the Federal Election Commission electronic database of campaign donors at their Web site to see what politicians or political action committees (PACs) someone donates money to, or to search by politician or PAC name to find a list of donors. Exhibit 3.9 shows a search page of the FEC site.

You could also check out the documents of incorporation businesses must file with the secretary of state's office in your state or a nonprofit organization's Form 990, the document they must file with the Internal Revenue Service so that they don't have to pay federal taxes. We will explain more about those documents in Chapter 8. As you can see in Exhibit 3.10, the U.S. Census Bureau's American Factfinder program will give you a nice snapshot of a community. By plugging a city or county name or zip code into American Factfinder, you can quickly find out information about household size, gender, age breakdowns, school enrollment, education level of citizenry, ethnicities, number of foreign-born people and percent of people living with disabilities. And that's just a small sample of the information you can get through the U.S. Census.

EXHIBIT 3.9	A search on the FEC Web site.

A search for Wal-Mart yields a list of contributions the retail giant made to both Republican and Democratic politicians in the 2007 and 2008 election cycles.

FEDERAL ELECTION COMMISSION   Skip Navigation

ABOUT THE FEC   PRESS OFFICE   QUICK ANSWERS   SITE MAP   SEARCH   enter search here →

HOME / CAMPAIGN FINANCE RPTS AND DATA / DATA SEARCH / SUMMARY REPORTS SEARCH

Summary Reports Search

Campaign Finance Reports and Data

Meetings and Hearings

Enforcement Matters

Help with Reporting and Compliance

Law & Regulations

Commission Calendar

Search From the Following Criteria:

Election Cycle: ○ 1999 - 2000   ○ 2001 - 2002   ○ 2003 - 2004   ○ 2005 - 2006   ○ 2007 - 2008   ◉ 2009 - 2010
Display: ○ Candidate Campaigns   ○ PACs & Parties   ◉ All

Name: wal-mart
State: (Select as many as appropriate)
         ALL
         ALABAMA
         ALASKA
         AMERICAN SAMOA

Office: ○ U.S. House   ○ U.S. Senate   ○ U.S. President   ◉ All
District:

Party: ○ Democratic   ○ Republican   ○ Other   ◉ All
Candidate Status: ○ Incumbent   ○ Challenger   ○ Open Seat   ◉ All

(Send Query)   (Clear Form)

What's New   Library   FOIA   USA.gov   Privacy   Links   eFiling   Inspector General   Subscribe

Federal Election Commission, 999 E Street, NW, Washington, DC 20463 (800) 424-9530 In Washington (202) 694-1000
For the hearing impaired, TTY (202) 219-3336 Send comments and suggestions about this site to the web manager.

Basic facts from Factfinder.   **EXHIBIT 3.10**

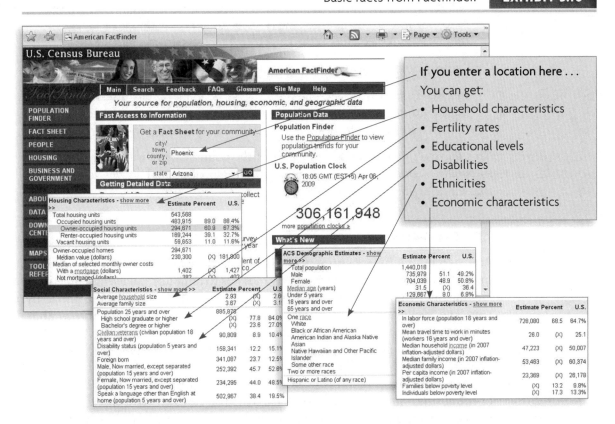

On the local government level, agendas and minutes of government meetings will tell you about problems people think their government representatives need to fix or plans or projects a government agency is considering or has considered. State or federal legislative or executive actions often lead to, or are preceded by, hearings and a period for public comments. All these documents provide background information as well as names of people who might be good to interview.

You can also plug a search term into the home page for the U.S. Senate or the House of Representatives. Often, when a problem that people cannot solve confronts them, they turn in frustration to their representative or senator. If the senator or representative took some action to solve the problem, you can bet he or she publicized it in some way. Let's return to the elevator story. You enter "elevators" into the search box on the House of Representatives page. Among the listings that result is a notice from the office of Rep. Anthony Weiner of New York's 9th District:[6]

U.S. Legislature Pages
www.senate.gov
www.house.gov

> New York City—New York City Housing Authority should take immediate steps to secure the safety of elevators in Pomonok Housing, Representative Anthony Weiner

(D-Brooklyn and Queens) today demanded. Rep. Weiner cited a recent Daily News report showing that there were 263 security lapses in Pomonok elevators last year. According to the report, it took the Housing Authority an average of 10 hours to repair Pomonok's elevators — the longest wait time in the borough.

And it provides this news update as well:

Last week, a Brooklyn infant, who was being rushed to the hospital after he stopped breathing, died after an elevator stalled 20 to 30 seconds. In August, a 5-year-old Brooklyn boy fell ten stories to his death when an elevator stopped between floors.

This tells you that at least in one part of the country there were concerns about the safety of elevators in a large public housing project, and it gives you evidence that elevator safety is important.

Press releases

A press release is an announcement issued by a company or organization. Sometimes it is about a new product, other times it is to announce an event. Sometimes a company issues it because it has information it must release to the public by law. The Securities and Exchange Commission, for example, requires public companies to announce quarterly and yearly earnings to the public, as well as major actions such as mergers or acquisitions. If you understand the limitations of a press release, it can be a good starting point.

Factiva
http://factiva.com

You can search for press releases in a number of places. Check LexisNexis or the business news site Dow Jones Factiva. You can also go to the sites of press release distributors like prnewswire.com or businesswire.com and search by the name of a company or organization, or by keywords. Searching through several months' worth of press releases could tell you a number of things, such as recent activities and news events, which could give you a news angle for your project. Press releases can also give you the names and positions of company officials, which could help you to navigate corporate mazes and get past public relations people. Sometimes they alert you to alliances the company has with other businesses, which could give you outside sources of information. Reading press releases before interviewing officials from a company or organization is important. They could expect you to be familiar with the company's recent activities and even if they don't, in demonstrating your familiarity you will come across as competent and professional.

A timely press release gives you the opportunity to call company officials and improves your chances of getting them to call you back. Often, the company has issued the press release because it has news it wants to talk about. Be prepared to talk about the release of the new product for a few minutes, before asking for information about the topic on which you plan to focus. If your investigation involves a public corporation, you will want to scan recent public filings such as annual and quarterly reports and press releases to get a handle on what the company has been up to. You can get those through the company's Web site or from a database of financial filings the U.S. Security and Exchange Commission maintains at www.sec.gov. We will look more closely at corporate financial reports later on in the book as you progress in your investigation.

Listservs

Listservs are e-mail lists people sign up for so that they can contact other people who are members of the same group or who share a similar interest. Patricia Simms, a reporter at the Wisconsin State Journal, likened the use of listservs for investigative reporting to eavesdropping at the dinner table. She has used them to find out information on health and medical issues. While some of them are private — you need to be invited in order to join — many of them are public. Once you find the listserv, you can join it to receive any messages sent to the group.[7] It will also allow you to send out inquiries, although you won't know who else is on the listserv so be careful what you broadcast. You can search for listservs by subject at L-Soft's CataList, which boasts more than 50,000 public listservs. A search for "elevators" in CataList produced the result in Exhibit 3.11.

CataList Listservs
www.lsoft.com/lists/
listref.html

Search result for "elevators" using L-Soft's CataList   **EXHIBIT 3.11**

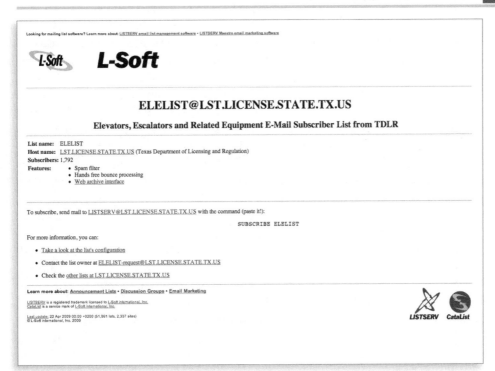

Financial Web sites

If you are interested in a public corporation or a business sector, you can get some great summary information from sites such as Yahoo! Finance, marketwatch.com and Hoovers.com. If you plug the company's name into their search box, you can find their latest financial information, whether they have posted profits or losses, a list of their top executives and names of their main investors and competitors. Hoovers allows you to search by geographic region if you simply want to find any corporations headquartered in and around your city. A search in Hoovers for "Peoria, Illinois," for example, yields a list of 23 companies that call Peoria home.

Forums

Google Groups
http://groups.
google.com

Also known as Usenet, chat boards, discussion boards or groups, forums are places on the Internet where people can post comments and hold online discussions. You can search these boards through Google Groups. Forums are a great place to find the people tucked inside corporations and other organizations. These are the people who tend to know what's really going on, and they don't always toe the corporate line. Use forums to discover what people are talking about and to find people worth talking to.

Social networking sites

Sites such as Facebook, MySpace and Twitter are quickly replacing listservs and Usenet because it is so easy to set up a group within these sites. They are becoming the first step for any organized activity. You can use social networking sites when you want to try throwing a question out to the crowd, a technique known as *crowdsourcing*. When you broadcast to the world that you are investigating something, you risk having your target take defensive steps that could include gagging anyone it has influence over. On the other hand, if you shoot out a question over the Internet, it may end up on the desk of someone who has valuable information to offer you, whom you would not have found any other way. Be careful that your question does not accuse anyone of wrongdoing. When you send out a question over the Internet, it is considered publishing; therefore, you want to make sure you don't libel anyone. Don't publish any accusations against any individual until you have proved those allegations.

You can use social networking sites to do a limited broadcast. Say you wanted to find people who work at McDonald's. If you have 100 friends on Facebook, you can post a message in your status box asking all your Facebook friends if they know anyone who works for McDonald's and asking them to relay your question to everyone on their Facebook friends list and so on. Within a day at least 1,000 people will know that you seek people who work at McDonald's, and you will likely get at least a few comments back. You might find your News Feed full of them.

Blogs

It seems as if you can't claim to be an expert on a topic if you don't blog about it. Blogs are sites on the Internet where people post their thoughts. When you search for information via blogs you face the same problem as when you use a search engine — too much information. Blogs are so numerous that many blogs can suck you in without yielding the information you are actually looking for.

Don't dive into blogs without a sense of the type of person or information you need to find. When you find yourself reading about the dating experiences of some 17-year-old in Scotland, it is time to mentally slap yourself. Stick to your subject and to sources who seem credible: Trustworthy sources provide their names and contact numbers, to begin with, and are affiliated with an organization that you've heard of or at least that you can track down through reputable sources to make sure it exists. Use information from the Internet as a starting point, but never use information that you cannot double-check with at least one reputable source.

Consider what happened to MSNBC and Fox News shortly after the 2008 presidential election. Fox News reported that in preparations for a televised debate prior to the election, Republican vice presidential candidate Sarah Palin did not seem to know that Africa was a continent. Fox News said the information came from a campaign insider but did not identify the person. MSNBC television anchor David Shuster identified the person as Martin Eisenstadt, an adviser for John McCain's campaign and a senior fellow at a think tank called the Harding Institute for Freedom and Democracy. But neither Eisenstadt nor the Harding Institute existed. As the New York Times reported later that week, they were the creation of two pranksters who had set up a Web site for the fictional Harding Institute, created a blog for the fictional Eisenstadt and even created a YouTube video for him, which starred one of the pranksters, Eitan Gorlin. Someone had e-mailed a blog posting purportedly from Eisenstadt to an MSNBC producer, who failed to double-check the source. It was particularly embarrassing for the network, considering that publications such as The Huffington Post and Mother Jones previously admitted that they had been duped by the hoax. The LA Times and the New Republic had fallen for it as well.[8]

Social Sites for Crowdsourcing
www.facebook.com
www.myspace.com
www.twitter.com
www.linkedin.com
www.yelp.com
www.craigslist.com

TEAM REPORTING

P reliminary research should give you a sense of how big your investigation might be. Depending on its potential size and scope, you might consider doing it as a team project. This decision needs to be made early in the investigative process so it can be set up to take advantage of a team approach. News organizations tend to handle big investigations by assigning them to teams. The team might be a pair of reporters or one that involves as many as eight dedicated reporters and researchers. Few organizations can afford to have one or more reporters work full time on only one story for long. With multiple members on a long project, each reporter can still cover breaking news even as the group continues the investigation. Some news organizations partner with others on investigations; reporters from a television station work with their newspaper counterparts, for example. That way the organizations don't have to sacrifice too great a portion of their staffs for the project. But other reasons for turning an investigation into a team project might be considered.

Why collaborate?

Teams build on each other's strengths. "You can do more things faster," said Joe Demma, a former investigations editor at the Sun-Sentinel newspaper in South Florida. "You can have different perspectives and strengths that complement each other. This gives the project not only speed, but scope, breadth and insights that one reporter alone is lacking."[9]

Each person on your team will bring different skills and ideas to it. You might have someone great at filing and managing public records requests, plowing through documents and putting together databases, while others on the team handle the interviews. Sometimes reporters are great at gathering information but they can't organize it; in that case, a good project manager can mean the difference between success and failure.

Maud Beelman, a projects editor at The Dallas Morning News, likened team investigations to compounded interest. "When individual knowledge is shared and leveraged," she wrote, "the overall effort is strengthened."[10]

With a team, you can send people out in multiple directions. Paul Williams successfully directed a team at the Omaha Sun in the 1970s. One series of stories by his team exposed how Boys Town, a home for troubled youth made famous by a Spencer Tracy movie of the same name, raised far more money from the public than it needed. He later wrote that it helped to be able to work on different lines of inquiry at the same time. While one reporter examined how Boys Town created and sustained the Boys Town image, others gathered and examined documents that the organization had to file with the state and federal governments about its operations and fund-raising activities.[11] "The lone reporter may be simply outpaced by events," he wrote. "Changes in policy, elections, personnel turnover, death or transfer of key persons, loss of sources—these may cloud or negate the meaning of facts gathered nine or ten months (or two years) earlier."[12]

Teams can create large multimedia projects. Stories geared for the Internet alone or for both print and Internet or broadcast and Internet demand collaboration. When the Miami Herald investigated the waste of sales tax dollars that were supposed to improve mass transit, it presented the investigation using a wide variety of multimedia and interactive story elements, called a story package. The story package mentioned in Chapter 2, titled "Taken for a Ride," included multiple stories, a video overview, graphic charts, a slideshow, a timeline, and a video interview.[13] Often, one reporter working alone cannot produce that kind of a presentation. Exhibit 3.12 shows the possible structure of a team responsible for a multimedia project. Note that team members may fill multiple roles.

Taken for a Ride
www.miamiherald.
com/multimedia/
news/transit/index.
html

The investigative team for a multimedia presentation.   **EXHIBIT 3.12**

Choosing the size of the team

How many people you put on a team will depend on the scope of the project, and how much time and what resources you have. A team might be one reporter and a Web developer. Or it might be a reporter and a photographer. Five reporters might form a team in which each one takes photos and video and they all work together on a Web presentation. You won't likely find big teams at small papers. Demma said that he managed teams as large as 19 reporters and three photographers and as small as two reporters. "One of our [projects in 2007] started out with two reporters and grew to three, then four, then five, then six, then more or less settled into three and a half," he said.[14]

Teams work particularly well for college classes. Class investigations led by David Protess in the Innocence Project, at the Medill Graduate School of Journalism at Northwestern University, have freed 11 people scheduled for execution. In George-

How the Pearl Project team uses technology for communication[15]	BOX 3.1

I n 2002, terrorists kidnapped Wall Street Journal reporter Daniel Pearl on the streets of Karachi, Pakistan, and later beheaded him. His colleague in Karachi, Asra Nomani, vowed to investigate his death and bring his killers to justice. But that proved to be a huge undertaking as the names of suspects grew and the connections between them became complex. In 2007 she teamed up with Georgetown University Professor Barbara Feinmann Todd to take the investigation into the classroom. The idea was to launch the Pearl Project to bring together the collective strengths of a group of journalism students to show the world once again that anyone who goes after a journalist will be brought to justice. The collaboration was based on the Arizona Project, the group formed to investigate the death of Arizona Republic reporter Don Bolles.

One problem was the size of the group — 32 undergraduate and graduate students. Another was that the source list was long. Many of the people they would need to interview were thousands of miles and five time zones away. To speak to them by phone would involve phone calls in the middle of the night. In addition, the class met just once a week for 2.5 hours. How could they coordinate all the activity among so many people and keep them all abreast? The solution lay in what they called Pearlpedia. They created a password-protected wiki to which team members would deposit interview transcripts, documents, reporting plans, assignments, articles and Web links. They appointed one person to keep everything on the site consistent in style. The students would each check the site for updates and communicate with each other at all hours of the day and night. They would "meet" with faraway sources in electronic chat rooms. "We plan to publish our work in traditional narrative form in national media outlets but also to make the Pearlpedia public someday as a sort of digital archive of a murder that marked a tragic milestone in modern-day journalism," Nomani wrote.

Find the Pearl Project at http://scs.georgetown.edu/pearlproject.   Reprinted with permission.

town University, the Pearl Project was started as a class investigation involving 32 students who looked into the killing of Wall Street Journal reporter Daniel Pearl in Pakistan in 2002. A closer look at that team is provided in Box 3.1.

Leading the team

If you choose to work as a team you need a leader. "A group with no designated leader will not produce good work," advises Mindy McAdams, a professor at the University of Florida at Gainesville. "The leader is the ultimate decision-maker for the team. The leader checks in with everyone often to ensure that they are getting what they need and staying in touch with the others. The leader must bring the project in on time. A leader is not a boss or a dictator. A leader doesn't do others' work for them but redistributes the work as needed."[16]

Some team leaders are more involved in the project than others. At times a team forms out of a group of reporters who each express interest in exploring the same issue and they choose the leader. At other times, the editor will form the team. Regardless, good leaders share common characteristics that help make the project a success. Exhibit 3.13 lists some of those traits.

Characteristics of a good team leader.   **EXHIBIT 3.13**

1. **Commands respect.** The leader should be someone with some experience or authority. There will be times when a decision must be made that some people on the team won't like. The leader is the type of person who can get people to accept a decision they won't like. In the professional world, the leader needs to act as a liaison and work with the rest of the news organization, be able to control time and resource issues and get approval from management for risky or controversial decisions.

2. **Is committed.** The leader considers the project his top priority. While no journalist should sacrifice family, health, other job responsibilities or a social life completely to a story, you don't want as leader someone who will abandon the project as soon as something else comes up.

3. **Holds tightly to a loose leash.** The leader is someone who understands she is actively involved even when each of the members seem to be operating on [his or her] own.

4. **Is a delegator, not a do-it-yourselfer.** The leader has to be someone who has enough confidence in the team members to assign them to what needs to be done and then lets them do it.

5. **Likes to solve puzzles.** You want someone who has a can-do attitude. When faced with a problem, the leader tries to figure out how to get it done rather than accept the idea that it can't be done.

6. **Has backbone.** That means that the person is someone willing to live with negative repercussions. When you come out with a story that aims to spur change, it will anger a number of people. People don't like to be forced to change the way they live their lives or do business. You want a leader who remains enthusiastic even after he realizes what's at stake.

7. **Accepts leadership but doesn't thrive on it.** You don't want someone who likes the feeling of power. Former New York Times Magazine food writer Molly O'Neill once wrote how when she was a chef running her own kitchen, she liked to peel garlic cloves, even though it was considered one of the lowliest tasks in the restaurant.

8. **Knows how to listen.** The team leader sits back while everyone else talks, and takes it all in. Reporters who talk a good game rarely make great team leaders.

9. **Is open-minded but realistic.** You don't want someone in charge who gets defensive when someone disagrees with a decision or with a direction. Open-minded also means open to crazy suggestions. On the other hand, she must keep the team grounded in reality when members start planning where to hang the Pulitzer even before the project ends.

10. **Has wide-angled vision.** The team leader should be someone capable of seeing the big picture out of the information gathered.

11. **Is a motivator and counselor.** The leader needs to be able to energize the team when the going gets tedious and talk them through frustrations.

Source: Based on Monica Moses.[17]

Dividing up responsibilities

Demma says that when you sit down to figure out who should do what, play to strengths. "The database reporter sometimes is not as polished at developing sources and interviewing sources and subjects," he said. "So, you need a good source developer and interviewer to go along with the database person. Then, you always could use a good document person, not only someone who knows how to read them, but what's out there and where to find them." One project he oversaw in 2007 involved four people:

1. A hard-hitting reporter who knew documents, was good at source development and could write well
2. A database reporter
3. Someone who could read and understand financial documents
4. A great, mild-mannered feature writer who could lay the groundwork for future source development

"Mostly reporters will start to drift off to their strengths and start to complement or play off each other," Demma said.[18]

Coordinating the gathering of information

Most reporters work best on their own. They protect their information until publication and even after publication. Working collaboratively means that you must share all notes and thoughts, and for some, that's an entirely new experience.

Even if some people perform only peripheral tasks, it is important that all individuals involved in the project meet regularly throughout the process. As the project evolves and changes shape, every member needs to know when direction changes and tangents drop. The leader needs to remind everyone of the big picture as they each get steeped in the gritty details. The reporters should each brief the team on the interviews they did since the last meeting, lay out the major points they think the interviews touched on and interesting facts that came out, and the next step—new people or new directions the interviews suggest.

Organizing and sharing information electronically

The team leader also will need to develop early on a system to share information, observations, interview notes, data and documents. More stories are done these days with big teams because technology provides us with new ways to share information. Some basic tools that you can use for your own investigation are discussed below.

Listservs. Google and Yahoo! both allow you to set up mailing lists whereby members can communicate to all other members of the group.

Private discussion forums. With a discussion forum, all members of the group can post notes to the same site and then comment on those notes. If you post interviews as part of a single thread, you can search through all the notes by name or phrase. Google and Yahoo! both offer online discussion forums that you can set up as private. Online courseware, such as Moodle, which is an open-source software package that many universities offer for free, have online forums that are easy to set up and use.

Moodle
http://moodle.org

Google Docs
http:// docs.google.com

Google Documents. With Google Docs, all members can upload documents, images and maintain spreadsheets and databases. This allows everyone to input information as it is gathered and analyze it as the project proceeds.

Wikis. A wiki is software that is designed to allow multiple people to work on one document simultaneously without fear of losing information as it gets edited and changed. They are great for working on story outlines that will keep changing, for story drafts, and for recording thoughts and observations. As mentioned in Box 3.1, the team working on the Pearl Project used their Pearlpedia wiki to keep the story organized. A number of sites offer free wikis, including Wikidot and Wetpaint.

Free Wikis
www.wikidot.com
www.wetpaint.com

Calendar Groupware
www.zimbra.com

Calendars. Google and Web-based e-mail and calendaring programs such as Zimbra all offer collaborative calendars so that team members can stay on top of scheduled interview, deadlines, and the different work and vacation schedules of each member.

Maps. Google allows you to create collaborative mashup maps. When a project has a geographic element to it, members can add information they gather to a map, allowing the group to look at different places where something relevant to the investigation occurs. We will see how to do a Google Mashup later in this book.

Timelines. Dipity.com is a free online tool that allows you to create a multimedia timeline. You can create one that is collaborative. You can see in Exhibit 3.14 how members can note on a Dipity timeline any information they gather as the project progresses. They can also add video or photos or link to files stored elsewhere. And if you note a location when you create each event on your timeline, Dipity will automatically create a Google Mashup for you, as you can see in Exhibit 3.15. A mashup is an integrated tool that combines data from a variety of sources. Finally, if each team member enters his notes on a blog, you set Dipity to grab from those blog postings and add them to the timeline. So if reporters store their interviews or PDF documents on a blog, the interviews and documents also will show up on the collaborative timeline.

Dipity Timelines
www.dipity.com

EXHIBIT 3.14   Organizing a team using a Dipity timeline.

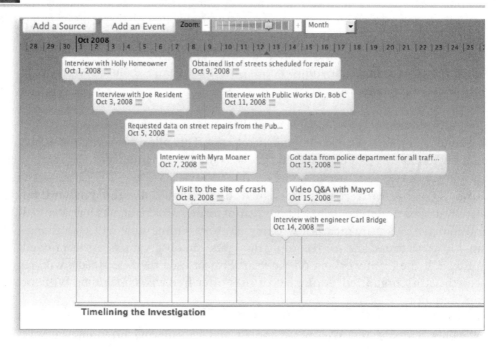

EXHIBIT 3.15   A Google Mashup created from the Dipity timeline.

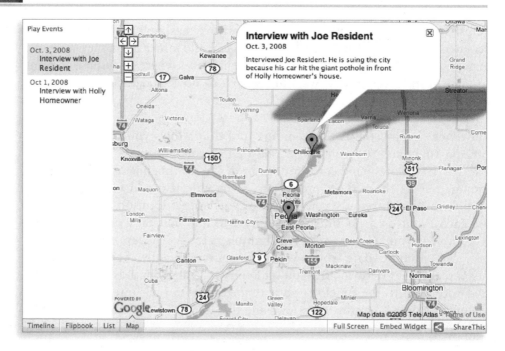

Writing the stories

Journalists often are known for big and easily bruised egos. That makes the decision on who will write the stories a tricky one for team reporting. On some teams, the person most familiar with the story writes it. On other teams, reporters each write separate articles, tackling different aspects of the story. Yet another method is to appoint one person lead writer. The reporters file copy to that person, who then compiles all copy into one or more stories. For the byline, you might put together a credit box, with each person's role defined in it. Writing as a team will be discussed in more detail in Chapter 11.

Fact-checking

Because of the short production cycle, daily newspapers tend not to verify quotes and paraphrases with sources. But on long stories, there is enough time for verification and it is an essential part of the process. If you have multiple members of a team, have reporters fact-check each other's quotes and information. Some teams build this into the information-gathering process.

Managing conflicts

Reporters tend to be self-starters and that could make for conflicts when they are forced to work as part of a team. To manage conflicts you need to see them as an inevitable part of the process, anticipate them and confront them. People will have different styles of working and reporting. Make sure everyone on the team is prepared to talk about their differences and to cede to a leader whenever team members cannot agree.

CONCLUSION

Starting an investigation is a little like starting off on an expedition. You want to have some sense of what you seek, even though you know that you will encounter unexpected things along the way. Background research helps you develop a rough plan of action you can follow. By reading articles of other publications on the same subject, academic papers, blogs and other information available in databases and over the Internet, you can get a sense of the people you will need to interview, the questions you will need to ask and the subtopics you will need to explore. If you plan to do your investigation as part of a team, this is the time to set up an organizational structure. You want to structure it in a way that leverages each person's skills and abilities. It is important to establish a communication system and a method for sharing the information that each person gathers. The preparation you take at this early stage will pay off in efficiency. It will prevent frustration later, as your investigation becomes complex, and it will help you prevent your project from becoming a disorganized mess.

1. Using LexisNexis, ProQuest Newstand, Factiva, News Bank Inc. or any news database that your college, university or public library gives you access to, answer the following questions:

    a. In 1991, the body of media mogul Ian Robert Maxwell was found floating in the Atlantic Ocean. He was thought to have fallen off his luxury yacht. What were some of the legal problems he faced prior to his death?

    b. In 1993, newspaper publisher Dean Lesher died, leaving the Contra Costa Times to his wife, Margaret Lesher. She sold it to Knight-Ridder, which later sold it to the MediaNews Group. What were the circumstances surrounding Margaret Lesher's death?

    c. What were the circumstances that led newspaper publisher Jay T. Harris to resign from the San Jose Mercury News in 2001?

    d. What were the circumstances that led five editors and a long-time columnist to resign from the Santa Barbara News Press in 2006?

2. Using Google Scholar, compile a list of people on one or more of the following topics, but only include those for whom you can find contact information:

    a. Racial profiling

    b. Discriminatory hiring practices at colleges and universities

    c. Unsafe building construction

    d. Predatory lending practices

    e. Financial mismanagement of charitable enterprises

    f. Ponzi schemes

3. Do a background search on your local congressman or congresswoman using Google/unclesam.

    a. What bills has he or she sponsored?

    b. What committees and subcommittees does he or she serve on?

    c. When the local or regional papers mention your representative in news stories, what issues is he or she connected to?

    d. Who opposed him or her in the last three elections?

THE BIG STORY Project · THE BIG STORY Project · STEP 3

3.1 Continue your preliminary research. Consider various places you might find information to help you better understand the topic and that could lead you to the proof of your premise. If you are working on a team project, each team member should concentrate on a different type of research material: government Web sites, news databases, blogs and chat rooms, scholarly research and so on.

3.2   Out of your research, try to come up with the following:

a. The government, industry or watchdog organization that regulates or monitors the problem you are investigating

b. A list of names and contact information of people to interview

c. The initial questions you need to ask these people in the interviews

d. The basic information that you will need to understand the answers they give you

e. Initial data and suggestions for data you might need to track down

3.3   Enter the information you collected through your preliminary research into a spreadsheet. (As team members conduct preliminary research, each should maintain his or her own spreadsheet with the information gathered and post it to the team spreadsheet.) Include the following columns:

- **Name:** The team member who collected it

- **Source:** The title of the news story or document or the name of the Web site found

- **Person to contact:** The name of someone cited in the article or Web site who is worth interviewing

- **News angle:** Anything the source mentions that could make your story timely or move it forward

- **Questions:** The initial questions to ask in the interviews

3.4   If working as part of a team, decide what roles in the investigation each team member will play: interviewing, gathering and plowing through reports, data analysis, writing the stories, designing graphic elements or information organization.

3.5   Think of ways to break up your long story into smaller pieces. If you are working as a team, assign the tasks to the team members most capable of producing those story elements.

a. Can you compile a chronology that you can turn into a timeline?

b. Are there geographic elements that you can map?

c. Do you anticipate collecting any documents that you could post online?

d. Will you record or videorecord your interviews so that you can upload them on a Web site?

e. Can you take your readers on a video or slide-show journey?

3.6   Set up your initial interviews with people you found through your research.

NOTES

1. Dawn MacKeen. Phone interview April 4, 2008.

2. Kelli Kennedy. "Despite 'net rumors, Sinbad NOT dead." *The Associated Press,* March 17, 2007. See also Donna Shaw. "Wikipedia in the newsroom." *American Journalism Review* (Feb./March 2008). And Janet Kornblum. "It's online but is it true?" *USA Today,* Dec. 6, 2005.

3. John Borland. "See who's editing Wikipedia— Diebold, the CIA, a campaign." *Wired News,* Aug. 14, 2007.

4. National Public Radio, Morning Edition. "Scanner tracks who's changing what on Wikipedia," Aug. 16, 2007. http://www.base-search.net/index. php?i=b&I=en.

5. Bielefield Academic Search Engine.

6. U.S. House of Representatives Web site, www. house.gov.

7. Patricia Simms. "5 Ways you can look good on the health beat." Prepared for the 2004 IRE Conference, Atlanta. Available at the IRE Resource Center, Tipsheet No. 2188.

8. Richard Pèrez-Peña. "A senior fellow at the institute of nonexistence." *The New York Times,* Nov. 12, 2008. See also David Bauder. "MSNBC retracts story sourced by hoax Martin Eisenstadt." *The Associated Press,* Nov. 12, 2008.

9. Joe Demma. E-mail correspondence, Nov. 19, 2007.

10. Maud Beelman. "Conceiving the investigation." Distributed in conjunction with the 2007 IRE Conference, Phoenix. Available at the IRE Resource Center, Tipsheet No. 2925.

11. Paul Williams. *Investigative Reporting and Editing.* Prentice-Hall, 1978, p. 161.

12. Ibid.

13. Larry Lebowitz. "Taken for a Ride." *The Miami Herald,* June 8, 2008.

14. Joe Demma. E-mail correspondence, Nov. 19, 2007.

15. Asra Nomani. "The Pearl Project: Wikis and social network software used to track Daniel Pearl's killers." *IRE Journal* (March/April 2008), pp. 29–31.

16. Mindy McAdams. "5 Steps for teams producing journalism," Teaching Online Journalism, Aug. 15, 2007, http://mindymcadams.com/tojou/2007/ 5-steps-for-teams-producing-journalism.

17. Monica Moses. "Principles of collaborative story planning," Poynter.org, Feb. 19, 2001, http://poynter.org/content/content_view.asp? id-4337.

18. Demma. E-mail correspondence, Nov. 19, 2007.

Requesting Public Records

CHAPTER PREVIEW Most actions taken by federal or state government officials are recorded somewhere. Government databases also record much of the actions of businesses and individuals. Some information, like voter registration, health inspections and census statistics, are readily available through the Internet or local offices. But other information that the government has is not easily available. You have to ask for it and sometimes you must sue to get it. Both the federal Freedom of Information Act and state public records acts give you access to public documents — if you know how to use them, what you are entitled to get and what the government can withhold. Because the process can take time, you should file public records requests as early as possible in your investigation. Follow the steps of a successful investigation that relied on public records to find out how you can best use similar documents in investigative reporting.

4

PUBLIC RECORDS: A RIGHT AND A NECESSITY

On August 1, 2007, thousands of people in Minneapolis were on their way home from work and thousands more headed to the Minnesota Twins game at the Metrodome, when the I-35W Bridge collapsed, sending cars plummeting into the Mississippi River. The tragedy spurred the federal government to reexamine its system for ensuring the safety of bridges around the country. Journalists across the nation began poring through government records to assess the safety of bridges in their own regions.

Using the U.S. Freedom of Information Act (FOIA), a team from television network MSNBC requested internal e-mails between federal and state highway officials. The 500 e-mails they received showed that the problem around the country was worse than anyone had expected. On the one-year anniversary of the Minneapolis bridge collapse, investigative reporter Bill Dedman reported that not only had many states failed to inspect their bridges on a regular basis, they didn't even know the number of bridges they had or the structure of some of the bridges they did know existed.

> At first, officials thought there were 756 steel deck truss bridges like the one that fell. That's how many they found in the official federal database of bridges, the National Bridge Inventory, which gets its records from the states. Then state engineers found 32 more to add to the list. But when states started the inspections, they found that 280 of the bridges weren't steel deck trusses at all — including 13 bridges made of wood timbers. Another 16 no longer existed; a bridge in Pennsylvania had been closed in 1982. Another 11 were private bridges, not subject to federal inspection. One in New Mexico was a pedestrian bridge. And a Maryland bridge had been double counted; it was actually in Pennsylvania.[1]

Bridge Collapse Story
www.msnbc.msn.com/
id/25956395

What Dedman and the MSNBC team did could be duplicated by any reporter anywhere in the country, after any major emergency. Next time an event requires some kind of immediate response, request the records of communication between safety officials, rescue personnel and inspectors. In this way you, too, might uncover problems that government officials would prefer to keep under wraps.

THE FOIA

In the United States we have a government that is of the people and for the people. That means that the people are presumed entitled to any documents the government creates. In 1966, Congress put that presumption into law. It passed the Freedom of Information Act, which states that the government can withhold documents from the public only if it can prove the need to do so. That put the burden of proof on the government holding the information rather than the public that might want to see it.[2]

This federal law and many state laws that mirror and expand upon it give reporters a process by which they can request public records. It lays out the specific reasons the government can cite to keep documents from you and forces the government to tell you these reasons when public records are not released. The law also provides the opportunity to appeal decisions to keep information secret.

What the act does

Under the FOIA, the government must publish in the Federal Register a description of each agency and how it is organized, how it generally operates, where it can be found and its rules of procedure. It must disclose and describe any forms it maintains. Why is that important? The U.S. government has more employees than the combined populations of Vermont, Wyoming, Delaware and the District of Columbia spread over a maze of agencies and departments. Imagine if you needed information from someone in Delaware, but you didn't know where the person lived, you had no map, there were no signs and everyone in the state was prohibited from helping you. You'd never be able to get the information.[3]

The information provided in the Federal Register can help you find and understand the numerous government agencies. It is searchable online, as shown in Exhibit 4.1. The act also requires agencies to make a whole range of documents

The Federal Register is searchable online at www.gpoaccess.gov. **EXHIBIT 4.1**

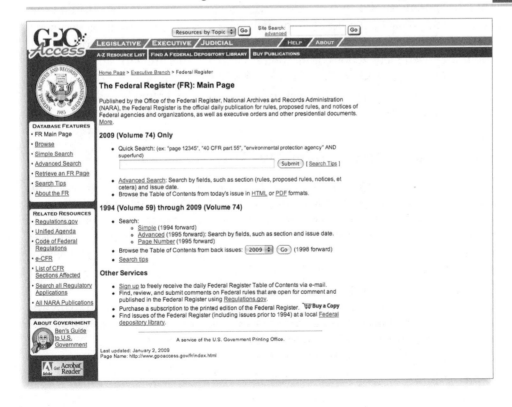

available for public inspection and copying without requiring you to file a formal FOIA request, including the following:

- Final opinions made in the adjudication of cases; statements of policy and interpretations adopted by an agency but not published in the Federal Register
- Administrative staff manuals that affect the public
- Copies of records an agency has already made public and that an agency determines will likely be the subject of additional requests
- A general index of released records deemed likely to be requested again

If an agency is required to make some documents available without a formal FOIA request, it must publish them electronically as well as in print. Availability of information is important. Considering the size and scale of the government, if it weren't forced to make documents easily available once they are deemed public, then the process would become burdensome and slow. Basically, the law says to the government: If a piece of information is public and popular, make it easy to obtain.

How the act is used

All kinds of people and organizations use the FOIA for all kinds of reasons. Journalists use it to find evidence of government actions or inactions, or to get information about corporations and their relations with government. They use it to find out information about public health and safety issues or about how the government spends or misspends taxpayer dollars. Businesses use it to monitor their competitors and track government actions or inactions that might affect their business. Lawyers use the FOIA to get evidence in the course of prosecuting or defending lawsuits.

Many agencies, especially larger federal ones, offer online forms for submitting FOIA requests. For others, you can submit a written request.

Who makes requests under the FOIA

The law considers three categories of users: (1) the news media and educational or noncommercial scientific organizations that need the information for scholarly or scientific research, (2) commercial users and (3) members of the public or nonprofit organizations who want the information for something other than research. But journalists file only a few of the gazillion FOIA requests made each year; lawyers and businesspeople account for the bulk. In fiscal year 2007, the Environmental Protection Agency alone processed more than 12,000 FOIA requests.

It's a good thing that many groups other than journalists make so many requests. Now remember that the government must make information *easily available* once someone requests it. That means that you don't have to start from scratch each time you want information from the government. You can capitalize on the work of the lawyers and businesspeople and their drafting of FOIA requests. You can get the same information they already requested, usually based on some background knowledge that told them there was information they needed to get.

A useful step in a search for public documents is to get a sense of the documents and data that an agency has. One way to do this is to "FOIA the FOIAs": You file a Freedom of Information Act or state public records act request for a list of all requests the agency has received over a certain time period and the status of that request. The list is called a *log,* or an *index,* of FOIA. Exhibit 4.2 shows a page from a FOIA log for 2008 from the Defense Nuclear Facilities Safety Board. Some agencies, such as the Department of Defense, post their FOIA logs online. Others can be found at a site like Government Attic, which is an independent, nonprofit repository of government documents already obtained by other users.

Box 4.1 provides a handy guide, put together by the National Freedom of Information Coalition, on how to FOIA the FOIAs.[4]

Government Attic
http://government
attic.org

Example of a FOIA log.　**EXHIBIT 4.2**

Freedom of Information Act Requests Log
Defense Nuclear Facilities Safety Board
2008

FOIA No.	Rec'd Date	Nature of Request	Resolution	Response Date
08-01	Jan 2	Request for information concerning "Council on American-Islamic Relations," and a list of individuals associated with "CAIR"	No records.	Jan 8
08-02	Jan 8	Request for information relating to the New Age Systems contract.	Provided.	Feb 1
08-03	Jan 24	Request for information concerning beryllium ore stockpile at a facility in Reading, PA	No records	Jan 29
08-04	Feb 5	Request for copy of awarded contract, and related attachments and modifications for New Age.	Records previously provided; duplicate request.	Feb 27
08-05	Feb 14	Request for information concerning Sen. John McCain.	No records.	Feb 15
08-06	Feb 18	Request for correspondence between members of Congress & DNFSB from 11/1/07-1/31/08.	Provided.	Feb 20
08-07	Feb 20	Request for records concerning Project NERVA.	No records.	Feb 20
08-08	Feb 26	Information concerning Schedule A employees	No records.	Mar 13
08-09	Mar 31	Information concerning Federal Employee ID No. Records	No records. Provided appeals officer's name	April 8
08-10	April 2	Info on Pinellas Plant	No records.	April 7

How to FOIA the FOIAs

BOX 4.1

WHAT YOU'LL GET:

- The log or file number
- The date the request was received
- The name of the person or organization making the request
- A description of the information sought
- The date the response was sent
- The type of response sent (granted, denied or partial release)

WHY MAKE SUCH A REQUEST?

A FOIA log is a treasure trove of information, invaluable for seeing:

1. What information is requested from agencies
2. Whether multiple requests for the same information are being received—indicating a hot issue that may merit further investigation and
3. Who is requesting the information

The key benefit is that any information previously released under a FOIA request is, in most instances, available for you to request immediately. With the information from the log, you can pinpoint requested material down to the case log file. These specifics reduce guesswork on your part and possible foot-dragging by officials processing your request.

SET YOUR PARAMETERS

The request can be narrowed by time length, although using a time length of a year or more is the most effective way to retrieve the information. You can also limit other elements of the log. For example, you could file a request for all requests on the subject of the Branch Davidians or the Persian Gulf War.

If you keep the request as broad as possible, limited by date only, you can discover information on various subjects. This is true particularly if the logs can be obtained in an electronic format, which we discuss below.

SHOULD I REQUEST THE LOG IN AN ELECTRONIC FORMAT?

If the log is available in an electronic format, request it. You are allowed to request an electronic copy, if it exists in that format, under the 1996 amendments to the FOIA, also known as the Electronic Freedom of Information Amendments.

Once you have the electronic document, you can use a variety of computer programs to explore patterns. For instance, a database program such as Access can find all the occurrences of certain words under the *"Subject" heading,* or *field.* Or the program can find the number of times a particular requestor made requests. Any of these sets of entries could prove useful for further research.

WHAT RIGHT DO I HAVE TO ACCESS THESE LOGS?

The Freedom of Information Act's generalized description of government records covers FOIA logs. However, exemptions one through nine of the FOIA may be used to prevent release of certain entries or material, such as material that would jeopardize personal privacy.

The logs' status as open records has been strengthened by federal departments selling their logs to commercial providers. The Department of Justice's Antitrust Division and the Federal

Trade Commission have sold copies of their logs to Newsnet of Bryn Mawr, Pa., which resells the material to online database providers like Dialog. Access to FOIA logs is not limited to those maintained at the federal level. Unless otherwise exempted, logs of state records can be obtained under state open records laws.

BUT ISN'T THAT UNETHICAL?

And in case we didn't mention it, here is another good reason to FOIA the FOIAs: it is a good way of checking up on the competition, whatever your profession might be. From time to time, we hear complaints that obtaining FOIA logs violates some code of ethics. Journalists, in particular, tend to think that a record of their FOIA request should be shielded from prying eyes, i.e., competing reporters working on the same story.

We, however, believe that an open record is an open record—which is what a FOIA request becomes once it is filed.

Reprinted with permission from the National Freedom of Information Coalition.

How much a FOIA request can cost

Government agencies can determine how much they will charge for copies of requested information. But they are supposed to be more accommodating if you are a member of the press or represent a nonprofit organization rather than a lawyer or businessperson. In 1986, Congress required that the government waive or reduce fees if the disclosure of the information is in the public interest and if you don't have a commercial interest in the information.

Agencies are not supposed to charge you anything for the first two hours of search time or the first 100 pages of documents if you are a journalist, a scholar, a private citizen, or a member of a nonprofit organization. That means that if you keep your request tightly focused, you might not pay any fees at all. Again, that's where having a map of the place and a peek at someone else's previous requests will come in handy. If you want the information for free, you will need to know exactly what you want.

How long it takes

The law requires the federal agency to determine within 20 business days whether or not it can deny giving you the information by justifying under the law the need to withhold it. If the agency can't do that, it has to get you the information promptly. If it denies your request, it must explain why and tell you that you can appeal the decision to the head of the agency. If you ask for a significant amount of information or your request is complicated, the agency has 10 more days to make this determination.

But the reality can be much different. Agencies stall, figuring you might give up. San Francisco Chronicle reporter Seth Rosenfeld first requested FBI records in 1981 that pertained to investigations into protests at the University of California at Berkeley in the 1960s. He waited years. After he sued in court for the documents, the U.S. Court of Appeals for the Ninth Circuit decided in 1995 that he had a right to most of the files he wanted. Although he ended up getting tens of thousands of pages, the FBI continued to withhold documents from the case even after the court decision. The National Security Archives, which is an independent research organization at George Washington University, did an audit of FOIA requests; it found one so old that the person who made the request in 1989, a graduate student at the University of Southern California, had not only graduated but had become a tenured professor at the California Western School of Law while still waiting for the documents.[5]

The federal government is so good at delaying the release of documents required under the FOIA that some reporters and editors joke that they must have more than one person at the news organization sign the FOIA letter — it is likely the reporter will be at another job, retire or die before the documents arrive. At the other extreme, some federal agencies might try to throw off a nosy reporter by burying her in documents and thereby making the one thing she wants difficult to find. That's why it is important to request any records in electronic format. These documents can be searched for names and keywords and sifted by database programs.

Understanding the limitations of the FOIA

On paper, the FOIA seems extensive. But it includes a number of loopholes that government agencies and officials use to delay the release of records and limit what they must release. Many reporters find they can't predict when a government agency might grant a FOIA request or try to stymie it. Let's look at some of the reasons officials might reject your request.

The FOIA doesn't apply to everyone.   Information about elected officials of the federal government is exempt. That includes the president, vice president, senators and representatives and the federal judiciary. Until recently, private companies that received federal contracts or grants were also exempt, but the Open Government Act of 2007 now entitles you to their nonproprietary information if it relates to a government contract.

You won't get records that don't exist.   That seems self-evident. But just because government bureaucrats know something, they might not have put it in writing. If it isn't on paper or in some electronic equivalent, you don't have the right to it. The government does not have to create any new records in order to comply with your request for information, and it doesn't have to do any research or analyze information for you.

You must know what you want.   The law doesn't require the government to help you figure out where or in what form the information might reside. In order for the government to find you the records you want, the law requires you to adequately describe the types of records the government must look for. If you ask for a letter and the information is in an electronic spreadsheet, you might not get it and the government isn't required to find it for you. And the government doesn't have to give you information if your request is too broad. Your request must be specific enough that a government worker familiar with the subject matter could locate it in a reasonable period of time.

You won't get anything that's classified.   Under the administration of George W. Bush, obtaining documents became extremely problematic because the federal government started retroactively classifying documents already in the public domain. The reclassification of documents violated the spirit of the Freedom of Information Act, which was supposed to force government to prove the need to keep documents secret before denying the public access to them. Exhibit 4.3 contains a document that was declassified and then reclassified in 2001. This declassified document was obtained by the National Security Archives, a nongovernmental research library at George Washington University. One of President Obama's first acts was to reverse the Bush administration policy of reclassification. In a memorandum to heads of federal agencies he wrote: "The Freedom of Information Act should be administered with a clear presumption: In the face of doubt, openness prevails."[6]

National Security Archives
www.gwu.edu/
-nsarchiv

You might not get information that identifies individual citizens.   The FOIA does not override the Privacy Act, which prohibits the disclosure of identifying information about individuals unless the information concerns some action that is public, such as paying property taxes or registering to vote. The government has wide latitude to deny you access to records when they pertain to individuals and you don't have permission from those people. Under what's known as the Stigmatization Doctrine, individual privacy rights can outweigh the public interest in the release of records. If the release of information could result in the stigmatizing of certain individuals, the government can withhold the records.

The U.S. Department of Justice successfully used the stigmatization argument after September 11, 2001, to keep out of public disclosure the names of people detained under suspicion of being terrorists.[7] The government also withholds records when officials believe that the release could violate the Health Insurance Portability and Accountability Act (HIPAA) of 2003, which protects the privacy of health records. This argument for withholding records becomes problematic in any journalistic investigation that involves doctors, hospitals, mental health systems or public administration of health facilities.

HIPAA FAQs
www.rtnda.org/
pages/media_items/
rtndas-guide-to-
health-coverage-
under-hipaa427.php

You won't get some documents that pertain to proprietary information, internal decision making or ongoing investigations.   The FOIA doesn't override other

EXHIBIT 4.3   This 1950 report miscalculated the chance that the Chinese army would invade Korea.

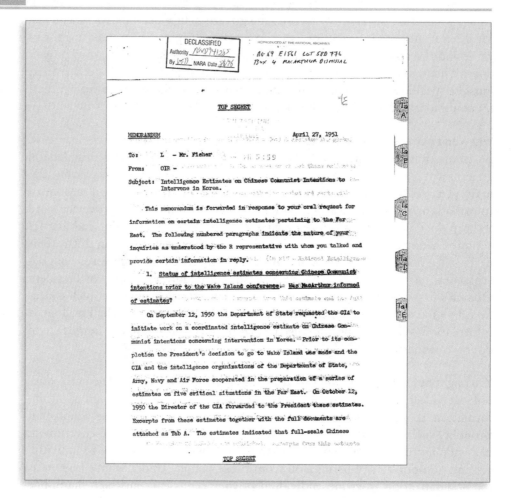

laws that might prevent public disclosure, such as laws protecting tax or census information. The government is allowed to restrict disclosure of material if it contains proprietary information submitted by and about a business or other outside entity. This exemption is important when you consider that the vast majority of FOIA requests are not made by journalists seeking information about the government but by businesses seeking information about their competitors. But it doesn't exempt information about a business or organization the government itself collects, say in the course of doing an audit. The government, however, can withhold documents that pertain to an internal decision-making process before a decision has been reached.

Law enforcement agencies can deny requests for information if it concerns ongoing investigations, confidential informants, individual privacy or if disclosure would help people circumvent the law. Bank regulators, such as the Federal Deposit Insurance Corp., have broad exemptions intended to protect the financial privacy of individuals as well as the integrity of the financial system.

Redactions

Sometimes a government agency will release some records but deny others. And sometimes within the records it releases it will take out or redact words, names, sentences, paragraphs or whole pages. The agency might do that by deleting columns in a spreadsheet, by taking a big black marker over the material, or by whiting out material before photocopying it. Some reporters have gotten records released only to find more words have been redacted than left untouched. Exhibit 4.4 is an example page from a redacted document released by the CIA in response to a Freedom of Information Act request. In the days

A redacted CIA document.   **EXHIBIT 4.4**

QUESTIONS ABOUT LIBYAN INTELLIGENCE MATTERS. AS A DISTANT RELATIVE OF KING IDRIS, HE EXPLAINED THAT HE HAS WANTED TO WORK AGAINST THE QADHAFI REGIME FOR MANY YEARS.

3. AT THE END OF THE DISCUSSION GIAKA AGREED TO MEET C/O OUTSIDE OF [   ] AND HE ACCEPTED A VERY SIMPLE RECONTACT PLAN. GIAKA STATED THAT HE WOULD PREFER TO DEAL ONLY WITH C/O [   ] IN THE NEAR TERM, BUT AGREED ULTIMATELY TO MEET WITH AN ARABIC SPECIALIST. C/O ASSURED HIM OF THE CONFIDENTIALITY OF THE RELATIONSHIP AND SET UP A NEXT MEETING FOR 14 SEP

4. [   ] GIAKA IDENTIFIED SEVERAL LIBYAN INTELLIGENCE OFFICERS, SEVERAL LIBYAN INTEL COOPTEES, AND REVCOM MEMBERS IN MALTA. HE IS UNAWARE OF ANY LIBYAN-SPONSORED SURVEILLANCE ON [   ] CITIZENS, BUT NOTED THAT THE COLLECTION OF ANY INFORMATION BY LIBYAN OPERATIVES WAS PROFESSIONALLY REQARDING. HE CLAIMS TO BE WELL ACQUAINTED WITH ESO OFFICER ABDALLAH ((KSANUSSI)) ON WHOM HE GAVE BONA FIDES INFORMATION. HE WAS FAMILIAR WITH SIX OF THE SEVEN NAMES PROVIDED [   ] AND CONFIRMD THEIR INTEL AFFILIATION. HE DESCRIBED THE BASIC STRUCTURE OF HAYYIT AL JAMN AL JAMAHIRIYAH AND PROVIDED THE NAMES AND BASIC BIO DATA FOR SEVERAL ESO OFFICERS ASSIGNED ABROAD. FINALLY, HE IDENTIFIED THE TRAINING SITE USED BY LIBYAN SECURITY SERVICES TO TRAIN PROVISIONAL IRISH REPUBLICAN ARMY MEMBERS IN ADDITION TO GIVING DETAILS OF HIS OWN KGB TRAINING. DETAILS ON THESE AND OTHER TOPICS COVERED DURING THE DEBRIEFING ARE BEING REPORTED SEPARATELY.

5.

before electronic copies, some reporters could occasionally discover redacted material by photocopying a photocopy of a redacted page. Sometimes the typed information beneath the whited-out section would appear in the photocopied page.

FOIA successes

News outlets get some great stories through the federal Freedom of Information Act. Following are some examples of some FOIA-based news broadcasts.

- *WOAI-TV, May 2006.* WOAI-TV reporter Mandi Johnston in San Antonio requested records from the Transportation Security Administration and discovered that badges, uniforms and other identification that would allow someone to slip through airport security had been reported stolen from more than 1,400 TSA employees over three years.[8]

- *CBS News, November 2007.* CBS News requested data from the Department of Defense and the Department of Veterans Affairs and found a suicide rate among veterans so high that it even surprised people who work on veterans' issues. In particular they found that veterans ages 20–24 had a rate between two and four times as high as their nonveteran peers.[9]

- *NBC News, April 2008.* Reporter Tim Sandler of NBC News obtained records from the U.S. Department of Defense that showed ties between companies that received millions of dollars in defense contracts and a religious sect in Texas raided by federal agents in response to accusations of child abuse and polygamous practices.[10]

- *WTTG-TV, May 2008.* Television reporter Tisha Thompson of Fox station WTTG -TV in Washington, D.C., looked into the types of personal information the FBI keeps on individuals by using the FOIA to obtain files kept on famous deceased people such as football coach Vince Lombardi, Washington Post publisher Katherine Graham and ABC News anchor Peter Jennings.[11]

Tisha Thompson's Story

http://media. myfoxdc.com/fbifiles/ main/index.html

STATE OPEN RECORDS ACTS

Each state has different laws requiring disclosure of public records; therefore, they vary from state to state. In Alabama, it is Section 36-12-40, just a clause in the state code, that gives citizens the right to inspect and copy public writing. It grants state officials wide latitude in withholding information:[12]

. . . records concerning security plans, procedures, assessments, measures, or systems, and any other records relating to, or having an impact upon, the security or safety of persons, structures, facilities, or other infrastructures, including without limitation information concerning critical infrastructure (as defined at 42 U.S.C. ß5195c(e) as amended) and critical energy infrastructure information (as defined at 18 C.F.R. ß388.113(c)(1) as amended), the public disclosure of which could reasonably be expected to be detrimental to the public safety or welfare, and records the disclosure of which would otherwise be detrimental to the best interests of the public shall be exempted from this section. . . .

In Florida, however, the Open Records Act is more than 18,000 words long and minutely details each exemption. Consider this clause:[13]

Criminal intelligence or investigative information obtained from out-of-state agencies: Whenever criminal intelligence information or criminal investigative information held by a non-Florida criminal justice agency is available to a Florida criminal justice agency only on a confidential or similarly restricted basis, the Florida criminal justice agency may obtain and use such information in accordance with the conditions imposed by the providing agency.

You can find your state's law regarding public records at the Web site of the National Freedom of Information Coalition, which maintains a database of the different state laws. You can also find an automated letter generator for filing FOIA requests and state public records act requests at the Web site of the Student Press Law Center. As long as you know what you want and who you need to send the request to, you simply select the state that applies and it will tailor the letter according to that state's laws. You then print out the letter and sign it. Exhibit 4.5 is a sample state public records act request created using the automatic letter generator.

State Public Record Laws
www.nfoic.org

Letter Generator
www.splc.foiletter.asp

Getting around the state bureaucracy

Even when you clearly have a right to public information under state laws you may have a difficult time getting the information if those who hold the information don't understand the law's requirements.

For some investigative reporters, getting around difficult bureaucracy is part diplomacy, part battle strategy. Consider a chain of e-mails on a listserv for investigative reporters in 2008, which resulted after a reporter expressed frustration when a local agency told him he could look at documents but couldn't use the agency's copy machines and if he brought in his own equipment for that task, he couldn't plug it into the agency's electrical outlets. He said he was going to bring in a handheld scanner that operates on batteries or on his laptop's battery power, counting on the batteries to hold up. He wondered whether they would let him sit down on their chairs or whether he would have to stand the whole time. Other tongue-in-cheek suggestions from the forum included bringing his own lights so he wouldn't have to use the ones overhead, running a series of 100-foot extension cords out the door,

EXHIBIT 4.5   Sample state public records request letter.

Get the name of the person who handles public records requests. It is usually the public affairs or public information officer.

Provide your phone number and e-mail address. You might have to negotiate for records. A back and forth by snail mail would take forever.

Your Full Name
Your Street Address Your Town, ST Zip
(your) phone number
Your_email@yourdomain.com

June 14, 2009
Joe Smith
Office of Public Affairs
Department of Public Safety
1 State Street
Your town, 90000

Request that they give you the records in an electronic format. That way, they can't charge you for copy costs and you can work with the data in spreadsheet programs.

Dear Mr. Smith,

Pursuant to the state open records law, Ala. Code Sec. 36-12-40 to 36-12-41, I write to request access to and a copy of all data concerning financial aid and scholarship awards given to students of Anywhere University between 2002 and 2009. Please provide the records in an electronic format that is exportable to Microsoft Word, Excel, Outlook or some other commonly used program. If your agency does not maintain these public records, please let me know who does and include the proper custodian's name and address.

I agree to pay any reasonable copying and postage fees of not more than $25. If the cost would be greater than this amount, please notify me. Please provide a receipt indicating the charges for each document. But as I am a student and I seek the information for a project that is in the public interest, I request a waiver of any fees you might otherwise charge.

I would request your response within ten (10) business days. If you choose to deny this request, please provide a written explanation for the denial including a reference to the specific statutory exemption(s) upon which you rely. Also, please provide all segregable portions of otherwise exempt material.

Please be advised that I am prepared to pursue whatever legal remedy necessary to obtain access to the requested records. I would note that Alabama courts have awarded court costs and attorney fees to parties who have successfully sued for access to public information. In addition, state law imposes criminal penalties, including fines and imprisonment upon those who knowingly fail to comply with a lawful request for records. Ala. Code Secs. 13A-10-12(a)(3) and 36-12-64.

Thank you for your assistance.

Sincerely,

They must put in writing why they deny the request. Make them cite the section of the law that gives them that authority.

They can charge you reasonable fees for copying and postage. Set a limit on what you will pay and request a waiver in case they can use discretion.

Your Name

down the hall and through the parking lot to his car's cigarette lighter, or asking for volunteers to take one photo for every page he needed copied.[14]

The best defense against lagging agencies and request run-arounds is to know how to get the most out of your records requests. Box 4.2 offers some basic tips for getting what you need.

| **Records request tipsheet** | BOX 4.2 |

In 1985, the Illinois Legislature passed school reforms intended, among other things, to improve the overall quality of the teaching force. Twenty years later, Scott Reeder, capital bureau chief for Small Newspaper Group, spent more than six months examining the practical impact of that effort. To evaluate the school reforms, he filed 1,500 requests for public records with 876 school districts in the state of Illinois. He requested teacher job-performance evaluations, confidential employment termination settlement agreements, and details of cases in which teachers were dismissed. He got every school district to comply. Here are his suggestions for making your public records requests equally effective:

- **Know what to ask for.** Sit down with an expert who would know what kinds of documents would have the information you seek and what agency would hold them.

- **Be as specific as possible.** Instead of asking for all public documents pertaining to teachers who have received an unsatisfactory performance rating during the past 10 years, this is how he worded one letter: "Please provide all school board minutes for meetings during the last decade in which a tenured teacher was placed on formal remediation under 24a of the Illinois School Code."

- **Ask with confidence.** He'd copy the law and staple it to the request to convince school officials they should not ignore it.

- **Be considerate.** Understanding that bureaucrats are often overworked and others are lazy, he provided them a way to give him the information in the easiest manner possible: "In lieu of the actual meeting minutes please feel free to provide the number of remediations that the school district has engaged in over the last decade, the year that it took place and the outcome of the remediation — whether the person quit, was fired or was retained."

- **Try various strategies.** Sometimes he pestered district officials until they complied just to get him off their backs. Other times he sought allies: the mayor's office, local school board members, or the state attorney general's public access counselor. He even sued one district and obtained a court order forcing it to comply.

- **If at first you don't succeed . . .** For one request he received a document in which the names and financial information that he wanted had been redacted. But it did show identifying dates. He filed a second request that did not mention names at all and only mentioned the type of document and date. That yielded the same document with none of the information redacted.[15]

BOX 4.3

How Ziva Branstetter used public documents to reveal the preventable deaths of abused children[16]

"I n a six-month investigation, the World reviewed medical examiner's reports, death certificates, court records and other public records to identify children who have died from abuse and neglect since July 1, 1999. State law allows DHS to release summaries of its prior contacts with a family if a primary caretaker is charged.

"Of the 72 cases, DHS had prior reports of abuse, neglect or contact involving 26 children, the World found. DHS also released records showing the agency had prior contact with four more children whose deaths were reported in 2005.

"The documents show that among the 30 cases, DHS received a total of 77 reports the children or their siblings were being abused or neglected. Some cases had as many as seven prior reports of abuse or neglect in the household while others received only a single report. In every case, the children were allowed to remain in the home and ultimately died from abuse or neglect."

Find the full story in Appendix A.9.

State public records request successes

Regardless of the challenges, television, newspaper, magazine and online journalists across the country use state public records acts for all kinds of stories:

- Kate Alexander of the Atlanta Journal-Constitution decided to see if she could document the danger involved in taking a taxi. She requested the driving records of taxicab drivers in Georgia and found that in a seven-year period, the Georgia Department of Motor Services suspended the licenses of 622 taxi drivers. She found that 72 percent of all the cab drivers had serious violations on their driving records. Of 2,860 cab drivers, only 121 had spotless records.[17]

- Charlotte Observer reporter Adam Bell was able to detail the costs to taxpayers for keeping a local racetrack from closing and moving to another city. He read some 1,000 pages of documents that showed that the government gave the racetrack owner millions of dollars in unpublicized incentives.[18]

- Scott Reeder, capital bureau chief for Small Newspaper Group, filed 1,500 requests for public records with 876 school districts in the state of Illinois to determine whether major school reforms instituted two decades earlier had had any practical effect. The complete story package appeared in 2005 as "The hidden costs of tenure."[19]

- Through public records requests, investigative reporter Ziva Branstetter was able to document the failure of the Oklahoma Department of Human Services to stop the deaths of children even after social workers discovered cases of abuse. Her story appeared in the Tulsa World newspaper in 2005. An excerpt from her story "DHS reports didn't save 30 children" is in Box 4.3, and the full story is available in Appendix A.9.

Scott Reeder's Story
http://thehidden
costsoftenure.com

KEEP TRACK OF YOUR RECORDS

Once you file public records requests, you will need to stay on top of them. Call the agencies as soon as the time period for their response according to the state or federal law runs out. If you are submitting multiple requests, it is a good idea to create a spreadsheet. In it, set up columns for the agency you sent the request to, what you requested, when you sent it, the date the agency responds, the name and contact information for the person you addressed it to, and a summary of information it produces.

CONCLUSION

What Branstetter did was a classic example of how a reporter can use a state's public records act to get information about a topic that is difficult to get through interviews alone. People are often reluctant to talk about sensitive topics such as crime and corruption, and when you find yourself making little headway when you call people for information, consider whether and how you could find the answers through government documents. Once you determine the government agencies that might have collected information on the matter that interests you, send out a request under your state's public records act or the federal Freedom of Information Act. While such requests aren't always successful, when they are, they can yield invaluable information that few people have seen.

EXERCISES

1. Go to the http://usa.gov and find the A–Z list of government agencies. Select one and file a public records request with the agency's FOIA administer requesting the logs of all FOIA requests made to the agency over the past two years. You can create the letter using the automatic letter generator at the Web site of the Student Press Law Center at http://splc.org.

2. Go to the home page of your state government. Find a listing of state agencies. Select one and file a public records request with the agency's public records request administrator for the logs of all public records requests made to the agency over the past two years. You can create the letter using the automatic letter generator at the Web site of the Student Press Law Center at http://splc.org.

3. Go to the Extra!Extra! page on the Web site of Investigative Reporters & Editors, at http://ire.org. Find a story based on state or federal public records requests. What information was the news organization able to find? Could the story have been done without getting those documents?

4. Using an Internet search engine or http://foia.cia.gov, search for frequently requested FOIA documents from the CIA. What are some of the most sought-after records people request from the Central Intelligence Agency?

4.1 As a group, discuss what documents you might be able to request from the government that could help you document and prove your premise.

4.2 Go to the Web site of the Student Press Law Center, http://splc.org. Using the automatic letter generator, write the necessary public records requests that you think might yield pertinent documents and data for your story. Make copies; sign and mail the originals. Have at least two people sign each letter.

4.3 Create a spreadsheet to keep track of your public records requests. In it create columns for the agency you sent the request to, what you requested, when you sent it, the date the agency responds and a summary of information it produces. Add your public records spreadsheet to your Master Sourcelist and anchor it there by creating a hyperlink.

NOTES

1. Bill Dedman. "Bridge collapse revealed holes in federal data: Internal e-mails show confusion in the hunt to inspect similar spans." MSNBC, posted Aug. 1, 2008 at http://www.msnbc.msn.com/id/25956395.

2. A citizen's guide on using the Freedom of Information Act and the Privacy Act of 1974 to request government records. Second report by the Committee on Government Reform, U.S. House of Representatives, Sept. 20, 2005. Online at http://sro.srs.gov/citizensguidefoiapa.pdf.

3. U.S. Census Bureau and *The Fact Book* published by the U.S. Office of Personnel Management.

4. National Freedom of Information Coalition, http://www.nfoic.org/foi-center/foia-the-foias.html. Reprinted with permission.

5. National Security Archives. "A report on Federal Agency FOIA backlog: Oldest unanswered Freedom of Information Act requests were filed in 1989." 2006.

6. Retrieved February 12, 2008, from http://www.whitehouse.gov/the_press_office/FreedomofInformationAct.

7. Charles N. Davis. "Expanding privacy rationales under the Federal Freedom of Information Act: Stigmatization as talisman." *Social Science Computer Review 23* (Winter 2005): 453–462.

8. Mandi Johnston. "More than 1,400 TSA employee badges & uniform items have been reported lost or stolen since 2003." WOIA-TV San Antonio, May 25, 2006.

9. Armen Keteyian. "Suicide epidemic among veterans: A CBS News investigation uncovers a suicide rate for veterans twice that of other Americans." CBS News, Nov. 13, 2007.

10. Tim Sandler. "Pentagon funds aid polygamous sect." NBC News Investigative Unit, April 13, 2008.

11. Tisha Thompson. "FBI files: Mismanaged secrets." Fox News WTTG, May 14, 2008.

12. Code of Alabama, Section 36-12-40, 1975.

13. Florida Open Records Act, Florida Statutes Title X, Chapter 119.071(2)(b).

14. Members of the National Institute for Computer Assisted Reporting. E-mail communications, Oct. 22–23, 2008.

15. Scott Reeder. "FOIA." Available through the IRE Resource Center, Tipsheet 2772. Reprinted with permission from Scott Reeder.

16. Ziva Branstetter. "DHS reports didn't save 30 children." *Tulsa World,* Dec. 18, 2005. Reprinted with permission of the Tulsa World.

17. Kate Alexander. "Outrunning a bad record series: Atlanta's taxis; A rough ride." *Atlanta Journal-Constitution,* Dec. 16, 2001.

18. Adam Bell. "Inside the drag strip deal: Bruton Smith's $80 million incentive." *Charlotte Observer,* May 12, 2008.

19. Scott Reeder. "The hidden costs of tenure," Small Newspaper Group. This series of stories was published throughout 2006.

The Game Plan

CHAPTER PREVIEW After you find your story idea, you need an action plan to develop the story. A good organizational system is essential to the success of an investigative project. You will learn to use a step-by-step methodology for your investigative project. An investigation can be a big story and can take time to develop, so that even with a methodology to keep you focused, you will need guidelines for keeping an investigative story manageable. Finally, you will learn how to visualize your story.

5

THE SCIENTIFIC METHOD

S ome investigative reporters like to think of themselves as detectives. However, their methods of investigation are more like those used in scientific inquiry than in a murder investigation. You may find it helpful to think of any investigation in terms of the classic model known as the *scientific method*. In its simplest form, the steps look like this:

- Develop a hypothesis.
- Test the hypothesis.
- Analyze the data.
- Repeat the experiment.
- Publish the results.

You can see how this method would apply in scientific experimentation. You stand in a lab dressed in a white coat and you hold a flask that contains a glowing substance. You think to yourself: "If I add a drop of gasoline to this liquid, it will blow up." That's your hypothesis. To test it you add the drop, observe whether it blows up and measure how powerful an explosion it was. You collect the data, analyze it and repeat the experiment to see whether it happens another time or was a fluke. After going through enough beakers, you publish the results.

How does that method work with journalism, where your subjects are usually people and much of the information you gather comes in the form of anecdotes, opinions and observations? The method can be applied through the whole investigative reporting process, from testing a hypothesis to analyzing the data and publishing the results. Even though they don't conduct experiments, journalists in investigative reporting do follow a similar method to the one scientists apply in their labs.

THE GAME PLAN FOR DEVELOPING A BIG STORY

A s you gather information on an important subject, you will find that it gets more and more complicated. As you gather more data from more diverse sources, you will stumble on contradictions and find yourself confused. The tangents that seem important will pile up, but they won't seem to connect. When you get to the point where you have information that is little known, you will second-guess yourself and begin to doubt your sources, your information, your instinct and your logic. Notebooks will fill with notes from interviews that yielded little useful information. At some point you might find yourself chasing a very different story than the one you set out to report. If you make it far enough along that you are ready to write the story, you won't know where to start, what to focus on, or even what story you need to tell. How in the world will you hook your readers and keep them reading to the very end? It's easy to get lost within a big story.

A basic game plan.   **EXHIBIT 5.1**

1. Develop a story premise (Chapter 3)

2. Gather the data (Chapters 6, 8 and 9)

3. Analyze the information gathered (Chapters 6, 8 and 9)

4. Outline the story (Chapter 10)

5. Draft the story (Chapter 11)

6. Verify the information (Chapters 11 and 12)

7. Publish the story (Chapters 11 and 14)

University of Florida Professor Mindy McAdams says good projects are planned out and crafted. "Do not for one minute think the structure will magically suggest itself when all the reporting and asset-gathering is finished," she wrote. "It will not. Good structure is never accidental. Structure is the segments or pieces that together make the whole — as well as the arrangement, or order, of those pieces."[1]

You need a game plan you can follow. It needs to be flexible enough so that as the story shifts you can follow it without having to return to square one. Exhibit 5.1 lists one methodology and indicates where the steps are discussed in the book. This methodology is designed to get you started and to keep you focused as you report and write your story. It is geared toward the execution of a big project story. As you gain experience you will develop your own system that works. Ask an experienced investigative reporter to break down her methodology and she might not be able to do it, because over time her process became automatic, almost instinctual. But in the beginning it helps to follow a step-by-step plan. The plan is also available for quick reference in Appendix B.

In addition to this basic game plan, it helps to plan your visuals early on. With stories increasingly utilizing multimedia elements, or converging print, broadcast and web elements, the information you gather must be thought of in terms of how it can be presented — both in the main story and any supporting pieces. Specific ideas for these elements will be talked about later in the chapter, but keep them in mind throughout your plan.

1. Develop a story premise

Unless you are your own publisher, investigative stories need to be greenlighted — an editor, editors and/or publisher must agree to give you the time and resources to report and write it and they must budget airtime, Web space or newsprint for the story.

As we saw in Chapter 3, you develop your premise before you do your preliminary research. The premise is similar to the hypothesis in the scientific method. It is a statement that makes a tentative assumption and that can be tested against evidence. In Chapter 4, we read an excerpt from a story by Tulsa World reporter Ziva Branstetter about the deaths of abused children.[2] She believed that the Oklahoma Department of Human Services too often left children in homes where abuse and neglect occurred. That was her premise. It makes a tentative assumption. To test it, she needed to get documents and data that would show that child abuse kept happening even after the cases were reported to the health department.

If you can't frame your story in a focused premise, you will have a difficult time convincing an editor to back your investigation by giving you time, resources or a commitment to publish or air it. While editors and producers love award-winning investigative stories, they hate when reporters waste valuable time.

To develop a premise you start with a question that can't be answered without significant reporting. Branstetter didn't set out to do a story about the Department of Human Services. Instead she asked if we are doing enough to make sure that children are protected from abusive relatives. As she researched that question, her story remained focused on that question.

Remember that the most interesting stories start from questions that have to do with people. In Branstetter's story it was children. If you shape your premise around a person or people, you will put a human face to your story. It will help you to keep your investigation focused, it will give you a thread to structure your story and visuals around, and it will help you produce a story with which your readers can identify.

2. Gather the data

You test your premise by gathering your data, just as scientists do in the scientific method. But forget the beakers and the white coat. Think of the world around you as your laboratory. The interviewing and data gathering is the testing. Your notebook is your beaker, and you will fill it with information you gather from the people you interview and the data gathered from reports, case files and other documents. You'll shake some of that information together — anecdotes with data, informed opinions with personal observations. The results will either support your premise or refute it and force you to either drop the investigation or alter your original question. This stage of the investigation has two components:

1. Gather data about the problem from media, government, academic, corporate or nonprofit organizations.
2. Interview people involved in and knowledgeable about the problem.

As you contact your sources and read through reports, don't lose sight of your premise. Every time you get confused or find yourself going in multiple directions, return to it. Ask yourself:

- What was my story to begin with, and is it still the story?
- If my story has changed, is it because I disproved my premise?

■ Do I now need to alter it?

■ In order to prove it, what do I still need to find out?

■ Who has that information, and how can I reach them?

Stay focused on your premise. It will help guide you in developing questions to ask the people you interview.

3. Analyze the information gathered

You can gather all the information in the world about a subject, but if you don't analyze it and help the reader understand what it all means, you haven't done your job. For a reporter, analyzing the data can be the toughest part of the investigation. Figuring out how to find patterns out of seemingly unconnected anecdotes, opinions, and facts is like trying to find a clear image in an abstract painting. It helps to think of this process in four steps:

1. Reread and examine all of the information you've gathered.
2. Draw a conclusion from the information you've gathered.
3. Decide whether your hypothesis is correct or incorrect.
4. Explain the cause or causes of the problem, its ramifications and possible solutions.

If you wait to finish gathering information before analyzing what you've got, your project will never end. After you've made some headway, such as finishing initial interviews, and when you begin to feel that you are getting a handle on the story, that's when it is time to consider the information you gathered.

Go through every page of your notes. On a clean sheet of paper or on sticky notes jot down anything you think is important. Try grouping them together. Through this process of extracting and grouping relevant facts, anecdotes, opinions and data, you will begin to spot patterns and contradictions. Your story will begin to emerge, and you will get a better idea of the people you now need to interview and the additional data you require. Once you've gone over everything you've got, then it's time to outline your story.

4. Outline the story

A big project story that is not adequately outlined turns into a disorganized mess and a tedious read. Your goal should be to produce a clear, compelling story, not a stream of consciousness. To achieve this, you need to outline the story over and over again. Your premise might be dead on — all the information you gather and all the sources you interviewed confirm it. But stories tend to emerge in surprising ways. The most effective way to get it to emerge is by outlining and re-outlining. Don't wait to outline. Just after you complete a first round of interviews, for example, sketch out what you have.

An outline forces you to examine all the information you gathered and organize it in your head and on paper. This framework helps you spot holes and contradictions. That's something you don't want to discover when you near deadline. It will also help you determine which issues are more important and which ones require only a quick mention. Outlining will help you test whether your narrative thread will work or if you have to find a different one. It will help you crystallize a potential lead. Finally, it will help you visualize the final story and show you how to proceed in your advanced reporting and information stage of the project. In Exhibit 5.2 you see a template for a possible early outline. Later, instead

---

EXHIBIT 5.2   An outline forces you to fit your information into a framework and find the logical connections.

THE CUT-AND-PASTE STORY OUTLINE

First Point
  Citizen said:
  Politician said:
  Expert said:

Second Point
  Document said:
  Citizen said:
  Business leader said:

Third Point
  Former employee said:
  Expert said:
  Data said:

Fourth Point
  Citizen said:
  Politician said:
  Lawyer said:

Fifth Point
  Historical trend showed:
  Estimates of future show:
  Comparisons with other piece show:

Instructions:

1. Identify the major points. Insert information you collected into the different boxes according to the point they support or refute.

2. Organize the points in order of importance.

3. See if you can spot your lead and ending.

4. See if you can spot the thread that connects all your major points.

of first point, second point and third point, it will look more like a story structure with a tentative lead, secondary leads and a proposed ending. Later in the book, we will look at ways to collect your information in a database that will allow you to keep a running outline of major points and tangential issues.

Outlining also forces you to ask yourself the question you should ask throughout your investigation: What's my story?

If you outline your story and then do it again at each stage in your investigation, you will be able to assess your material and figure out what you need.

5. Draft the story

A compelling story not only has a beginning, middle and an end, but it grabs readers and keeps them reading throughout, no matter the length. If you set out to do an investigative story, it will likely be complicated and involve tedious information. So how do you keep readers hooked and make the story relevant to them? Focus the story around a narrative thread, a single storyline or a strand that continues throughout the entire piece even as the story winds and digresses. This thread will ground your readers and bring them back to a point of familiarity. A narrative thread can be a person. It could be a place that you keep returning to in the story. It could be a piece of legislation you follow or a timeline of events. It is a central element that serves to ground readers and remind them, just as they start to get confused, what the story is about.

Don't wait until you think you are finished with your reporting before you begin to write the story. You should write your first draft just when you feel confident you are on the right track and that you have a substantial amount of information, but by no means all the information.

In the first draft, you will try to make the story as complete as possible. In the second draft, you will concentrate on clarity, making sure the reader fully understands the central problem. In the third draft, you will make sure you prove your case. Readers need to be convinced they should care. In the final draft, you craft the story into a compelling read so that readers can't *help* but care. As you work through each draft, you will find holes you need to fill. Reporting doesn't stop during the writing process. It will continue until all of those holes are filled. At that point, the story should be airtight.

6. Verify the information

After you draw a set of conclusions from the information you gathered, making sure those conclusions are correct is essential. Scientists repeat an experiment to confirm their results. So go back to the key people you interviewed, the experts you relied on, the people intimately involved, and policy or decision makers. Run your conclusions by them. Do they agree with your take? Have their recollections, opinions or ideas changed in light of what you now know? You might want to find independent sources to examine your method of analysis and your conclusions. You might need to amend your conclusions based on what they say. You need to be certain you haven't gotten it all wrong. In science you retest to uncover errors. In investigative journalism, you retest your conclusions for the same purpose.

Now is the time to check every single one of your facts. It is healthy to doubt yourself and your information. Take out a calculator and redo all your math. Double-check the spellings of the names and locations you cite. Run any logic and assumptions you made by your experts for a second opinion. Look for any assumptions you may have inadvertently made that you can't back up.

7. Publish the results

Whether you are a scientist or journalist, the end goal is to publish the results or story. This sounds obvious, but one frustrating thing about investigative reporting is that every question you ask leads to more questions. It is why many investigative projects that people start never get published; the reporter simply couldn't break off the process. To do so is difficult. It may mean that you must leave some questions unanswered. A general rule of thumb you can follow is this: Stop when . . .

1. You answered your central question, *and*
2. You can present sufficient evidence to prove convincingly your conclusion, *and*
3. You know that any more information you gather will only further prove the same point or take you in a new direction.

Repeat the experiment

Scientists repeat experiments before they publish. Reporters sometimes repeat a story after they publish. After high school senior J. David MacSwane went undercover to see how far Army recruiters would go to get him to enlist, news organizations across the country sent their own employees undercover to Army recruiting stations to see whether they'd find similar situations in their local areas. You can read MacSwane's story "An Army of One" in full in Appendix A.4 of this book. This is just one example of how an investigative story may be repeated in various ways.

GUIDELINES FOR KEEPING YOUR STORY MANAGEABLE

W ith an investigative story, you might gather so many quotes and anecdotes, names and numbers, statistics and bits of history, that it all can become one big jumble of notebooks and documents. The following general guidelines can help you keep your story focused and on track.

First determine whether the story is doable

Be realistic. Don't waste time chasing a story you can't do and don't waste other people's time. Consider how your sources will feel if you abandon a project after you spend a significant amount of time with them. This might be just a story for you, but for the people at the heart of the story it is their life. For help in determining if a story is doable, ask yourself the questions that follow.

What key pieces of information will I need, where can I get it, how difficult will it be to obtain and how long will it take?

Perhaps your story depends on certain data from a federal agency and you won't get that without filing a public records request. Getting the information could take a month or longer. Perhaps you won't get it at all. Maybe your story involves a private corporation and you aren't entitled to their financial information. If your story depends on that, it may not be doable.

Will I have access to the people essential to the story?

Sometimes this sounds easier on a checklist than it is in practice. But it's crucial that you talk to a variety of key sources for your story. Author and scholar Mark Kramer wrote that if you want to write a powerful story, you talk to people for extended periods of time and in different settings. "The best idea will become a lousy story without deep access to people living their lives," he wrote.[3]

You might want to investigate how your local government responded to a disaster. You learn of many frustrated victims and a long list of people suing. But interviewing these people could be painful. You have to ask yourself honestly whether you have the strength of spirit to interview people who are emotional and angry. To be an effective reporter you need to empathize, and that means sometimes you feel a portion of the pain someone else feels.

Or the entire story may hinge on whether one key person will open up to you. If she won't, you won't have a story. Don't wait to consider that until *after* you have interviewed 20 other people.

Avoid using your friends or family as a source in your story. Because you have a relationship with those people, that could taint how you view the information. Instead, you can let your friend or relative point you to someone else to interview. If you use someone you already know as a primary source, you could lose credibility in the eyes of your readers who could see it as lazy reporting.

Will I need to travel far to get information?

The people you need to interview and the documents you need to get might be hundreds of miles away. If so, consider whether you can find the time, money and energy to travel. Consider how much you will mind being away from your partner or family.

Does my story depend on granting anonymity, and will that affect whether I can get the story published?

News organizations have tightened up on the use of anonymous sources. It is unlikely that as a student journalist you would be able to get a story published in a mainstream publication if it depends on unnamed sources. We will explore in more detail how to work with reluctant sources in Chapter 6. But you should reconsider doing a story that must be based in large part on unnamed sources.

Do I have the nerve to ask difficult questions?

On paper it might seem easy: Get evidence that shows that so-and-so is doing this and that. But at some point, you will have to confront so-and-so. If you are the type of person who avoids confrontation, think twice about a project that will demand confrontation interviews. That said, people often find they are good at something only after they face up to their fear of doing it.

If my story depends on poring through reports, do I have the time and patience to do that?

Be realistic. Perhaps you find a long list of legal cases on LexisNexis that point to a big problem. That part was easy. But now you must read through those cases. Do you want to spend your time doing that? How you answer that question is a great measure of how important you think your story is.

Will I be able to analyze the data?

Few journalists are data nerds, but don't let inexperience stop you from taking on a project. Experts, from IRE to professional number crunchers, can help you with your analysis. You might find someone who will help you as a way to gain publicity for his business, or because working with a journalist on a story is a change of pace. You can find expertise if and when you need it, but you must consider at the beginning if that will be possible and how hard it will be to do. Don't think people won't help you because you are only a student. Sometimes people will help you *because* you are a student.

Will the story depend on someone giving you secret information?

In 1980, two reporters from the Long Beach independent Press-Telegram investigated how private hospitals transferred poor people with serious medical problems to county hospitals instead of treating them, as required by law. Much of their evidence came from medical reports. Now state and federal laws tightly protect individual medical records. While occasionally people leak information that they are supposed to keep secret to reporters, you can't base your project on that possibility. You must consider, too, that were you to get secret information protected by law, your sources could risk going to jail and you might be hit with a subpoena from police or government investigators who want to know where you obtained your information. And if you fail to disclose it, you could risk jail yourself. An award-winning series on steroid use that ran in the San Francisco Chronicle in 2005 was based on secret grand jury testimony. But reporters Lance Williams and Mark Fainaru-Wada spent two years fighting subpoenas and a prison sentence from federal investigators who wanted them to disclose their source of the information.

You could also face subpoenas if your sources are drug dealers, illegal immigrants or anyone else who violates the law. As of the writing of this book, no federal shield law protects journalists from subpoenas or contempt of court citations for refusing to turn over notes, identify sources or testify in court. We will look more closely at legal issues that affect investigative reporting in Chapter 12.

Will my editors give me the space necessary to tell the story?

If your organization never runs stories longer than 400 words or never broadcasts longer than a few minutes, you won't be able to publish a long article or broadcast. Still, just as you can find the expertise you lack when you need it, you can get around limitations on space or time if you are creative. There are alternative ways to tell complex stories, and we will explore some of those in the second half of this chapter. But you want to be realistic from the get-go about what your news organization will permit you to do. If you will need to tell your story in small chunks with lots of photos, video or audio, be prepared to gather that material throughout the reporting process.

Will I have to spend time with people in a setting that makes me uncomfortable?

Two reporters from my local newspaper took on an enterprising story on homeless people. They decided they would experience firsthand what it is like living on the streets. So they donned what they thought homeless people would wear and went out of their homes with little money. But over the course of the next two days, the reporters talked to few homeless people, and they admitted in the stories they published that they felt intimidated. They almost cut their two-day venture short because they found sleeping on the beach to be cold and uncomfortable. Your story might require you to spend time in a bad neighborhood or among sick people or people who hold extreme political or religious beliefs. You need to be able to do that and still report on it as objectively as possible.

Establish parameters

Before you go for that Pulitzer Prize-winning story, make a deal with yourself to settle for less if necessary. When you do that, establish parameters. Ask yourself, "What is the most I want to accomplish in this story?" Then consider, "What is

EXHIBIT 5.3   Establishing parameters for the elevator safety story.

1. What is the most I want to accomplish?
   - Determine that problems exist with the maintenance of elevators.
   - Determine how elevator safety is regulated and enforced.
   - Determine whether laws need to be passed or enforced.
   - Find out who is responsible for enforcing safety regulations or failing to do so.
   - Determine if a connection exists between lack of enforcement and safety risks.
   - Discover how often elevators on campus break down and try to correlate that with overdue inspections.
   - Find out whether people were seriously hurt or died on poorly maintained elevators.

2. What is the least I want to accomplish?
   - Determine how many elevators are overdue for inspection and what that means.
   - Find out how often elevators on campus break down.

the least I should accomplish?" As an example, consider how you would answer those questions if you decided to investigate elevator safety on your campus. Exhibit 5.3 shows possible answers to those questions.

After setting these parameters, you then need to ask yourself:

- Will it be enough that I show that laws are outdated or that a problem exists?
- Will it be enough that I give people who are affected a voice?

With set parameters, even if can't prove what you wanted to prove, you will still have a valid story to tell. After you spend time, energy and resources on a story, you don't want to scrap it just because it isn't earthshaking. If you spend time talking to people and digging through documents, you will more than likely end up with something that is relevant and interesting.

Use a To Do list

Organization is the key to a successful investigation. And the key to organization is a To Do list. It is a flexible document that grows as you proceed with your research. You will put things on it and take them off it as you become more certain of what information you need to acquire and the people you need to interview.

Make it as thorough as possible. Consider all possible sources for your story, and write down each person and document needed. Where do you need to go, and what observations do you need to make? List them. What reports must you get? List them. A good To Do list will help you measure your progress at every stage. It will keep you from feeling discouraged when publication is a long way off. It will also help you spot problems with your premise. When you take many

What goes on your To Do list.   **EXHIBIT 5.4**

- Background research
- People to interview
- Data to get
- History to track down
- Observations to make
- Meetings or events to attend
- Experts to find

sources off the list because they aren't relevant and replace them with very different sources, it could be that your story has changed.

The To Do list helps you break a complicated project into small, doable tasks. It will help you stay productive when you begin to feel overwhelmed. While waiting two weeks for a hard-to-get interview, for example, you can gather supporting data, hunt down legal documents or read through tedious reports. A good list makes you more efficient and keeps you focused. The basics of your To Do list are included in Exhibit 5.4.

Let's go back to the investigation into elevator inspections. For that investigation you need to talk to someone on campus who works at property and maintenance. You need an elevator expert and elevator riders, particularly those in wheelchairs. To find out what the laws are, you will need to talk to someone at the state or federal level who is knowledgeable about elevator safety regulations. You might track down an elevator company to do a comparison on the types of elevators the campus has and new elevators on the market. Besides needing more frequent inspections, the elevators could be outdated in terms of safety and reliability. You might want state and national numbers for elevator breakdowns or inspections. Exhibit 5.5 shows your To Do list for that project.

Before you add a new task to your To Do list, evaluate whether you need to do it. That will prevent you from veering off on unnecessary tangents and wild goose chases. Don't put something on your To Do list that you can't reasonably do. If you plan to investigate how companies outsource jobs, don't write that you will interview workers in Bangladesh if you don't have a way to travel to Bangladesh or know an alternative way of contacting the workers. Instead, put on the list that you will interview U.S. representatives of companies that outsource to Bangladesh.

At the same time, just because you put something on your To Do list doesn't mean it must get done for the story to work. Just as the list will grow, it will also shrink. Tasks you think you need at the beginning might turn into tangential information that isn't necessary by the end. Your story concept might change; some of the information you now think you need will later become irrelevant.

EXHIBIT 5.5   Elevator story To Do list.

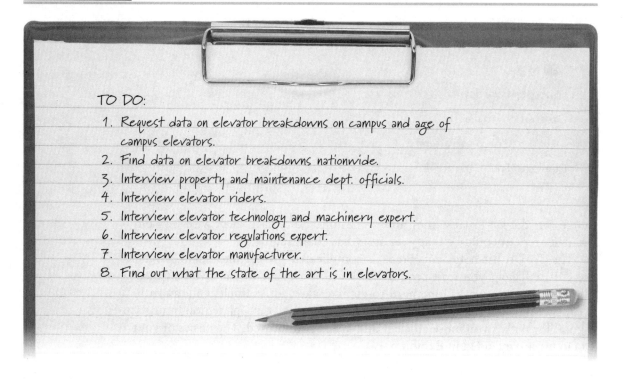

TO DO:

1. Request data on elevator breakdowns on campus and age of campus elevators.
2. Find data on elevator breakdowns nationwide.
3. Interview property and maintenance dept. officials.
4. Interview elevator riders.
5. Interview elevator technology and machinery expert.
6. Interview elevator regulations expert.
7. Interview elevator manufacturer.
8. Find out what the state of the art is in elevators.

Mary Shanklin, a senior reporter for the Orlando Sentinel, suggests that once you begin working on your project, don't come into the office without a daily plan for advancing your project. Set up interviews, make plans to go out to places you need to visit or to go through records. Book your time, she says, so that editors won't book it for you with other assignments.[4]

Keep it organized

As you tick off the tasks on the To Do list, set up an organizational system to keep track of the information you collect. Every journalist has his or her own. Some reporters designate notebooks for each investigation and note down the time and date on every page whenever they take notes. I have a tendency to take notes on the backs of flyers and on the envelope my phone bill comes in, but then I copy them onto a computer file, which then makes it electronically searchable. Some people have systems that involve colored file folders. If you work as part of a large team and you will share notes from dozens of interviews between you, it will help to post interviews to the online forums or wikis discussed in Chapter 3. Disorganization can kill a big story. A good way to organize notes is by using a spreadsheet program such as Excel — follow the steps in Box 5.1 to set up your Master Sourcelist.

| Using Excel to organize your data | BOX 5.1 |

First Step.   Consider where you will keep the various forms of your notes and data. Some of your information you will store as word processing documents. Some will be PDFs. You might have photos or documents saved as JPEG images. You will get information via e-mail. You might save screen shots of Web pages or download copies of Web sites to your computer and save them as HTML files. Try to keep as much of that as possible in one designated file on your computer. If you use a flash drive, make sure you back it up onto a desktop somewhere. People lose flash drives or drop them into water by mistake. In your e-mail program, create a separate file folder for all e-mails related to your investigation.

Second Step.   Open up an Excel spreadsheet. That will be your Master Sourcelist. Every time you create any file on your computer or flash drive related to your investigation, create a nickname for it, such as "Expert Interview," and enter that nickname into a row in the first column of the Master Sourcelist spreadsheet. Then create a hyperlink to each listing:

1. Click on the nickname you just plugged in. Go to the **Insert** menu and click on **Hyperlink**. That brings you a box that allows you to select a file from your computer.

2. Click on **Select** and then **Document**. You will be able to browse from your computer files and select the source document file.

3. To create a label for the listing, click on **ScreenTip** and then enter a label in the box that appears (see Exhibit 5.6 on the following page).

When you or a member of your team receive an e-mail that includes information you will need for your project, save a copy to your project file and do the same as you did with the Expert Interview file. Plug a nickname for it into a new row in your spreadsheet and create a hyperlink to that e-mail file you copied onto your desktop. If you are part of a team, create a screen name to identify who on the team created the source document.

In your Master Sourcelist, you can also link to digital audio interviews and videos stored on your computer. You can also catalog anything you find on the Internet by clicking on **Web Page** instead of **Document** in the **Insert Hyperlink** box.

And remember that spreadsheet that was recommended in Chapter 3 to keep track of your public records requests? List the spreadsheet in your Master Sourcelist and anchor it with a hyperlink.

Note, however, that when you create this master file, you are not actually storing any of these files in the Master Sourcelist. If you delete the source file from your computer or if the Internet site you link to disappears, the source will no longer be available through the Master Sourcelist and the hyperlink won't work.

If you find relevant information over the Internet, take a screen shot of it through the Print Screen function on Windows or the Grab program on a Macintosh and paste it into a document, or save the Web site as an HTML document.

EXHIBIT 5.6   Use ScreenTip to label a listing.

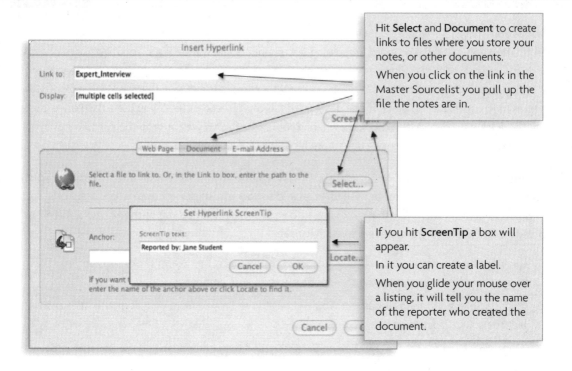

Set a timetable

Stories that lack a deadline will evaporate. So set a final deadline and then create a reasonable timeline that considers your available time and resources and meets the deadline. Ask yourself:

- Will you be able to work on this project full time or will you have to work it around daily stories?
- Is there a time element to your story that requires you to get it published by a certain date?
- Will you need to interview sources who are hard to get hold of?

Determine your time constraints. You might have other classes and a job. You might be a parent with a small child or taking care of an elderly relative. Maybe you work on the student or local newspaper and have daily or weekly stories you will need to file even as you work on your investigative project. Take all of that into account. Figure out how much time you have and when you will fit in time for your project. If you work during the week, consider whether you will be able to find people to interview on the weekends. If you plan to work as part of a team, consider how difficult it will be to coordinate your time schedule with their schedules.

A one-month plan for carrying out an investigation.   **EXHIBIT 5.7**

Week 1:	Start with a premise. Interview campus officials and riders. Write up a preliminary outline based on the information. Reevaluate your premise.
Week 2:	Track down state and federal officials. Re-outline with the new information. Reevaluate your premise.
Week 3:	Track down an independent expert and an elevator company. Re-outline. Look for a narrative thread that connects all your points. Reevaluate your premise.
Week 4:	Track down data. Re-outline. Look for lead and ending. Go back to your sources and confirm the information they gave you in light of what you now know.
Week 5:	Write story and fill in holes. Double-check all facts you use and verify all quotes you include. Publish!

Let's go back to the To Do list for the elevator story for an example. Consider how difficult it will be to accomplish each task, and try to set a realistic timetable that gives you enough of a cushion in case you encounter more problems than you expect. If you intend to publish the story within one semester, you have about four months to complete it. Look at Exhibit 5.7 to see a sample week-by-week plan for carrying out that investigation within a one-month period.

That's a rough plan. You might interview riders through all five weeks and interview experts directly before or after you talk to officials. Your data might come first or at every stage. You might write drafts of the story at different stages. But a rough game plan will tell you from the get-go whether you have enough time to do the work.

As shown in Exhibit 5.8, Maud Beelman, assistant managing editor for investigations/projects at The Dallas Morning News, suggests that you break your investigative process into sections and create benchmarks for each.

You need to be able to judge your progress and know when you stagnate. You need to be able to determine when to publish the story as well as when the evidence

The Beelman three-phase plan.[5]   **EXHIBIT 5.8**

I. **Research and planning.** Outline your project according to a proposed methodology. In other words, how do you propose finding the information, and how long will it take? In this stage you file public records requests and get easily obtainable data and documents. You also meet with photographers, graphic artists, and Web editors to discuss different ways to present the story.

II. **Report the story.** Retooling the project outline. Outline and write the story.

III. **Edit the story.** Check facts. Make final decisions about layout and presentation. Submit story to lawyers for pre-publication legal review.

refutes your premise and you must bail on it altogether. Never promise your editor something you can't deliver. Whether you make the deadline for tomorrow, a week from tomorrow, one month from now or in six months, plan to meet that deadline.

A game plan in action

In 2007 Doug Pardue and Tony Bartelme of the Post and Courier of Charleston, S.C., decided to see whether mercury from coal-burning plants ended up in the bodies of people who eat fish they catch in the state's rivers and streams. Box 5.2 is a breakdown of how they went about exposing a problem that the state had ignored.

Anatomy of an investigative project   BOX 5.2

HOW THE POST AND COURIER IN SOUTH CAROLINA INVESTIGATED "THE MERCURY CONNECTION"[6]

Step 1: The tip.   Representatives from the Southern Poverty Law Center visited the Post and Courier in South Carolina to discuss how mercury from coal-fired plants kills fish and may affect people who eat the contaminated fish. Recalling stories that had been done about lead contamination, reporters Tony Bartelme and Doug Pardue remembered that those stories were powerful because they focused on children. They asked if the SPLC had any cases of people getting sick from the mercury but the center couldn't cite any human cases. Bartelme and Pardue decided to see if they could find the people.

Step 2: The scouting expedition.   The reporters knew that, for years, the state had tested mercury levels in fish taken from various parts of the state's rivers and streams. So they decided that they would try to test people who eat fish from the most mercury-contaminated rivers and streams. They needed to find out how they would test the people. They found a laboratory at the University of North Carolina at Ashville that agreed to run tests

at $25 a shot. They felt that the paper could afford enough tests to make the story convincing if the tests showed mercury contamination.

Step 3: The search for other relevant data.   It turned out that the state of South Carolina had been running around to places where people fish and testing the fish for mercury in rivers and streams. While there was no data on mercury in people, there was abundant information about fish contamination.

Step 4: They go for it.   They first mapped the fish test information from the state database and located the places with the highest levels of mercury contamination in fish. Three locations in particular formed what they dubbed "The Mercury Triangle." They went out to test people who fish in that area.

Step 5: The first snag.   It turned out that they went looking for people in an off-season for fishing and found no one. "We had to wait for spring," Pardue said.

Step 6: The second snag.   They returned in the spring to fishing spots in "The Mercury Triangle" and found two types of people who fish—people who depend on the fish for their subsistence and those who fish recreationally. They went out to both sets and asked if they would be willing to be tested for mercury levels. That required the reporters to cut off locks of their hair, since that's a place where mercury accumulates, and put them in sealed packets to send to the lab. About half of the people agreed to do it. The first tests showed negligible amounts of mercury.

Step 7: They rethink the methodology.   They realized that they didn't focus on people who actually eat substantial amounts of fish from the local rivers and streams. They also realized they had to eliminate people who ate significant amounts of seafood, because the mercury in seafood most likely wouldn't come from the region's coal-fired plants. When they went back to the rivers to redo the hair clippings, they made sure to ask people first about how much and what kind of fish they consumed on a regular basis. "Soon we were running into people with eight times the level of mercury considered safe," Pardue said.

Step 8: They round out the story.   They realized that while they had focused on trying to make the connection between mercury pollution, high levels of mercury in fish and the people who eat them, they also needed to take a look at the best available technology to see if there were adoptable solutions. They found that even plants with high-tech scrubbers would still leak small amounts of mercury.

Step 9: They end the project.   After testing between 40 and 50 people they wondered, "Is that enough?" They decided that since their tests were the first conducted in the state they didn't need the study to be scientific, just convincing.

Step 10: They present the story.   They divided it into three parts:

1. The data,
2. The battle over coal-fired plants,
3. What the state was doing about the problem.

The results.   The state quickly began posting signs at various sites warning people not to eat the fish, and they began for the first time a program to test people. "We had an amazing immediate impact," Pardue said.[7]

Find the "The Mercury Connection" at www. charleston.net/news/2007/oct/28/the_mercury_ connectionwe_know_mercury_ta20361

TOOLS AND MEDIA: VISUALIZING THE STORY

A big part of planning your story is planning how the story will be presented. Today's big story is likely to incorporate multimedia, so begin "visualizing" your story even before you gather your data and conduct your interviews. You will be able to create a great visual presentation at publication or broadcast only if you collect the information for graphics and media all along the way. Good graphics and interactive media take time to create and the background information can't be gathered at the last minute. When you launch an investigative project, if possible, include graphic artists, photographers and videographers as part of the team at the outset, or designate which team members will fill those roles based on their skills. If you work alone and must shoot your own video and photos and create your own content, then it is critical to plan these elements of your story. If you think of multimedia elements as you gather information, you will make sure to gather the information you will need. Planning is everything.

Start early on the art

When you start writing that story in your head, picture the art and video that could go with it. Tim Harrower, the former page designer for the Oregonian newspaper and author of the "Newspaper Designer's Handbook," said that art will account for one-third of a well-designed page and every page should feature one dominant piece of art. On an online site, a small photo or a large slideshow might accompany the story. Broadcasts call for striking images that keep the viewers' attention. So when you ask yourself, "What's the story?" follow the answer with the question "How can I illustrate that story?"

The best photos and videos involve people and action. The best audio involves different sounds. To get those great shots and sounds, you need to give yourself ample opportunity. When you see stories illustrated with buildings and landscapes instead of people and actions, you can bet the reporter waited too long to bring the photographers into the project.

Create a storyboard

A storyboard is a diagram of the potential elements of your story. Think of it as you would your visual To Do list. It will change as your story changes, but it helps structure how you go about gathering information. If you draw a preliminary diagram of a story package on the chalkboard, it might look like the sample given in Exhibit 5.9.

EXHIBIT 5.9   A sample storyboard.

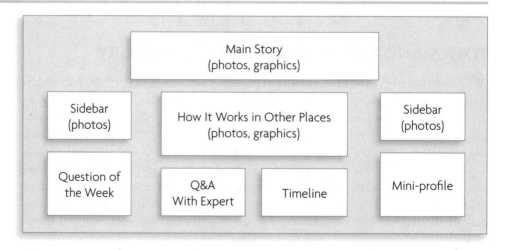

ELEMENTS OF A MULTIMEDIA STORY PACKAGE

One way to think about possible elements in your package is to think about the basics of any journalistic story: the who, what, where, when, how and why. How can you illustrate and explore those aspects of the story visually and otherwise?

Illustrating the "What"

Let's take the what first because that's at the heart of the story.

Overview

If you plan to tell a story in chunks, you are going to need to tie them all together. In an overview you summarize, for the reader, viewer or listener, the gist of the story — *what* it is about. An overview summarizes all the pieces of the package and focuses on the big picture. Think of the overview as the nut graph of the package. You'll also want to summarize all the other elements of the story — the who, where, when, why and how — in a tight frame. Exhibit 5.10 is a screen shot of the opening overview to the Times Herald Record story "I didn't do that murder: LeBrew Jones and the death of Micki Hall."[8] Notice that the overview summarizes all the important elements and encourages the reader to keep going.

In addition, you'll need to emphasize the relevance to your readers, the news angle and what moves the story forward. If the story will necessitate educating

Online overview of "I didn't do that murder: LeBrew Jones and the death of Micki Hall" by Christine Young.

EXHIBIT 5.10

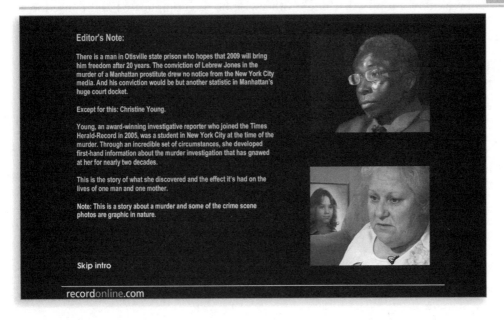

Editor's Note:

There is a man in Otisville state prison who hopes that 2009 will bring him freedom after 20 years. The conviction of Lebrew Jones in the murder of a Manhattan prostitute drew no notice from the New York City media. And his conviction would be but another statistic in Manhattan's huge court docket.

Except for this: Christine Young.

Young, an award-winning investigative reporter who joined the Times Herald-Record in 2005, was a student in New York City at the time of the murder. Through an incredible set of circumstances, she developed first-hand information about the murder investigation that has gnawed at her for nearly two decades.

This is the story of what she discovered and the effect it's had on the lives of one man and one mother.

Note: This is a story about a murder and some of the crime scene photos are graphic in nature.

Skip intro

recordonline.com

your reader about tedious terminology or you think it will be difficult to get readers to care about a big problem, consider creating a glossary and zeroing in on the problem through a case study.

Glossary

Complicated stories often require you to educate your reader and that, too, disrupts a narrative flow. You can't simply leave out the legal technicalities or the explanation of technological, scientific or financial terms. But you can break them out of the main bar. That's what student journalist Brady Averill did for her story in the Minnesota Daily about inadequate housing conditions. She provided definitions for the terms "provisional license," "rental license," "rental dwelling license," "landlord" and "tenant." The glossary in Exhibit 5.11 appeared as part of her story package, which is presented at the end of this chapter.

Case study

In your story, you will likely have room for only short summaries of the cases you cite as evidence of the problem. You can take one or more out and explore it in more depth as a case study sidebar or box. Again, this allows the reader who wants to learn more to find out the details about a particular case, without slowing down the reader who just wants the pertinent facts about the overall situation.

Flash illustration

On the Internet, programs like Flash allow reporters to use audio and animation to break down topics that might otherwise be too complicated and dense for a reader to wade through.

EXHIBIT 5.11   Glossary from "If these walls could talk . . ."

HOUSING VOCABULARY

LANDLORD
Someone who rents a building or dwelling unit.

TENANT
Someone who pays rent to live in a dwelling unit or building.

DWELLING UNIT
A living space that contains bathrooms, bedrooms and a kitchen.

FIVE-YEAR PLAN
It's a business plan Minneapolis implemented in 2005 in which the Minneapolis Fire Department and housing inspection services will try to inspect about 16,795 rental buildings in the next five years.

PROVISIONAL LICENSE
Landlords apply and pay for provisional licenses until a rental license inspection occurs.

RENTAL LICENSE INSPECTION
Inspectors look at anything on the interior and exterior of the property that could violate the city's rental maintenance code. The landlord must pass the inspection without violations — or correct violations if they are found — before he or she can get an approved rental license.

RENTAL DWELLING LICENSE
A rental dwelling license is approved after passing a license inspection.

SOURCE: MINNEAPOLIS REGULATORY SERVICES; HOUSING DIVISION; DICTIONARY

Consider a story the New York Times did in 2007. Reporter Charles Duhigg compared the level of care at more than a thousand nursing homes owned by investment banks versus ones owned by companies that specialized in health care management. The stories that resulted dealt with complicated corporate structures and dense financial data. For one story, Duhigg had to explain how difficult it was for the family of one deceased patient to sue because deep layers of corporate ownership shielded the nursing home. This could be dry, tedious stuff that some readers would have trouble understanding in print. But on the Web, he was able to show the circles in a multimedia presentation. In it, his short audio explanation makes viewers feel as if he is taking the time to explain the problem directly to them.[9]

Charles Duhigg's Story
www.nytimes.com/
2007/09/23/business/
23nursing.html?_r=1&
scp=1&sq=layers+of+
ownership+duhigg&st=
nyt&oref=slogin

Illustrating the "Who"

Introduce your readers to the people in charge or to the people the problem directly affects. When readers get to know a victim in a three-dimensional sense, they identify with the person and will care more about the problem. So think about profiles and Question & Answer interviews as part of the story. These can be done through written words, digital audio or video.

The profile

Let's turn to the story about housing. One of the examples you might cite is an apartment rented by a college junior. In the main bar, you explain how she woke up to find a rat in her kitchen. The ceiling above her bathroom leaks, her bedroom window won't open, in violation of housing codes, and the heat rarely works. In the profile, the reader learns that she wants to get into a good medical school, but the apartment is often so cold she can't sleep. She has been falling asleep in her classes as a result, and she can't study. Readers learn how hard she has to work to pay the rent, and how difficult it was for her to find the apartment. It turns out that she spent a week living out of her car and doesn't ever want to have to do that again. A profile brings to life a problem and makes it more real than just a discussion of laws and facts.

The Q&A

If you want the person to speak for himself, you can use a Q&A format. In a Q&A you can ask someone straight questions the readers would want answered, and you can have the person answer in his own words, including any admissions, denials, answer-fudging, obfuscations and refusals to answer. This format can also work well as a video interview, if you are able to set up a camera and get the agreement of your subject to be filmed, or it makes an excellent podcast. When a topic has at least two clearly opposed sides, you can invite representatives to submit short commentaries explaining their position in a point/counterpoint box or in contrary Q&A interviews.

Who's Who list

Sometimes complex investigative stories involve so many key players that they read like a Dostoevsky novel. When you have many players, each of whom serve different and equally important roles in your story and you must go back and forth between them, it helps to give your readers a Who's Who list. It's a collection of names and explanations of what role they play in the story. You could design it as a set of mug shots with biographical summaries and a statement of what key role they play.

Man on the street

You see this format in many daily newspapers: Five or six photos of everyday citizens above or next to a quote from them that answers the same question. When a newspaper asks substantive questions, the result is insightful. This element is good to include when your investigative project includes information that will affect the general community. For example, the local government will soon take some action, a state agency proposes a change in rules, the police plan a change in procedure. By asking everyday people a question related to your investigative project, you allow them to serve as proxies that bring your readers into the story. It also sends readers the message that you aren't preaching to them; instead, you are trying to give them information to help them take a stand.

Illustrating the "Where"

In the Internet age, your reader or viewer might be anywhere. That means that they may not be familiar with the locations in your story. Whenever you can, map out your data.

Information map

Throughout your project, keep track of any geographic locations. You can plot them on a Google map and combine them with information from the story that's related to each location. You can create a sophisticated-looking interactive map of your own, by inserting photos, descriptive information and small data charts in the map, which will be discussed in more detail in Chapter 9.

Earmarks Map
http://sunlightlabs.
com/earmarks

Exhibit 5.12 is a map that the Sunlight Foundation created to show readers how Congress spends taxpayer funds through earmarks — a way to sneak allocations for pet projects into bills already passed by the House and Senate.

Illustrating the "When"

Telling a story chronologically could get tedious, but it can make a great infographic that will keep readers grounded through a complicated story that has many twists and turns.

The Sunlight Foundation's mashup map of congressional earmarks.   **EXHIBIT 5.12**

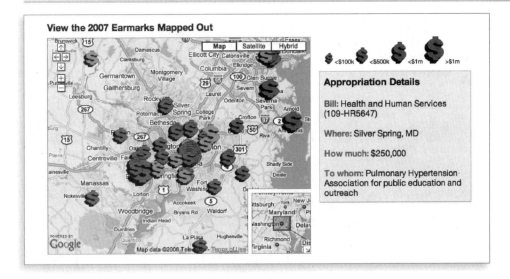

Timelines

You can put all kinds of information along a timeline — you can insert photographs, mini charts, and little stories about key developments into it. Look at Exhibit 5.13 to see how a timeline can be made from the steps in an investigative story.

As mentioned earlier, an easy timeline creator is available at dipity.com. It gives you the added benefit of turning your timeline into a map mashup. And if you decide to involve the public in your project, you can wiki your timeline, which will allow anyone to add and edit. The tool allows you to incorporate images and link to audio and video.

Illustrating the "How" and the "Why"

The how and why often tie together. They can both be explanations of a process, such as how something works and why it happened, or how we got here and why we should fix things. So it's important to explain both the how and the why. You can present these visually in a number of ways: through diagrams, pro/con arguments, slide shows and so on. Let's look at just a sample of possibilities:

Information layers

These work when the timing isn't as important as the order of the events; when one event or factor builds on another and another and another, you can lay them out as strata or levels of a pyramid.

Consider an economic recession. Its occurrence depends on a series of conditions, each depending on another condition. You can show them as geologic

EXHIBIT 5.13   Timeline of a big story project.

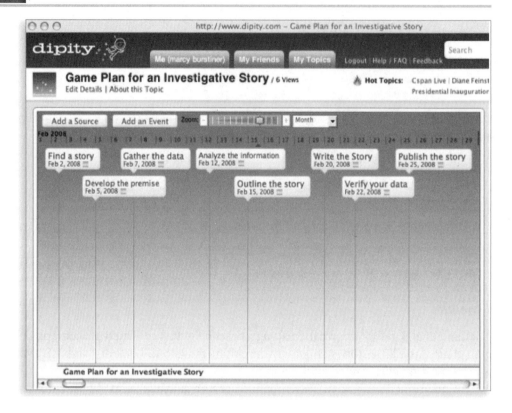

strata, one on top of each other. At the bottom is a layer of government deregulation. On top of that is huge consumer demand. That leads to job growth. The next layer is rising housing prices. Over that is a loosening of credit restrictions on the part of the banks. You can see through a diagram of layers that if a component at the bottom collapses, the whole structure topples or caves in. You can use this example to show that an investigative story rests on the quality of the layers it sits on. The story will collapse if any of the following occur: the premise is wrong, you fail to gather information that reveals the problems, your analysis is screwy, or you fail to verify your information. These information layers are illustrated in Exhibit 5.14.

Concentric circles

By creating circular layers of information, you can show how one factor affects another. Note that every time you create a map with layers or with circles, you can turn each section of information into a hyperlink that takes the reader to a sidebar story, or another illustration. Or it can activate audio or video that explains each layer and the connections between them. In the diagram in Exhibit

Using information layers to show connections.   **EXHIBIT 5.14**

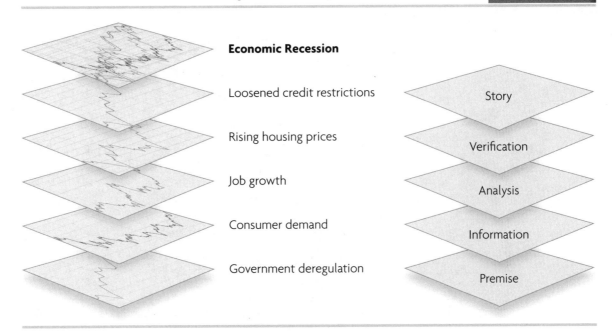

Economic Recession

Loosened credit restrictions — Story

Rising housing prices — Verification

Job growth — Analysis

Consumer demand — Information

Government deregulation — Premise

5.15, the innermost circle for "elevator" could take the reader to a sidebar about elevator breakdowns on your campus or to a comparison of the specifications, age and capabilities of the typical elevator on your campus with a state-of-the-art elevator. The circle for "elevator maker" could take a reader to a sidebar about the troubled history of the maker of the elevators on campus or about the connections between the elevator maker and government regulators.

Video or slide-show journey

A video journey takes a viewer along on an information tour. When the Miami Herald wanted to show readers how the county wasted taxpayer dollars, it sent a reporter and photographer to ride a nearly empty bus line round trip. They created a dramatic slide show that began with this narration:

> This is the story of a little used Miami Dade Transit bus route paid for with your tax dollars to appease a county commissioner named Javier Soto. Since late 2005, Route 82 has run virtually empty through the streets of Westchester. When we rode in April, six people boarded in one hour, mostly seniors riding for free. Voters who approved the half-cent tax in 2002 didn't request this route . . . [10]

The accompanying slide show showed the viewer the emptiness of the bus in time increments from the moment the photographer and reporter boarded, to the end of the long route.

Empty Bus Slide Show
www.miamiherald.
com/multimedia/
news/transit/
slideshow2/index.html

EXHIBIT 5.15   Each circle in this diagram of concentric circles can become a link to more information.

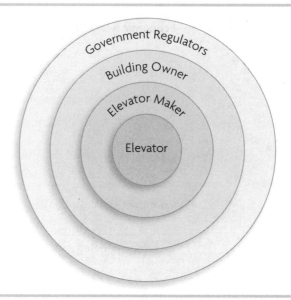

How-to guide

Rich Somerville, the former managing editor of the Times-Standard newspaper in Eureka, Calif., said that newspapers should aim to make their readers smarter and show them ways they can improve their lives. You can do that with a how-to guide whenever the story involves action that people can take. This type of feature engages your readers, listeners or viewers, and lengthens the life of the story on the Web, as people return to the site for the handy guide and find it through search engines. For a story about hazardous toys you could include a guide to spotting dangers in toys, tracking down the manufacturer or even how to get products tested for lead or dangerous chemicals.

"Where to get help" box

You should always consider including a list of people and organizations that your readers could go for help, with contact information and Internet links. This smaller version of a how-to guide is also the type of information that will lengthen the story's shelf life.

Games

Sometimes to understand the why of a story, readers need to understand how difficult it is for decision makers to weigh potential options. To explain how impossible it is to satisfy all residents when planning a new park, The Gotham Gazette, a Web site about New York City published by the Citizens Union Foundation, came up with an interactive game that takes readers through the complicated issues such as city park planning. Each step presents four options, and each option leads to problems that must be solved by choosing one of four more options, which in turn leads to other difficult issues. Exhibit 5.16 is a screen shot of the "Plan Your Future Park" game.

Plan Your Future Park!
www.gothamgazette.
com/parksgame

Presenting key data in tables, charts and lists

Readers' eyes tend to gloss over numbers in stories. But those same numbers in a visually striking bar chart or pie chart can demonstrate at a glance inequity, severity and trend. You can design a variety of charts off the data you collect using a spreadsheet.

Be careful, though. When too many tables are grouped together, the information in them can seem as dense as if you just presented all the numbers within the story. But when spread out, one by one or two per story segment, for example, they can be dramatic. They can help *show* readers what you are trying to tell them.

City park issues presented as a game from The Gotham Gazette.   **EXHIBIT 5.16**

Reprinted with permission from Gotham Gazette, an online publication on New York City issues.

Rankings and ratings lists

People like top-ten lists. If your story involves levels of acceptability that you have been able to quantify — such as water or air quality or building safety — you could provide a list with rankings or ratings that show which things or places are better or worse than others and which explain why. You could also juxtapose photos or videos of best and worst cases.

Flow charts

If your story involves a process, you can diagram it with a flow chart. The one in Exhibit 5.17 describes the criminal court process in the state of Alaska. But you can get creative with flow charts, by substituting photographs or other graphic elements for the boxes, circles and diamonds and by inserting Web links or even video into the boxes.

Comparison tables

A comparison table is a good way to explore options for solutions or explain steps a government could have taken. A free online tool called Tablefy allows you to easily create comparison tables. Designed for a multimedia presentation, this software enables you to insert video from YouTube, photos or links in the columns or rows. It also lets you surf for data and information to insert into your table. And if you fill the columns or rows with data, Tablefy can sort and tabulate in a way that mimics a spreadsheet. Once you create the table, you can embed it on your Web page. Exhibit 5.18 is an example of a simple table created using Tablefy. You can compare costs and benefits of a proposed infrastructure project, advantages and disadvantages of proposed legislation, stands on issues during an election, and so on.

**Chart and
Table Creator**
http://tablefy.com

Quizzes

Quiz maker
http://hotpot.uvic.ca

One way to lead a reader into consuming data or facts they might otherwise avoid as tedious is to present the information as a quiz. While college students may avoid a quiz whenever possible, online readers are mysteriously drawn to them. Download free quiz-making software from a company called Hot Potatoes and others.

VISUALIZING HOW THE PIECES WILL FIT

Now that you have an idea of what visual elements your story will include, the next step is to think about how they will all fit together. Choose the elements that will be the dominant pieces of your presentation and then arrange the supporting pieces, creating a hierarchy. The most important pieces need to stand out. The reader or viewer should see the primary elements first and then move to the secondary elements.[11]

Using a flow chart to break down a complicated process.   **EXHIBIT 5.17**

STAGES OF A TYPICAL ADULT CRIMINAL CASE

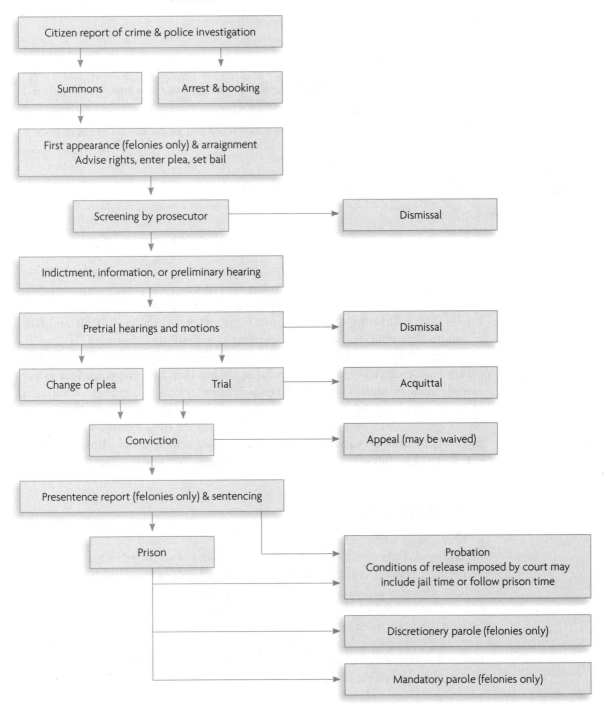

EXHIBIT 5.18   A simple comparison table created with Tablefy.

⇕	Apples ⇕	Oranges ⇕
Looks		
Health benefits	Just one a day keeps the doctor away	Will stave off scurvy when you take a slow boat from Portugal to India via the Cape of Good Hope
Small Pleasures	The crunch when you first bite into it	Fun to stuff a big slice in your mouth so that it forms an orange smile
Annoyances	The core	The peel and pits
Other benefits	Surprisingly satisfying for the appetite	Rehydrates and energizes

0 comments 0 views   0 ⊞ 0 ⊠

You will need to consider the space and time that you have available to use. Know that an element that you have prepared may not make it into the final product. However, it is better to have some extra elements prepared, as other stories may fall through, allowing you more space. It can be difficult and frustrating to try to pull together more content as a deadline is looming.

A great way to learn how pieces of a story best fit together is to look at what others have created. Note what works and what could be changed. Just as you can glean story ideas from other people's stories, you can gather visual ideas from other people's story packages.

In Exhibit 5.19 (see pages 114–115) you can see the elements Brady Averill used for her story on substandard student housing and how the Minnesota Daily laid it out. The full text of the story is available in Appendix A.5.

CONCLUSION

With your game plan and storyboard, you now should see clearly the steps ahead. Depending on your premise and what you found out through your preliminary research, you should have a long list of people to interview. You should have an idea of what data will support your premise, what comparisons you need to make and what historical information you will need to track down. You should understand how to organize all the information you gather using outlines and spreadsheet programs. You should have an idea of ways that you will be able to lay out the information once you gather it in visual and possibly interactive ways. Now you just have to gather the information. We will see how that is done, in Part II.

EXERCISES

1. Go to the Extra!Extra! section of the ire.org Web site. Select an investigative story to read. What do you think was the premise the reporters started with? How did they test it? What data did they analyze?

2. Imagine that you are going to replicate that investigation. Develop a game plan for it and write up a preliminary To Do list. Set your parameters: What is the most you might be able to accomplish, and what is the minimum you could base a story on?

THE BIG STORY Project   •   THE BIG STORY Project   •   STEP 5

5.1   Considering what you learned from your preliminary research, assess the doability of your proposed project.

   a. What key pieces of information will you need, where can you get them, how difficult will they be to obtain and how long will that take?

   b. Who are the people who are essential to the story, and will you have access to them?

   c. Will you need to travel far to get information?

   d. Will you need to grant anonymity, and will that affect whether you can get the story published?

   e. Do you have the nerve to ask difficult questions?

   f. Is it necessary to pore through reams of reports, and do you have the time and patience to do that?

   g. Will you be able to analyze the data, or will you need to seek help from experts such as the people at the National Institute of Computer Assisted Reporting?

   h. Will the story depend on your getting secret information?

5.2   If the answers to these questions lead you to believe that the story is not doable as you proposed, try to alter the premise in such a way as to avoid the problems and still turn out a good story.

5.3   Determine the maximum you think you can accomplish with your project and come up with a minimum you can produce that will still result in an informative article.

5.4   From your preliminary research and interviews map out a detailed list of people to interview according to this formula:

   a. People affected by the problem you are investigating

EXHIBIT 5.19   Visual story package "If these walls could talk . . ."

Overview

Main Story

Methodology

Get Help Box

List

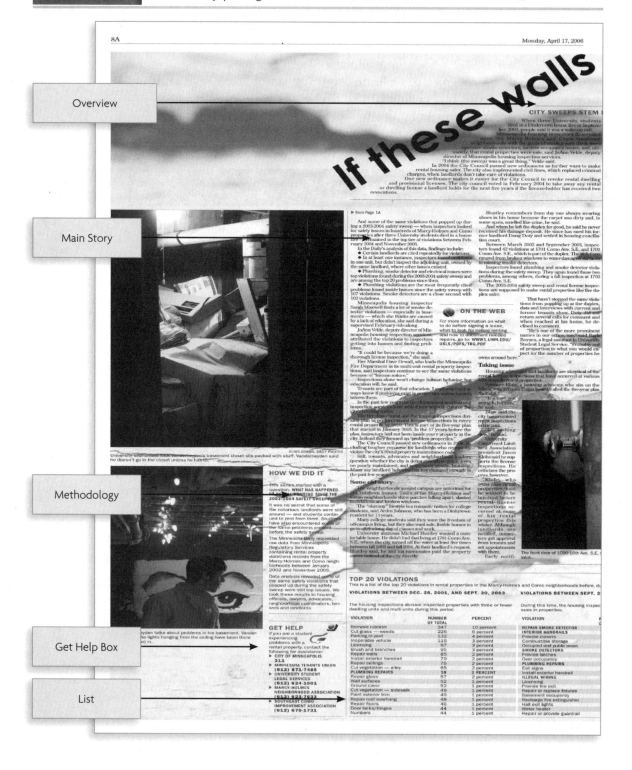

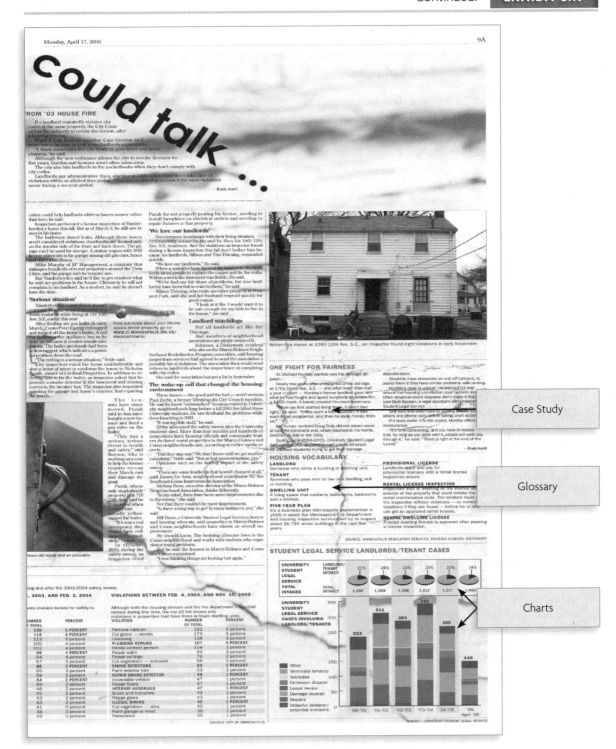

Case Study

Glossary

Charts

Reprinted with permission.

b. The people responsible

c. Any policy makers who have the authority to change the situation

d. Independent experts who can help you explain the problem

e. People who will be able to fill in holes after you have done a significant amount of reporting

5.5   Create a To Do list. If the investigation is a team effort, post the To Do list on a wiki. Include all the things you think you will need to get to prove your premise and make your story compelling: background research, people to interview, data to get, history to track down, observations to make, meetings or events to attend and experts to find.

5.6   Create a Master Sourcelist spreadsheet. If your investigation is a group project, designate a place where all team members will store a copy of any information they gather; it could be a particular computer or a wiki stored on the Internet. Store the Master Sourcelist there as well to keep track of all information collected for the project. Every time someone adds a listing to the Master Sourcelist, turn it into a hyperlink to the source of the information.

NOTES

1. Mindy McAdams. "5 Steps for teams producing journalism." Teaching Online Journalism, Aug. 15, 2007, http://mindymcadams.com/tojou/2007/5-steps-for-teams-producing-journalism.

2. Ziva Branstetter. "DHS reports didn't save 30 children." *Tulsa World,* Dec. 18, 2005.

3. Mark Kramer. "Reporting for narrative: Ten tips." In *Telling True Stories: A Non-fiction Writer's Guide.* Plume, 2007, p. 26.

4. Mary Shanklin. "Managing and juggling: How to cover a beat and still produce." IRE Better Watch-dog Workshop, Feb. 2005. IRE Tipsheet No. 2271. E-mail communication with Mary Shanklin, June 18, 2008.

5. Maud Beelman. "Conceiving and managing the investigation." IRE Conference, Phoenix, 2007, Tipsheet No. 2925. Available through the IRE Resource Center at http://ire.org.

6. Doug Pardue and Tony Bartelme. "The mercury connection." *The Post and Courier,* Oct. 28, 2007.

7. Doug Pardue gave his account at the IRE National Conference in Miami in June 2008 and clarified some points in an e-mail exchange, July 29, 2008.

8. Christine Young. "I didn't do that murder: LeBrew Jones and the death of Micki Hall." *The Times Herald Record.* At http://thr-investigations.com/lebrewjones.

9. You can check out Duhigg's story "At many homes, more profit and less nursing" and the accompanying multimedia graphic at the *New York Times,* http://www.nytimes.com/2007/09/23/business/23nursing.html?_r=1&scp=1&sq=layers+of+ownership+duhigg&st=nyt&oref=slogin.

10. Larry Liebowitz. "Empty bus: One hour on metrobus route 82." *Miami Herald,* http://www.miamiherald.com/multimedia/news/transit/slideshow2/index.html.

11. James Foust. *Online Journalism: Principles and Practices of News for the Web.* Second Edition. Scottsdale, Ariz.: Holcomb Hathaway, 2009.

Gathering Information

P A R T   T W O

The Interview Process

CHAPTER PREVIEW Interviewing is a process. In the investigative project, one question leads to more questions and one interview leads to another interview. No one interview will yield all the information you need, so knowing how to connect with many people is important. To do that, reporters must understand that people are three-dimensional. Reporters must genuinely care about the story they investigate and demonstrate their sincere interest in the information a person has to offer. Care and interest result from doing background research about the topic you will talk about (which is step one in getting good interviews). You must be able to listen to people's answers and follow up with more questions. It also helps over the course of a long project to develop a system for scheduling your interviews. Methods of interviewing will vary depending on what type of information you seek and how much information you need from a particular source.

As you gather your information from interviews, you need to develop a system for storing and organizing your notes, which will help later as you analyze and write the story.

6

THE MYTH OF THE KILLER INTERVIEW

Rarely does a reporter go out to interview someone and come away with every question answered and a story all wrapped up. What makes an interview good is the quality more than the quantity of information you gather. Sometimes a two-hour interview will yield little useful, unique or relevant information while a five-minute interview will net you something essential. You might need to interview someone more than once to get the information you need. Your source might only feel comfortable with you after multiple interviews. Or your source will only explain information you gathered elsewhere. A source may not be reluctant at all but too busy to sit down for several hours at a time and can only fit in interviews in five-minute sessions over many days. Some people may talk more comfortably over the phone, while others prefer that you interview them in person. Investigative reporters tend to interview many, many people in all kinds of settings — on the way to the airport, in jail cells, in restaurants, or while accompanying a doctor on hospital rounds. Only from interviews with many different people do you gather enough pieces of information to form the basis of your story and provide the evidence for the case you need to make. To be effective as an interviewer, you have to understand how to work with and vary your questions for different types of people and personalities.

The interview process can be frustrating. You can't predict what you will end up finding out, so it may not be until much later in the project that you understand the value of the information someone gave you. What seemed unimportant in the beginning might become crucial by the end. Your story will emerge out of the little pieces of information you gather. Sometimes each piece alone isn't worth much, but put them together and the picture they form may startle you.

Each question you ask generates more questions. So you could walk away from even the most informative interview feeling more ignorant and confused than when you walked in. You might come away with just one nugget of new, useful information and consider the interview fruitful. Or you might come away from a long interview with only a sense of how the person you interviewed feels; that in itself might be important. Different people yield different types of information. Information can take various forms: Emotions, descriptions, details, facts, opinions, historical knowledge, names, dates, or simply confirmation of a guess or of something you already know can all be equally important.

DEVELOPING SOURCES

Source development is the building of a relationship with an individual through repeated contact. Individuals tend to distrust people they don't know, so it helps if they can get to know you. That process takes time and effort. It helps to develop relationships with people *before* you need them for a particular story. Call them from time to time and ask about their job, their lives and the issues that affect or interest them. If you treat people with respect, it doesn't take long to develop trust. The first time people talk to you they might be reticent. If you don't rush the first interview, then the second time they will feel more comfortable with you. By the third they will want to help you, and by the fourth it's as if they've known you for years.

When you meet people, get their business cards or contact information. Put it into a card file, address book, or spreadsheet. Some reporters collect thousands of names and phone numbers. When you build sources this way, you create relationships with people that last over time. Bob Woodward's relationship with Deep Throat, the most famous reporter-source relationship in the history of journalism, began years before the Watergate crisis broke.

People won't talk if they fear a reporter is incompetent or disinterested. Even if you only need to talk to someone for the most tangential part of your story, you need to treat the issue with the same amount of interest and respect as you would the central issue. That's because to the person you interview, it *may be* the central issue. To treat the subject in a disinterested, superficial or impatient manner also is to treat that person in a disinterested, superficial or impatient manner. You can't fake interest or respect. To convince someone that you think a particular topic is important and interesting, you must believe it yourself.

Connect with people

To build source relationships and get good information from your interviews, you need to connect with the people you interview. Show a genuine interest in their work and their lives. Throughout the world you will encounter top scientists whose families show little interest in their research, successful lawyers whose cases bore their spouses, and renowned engineers whose friends don't understand what they do. Outside of work, those who rarely run into people who show genuine interest in what they do may get into the habit of keeping information to themselves. They may assume people aren't interested, so you need to convince them that you are. If you can do that, you may become one of the few persons outside of their field with whom they can talk about their work. You will be a refreshing change of pace.

Conversely, people leave their families behind when they go to work. Most of the people they encounter throughout the day will show little interest in how adorable their daughters look, the great places they discover as they walk their dogs, how well they golfed last weekend or how many fish they caught on vacation. I know two reporters who compete on the same beat for different papers. A government official key to their beat used to favor one reporter over the other. Why? One reporter routinely enquired about each of his three children by their names.

People are multidimensional. They spend most of the day at work and then go home to their family and watch movies, read books, play video games or follow sports. Some people garden, others cook or knit, paint or carve furniture.

You connect with someone when you find that you are both interested in the same subject or engage in the same activity. If you are genuinely interested in a variety of areas, you will find it easy to connect with different kinds of people.

Keep your contacts discreet and professional

Ken Metzler, author of a classic text on interviewing techniques titled "Creative Interviewing," warned that you have to be careful when you interview many people for one story in a small community. Where everyone knows everyone, he warned, word of your first interview will spread to everyone else you need to interview. If you botch the first one by appearing callous, sneaky or biased, you will have a difficult time getting subsequent interviews. Even if you get the interviews, the people you talk to may be less open.[1]

Metzler's advice doesn't just apply to physical towns. Small communities can cross geographic boundaries; they are defined by occupation, religion, politics, sports, hobbies and ethnicities. People often belong to many different small communities at the same time. Within each one, people tend to know each other or at least know of each other. Investigative reporters are a small community, for example. So are orchid growers, insurance defense lawyers, people who play pedal steel guitar and triathletes.

To prevent messing up on your first interview, or subsequent ones for that matter, Metzler says to be discreet. Avoid gossip, even when your interview subject wants to dish it. Don't be tempted to tell someone what someone else said in a previous interview and don't take sides. Once you talk to enough people, however, you will gain expertise. Once that happens, he said, you can trade information with sources as long as you don't break promises or expectations of confidentiality.

Metzler also suggests that to navigate a small community, seek out the leaders. But recognize that leadership is sometimes unofficial, especially in bureaucracies where the official leader is appointed and changes with each shift in executive administration.[2] Police officers might respect and follow a lieutenant who rose from the ranks and has been in the department longer than a chief who was hired recently from a different city. An unofficial leader is someone who is most respected, or is the organizer of activities or the historian. Look for the person who has been around forever, knows everyone, and keeps track of everything. He keeps locked inside his head the history of the community or organization and all the people in it, and can lay out for you all the battles they wage.

DEVELOPING AN INTERVIEWING SYSTEM

When you ask people for interviews, tell them what information you seek. Deciding what information you need is something you must figure out yourself. For a story on dangerous streets, you might decide to talk to the mayor. But you need to ask yourself why he would make a good subject. As mayor, does he have

Two systems for planning an interview.   **EXHIBIT 6.1**

THE 5Ws SYSTEM	THE INDUCTIVE APPROACH
1. The What	1. The fishing expedition
2. The Who	2. The stakeholders
3. The Where	3. The experts
4. The When	4. The decision makers
5. The Why	5. Filling in holes

decision-making power over street repair projects? Is the issue one he campaigned on? You may have good reasons to interview him. If you tell him why you think he is important for your story, you will demonstrate that you have a good handle on your story. And you will give him an idea of what you want from the interview.

Once you decide why a person is a good interview subject, you need to figure out how and when to talk to him. You might try dividing your interviews into rounds, with each round of interviews focused on a different facet of information that you need. Exhibit 6.1 shows two systems you can use for approaching an interview.

The 5Ws system

The 5Ws system is a useful way to organize information and to direct your investigation. Just as it is useful in planning visual elements, it is useful in planning interviews as well.

Round 1: The What. Interview people who can help you identify the problem. Consider the story about a dangerous street. Do a high number of car accidents occur? Are pedestrians or bicyclists getting hit? What data are available to quantify the problem? Is the problem getting worse?

Round 2: The Who. Interview people most affected by the problem or who can help you identify the people affected: victims of car accidents, residents who complained to the city about dangerous intersections or streets in need of repair, police who patrol the streets and maintenance crews who repair them.

Round 3: The Where. Interview people who can put the significance of a location into perspective. Are some streets more dangerous than others? Is an inequity involved? Does the city maintain the streets more in one area than it does in another area? Does one area have better signage or more traffic enforcement than another?

Round 4: The When. Interview people who can explain the historical context or make estimates about when something will happen. Is this a new problem or one long ignored? Is there something relevant about the current timing? Has the city recently slashed its budget for street repairs? When did the police department suddenly become shorthanded?

Round 5: The Why. By this round you know an awful lot about city streets. You know about residents most affected, the size and intensity of the problem, and the historical and geographic contexts. Now you need to know the causes of the problem and possible solutions to it. Go to the people directly involved and find out why they are doing what they are doing or not doing what they should be doing. You may already have a pretty good guess as to what their answers will be. Find an outside expert who can explain how it all works, who can help you connect all the pieces of information you collected and help you spot any holes in your knowledge of the subject or situation. The expert may be a psychologist, sociologist, economist, hydrologist or zoologist; he or she is someone who can help you nail down why things are happening the way they are and how it all works. In a story about dangerous streets, the expert might be a civil engineer, a professor who studies transportation issues or a consultant who works with municipalities on street design. For help on finding an expert, look at Box 6.1.

List of Professional Organizations
www.google.com/
Top/Society/
Organizations/
Professional

The inductive approach

Inductive inquiry is a more exploratory process. You start with a very general premise and narrow it down as you go along. While an editor generally wants you to be as focused as possible, you would use an inductive approach to planning interviews when you think something smells fishy but you won't know what is wrong until you investigate. An example inductive premise might be: There is a problem with how the city repairs streets.

Round 1: The fishing expedition. For the first go-around, line up interviews with a diverse assortment of people who can help point you in the right direction. If you follow this approach, let people know that you aren't certain at this point exactly where your story is going. Notice where the information people give you overlaps — that becomes your focus, as shown in Exhibit 6.2 (page 126). In the pothole story, consider the different areas your sources point to: Some people tell you to look at the size and number of potholes, some tell you to look into car accidents, others tell you the problem is with the new public works director and still others say the problem rests with budget cuts. You should take all of these interviews into account, and you could focus on whether the new *public works director* is implementing *budget cuts* in such a way that streets are getting neglected, *creating potholes* and causing *accidents* to increase.

Round 2: The stakeholders. Find the people directly affected by the problem: residents, victims and families of victims and anyone who must drive on bad roads. These people may be the ones who are also most affected by your story, so getting their input, or side of the story, is important.

| Finding and contacting experts | BOX 6.1 |

Potential places to look:

- Plug a topic into an academic search engine (such as Google Scholar or Google Book Search) with the term "professor," and you are likely to find the person who wrote the book, or at least a journal article, on the subject. For example, if you need a mathematician to talk about a lottery story, you can try entering the terms "lottery" and "math" or "statistics." Use the advanced search feature to limit the years of publication so that you will find someone who is still working in the field.

- Try a public relations news site such as Profnet, an offshoot of prnewswire.com. The site enables reporters to send out an e-mail about their story to every university public relations person and every professor who is a member of the network. While Profnet won't help you if you aren't affiliated with a publication, it will likely help you out if you expect to publish your story in your campus newspaper or a local newspaper.

- Using research databases such as LexisNexis or EbscoHost, look for papers or articles written about your topic. Look at both the authors and the citations lists for possible contacts. Access to these kinds of sites is usually available through your university or local library.

- Visit the Web sites of the academic and professional organizations related to your field of interest.

Keep in mind:

- Make sure the expert has knowledge that is directly related to the field you need. Think of the diversity of the communications field alone. You probably would not contact a rhetorical theory professor for a story about embedded reporters.

- When speaking with the experts, mention some of the data or information you found in your preliminary research to let them know that you did your homework and that you already know basic information.

- If you are e-mailing, write a subject line that is clear and to the point, such as "Interview regarding (topic)." Send it using an e-mail account with a university address or one that sounds professional (think how "JoeJones@university.edu" looks in an inbox versus "superawesomeguy123@myemail.com").

- Take care to have a professional tone in your e-mail. Make sure you correct all typos and other errors, and double-check all names.

- If possible, find out if the experts have a title before their name, such as Doctor, Professor, The Honorable, and so on. Many put a lot of pride in earning the title and will have a better response to those who use it.

Round 3: The experts. At this point you need to talk to independent experts who can inform you about the facts and issues that the stakeholders aren't aware of or don't understand. They can tell you about possible solutions and why the solutions have not been implemented or likely won't be implemented. They can also help you understand the historical context, make comparisons with how things work elsewhere and help you understand any confusing contradictions arising from your previous interviews.

EXHIBIT 6.2   Finding the focus in the pothole story.

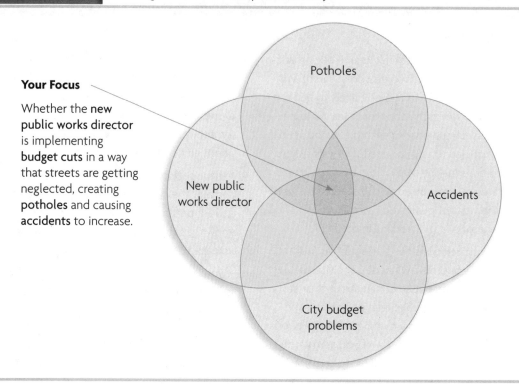

Your Focus

Whether the **new public works director** is implementing **budget cuts** in a way that streets are getting neglected, creating **potholes** and causing **accidents** to increase.

Potholes

New public works director

Accidents

City budget problems

Round 4: The decision makers. The people in the first three rounds should be able to point you to the people who are likely responsible for the problem, and it is time to talk to them. You will want to ask them why they are doing what they are doing, what actions they plan to take to solve the problem or why they haven't solved it. For road repairs you would want to talk to city or county politicians and the director of the public works department.

Round 5: Filling in holes. Now you likely will have questions that still need to be answered. You need to go back to people you already have talked with and to find others who can help you answer your questions or explain any confusing points or contradictions that you haven't been able to reconcile.

SETTING UP THE INTERVIEW

S chedule your interviews as soon as you complete your preliminary research, even if you aren't ready yet to do a particular interview. If your story revolves around one key person, you might not want to interview that person until you've first interviewed people who know him and read relevant biographical or business documents. But you should still make the calls now to set up the interview for a later time. Estimate how long it will take you to prepare yourself for the interview. Figure out where in your schedule you will be able to block out the necessary time to sit down with the person or when you can make room for a long phone interview. Then call him and set it up. You will come across as professional if you tell someone that you aren't ready to talk to him now, but you want to talk to him two weeks from today if possible. If you wait too long to try to schedule an interview, you risk no interview at all. So get yourself on people's appointment schedules as soon as possible.

Timing can be a deciding factor in whether a person will talk. People juggle busy work schedules, family responsibilities and their own personal activities. Even though interviewing this person may be high on your priority list, being interviewed by you may be very low priority to him or her. Give these people plenty of time to fit you in. If you insist that someone has to talk to you the next day, the person may feel rushed and the interview will be forced. You don't want to interview people just before they have to pick up their kids from day care. They won't give you any extra time. And you don't want to interview them before an important meeting — they will be distracted or nervous or both.

You will have more success in landing interviews if you are flexible. You might need to schedule it early in the morning or late at night. Some people are more comfortable talking outside of their work hours, so you need to be prepared to talk to them in the evenings or on weekends. You want them to give you information. So help them do that in any way you can.

Seattle Times reporter Eric Nalder says where you interview people can also make a difference. "Whenever possible, I interview people close to the action, while they are actually doing whatever it is I am writing about," he wrote. "However, whistle-blowers and reluctant targets are best contacted at home. You can calm a nervous source by taking him or her for a walk. If you arrange a lunch appointment you can force a person to spend at least an hour with you."[3]

When sources won't get back to you

Be polite, professional and persistent. Call *and* e-mail. Don't be afraid to call people at home, but be considerate: One sure way to turn off a potential source is to wake him up out of bed or worse, wake his colicky baby.

Sometimes sheer persistence can wear reluctant sources down. Become the "Terminator": You absolutely will not stop until the person grants you the interview you need or gives you the information you seek. But be a pleasant Terminator, and don't cross the invisible line between journalistic pestering and harassment or stalking. Be persistent, not obnoxious.

Sometimes the best information comes from what you see, rather than what people tell you. While anecdotal leads are great ways of starting stories, so are descriptive leads in which you describe to the reader what you see. Capture settings and action. Writer Mark Kramer suggests that when you schedule some time with your interview source, ask for a day that they expect to be the *busiest* and *not* when they expect to be free. He says to tell the person that you promise not to be a bother, that you just want to tag along.[4]

Which type of interview?

Different types of interviews yield different information. You won't get a sense of the setting a person works in if you talk to her over the phone. And it is very difficult to get a sense of someone's personality in an e-mail. At the same time, if you need specific answers to very specific questions, you may not want to bother someone in person when a short phone call or an e-mail message will do. Understanding what you need to get and what type of interview will work best to get that information will make your interviews more effective.

In person

This type of interview is essential if the person providing you with the information is as important to the story as the information itself. If you do a story on pesticide use and want to talk to a regulator about what the laws are and how they are enforced, you can probably do that over the phone. But if you discover that the degree to which the laws are enforced depends on who the chief regulator is, then you want to know all about the chief regulator. You won't be able to do that as well over the phone.

In-person interviews are essential if you want extended time. People don't expect you to come to their office for just a few minutes. But they often expect a phone call to last that long. In-person interviews also work to your advantage in dealing with people who think they are too busy to talk to you. It is more difficult to shoo you out of the office than to get you off the phone. Regardless of how busy a person says she is, once you are in her office, she will often grant you at least twice as much time as promised.

In-person interviews are more effective when dealing with people who are reluctant to talk. It is harder to gain someone's trust and confidence if you are just a voice over the phone. In person, you can look directly into someone's eyes and they can look into yours. You can use body language to show respect and interest. You can shake their hand, hand them your business card, or in the case of some cultures, put your palms together in a sign of greeting and respect. It is easier to delve into personal questions; in someone's home or office you can inquire about personal photos or mementos as a segue to a discussion of their personal lives or interests.

When you make an appointment to see someone in their home or office and take the time and effort to do so, you signal to them that the interview is important. That's a good technique when you know the person wants to feel important, but it might work against you if they want to keep a low profile.

Phone

Phone interviews work best when you have specific questions you need answered and you know the person can answer them. They also work well when you need information from busy people who already know you through previous interviews. Some people might feel more comfortable talking to you over the phone than being seen talking to a journalist. People who don't want to have a high profile in your story might feel better talking over the phone as well. Phone interviews are necessary when the person is far away and you lack the time or resources to travel to him or the person is too busy to do the interview in person. You can develop relationships with people over the phone, and you can gain their trust through multiple conversations.

But don't rely entirely on the phone for your story. You can't use all five senses over the phone, so you miss visual cues. You also eliminate the opportunity for personal observation of any action that might occur during your interview. A public relations official might even be sitting in the person's office as he talks to you over the phone and you wouldn't know it.

E-mail

With e-mail, not only do you miss out on body language over the phone, you lose voice inflections as well. E-mail communication is limiting and can lead more easily to miscommunication. You can't sense a joke over e-mail. You can't get prolonged silences. You can't be 100 percent sure the person you think wrote the e-mail actually wrote it. E-mails are effective for introducing yourself, for setting up an interview and for giving the person who you will interview a sense of what you want. It is a great way to follow up after interviews with those questions you forgot to ask during the interview. It is also a great source for fact-checking your quotes to verify you wrote them down correctly, making sure the person meant to say what he said, or if your investigation is taking some time, checking that the person still feels the same way. Keep in mind that if the person could get in trouble for communicating with you, you should think twice about e-mailing him on a corporate e-mail account. It could be monitored and he doesn't have the ability to delete it from his network.

Web interviews

As webcams and computer-to-computer phone programs like Skype become more ubiquitous, interviewing with these tools could bridge the gap between the phone and in-person interviews. You will be able to look someone in the eye and get some sense of body language. You can show interest and respect while getting some sense of their surroundings. But many people are not comfortable with this technology, and you should use it only if your source is used to it and an in-person interview is not feasible.

PREPARING FOR THE INTERVIEW

T he success of an interview depends on how much preparation you put into it. Good questions yield good answers, but good questions don't just materialize. They come from your knowledge of the subjects you will discuss in the interview and your knowledge about the person you will interview.

Building background

You already should have done some preparation for the interview by doing sufficient background research so that you are versed in the subject matter and are able to understand any lingo — legal, technological or scientific terminology — your interview subject will likely use. You should be familiar with the important players with whom the person likely interacts. If you were to interview your local state legislator, you should go in knowing the name of the mayor, the person who heads the local political parties, the head of the state legislature and any other key people from district and state politics. You should bone up on any issues that will affect that person's job, industry or cause and any important events in the recent past that affect his business, profession or life.

Preparing primary questions

Questions may be on different levels. On one level are the questions you know you need to ask. You pinpointed this person as a possible source for a reason. Don't lose sight of that reason when asking the questions. This point may seem obvious, but it is amazing how questions can disappear from your head once you meet a person face-to-face. Some people are charismatic; they have an inexplicable quality about them that makes you tend to believe what they say. Others are master manipulators; they know what to say and when to say it in a way that deflects any questions they don't want to answer. Others are effective by being unassuming; they seem so nice or innocent or ordinary that you forget that you suspected them of having done something wrong. If you don't go to an interview adequately prepared, you could find yourself steered to a direction you hadn't intended. You'll find that when you review your notes afterward, the source who was so helpful during the interview and gave you so much of her time hadn't actually given you any useful information at all. She'd somehow managed to avoid all your hard questions without you even noticing.

Before you pick up the phone or drive out to meet someone write out five questions you need to ask and five questions you want to ask. The list also comes in handy when at various moments in the interview, a thread of questioning ends and an awkward moment ensues when the source waits for you to ask another question.

What might you need and want to ask? Think on two levels:

1. What do you want to know at this point in your investigation?
2. What will you need for your final story?

You want information now that can help you prove or refute your premise. You want information that can help you progress in your investigation. But you also want to collect information that you may need later to turn your story into a compelling read and a visual multimedia presentation.

From the beginning you want to be able to visualize your story as much as possible. At every step in the information-gathering process, you want to do that as well. At every stage you will need facts about the Who, What, When, Where, How and Why of what happened and clarifications of contradictions or of things you don't understand. You will want personal recollections in the form of anecdotes; vivid details that will help you paint a picture for your readers; comparisons with other situations or with ideal situations; historical knowledge that will help you put the problem into context; and emotions told through not only words, but body language, intensity, and even silence.

Pulitzer Prize-winning author and historian David Halberstam said you can't rush the interview process. "The more reporting you do, the more authority your voice has," he wrote. "I can always tell when a journalist is cheating. I can tell when it's a two-phone-call-story." The most important question he would ask in every interview was, "Who else should I see?" He argued that time is the crucial ingredient for a good narrative story. "The more time, the more interviews you can do, and the greater the density of your work."[5]

Being ready for tough situations

People directly affected by a problem have a different perspective than the people the problem only indirectly affects. The truth emerges when many different perspectives converge. If you work a crime beat, for example, witnesses, victims and perpetrators are firsthand sources while the police are secondhand sources unless they too witnessed the crime as it took place. But even those who experience something directly will remember it in different ways. The classic Japanese movie "Rashomon" presented a possible rape/murder/suicide from the different perspectives of four people, and the viewer is left unsure of what happened. This subjectivity of accounts is now called the "Rashomon effect," and many criminal justice experts understand that eyewitness accounts are often the least reliable evidence of guilt or innocence. Even if two people both have 20-20 vision, they see things in different ways and they recall different things. That's why you need to talk to multiple sources at a variety of levels, so that you can get the full and accurate picture. Sometimes you must talk to people who are reluctant or unwilling to talk. As you set up and prepare for interviews, you have to be ready to deal with difficult or nervous sources. Knowing what you can do in tough situations is a critical part of getting the information you need.

Reluctant sources

Some people will insist on anonymity, which creates problems. Many newspapers have restricted the use of unnamed sources after both The New Republic magazine and the New York Times were forced to admit that they had published stories that quoted people who never existed; writers Stephen Glass in the New Republic and Jason Blair in the Times had made up the stories and the people in them.[6] These restrictions are hard on student reporters who have yet to earn the credibility and trust more seasoned journalists enjoy. If you want your clips to count, you should avoid unnamed sources. That means that you will have to work hard to convince your sources to tell their stories publicly.

Negotiate. Don't be afraid to negotiate. If a source insists on anonymity, agree to treat the interview as a conversation. Tell him that you will take notes and that after the conversation you will go over the various points that interest you and discuss with him whether he still feels that his name can't be attached to the statements you want to use. This way it will give him a chance to get to know you and feel more comfortable about your questions. Or try telling the person that the conversation can initially be not-for-attribution, and you won't take notes, but that after a short discussion you will take out your notepad and ask questions. At that time the person can decide whether to answer.

You might emphasize to your source that she will be only one of many people you will talk to for the story. Ask whether it might be okay to use her comments, with her name attached, on the condition that she won't be the main source of the story. You might even go so far as to say that you won't use her in the story at all, until you have quoted four or five other people. Some people just don't want to be seen as your main source, but they may not mind being a lesser source. Assure her that you won't use any quotes until you call her first and ask for permission. At that time you will read back the exact quotes you want to use, any paraphrases of her comments and explain exactly the context in which you will use the information she provides.

Perhaps she doesn't want to be in the story but won't mind if you only need her opinion on the general state of affairs and not on any particular case. It might go the other way. She doesn't mind offering her opinion about what happens on her own block, but you understand that she doesn't want to be quoted on what happens in the rest of the city. She might not mind talking to you if you identify her only as a resident of the town and are clear that her employment at a local company is irrelevant and won't be mentioned.

Use alternate identification. If the person still insists on anonymity, try to get her to agree to some sort of identification. While you could leave out her name, you would like to include relevant details about her: The company she works for, the government office she works at, the neighborhood she lives in, or her profession, political party, gang affiliation, or religion if they are relevant to the story.

Bring up what is already known. Work from documents. While some people might be reluctant to offer information that you don't know about, they might be willing to talk about something that is already written down somewhere in black and white. They might be unwilling to do an interview, but if you call just to check some facts, or you want to show them something and see if they can tell you whether the information is incorrect — well, that's a different story.

Don't depend on one person. Try not to overweigh your story with one source. This happens when all of the important information in the story comes from one person; the other sources you quote or cite simply clarify what that person told you or add tangential information. A story structured this way will collapse if the person decides to retract the information before publication. Your story will have little credibility if after publication your main source refutes the information your story depends on.

Always keep your promises. Never break a deal you made with a source, after the fact. Regardless of how much you regret having made the deal, a deal is a deal. You can try to get your source to change his mind and agree to alter the agreement, but your long-term credibility depends on your honoring all agreements you make. That's why it is essential that you carefully think through any restrictions placed on information before you agree to accept them.

Deep-background and off-the-record sources

Some sources will try to manipulate you. One of the key ways they might do that is to offer you information on *deep background*. That term means that it is for your information only — you cannot ask other people about it, it cannot be used in the reporting process and cannot be used in the story. Think very carefully before agreeing to that kind of deal. Some reporters like the feeling of importance they get by knowing otherwise secret information. But taking information you can't use in the reporting process goes against everything you set out to do, which is the dissemination of information. You *are* your readers and viewers and listeners. Your duty is to them, not your sources. Just as you should never violate an agreement you make with a source, don't enter into an agreement that violates the interests of your audience. Perhaps the only time you may accept deep-background information is when a source needs to warn you that your information is wrong and the only way to convince you is to share information that cannot be used under any circumstance.

Don't confuse an *off-the-record* agreement with deep background, and make sure before you accept information that your source understands the difference as well. When people say "off the record," they generally mean *not-for-attribution*, that is, their name cannot appear connected with the information in the story. Sometimes they mean that you can't use it from them at all, even without attribution; that for you to report it, you must get it from another source. In contrast to deep-background information, off-the-record material can still be useful.

Let's say someone wants to help you out, but if anyone found out that you got the information from her, she will get fired. Instead, she tells you who else has the same information, where you might likely find it or how to go about looking for it. You take the extra effort to get the same information all over again from another place even though you already have it; that way, the information will still get out and she will keep her job.

Hostile sources

Every reporter must from time to time deal with the person who flatly refuses to be interviewed. While reporters have their own tactics and strategy for gaining access to someone who refuses to give it, they seem to have one common tip: Hit the person with solid evidence. The more you already know, the less they can avoid talking to you. If the evidence you have makes them look bad, they will have to address it.

Try not to get fixated on the need to interview particular individuals if other people can give you the same information. Remind yourself that you can talk to other people. Before making phone calls on a story, write down the names and phone numbers of at least six people who could answer your questions. If one is hostile, go to the next name on your list.

INVESTIGATIVE INTERVIEWING TECHNIQUES

Few beginning reporters find interviewing natural or easy. Some of the most experienced reporters never find it easy. Joan Didion, in the foreword to her collection of essays "Slouching Towards Bethlehem," recalls how she would often find herself sitting on the edge of a bed in a motel steeling up her nerves to call some local district attorney. Many consider Didion a master storyteller and interviewer, but as she acknowledged in that book, each time she interviewed someone she'd never met before she had to overcome the willies.[7]

All reporters have their own styles that work for them. Most reporters use different approaches for different types of interviewees. For example, they have one for those who want publicity versus those who don't, or one for those sophisticated about the press versus those who have never been interviewed before. To make your interviews more effective, you can start with some common interviewing techniques.

Controlling the interview

Many people in politics and in business pay consultants large amounts of money to train them how to handle interviews. These consultants often advise interviewees to decide on three subjects to talk about. No matter what the interviewer asks, they should stick to those three points. That's a way for the person being interviewed to control the interview. You need to do the same from the other side. When both interviewer and subject are sophisticated about this process, the interview can be like tug of war.

One way to take control of an interview is to throw off the person you are interviewing. Be sharper and more knowledgeable than you look. If a reporter seems mousy, it throws people off when she asks hard questions. If a reporter looks clueless, it throws people off when she demonstrates thorough knowledge and an analytical mind. But don't confuse the ability to throw someone off with intimidation. If you try to intimidate someone, the person will likely become defensive and clam up, rather than open up.

If possible, be the one to establish the rules. This will set the tone of the interview. For example, your source might suggest a conference call with two other people. Try to insist that it be one-to-one; that multiple voices are confusing. Your source might request a phone interview, you could insist on it being in his office. More and more, sources try to get away with e-mail interviews. Insist that you must talk on the phone or in person. When you set rules, you send a signal that you know what you are doing and that you won't be intimidated or manipulated. Be insistent but not obnoxious. You want to know when to be flexible. In fact, it is good to be insistent *and* flexible at the same time. Here is an example: A source in the food industry says he is so busy all day he can't possibly take the time for a phone interview, but he can fit in an e-mail interview. You tell him that won't work, but that you are willing to do the interview at five in the morning before he opens his bakery or at midnight when his restaurant closes. Or he says he can't possibly find time to do an in-person interview as he is leaving for vacation and has work piled up until then. You tell him you will drive him to the airport, and since that is a 40-minute drive, you will have plenty of time to talk and the voice recorder will take it all down.

Take charge from the get-go. When you walk in, offer your hand and introduce yourself, rather than wait for the person you are interviewing to do so. Go over the format for the interview — whether you will start with personal or professional questions, whether you will ask general or more specific questions. Get the person to spell his name and make sure you have his correct title. Establish whether you need to record the interview and whether you will want to take photos afterward. Again, taking control sends the signal that you know what you are doing and that you are in charge of the interview.

Getting people to talk

Someone might not be able to tell you information for many reasons. Doing so could cost them a job, customers, friends, trust of their co-workers, their reputation, or their dignity and self-worth. They may be bound to confidentiality by an employment contract or by professional standards of conduct. It is not usually effective to get people to break contracts or professional or personal codes to give you the information you need or want. Instead, try to focus on what information the person can comfortably give you.

See the world their way

Try to understand the person's point of view. Different types of people see the world differently, and they have different abilities to answer different types of questions. An engineer makes a career out of designing and building things; he figures out how to make something work. He doesn't necessarily spend his time thinking about the politics of something. So asking an engineer a question about how something works might be more effective than asking him about the politics of why something is being done. A scientist might see the problem from a logical perspective; decisions that seem to make no sense might put him at a loss. A politician might be able to size up the pressures from multiple constituencies. A financial manager might see the problem from a cost-benefit perspective.

When you aren't sure how a person thinks or what language he speaks, try going back to the universal language: money. Almost everyone understands money, the shortage of it, and what could be done if they had more of it.

Phrase questions as if people aren't able to talk

Working with a source is far more effective than working against one. Instead of assuming that an individual doesn't want to give you information, try assuming that she does but can't. If that's the case, you may find a way to help her help you. Ask her three questions:

1. Why can't you? If you understand the answer to that question, you might be able to find a way the person can give you the information in a way that does not pose problems. Again, just because someone can't answer a particular question doesn't mean they want you to leave the interview uninformed. For example, lawyers are bound by *attorney-client privilege*. That means they can't give you information that might harm their client or give you information without the client's consent. Understanding that goes a long way. To get more information, try asking the next question:

2. What *can* you give me? Your source might not be able to give you details about a particular case, but she can talk in general about something. Some people won't admit to "problems," but they don't mind talking about "challenges." A person might not want to talk about what is happening now, but she doesn't mind talking about a problem if you pose it as a hypothetical case. It might help to say, "This is what I know." That statement will give your source something to work from and make her think she isn't offering you anything new, she is just clarifying what you already know or she is correcting your misinformation. Some reporters use that technique when they actually don't know. What they offer is a guess with the hope that the person they are interviewing will be able to confirm it as fact.

3. Where else could I find it out? It could be that while the person you are trying to interview could be fired for disclosing the information, he can point you to the guy in the office next door who is far too valuable to the company to be intimidated. While one lawyer can't talk to you because his client doesn't want the publicity, he can point you to a defendant in a case that he doesn't represent.

Repeat the question

If someone doesn't want to answer a question, or has trouble answering it, skip it. Later on in the interview, rephrase that question and ask it again. Or wait a day, call the person up and ask it as a follow-up question. Sometimes people simply forget that they had trouble answering the question earlier or that they hadn't wanted to answer it. Sometimes people's brains freeze on a piece of knowledge, and if you ask the same question at a different time, the mental block disappears. Often they don't want to answer because they don't feel comfortable with you, but they will be more open after they understand more about what you want.

Sometimes a little rewording works wonders. Asking someone "How could you have done this?" comes across as an accusation. But "How could this have happened?" is not as accusatory.

However, the more persistent you need to be, the more polite you must also be. In interviewing it might work this way: "I know I already asked you this and I'm sorry for having to ask it again, but I really need to know. Exactly what did you do and when did you do it?"

Ask for a step-by-step explanation

When information is complicated, your inability to understand what sources say or their inability to be clear will frustrate them. They may fear that in simplifying the issue, you will end up misunderstanding it and you will get it wrong. Watch for signs of frustration. When you see your source begin to feel frustrated through body language or by the way they sound, slow down. Get them to slow down their thinking. Ask them to take you through the issue one step at a time and make it clear to them that you understand how difficult it is to simplify a complicated problem.

Change your lens

If you ask a pointed question that a person doesn't feel he can answer, try a wider angle. Move from specifics to general, from actual to hypothetical. Sometimes it might work the other way. You want him to talk about how things work or why things are the way they are in general, but he doesn't feel comfortable doing that. In that case zoom in from the general to the specific. He might not think he is in a position to talk about cases in general but he can talk about his last case. You don't want to push people to connect dots for you who don't think that they are capable of doing so. So let them tell you about their individual dot. You can connect them yourself later by comparing what they told you with what others tell you.

Collecting anecdotes

Another interviewing technique is to get your subject to provide revealing anecdotes about themselves or a situation. An anecdote is a little story that demonstrates something about someone or recounts an important moment in someone's life. They are the key to bringing a story to life that some readers might otherwise dismiss. Anecdotes can crystallize the importance of a story. Former San Francisco Chronicle sportswriter Joan Ryan included the following anecdote, about a young gymnast who was under pressure to lose weight, in her book "Little Girls in Pretty Boxes," which was an investigation into the treatment of young girls training for the Olympics:

> Once, when she tried to buy a bagel and cream cheese at the deli near the rink, the man behind the counter wouldn't serve her. "Coaches orders," the man said. Elaine's coaches had instructed him not to sell her anything but tea and coffee. Humiliated, she drove to the 7-Eleven down the road, bought a pint of ice cream and ate it in the parking lot.[8]

Getting anecdotes is tricky. If you ask someone, "Tell me a story about yourself," she may not be able to think of a story. Broad questions cause the memory to lock. Little questions can open it up.

A great interviewer will ask for the smallest details. The more you press for details, the more details the person you are interviewing will provide. People hold back the minutiae of their experiences because they assume no one is interested in them. You must convince people that you want the mundane, because great anecdotes are built on them.

Ask for details in all five senses: sight, sound, touch, smell and taste. Was the shirt red, green, striped? Was the substance slimy, soft, hard or bumpy? Think extrasensory as well. Premonitions make for great anecdotes, but you rarely get them without asking. Let's look at types of questions that can help you pull anecdotes out of people's memories.

Ask about their firsts and lasts

People tend to remember the first time they did something and the last time they did it. Everything else might be fuzzy. Ask: Do you remember the first time you met him? What was it like the first time you did that? When was the last time that happened? What was that like? When you ask about the first time, the memory cabinet opens up. The person will likely recall a better example or an even better story.

Ask about their bests and worsts

These questions work in the same way as the first and last questions. What was the best job you ever had? What was your biggest win? What was the most difficult campaign you directed? What was the toughest case you argued?

Ask for comparisons

If someone can't put an experience into words, ask her to compare it with something else. "That campaign you directed to try to stop timber logging. Was it like the one you did earlier when you tried to stop the dam from being built?" Even when the answer is no, an anecdote will emerge from the differences between the two.

Listening closely

Another key interviewing technique is listening. Master the art of listening. Give people enough time to gather thoughts and put them into words. One of the things that make an in-person interview more effective than a phone interview is the use of silence. With cell phones especially, silence often confuses people; they wonder if the connection dropped. But in person, silence is one of the most effective tools you have. By waiting for people to continue their thoughts you will come across as considerate and thoughtful. Also, people try to fill the vacuum. They end up saying more than they intended or they say something other than what they intended.

While you wait, don't let your mind wander. Stay focused on the person you interview and on the things being said. As much as possible, keep your eyes on her eyes rather than on your notebook. Listening to what someone is saying and connecting to her as a person is more important than getting down everything she says, word for word. You can always ask someone to repeat something they said or clarify it. To avoid interrupting the flow of an interview, you might try jotting down a fragment, and when you sense it is something important, circle it or put a star next to it. Then come back to it later in the interview. You can say: "I keep thinking back to something you said earlier. Mind if we go back over it?"

If you treat someone with respect during an interview, if you ask them thoughtful questions and allow them time to reflect on your questions and to answer them carefully, they will return your calls and answer follow-up questions later.

To sharpen your focus during the interview, prepare before the interview to pick out the critical parts of the conversation that you can use in your story. What follows are particular elements to listen for.

Major points

You will find this easier if you prepare for your interview by jotting down (from your background research) the possible topics the person might cover and all the points you want him to hit. You might remind yourself of your story premise and what you need at that step in the interview process. Listen for the points and when they are raised, put an asterisk next to those comments, underline or circle them.

Evidence

Listen for any evidence that supports or refutes your premise. Be equally prepared for both possibilities; don't ignore statements that knock down your premise. Also be prepared for gradients of the two. Your premise might be correct in some ways and off the mark in others. Don't force the information into only black and white categories. Truth comes in all shades.

Patterns

Listen for patterns that connect different pieces of information within an interview. Say you talk to a business executive. You ask him about his family. He explains how he and his father always fought. Later, you ask him about his first job, and he says he liked the job but not his boss. Still later, you talk about the company he heads, and he says he loves the day-to-day management but doesn't like having to answer to a board of directors. You can see from his comments about different subjects that perhaps he has a problem with authority. That's an example of how different pieces of information can paint a picture or explain something that isn't explicitly said.

Once you spot a pattern in some of the comments, you might want to point that out to your interviewee and see what she thinks. Does she agree with your take, and if so, can she think of other examples that fit the pattern? If she disagrees with your take, then it means she thinks the experiences or opinions that you connected were unique occurrences. That might indicate that these instances are significant and warrant further exploration.

Killer quotes

When you are far from writing your story it is difficult to think about the actual quotes you will need. But if you fail to listen for quotes early on, you will make writing the story difficult. Colorful expressions filled with humor or emotion make great quotes. You also want to quote people when they offer insight.

Dana Priest and Anne Hull's story

www.washingtonpost.com/wp-dyn/content/article/2007/02/17/AR2007021701172.html

A powerful quote comes from the series of articles that Washington Post reporters Dana Priest and Anne Hull did in 2007 on the neglect and mistreatment of U.S. soldiers after their return from Iraq. The article contains a profile of a woman who suffers from paranoia and depression after serving two tours of duty. She describes how one day, after getting lost on the subway on her way to work, she went home and considered killing herself.

"If I cut this way, I'll survive and be embarrassed," she remembers thinking. "If I cut that way, there'll be a lot of blood. If I do it in the back yard, they might not find me for a couple of days. It will be icky. Maybe I'll have a blanket to cover up my body."[9]

Listen and ask for detailed descriptions, even if what the person is recalling is painful.

To get long quotes you need a tape recorder or you need to write fast. You can't possibly write fast enough to note everything the person says. That's why it is important to listen carefully for certain things. You want to be able to catch the great quotes when they fly by. To catch them the pen in your hand must always be at the ready, like a baseball mitt in your hands. You will jot down an expression here, a fact there. But as soon as the person says something that seems like a good quote your fingers take off, taking down every word. If you do that several times or more during each interview, you will have plenty of good quotes for your story when you are ready to write it.

What can be paraphrased?

The opposite of the killer quote is the garbled expression. Reporters love those who speak in perfectly quotable sentences. But often those with real knowledge don't have a way with words. So you must help them communicate the importance of the information they try to give you. Don't be afraid to paraphrase. It is the key to getting anecdotes and bringing readers into your story. Let's return to the war veteran that Priest and Hull introduced us to. After she considered killing herself, she sought help at a VA hospital. The reporters write:

> Blackwood shared Ward 3D East with 26 men and three other women; mixed-gender wards are common in VA psychiatric units. There was no exercise equipment. No outdoor courtyard. No treatment either, other than prescription medication. The linoleum corridor was 39 paces long, and Blackwood walked it many times a day.[10]

Blackwood's thought process about killing herself is in her own words. This story about Ward 3D is a paraphrase of what she told the reporters.

When you paraphrase you put words into someone else's mouth. So be careful. You need to accurately translate the words that come out of their mouths so that they best represent the thoughts in their heads. Always, before publication, read paraphrases back to the person whose statement you paraphrased.

Listen for the unspoken

Sometimes what is most important is what people don't say. Some people have a difficult time expressing emotions or talking about things that are personal. They keep their feelings bottled up. Often the information these types of people will offer up will be superficial. Other people will actively seek to avoid talking about difficult subjects because it will make them look bad or get them into trouble. They will force you to dig for that information, and that means that you first have to listen for what is not said. Just as you listen for patterns in the things they say, listen for a pattern to questions they seem to evade. Look at Box 6.2 for an example.

Follow up questions

Asking good questions isn't enough if you don't follow up on the answer. You need to question the answers that people give you. If someone says something that needs further explanation, ask for details with the following questions:

- Who was there at the time?
- Was that the first time it happened?
- Does that happen often?
- Why did it happen?

Finding the unspoken story in an interview   BOX 6.2

Imagine that you are interviewing Public Works Director Bob Cat about road maintenance for your dangerous streets story. Your questions and his responses might be as follows:

Question: How do you decide which roads get repaired when?

Bob Cat: We have 347 miles of roadway in this town. Obviously we take care of emergency situations first.

Question: Who decides if a road condition qualifies as an emergency?

Answer: Well, if there is a crack or hole that poses a danger to people's lives obviously that would be an emergency.

Question: And who determines that?

Answer: I do, based on what my guys on the street tell me.

Question: How many people do you have on the street?

Answer: Four.

Question: Four inspectors? And how many do you have doing the repairs?

Answer: No. I have four total.

Question: Four people to inspect and repair 347 miles of roadway?

Answer: Well, we've put them all to work on repairs.

Question: So you have no inspectors?

Answer: Not since the city cut our budget last year.

Question: How many inspectors did you have before that?

Answer: Four.

Question: So if you have no inspectors, how do you know about emergencies that need to be addressed?

Answer: Residents call us, and the city council makes suggestions.

Question: So you repair the roads that the most people complain about. That's the system for prioritizing repairs?

Answer: Not necessarily. Just because a lot of people complain doesn't mean it's the most dangerous problem. I also check out the streets myself as well.

Question: You schedule in tours of the different parts of the city?

Answer: Not exactly.

Question: When and where do you make these observations?

Answer: On my way to and from work. I live five miles away.

Question: You live on the west side of the city, don't you? When was the last time you drove five miles on the east side?

Answer: I'd have to think about that.

What Bob Cat is trying not to say is that he doesn't have a system for prioritizing road repairs. He ignores complaints from residents and orders repairs only for problems on the roads that he, his family, friends or important people he knows use. Budget cuts forced him to cut his road inspectors, and no officials have seemed to notice problems.

- How easy or difficult was it?
- How did it make him feel?
- Was it a good or bad thing?

Through follow-up questions, you can catch people in inconsistencies, exaggerations and hypocrisy. Although you should prepare a set of questions for every interview, don't get stuck on them. Try following each of the answers up with a how or why question. How did that work? How many people were there? How often did that happen? How did that make you feel? How bad was it? How much did that cost? Why did you do that? Why did that matter? Why is that important?

Asking the tough questions

If you gather information that points to embezzlement, at some point you must confront the person you believe stole the money. Or you discover a chain of patronage jobs that seems to originate with a high-ranking official, and it turns out that he gave the jobs to keep people quiet about his relationship with an under-aged girl. Or you discover that a person married for 20 years with three kids who led a campaign against gay rights in your state is a closet homosexual. You will have to confront these people with an accusation and your evidence for it.

It's probably not a good idea to start an interview with the most hot-button question. Patience in interviews will pay off.

The more difficult a question is, the more forthright you should ask it. You can ease into or build up to it. But once you get to the point where you need to ask the question, just ask it. Don't sneak around it, allude to it or avoid it. You can't expect people to be forthright with you if you aren't forthright with them.

Here's how you might pose a difficult question:

"Senator, you've campaigned for years against same-sex marriage and other legislation that would expand rights for homosexuals. But people who know you well told me that you've had homosexual relationships. I'm sorry, but I have to ask: Have you had sexual relationships with men?"

Make sure you have already asked any other important questions, in case he ends the interview at that point.

Interviewing survivors and victims

Investigative stories often deal with emotional topics. A story might require you to talk to people traumatized by something that happened to them. They might agree to talk to you only because they are too traumatized to know they shouldn't — their lives could be in danger if they talk to the press. Or they refuse to talk to you only because it would force them to relive a painful experience. Making your reader care about a problem is difficult if you can't introduce them to the actual people it harms. That means that you can't avoid talking to people who are victims.

Some of the toughest reporters in the world, those who have developed skin thick enough to deal with the most ruthless business people or hostile political figures, cringe at the thought of interviewing people who are in pain, who have been victims of violence or disease and those who have lost loved ones to it. But the best of them know that the people harmed deserve more than anybody else the chance to tell their story. Just as you can't write an investigative story attacking people without giving them the chance to refute any accusations and clarify their position, you can't write the story without giving the victims their due as well. Fortunately, experts have studied ways to cover traumatic and tragic situations, and Box 6.3 highlights their advice for handling these types of interviews.[11]

Documenting the interview

Record your interviews on a digital recorder if possible. I used to advise students against this practice because sometimes when you know the information is being recorded, you get lazy and fail to pay careful attention to what is being said. So here's my advice in the digital age: You will want the audio later for the Web, so you need to collect it. But to keep engaged and alert in the interviewing process, record *all* your interviews. Transcribing interviews is tedious; you will pay attention and take good notes to avoid having to do so.

Plan to bring along a digital camera or a video camera. You might have only one chance to interview this person. Snap photos and take video, and make sure you get the information needed for a photo caption (who is in the picture, what is going on, when did it happen and where). You may not have a chance later to collect the audio or visuals you will need.

Remember to ask your subject's permission before taking photos or video. If you are photographing or recording anyone under 18, get a parent's permission.

| Tips for working with survivors and victims | BOX 6.3 |

BE PREPARED FOR REJECTION

Chip Scanlan, a writing coach with the Poynter Institute, suggests that when a victim rejects your polite request for an interview, write a short note and ask a family member or friend of the person to deliver it to him or her.[12] Sometimes people react without thinking, but after they have a chance to think about it, they realize they want to tell their story. Famed crime reporter Edna Buchanan advised that when the family of a victim hangs up on you, which you should expect, give them a few minutes, steel yourself up, and call them back. That gives them time to reconsider whether they want to talk to you and what they want to say. Half the time they will now talk to you.[13]

GIVE THEM THE OPPORTUNITY TO TALK ON THEIR OWN TERMS

Earlier in this chapter, I discussed how controlling your interview is important. But that doesn't hold when you wish to interview victims of trauma. In that case, ceding control to them is important. Let them pick a time and place that allows them to feel most comfortable. Be as gentle with the questions as possible, even though you can't shy away from asking difficult ones. Don't press questions that they don't want to answer.

ALWAYS TREAT VICTIMS WITH DIGNITY AND RESPECT

Try not to sound skeptical. Treat them the way you would want someone treating members of your family under similar circumstances. Don't say you understand what they are going through or use other empty phrases.

CLEARLY IDENTIFY YOURSELF

Victims of crime and tragedies will likely have been interviewed by many different kinds of people — police, prosecutors, investigators, counselors, social workers, lawyers. They may lump them all together in their minds. Make sure they don't confuse you with some official and that they understand fully that you are a journalist and that what they tell you may end up in print.

START WITH GENTLE QUESTIONS

If you are interviewing someone who lost a loved one to violence, don't begin with asking about the incident that led to his death. Focus on his life and what he liked to do or what he was like as a person. Begin with questions that the person will likely feel most comfortable answering.

DON'T WRITE THE OBITUARIES OF MISSING PEOPLE

Even if you are convinced that the person you are writing about is dead, until the body is found his

friends and relatives cling to the hope that he is alive. Don't ask questions in such a way as to insinuate that the person won't come back.

LET PEOPLE CRY

When you interview people about something sad or traumatic, be prepared for the possibility that they will break down. There is no blueprint for what you do then — you must go with your instinct. You could stop the interview and tell the person you could come back at another time. Or you could try to find them a tissue and a glass of water and wait until they gain enough control over their emotions to talk. It is okay to ask the person if they want you to leave and then be prepared to do so. Let the person know that it is okay for them to cry. But don't ask them if they are okay; obviously they are not.

DETERMINE IF THE INTERVIEW IS NECESSARY

In their book on the ethics of covering violence, authors William Cotè and Roger Simpson talk about the "unthinkable option," that of not doing an interview or dropping a story when someone vital to the story has already been traumatized by an event or a problem and your interviewing them or doing the story will cause them further harm. They suggest that you discuss with your editor the difficulties and ethics of interviewing trauma victims before you begin a story that involves traumatic situations such as interviewing victims of child abuse, or investigating government response to natural disasters or the culpability of a corporation in the event of a workplace disaster. They warn:

> It is critical . . . that a deliberate decision replace a knee-jerk assumption that reporters must interview all victims, photographers must shoot all injured people, and pen and film should capture all tears and screams.[14]

Generally, you are free to take pictures in a public place as long as the subjects do not have a "reasonable expectation of privacy." While what falls under this legal guideline has been debated, it's best to use common sense. Pictures in a public park would be fine, but pictures in a park restroom should be avoided.

AFTER THE INTERVIEW

After you do an interview, type up your notes as soon as possible. Scribbles and your own custom shorthand likely will fill your notebooks. Typing your notes ensures that you will still be able to read and understand it all in the future. Don't risk misinterpreting your notes or forgetting that what you jotted down was something you don't fully understand.

Instead of typing your notes into a word processing program such as Microsoft Word, consider using a spreadsheet program like Excel. (Appendix C contains a basic Excel tipsheet for those who need a crash course.) Think about questions and answers as data to organize and analyze. Let's look at the advantages of plugging notes into a spreadsheet program. In Exhibit 6.3, you can see how information can be plugged in from a hypothetical interview with Joe Resident, a man you interviewed for your story about dangerous streets. To duplicate this worksheet, open up a spreadsheet. In the first row, name your columns: "Person Interviewed," "Date of Interview," "Question" and "Answer." Then devote each row to a different question and answer.

Add a "Major Points" column to summarize the main elements from the interviews. A *major point* is something important that a statement from an in-

EXHIBIT 6.3   Keeping your notes organized in a spreadsheet.

	Person Interviewed	Date of Interview	Question	Answer
1	Person Interviewed	Date of Interview	Question	Answer
2	Joe Resident	Aug. 19, 2008	What is your job?	Owns small hardware store.
3	Joe Resident	Aug. 19, 2008	Why are you suing the city?	"I crashed my car because I hit a pothole the city should have fixed."
4	Joe Resident	Aug. 19, 2008	Why do you think the city is responsible?	"A woman down the road said she had called the city three times to warn them about the pothole and get them to fix it."
5	Joe Resident	Aug. 19, 2008	What happened?	"I was driving along, hit the hole and my car popped up. I lost control of it and hit a telephone pole."
6	Joe Resident	Aug. 19, 2008	So why sue the city?	He thinks it might be the only way to get the city to take care of the roads.
7	Joe Resident	Aug. 19, 2008	How bad was the accident?	"My car was totaled. The front just accordioned in. My back has been killing me ever since. "

terview suggests or illustrates. For example, Joe Resident said this: "I crashed my car because I hit a pothole the city should have fixed." That suggests this major point: Potholes cause accidents. Someone else might say something later that also suggests the same idea—that potholes cause accidents, and the spreadsheet format will make it easy for you to spot repetition in these points. Try to keep the major points simple, using a few key words. Being concise now will make it easier later in the investigation when you start outlining your story.

From this process of summarizing, you may also see that some of the things Resident said raise other questions you now want to ask, and they make you think of people you need to track down. Create two more columns: one for "Questions Raised" and another for "To Do." Exhibit 6.4 includes those new columns and the title bars.

If you sort your information by the "To Do" column, you get a plan of the next steps in your investigation. Before you enter notes from other interviews into the spreadsheet, anchor your notes from Joe Resident by using hyperlinks. That way you can move parts of the interviews onto different sheets and sort your data without losing your frame of reference; Excel will transfer the links to the new spreadsheet. If you click on any of the hyperlinks, it will take you back to the unsorted spreadsheet you copied the information from. Or if you glide over a hyperlink with your mouse, you will see the name of the source interview in the form of a ScreenTip. This will be especially handy when you start connecting the dots, as we'll discuss in Chapter 9. Box 6.4 shows you how to create hyperlinks and screen tips to anchor the notes from an interview.

Adding "Questions Raised" and "To Do" columns.   **EXHIBIT 6.4**

Person Interviewed	Answer	Major Points	Questions Raised	To Do
Joe Resident	He thinks it might be the only way to get the city to take care of the roads.	People are suing.	How many lawsuits agains city over potholes?	Get Discovery documents. Check with city attorney.
Joe Resident	"A woman down the road said she had called the city three times to warn them about the pothole and get them to fix it."	People have complained to the city.	How many residents/ complaints filed with the city?	Interview Holly Homeowner.
Joe Resident	"I crashed my car because I hit a pothole the city should have fixed."	Potholes cause accidents.	How many pothole-related accidents over the past five years?	Get accident data from police.
Joe Resident	Owns small hardware store.			
Joe Resident	"I was driving along, hit the hole and my car popped up. I lost control of it and hit a telephone pole."			
Joe Resident	"My car was totaled. The front just accordioned in. My back has been killing			

Creating hyperlinks
BOX 6.4

1. Highlight all the cells that hold notes from a particular interview.

2. Name that group of cells by entering a name, such as "JoeResident," in the space to the left of the **Formula** bar. Make sure you don't include any blank spaces between the words in the name.

3. Now highlight the "Answers" column (whichever column you used to enter in the information from your notes). With the cells in the JoeResident interview still highlighted, go to the **Insert** menu and click on **Hyperlink**.

4. Enter a **ScreenTip** that will show up when you glide your mouse over a piece of information from that interview. Let's call it "Resident Interview."

5. Click on **Document** and then **Locate**, as shown in Exhibit 6.5.

6. Click on **Defined Names** and choose "JoeResident." Every time you name a range of cells, it will add that choice to the **Anchor** menu. Once you hit **OK** and return to your spreadsheet, you will see that every cell entry has turned into a hyperlink.

EXHIBIT 6.5   Using the Edit Hyperlink dialog box.

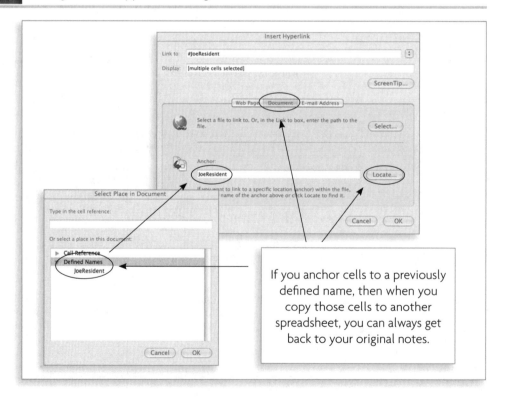

If you anchor cells to a previously defined name, then when you copy those cells to another spreadsheet, you can always get back to your original notes.

Now pull up your Master Sourcelist that we created in Chapter 5, add the Joe Resident interview to it and create a hyperlink to the interview file.

Finally, set up your notes for your next interview. Below the final row for the Joe Resident interview, create two new spaces for the name and date of the Holly Homeowner interview. Enter in your notes for that interview, and be sure to keep the columns the same. To visually distinguish between the Resident and Homeowner interviews, you can color-code them. Highlight all the cells from one interview and click the Paint Can Icon on the Formatting toolbar. That will give you a selection of background colors to choose for that interview. When you are done with the second interview, name and anchor those cells the same way you did for the Resident interview. That will allow you to use Excel or another spreadsheet program to outline your story, which we will do in Chapter 10. You can see how the finished product with hyperlinks might look in Exhibit 6.6.

Repeat all the steps for each interview you do. Box 6.5 offers tips for formatting your spreadsheet so that it will look like the ones in the examples included here.

We will come back to the Joe Resident and Holly Homeowner interviews in Chapter 10 when we need to connect the dots in our investigation.

Organizing multiple interviews on a spreadsheet. **EXHIBIT 6.6**

Person Interviewed	Date of Interview	Question	Answer	Major Points	Questions Raised	To Do
Joe Resident	8/19/08	What is your job?	Owns small hardware store.			
Joe Resident	8/19/08	Why are you suing the city?	"I crashed my car because I hit a pothole the city should have fixed."	Potholes cause accidents	How many pothole-related accidents over the past five years?	
Joe Resident	8/19/08	Why do you think the city is responsible?	"A woman down the road said she had called the city three times to warn them about the pothole and get them to fix it."	People have complained to the city	How many residents/complaints filed with the city?	Interview Holly Homeowner
Joe Resident	8/19/08	What happened?	"I was driving along, hit the hole and my car popped up. I lost control of it and hit a telephone pole."			
Joe Resident	8/19/08	So why sue the city?	He thinks it might be the only way to get the city to take care of the roads.	People are suing		Get Discovery documents
Joe Resident	8/19/08	How bad was the accident?	"My car was totaled. The front just accordioned in My back has been killing me ever since."			
Joe Resident	8/19/08	That woman down the street who complained three times. What's her name?	Holly Homeowner. "She's in the yellow house."			
Holly Homeowner	8/23/08	Have potholes been a problem?	"Well, there is that one that you can see right here from my front door. We call it the Grand Canyon."	The potholes are big		
Holly Homeowner	8/23/08	Did you call anyone about it?	She complained to the city three times. "Once I went down and filled out a form they had. But nothing happened."	People have complained to the city		Request data on complaints filed
Holly Homeowner	8/23/08	How long has it been like that?	Since the fall, at least. "Long enough for my kids to name it."	The problem has existed for some time		
Holly	8/23/08	Has it caused	Joe Resident crashed his car. "But every	Potholes cause		

| How to format a spreadsheet for an investigative story | BOX 6.5 |

These instructions use Excel, but other spreadsheet programs offer similar capabilities.

- **Wrap your text.** Highlight all the cells on the sheet and on the **Format** menu, select **Cells**, select **Alignment** and select **Wrap Text**. That will prevent long text from getting cut off by the next column.

- **Widen your rows and columns.** Highlight all the cells, go back to the **Format** menu, select **Columns** and **Width**. That will allow you to widen the columns. Do the same for **Rows**.

- **Create a title bar.** In the first cell, enter the name of the person you interviewed. Highlight the row and go to the **Formatting** toolbar (if you don't see it you will find it under **View** then **Toolbars**) and change the color.

- **Increase the magnification.** Using the zoom slider, increase the magnification to 150 percent or 200 percent. That will give you a screen that is easier to enter information into and that doesn't look like a plain spreadsheet. You can even change the font of the type you use to a handwriting script to make it look like handwritten notes.

CONCLUSION

Interviewing is a skill journalists work on and improve upon over the course of their entire careers. Reporters have different styles that work for them, and they vary styles when they interview different types of people. But all effective reporters seem to share some basic rules for all interviews: They treat people with respect, they demonstrate genuine interest in and curiosity about the person being interviewed and the topic being discussed and they try to be both flexible and persistent. If you prepare for your interviews by doing background research and developing a set of questions to work from, you will go into the interviews with confidence and show your interview subject that you know what you are doing. Train yourself to listen carefully for important information that you will need to tell a convincing and compelling story: evidence, anecdotes, quotes, comparisons and patterns. And finally, keep your notes organized: Type them into a word processing or spreadsheet program that lets you link back to your Master Sourcelist.

In the next chapter, we will look at a published story that involved many interviews, as well as data and documents, to see how complex information can be woven into a compelling story.

EXERCISES

1. Throughout the day turn every encounter into a mini interview.
   a. Ask each person you meet their name, where they are from, what they do for a living or what they hope to do for a living, and what they love

to do most when they are not at work or school. Then see how much more information you can learn through these casual interviews: where they grew up, whether they are married or single, whether they have children or pets, their religion, politics or favorite movies, and so on.

b. Get their business card if they have one, or find out if they are on Facebook, LinkedIn, MySpace or some other social networking site where they can be reached.

c. Create a spreadsheet and enter the names and contact information and other information you collected about them.

2. Pick someone who has an occupation or interest that might make for a good story. Call him or her up and ask if you can follow him or her around for a morning or afternoon. When you do follow that person, take notes as if you intend to make that person's actions the narrative thread in your story. Look for the scene that will open up the story and for scenes that provide telling details about the person.

3. In your library or through a Web search, find an article that profiles a prominent person. Magazines to look through include Vanity Fair, The New Yorker, New York Magazine, Esquire or Rolling Stone. How did the author of the article bring the person to life? What anecdotes can you spot? What telling details did the author include? What questions do you think the author had to ask to get the anecdotes and telling details?

THE BIG STORY Project   •   THE BIG STORY Project   •   STEP 6

6.1 From the information you got from your initial interviews, combined with the information you got from your preliminary research, map out a schedule for your next interviews according to the 5Ws System or the Inductive Approach as outlined in this chapter.

6.2 Create a spreadsheet for your interview notes. Make columns for the name of the person you interviewed, the questions you ask, the answers they give, the major points the answer suggests, questions raised, and To Do.

6.3 Anchor the information in the "Answers" column by creating a hyperlink and ScreenTip.

6.4 Enter the notes from interviews you have completed so far into the spreadsheet. Each time you complete new interviews, enter the notes into the spreadsheet.

6.5 Sort your spreadsheet by the To Do column and add those tasks to your To Do list.

NOTES

1. Ken Metzler. *Creative Interviewing: The Writer's Guide to Gathering Information by Asking Questions.* Third Edition. Allyn and Bacon, 1997, p. 167.

2. Ibid.

3. Eric Nalder. "Loosening lips: The art of the interview." Distributed to the 2006 IRE National Conference, Ft. Worth, Texas. Available at IRE Resource Center, Tipsheet 2720.

4. Mark Kramer and Wendy Call, eds. *Telling True Stories: A Nonfiction Writer's Guide.* Plume, 2007, p. 26.

5. David Halberstam. "The narrative idea." In *Telling True Stories: A Nonfiction Writer's Guide.* Ed. Mark Kramer and Wendy Call. Plume, 2007, pp. 12–13.

6. To learn more about the Glass story, see the 2003 movie "Shattered Glass," which starred Hayden Christensen. For more information on the Blair scandal, read "Correcting the record: Times reporter who resigned leaves long trail of deception." *New York Times,* May 11, 2003.

7. Joan Didion. *Slouching Towards Bethlehem.* Washington Square Press, 1981, pp. 13–14.

8. Joan Ryan. *Little Girls in Pretty Boxes: The Making and Breaking of Elite Gymnasts and Figure Skaters.* Warner Books, 1995, p. 156.

9. Dana Priest and Anne Hull. "Soldier finds comfort at dark journey's end." *Washington Post,* June 17, 2007.

10. Ibid.

11. Two good sources are the Victims and the Media Program at Michigan State University and the Dart Center for Journalism and Trauma at the University of Washington.

12. Chip Scanlan. "First rule of interviewing: Be human." Poynter Institute. Retrieved Sept. 16, 2001, from http://www.poynter.org/content/content_view.asp?id=5936.

13. Edna Buchanan. *The Corpse Had a Familiar Face.* Simon & Schuster, 2004, p. 406.

14. William Cotè and Roger Simpson. *Covering Violence: A Guide to Ethical Reporting About Victims and Trauma.* Columbia University Press, 2000, p. 9.

Analyzing the Big Story

CHAPTER PREVIEW Investigative stories often reveal a problem that people in a position of power would like to ignore or keep secret. Therefore, investigative journalists must be able to prove the case they make. The story must also be powerful enough to draw readers or viewers in and keep them until the end. When done right, an investigative story will lay out a problem so convincingly that readers and viewers will feel outraged and push corporations to change their ways and governments to take action. You will see how an investigative story can do this as you follow an example that is both convincing and compelling. I will explain some basic components of any investigative story and show you how the reporters incorporated these components into the published story.

7

CHAPTER

ANALYZING A SAMPLE STORY

Before delving deeper into your investigative story, it helps to take a look at an example that shows how one news organization reported a complicated, important problem and told the story in a compelling way. The following story was the first of a four-part series published in April 2004 by Newsday, a daily newspaper that covers the Long Island suburban communities in the New York City metro area. In "A Tragic Vulnerability," reporters Dawn MacKeen, Lauren Terrazzano, Amanda Harris and Eden Laikin explored the preventable deaths of elderly people who had wandered out of assisted living centers on Long Island. The stories that followed looked at violence against elderly residents with dementia and inappropriate medical treatment given to these patients.[1]

Read through the story (pages 155–166) and notice whether you as a reader find the story to be compelling and the information clear. Marginal notes of two types appear alongside the story: the italic items give background from the reporters and the boldface items point out the key components needed to make an investigative story strong. Exhibit 7.1 summarizes these basic components. After the story, these components will be broken down and further explained.

EXHIBIT 7.1	The seven components to any good investigative story.

1. Something important is at stake.
2. The problem affects people.
3. The story uncovers information that is not widely known.
4. The story identifies the cause of the problem.
5. The story identifies possible solutions and obstacles to those solutions.
6. The evidence backs up the case.
7. The story provides context.

A Tragic Vulnerability

By Dawn MacKeen, Lauren Terrazzano, Amanda Harris and Eden Laikin,
Newsday, Copyright 2004. Reprinted with permission.

Ethel Danzker was wearing a thin polyester dress, stockings and sneakers when she wandered out of Birchwood Assisted Living in East Northport and into the darkness. The average temperature that December day was 37 degrees.

A few years earlier, Danzker had suffered a series of small strokes that left her frail and disoriented, barely recognizable as the once mentally sharp woman known for her stuffed cabbage and soft hugs. Eventually, her family decided to place her at Birchwood in a special unit for people with dementia.

On this evening, the 89-year-old grandmother was able to slip outside unnoticed just after dinner. But she would walk only several feet farther before falling into a fish pond on the property. There, an aide would eventually find her lying face down in the knee-deep water, according to state records.

Rushed to Huntington Hospital, Danzker battled hypothermia and a lung infection that came from the cold, stagnant pond water she inhaled.

Three weeks later, she was dead.

"I never thought this would be the way she would die," said Danzker's youngest daughter, Sheila Shaw of East Northport, her anger still evident long after her mother's 1999 death. A Birchwood spokesman said its staff did nothing inappropriate, but Shaw says, "It was understood they were taking on a woman with dementia. They were supposed to be watching her."

Danzker's case is not unusual. Since 1998, at least 126 elderly people have been reported missing from centers that offer assisted living on Long Island, a Newsday investigation has found. And at least seven have died.

Some wanderers were found miles away, at train stations, on busy highways including the Long Island Expressway, and in New York City. But others didn't get far at all: Two elderly women with dementia were found dead in sub-freezing weather within feet of the centers where they lived.

Once, these frail and confused individuals might have died at a younger age from other causes, or received care at home or in nursing homes. But now, they are being placed, in rapidly growing numbers, in assisted living facilities that are often neither set up nor regulated to accommodate them.

Since Danzker's death, some centers have increased security for residents with dementia, many of whom have Alzheimer's disease. But the problem continues.

Questionable care

As recently as March 23, one resident, Emmy Eriksson, disappeared for eight hours after wandering from Castle Senior Living in Plainview. She was wearing only a T-shirt and jeans, on a day when the average temperature was 32 degrees.

The story is about people

The reporters decided late in their investigation to start the story with Ethel Danzker. Said MacKeen: "Our story really flipped. I believe we were going to make the medical care more of an up-front story. We were writing it — Lauren, Eden and I were all working on big pieces — I think it was toward the end that the wanderers were so compelling that we ended up making that the lead."[2]

Using numbers to support your case. The reporters needed to quantify the problem. Laikin suggested giving the addresses of the care centers to police. "We said, 'Can you show us any missing person calls?' They came back with six from here, 10 from there."[3] See Chapter 9 to see how you can use data as evidence.

Something important is at stake

One day, Laikin received a call at home from an officer. He said the helicopters were out on a case looking for an elderly person who had wandered out of her care facility. The officer was a valuable source and, "that ended up being a great find," she said.[4]

The problem affects people

The reporters make sure those people and their concerns don't get lost in the story.

Eriksson, 78, was found around 7 p.m. after police scoured the area with helicopters and a search dog. She was shivering, huddled in an unlocked car in the center's parking lot.

Eriksson, who has had Alzheimer's for 10 years, had soiled herself and "was shaking and cold," said daughter, Jeanne Widman of Lindenhurst. When she saw her, Widman said, all the elderly woman could say was "mommy, mommy, mommy."

"She calls me mommy," Widman explained.

In addition to the problem of wandering, Newsday found case after case in which residents with dementia have been victimized by bad health care, medication errors, theft and even violence at the hands of other residents with the same condition.

There's the former teacher's aide, 75, who died of heart disease after she refused 19 doses of heart medicine without a doctor or her family ever being told. And the 62-year-old woman whose family believes for eight days, she was mistakenly given a diuretic, used to help the body shed fluids, instead of the Prozac prescribed for her depression.

There's the 97-year-old great-grandmother whose platinum and diamond engagement ring, which she wore every day for more than 60 years, suddenly disappeared without her realizing it was gone. And the retired salesman, 84, who was beaten so badly by another resident with dementia that doctors had to place titanium screws in his cheek to keep his eye socket intact.

In some cases, these problems might have been avoided if the residents could remember medication schedules or recognize drugs they're supposed to take. If they could clearly communicate how they feel, or understand the need to avoid a resident displaying anger. But the percentage of residents who lack these basic abilities is growing as new therapies keep people alive longer, and busy, two-income families can't care for the elderly at home.

A growing segment

Four years ago, about 35 percent of assisted living residents nationally had dementia, experts say. Now, that percentage has grown to more than half, a figure that suggests that up to 3,500 seniors with dementia could be housed in centers on Long Island.

The story provides context: Scope

The reporters needed to show how widespread the problem was and who might be affected.

"The more I looked into it," said MacKeen, "it revealed itself as a massive problem."[5]

It's an exploding population that promises to create a surprising new class of health care victim: The elderly person with dementia who's able to pay for quality care, but who isn't getting it due to inadequate and outdated regulation, the lack of widely enforced standards and an inability to safely monitor the residents who need it most. Families pay thousands of dollars a month to keep relatives in assisted living, a cost not generally reimbursed by the government. But, government oversight of the industry is spotty, at best.

Out-of-date laws

On Long Island, 32 of the 41 centers offering assisted living are licensed by the state as "adult care facilities." This means they operate under rules initially aimed at a younger group, many with psychiatric problems, that were written 30 years ago by the state's social services agency, and not the health department. These rules do not mandate a nurse be on site; only one staffer is needed for every 40 residents; and health assessments are typically updated yearly rather than every six months, as in nursing homes.

Meanwhile, the nine centers run by Sunrise Senior Living, Inc., the nation's largest assisted living chain, aren't licensed at all. One result, critics say, is that residents with dementia can be cared for by low-paid workers with minimal training who sometimes act as substitutes for medical pros, and who are frequently spread so thin they can't keep track of some of the disorder's worrisome symptoms.

The story points to the cause of the problem

Issues that affect people rarely happen out of nowhere. You need to show who or what is responsible. It's something readers or viewers will want to know and can lead the way to finding solutions. Often there are multiple causes, as you will see as you continue reading the story.

"You have home health aides who are wonderful people, but you're asking too much of them professionally regarding matters that they have not been trained in," said Kathleen McNeill, a nurse with experience in several facilities. The result, she said, can be "disaster . . . and disaster can go on for years before it's even noticed. Who's going to tell?" McNeill asked. "You have a dementia resident who doesn't know what he's getting or what he's not getting."

To be sure, assisted living can be appropriate for residents who direct their own health care and don't have medically complicated cases. This includes the 50 percent who don't have dementia, and many at the beginning stages of the disorder.

"If residents are not in the more advanced stages of dementia," said Lisa Newcomb, executive director of the Empire State Association of Adult Homes and Assisted Living Facilities, "they don't need a lot of clinical intervention and nursing care . . . what they need is supervision and assistance with activities of daily living in order to maintain as much independence and choice as they can."

Get all sides of the story. You must give the accused a chance to speak for themselves and defend their actions. See Chapter 12 for what to consider when a person and organization is your target.

Newcomb believes problems with wandering and violence aren't widespread. She says dementia care is an evolving field, noting, "Things will go wrong, and people are learning from that all of the time. But I think the situation is continually improving."

A changing industry

When assisted living was conceived in the 1980s as a for-profit business, the industry focused on older people who needed more help with daily tasks than they'd get in a retirement community, but who didn't require the level of medical care provided in nursing homes.

This population was mostly fit, and able to keep track of their own care. "Years ago," said Rita Porwick, a former industry administrator who now counsels families on

The story provides context: History

Here the authors lay out what has happened in the past that contributed to the problem.

placements, "we were told that if there was any inkling of confusion, or wandering tendencies," that person should not be allowed in assisted living.

After 1990, though, that view changed when the U.S. Census showed a double-digit growth among people 85 and older, a demographic bubble that could only be expected to expand as the baby boom became the elder boom.

This shift prompted new owners to join industry pioneers in building centers, experts say. And in New York, it led many adult care facilities that previously served a younger group to re-invent themselves in order to capture their own piece of this rapidly developing new market.

Specialized services

Eventually, this activity translated into an overbuilt industry, experts say, and when the economy soured, the result was an increase in empty beds. Now, state officials say about 20 percent of the industry's beds are unfilled.

Recently, critics say, many centers have begun addressing those empty beds by marketing to people with dementia. Along with new services for the general population, some centers have created special units and weekend "respite centers" that include secure rooms and special programs.

The idea was that these services, linked to the often upscale housing, would appeal to adult children with busy lives and money to spend who may feel overwhelmed as caregivers and guilty about institutionalizing a parent.

Because this group is such a "major financial revenue source," Porwick said, "Everybody [in the industry] is pushing to come up with specialty dementia units without really researching it, or providing what needs to be provided for this population."

The wanderers

In Newsday's review of thousands of pages of state health documents, only nine cases of wanderers turned up. State law only requires that centers report people missing after 24 hours.

But reviews of legal and police records since 1998, as well as interviews with more than 100 family members, suggested the problem was far more widespread. Police on Long Island, for instance, responded at least 107 times to requests that they search for missing residents, records have shown.

The case is backed with evidence

The reporters requested these records under the New York Freedom of Information Law.

Said Laikin: "We had a lot of trouble with the State Health Department. We wanted the inspection reports. Inspector's notes. We had to get our lawyers involved. It was at least six months before we could go into their office and go through their files."[6]

Dorothy Rausch, 86, wandered from her center three times in just six months. The final time she walked about a mile down the road before she fell and hit her head, an injury that led to her death.

Marie Bond, 79, and Patricia O'Connor, 85, both died after exposure to cold weather as they lay just outside their centers. O'Connor was found five feet from her door, wearing only a striped pajama top and a bra, her body temperature 54 degrees. Bond was found 100 feet from the entrance of her center, dead of heart disease with hypothermia listed as a contributing factor.

Leonora Lizzo, 89, wandered outside and fell down 10 concrete steps in front of her center, her injuries leading to her death. And Mildred Curtiss, 83, broke her leg when she wandered off one evening to a nearby golf course, where she lay in the darkness until being discovered by a passerby.

Spotty state regulation

The problem, experts say, is that in New York State, the rules haven't kept up with the demographic realities. Even though more than half of assisted living residents now have some level of dementia, rules on security and surveillance remain largely unspecific and there are no set standards on what methods or equipment should be used.

In addition, an emerging class of assisted living facilities lack any government rules about how to handle wanderers because they're totally unlicensed by the New York state health department. These include the centers run on Long Island by Sunrise.

Though the state disagrees in at least two cases, these centers say they don't need licensing because they don't provide health care. That's handled by outside agencies. But it also means they don't have to follow state mandates on staffing, building security or surveillance.

The story points out the obstacles to the solutions

The reporters showed that the problem was systemic.

"When you look at a problem you look at the system that should be there to protect the individuals in the system," MacKeen said. "It was a very strange setup that allowed Sunrise to not have many inspections. But they were advertising themselves as safe havens for some of the most vulnerable members of society."[7]

A watchful eye?

Certainly, many centers have their own systems for keeping track of wanderers, some of which are effective.

For instance, Jamison Gosselin, a spokesman for Sunrise, said a variety of security devices are used at their centers, including locked units accessible only by a keypad at the door and electronic bracelets that trigger alarms when a resident leaves a specific area. However, "for competitive reasons," he refused to specify which centers use which devices.

Records show that residents have been reported missing from 30 of the 41 centers offering assisted living on Long Island. But a Newsday survey has found that only 13 of the licensed centers have locked dementia units, only five use alarm bracelets to help keep track of residents and only three have camera surveillance.

But these systems are often put in place only after a problem occurs.

For instance, Scott Steffens, who operates Birchwood, said that since the Ethel Danzker incident, the center has installed an elevator key system to prevent residents from leaving the dementia floor.

A 'tough old lady'

Dorothy Rausch's words still resonate with her grandson, Kevin Steiger. After she fell on a busy road one sweltering August day in 2001, she was bleeding profusely from her nose and deep cuts on her eyebrow and lip. She told him it would take "more than this" to keep her down. "I'm a tough old lady," she said.

But the next morning, Rausch lapsed into a coma from a blood clot in her brain, and she died 15 days later.

Rausch's family placed her at Atria East Northport the previous February, after she had fallen several times while living at her daughter's home, and because of concerns she was becoming increasingly confused. It had gotten so bad that her daughter, Carol Leffler, began hiding the knobs from the kitchen stove, so Rausch couldn't turn it on at night and start a fire.

Then Leffler, 65, was diagnosed with breast cancer, and the family made the agonizing decision to place Rausch in assisted living.

Family files lawsuit

In papers filed in a 2002 lawsuit against Atria, Steiger said he and Leffler were comforted by Atria's promises of 24-hour-security and felt the estimated $2,100 monthly price-tag was justified by the peace of mind they believed they would have.

Collecting evidence from the very beginning. The reporters started their investigation with lawsuits. They found citations of the cases through the LexisNexis database and obtained copies of the complaints and the discovery documents. "A lot of stuff is filed right in the county courthouse," Laikin said. "It's a gold mine."[8]

But there were no surveillance cameras or specific security staff, according to depositions given by the facility's executive director, Mario Mellino. And the center's system for keeping track of potential wanderers was a collection of photos tacked to a pillar near the reception desk.

In his deposition, Mellino, who has no prior experience working with health care, testified that it was his decision to take down the photos, but he didn't say why. And sometime around the time the photos disappeared, Rausch — whose picture was featured there, according to the family — would wander away for the third time in just six months.

This time, she never made it back. Rausch walked nearly a mile before falling near the busy intersection of Vernon Valley Road and Norton Drive.

When police responded, they called the family to the scene. When Leffler and Steiger arrived, her daughter asked Rausch where she thought she was heading. The answer was simple and sad: "I don't know," she said.

"I just thought that, because of the ages of these people . . . I assumed that there would be staff members who monitored their comings and goings," Steiger told Newsday recently. "I didn't think they could walk out, and walk into the main road."

Now, he says, he believes they are "no more than glorified motels."

A spokesman for Atria declined to comment on Rausch's death, citing confidentiality concerns. But Atria's vice president for New York, John Hartmayer, said, "At the end of the day, our goal is the safety and security of our residents. That is what we strive to do." State health officials said Atria never reported Rausch's death to them, as required by law, and they are now following up on the facility's reporting practices.

Rausch's family sued Atria for $10 million and it was settled in October 2003 for an undisclosed amount.

Who's at risk

Wandering is one of dementia's significant calling cards, medical experts say.

It can be triggered by stress, agitation coming from feelings of lost control, or a desire to fulfill obligations from the past, even as more recent memories fade and disappear. Some seek to return to places where they once worked or to homes where they once lived.

According to the national Alzheimer's Association, as many as 60 percent of people with the disease will wander and become lost at some point.

Meredeth Rowe, a nurse and researcher at the University of Florida, conducted two studies including 718 people with dementia. Ninety-three died after wandering from private homes, boarding homes, nursing homes and assisted living centers.

The study showed 22 percent of those found dead were from assisted living facilities, a significant number because only a small percentage studied typically reside in such places. "There's a significant over-representation of people who come from assisted living," Rowe said.

The story provides context: Comparisons

The reporters show that the problem is not unique to New York by looking to other studies done elsewhere in the country.

Overall, she said, wandering is "really under-reported, and really under-researched."

In New York, state regulators have only superficially addressed the problem of wandering, critics say. Many providers in licensed centers argue that state regulations, which were written for a different population, actually block them from keeping suspected wanderers under lock and key.

Seeking high-tech answers

"The licensing guidelines say we can't lock people in unless they're in a specific dementia unit," said Katherine Heaviside, a spokeswoman for Sterling Glen.

But experts say locked doors aren't the only answer. "There are electronic alternatives," said Charles Phillips, a gerontologist and author of numerous studies on assisted living and dementia. "Protecting individuals from injury or danger due to wandering does not demand locked doors."

Phillips argued that centers should use electronic sensor systems at doorways that can trigger an alert if a suspected wanderer is about to leave, and that there should be security staff that keep entrances and exits under constant observation.

Rules covering licensed centers that offer assisted living were written in 1974 by the Board of Social Welfare, an arm of the now defunct state Social Services department.

The state health department gained oversight responsibility for these facilities in 1998. In January, the department issued non-enforceable guidelines to adult care facilities that specifically address special new units now being touted by many facilities for residents with dementia.

The story identifies possible solutions at the microlevel

Whenever a story looks at a problem, solutions must be provided. These solutions are at the microlevel, meaning that individual organizations can implement them.

These units segregate people with the condition in a separate part of the building, and can cost residents as much as $2,000 extra per month. They frequently offer special programs designed to help residents cope with their symptoms, additional staffing and extra security, such as the use of keypads to open the doors.

The new state suggestions urge that these units be staffed by one worker for every six to eight residents during the day—figures that are significantly higher than the one-for-40 coverage existing regulations require for the general population.

Officials from the 14 licensed centers with dementia units on Long Island said they are following the new guidelines, as far as staffing ratios are concerned.

Gaps in oversight

Still, critics say that major gaps remain in the state's oversight process: While the special units can help residents deal with dementia, there's no guarantee that a resident with the condition will be placed in one. Because of the added costs, many families hold off placing relatives in these units as long as possible. The base cost of assisted living ranges from $1,500 to $7,410 a month, depending on the center, type of room and services.

Louise Fanning of Wantagh, whose 72-year-old mother, Catherine LoCoco, wandered away from Sterling Glen of Bay Shore on a cold night in January, said she struggled to keep up with the $2,700 monthly cost of her mother's basic care. She said she could not afford the secure Memory Care Unit that would have brought her total costs to about $5,000 a month.

When LoCoco wandered from Sterling Glen she was found about three miles away near Good Samaritan Hospital in West Islip by a passerby. Since that incident, Fanning said the center said she would have to transfer her mother into its special dementia unit, at a much higher cost, if she was going to continue to live there.

She has since moved her mother to a different center that has a dementia unit that costs less.

Sterling Glen's vice president of operations, Kevin Hunter, said the company's priority is to treat residents "with dignity and respect," but because assisted living is considered home, the company isn't allowed by law to restrict the comings and goings of the people who live there. He said LoCoco was fully dressed with her coat that day. Beyond the cost, only about half of assisted living centers offer these units. This limits the number of beds that are available.

A Newsday survey, in fact, found that only 23 of 41 centers have these special units, and that the number of beds available range between 756 and 792. Because of this, critics worry for-profit companies can't be expected to advise residents move somewhere else if a problem occurs and they can't immediately fit them in one of their special units.

One Suffolk doctor who regularly treats residents said that some administrators have become annoyed with him when he told families their relatives needed more care than was being provided in the general population.

"They'd say, 'why are you telling them that? Right now we can provide this [level of care]. Who knows what's going to happen next month,'" the doctor said, asking that his name not be used because he regularly sees patients who reside in assisted living.

The state also suggests that staff working these units be "appropriately trained" and "capable of meeting the needs" of residents with dementia, but even the latest recommendations offer no specific guidance on what training should include. And that, too, ignores the fact that it may be even more important for staff to be well-trained in how the disease presents itself in the general population, medical experts say.

False sense of security

Leonora Lizzo's family never even considered that she would slip out of Ambassador Manor in Long Beach in 2001. The adult home, which offered assisted living, urged the family to pay $42 a day extra for an aide to supervise Lizzo, who had been diagnosed with dementia several months earlier.

A former postal worker from Oceanside who retired at the age of 80, she was becoming forgetful and more combative. Still, she was afraid to venture far from her room, according to her family. But on that April evening, as the rest of the residents were eating dinner, she wandered past the front desk and out of the lobby. She was found lying on the sidewalk at the bottom of a cement staircase.

"We were told there would be people there to watch," her son, Justin, said, adding that the family — which is suing the facility — didn't know for three days about the fall because Ambassador initially notified the wrong family of the accident. One month later Lizzo died of pneumonia that followed severe blunt injuries to her head, stemming from the fall, according to a Nassau medical examiner's report.

Lizzo's daughter-in-law, Diane Lizzo, said she thought Ambassador would provide better care, especially for those with dementia. "All we know is that we were paying through the nose for it," she said.

Ambassador's former operator, Bianca Minelli, said that Lizzo's fall had nothing to do with her death and that she received good care while at the center, which has since closed.

Special programs for dementia patients are often sold by individual facilities as a panacea for vulnerable residents.

Problems persist

But being in a supervised program didn't keep Mildred Curtiss, 83, from hobbling away from Atria South Setauket one April evening in 2000, using a metal walker to make her way slowly along Nesconset Highway to a nearby golf course.

There, she fell and broke her leg. No one knows how long she lay there, but eventually someone found her crumpled figure on the side of the road, her walker well out of reach.

A bright, blue-eyed, atypically active octogenarian, Curtiss lived independently until her memory began to fade.

But after she fell in 1999 and lay alone in her Port Jefferson apartment for hours, her son, Joseph, decided she needed 24-hour care. He and his wife, Barbara, eventually decided to place her in Atria because, they said, it was clean, many of the residents seemed to be active, and it was close to their home in Miller Place.

Initially, the family said they paid about $2,200 a month. But after she fell one day and was sent to the hospital, they agreed to place her in Atria's extended day care program for Alzheimer's residents, at an additional cost of $500 a month. The idea was that Curtiss would receive more restrictive, one-on-one care during the day, while participating in recreational programs that were specifically designed by Atria to enhance memory. "We just wanted her safe," Joseph Curtiss said. But problems surfaced then, too.

Mildred, who used a walker because of an earlier leg injury, complained to her family that her roommate, who also had dementia, threatened to kill her. And on April 2, family said, she slipped out of the building during the early evening hours, and began her slow trek along the highway.

Hartmayer of Atria, citing confidentiality protections, wouldn't discuss the Curtiss case. But he noted that his company is "always looking to refine and improve our internal systems."

After the incident, the family moved Mildred Curtiss to a nursing home, and she has since died. They are currently suing Atria for negligence.

Barbara Curtiss said it wasn't enough to just move her mother-in-law into a special dementia program. "They should have had ankle or wrist bracelets that prevented her from going out," she said, and better staffing at the door.

She 'loved to walk'

The daughter of Emmy Eriksson, who wandered from Castle Senior Living last month, has similar concerns.

Her mother was living in a locked dementia unit at Castle, but she was able to wander from there at around 11 a.m., walking out through a gated courtyard that officials at the center said was normally locked.

Talking to the families. The most difficult part of the project was talking to families who were emotionally scarred.

"A lot of these people felt a lot of guilt," Laikin said. "Lauren did a lot of the interviews. She was good at talking to people and getting them to open up."[9]

Look back at Chapter 6 for suggestions on how to interview victims of trauma or violence.

"My mother loved to walk," said her daughter, Jeanne Widman. "She stayed with me for about a week and every day she'd be standing with her coat on, saying 'let's go.'" That hasn't changed she said, but her condition has worsened over the years and she is no longer able to have a clear conversation.

Now, Widman said, "she has her own language . . ."

"If someone would have asked her who are you, she couldn't even answer. All she could say was, maybe, 'Brooklyn' or my father's name, 'Walter.'"

That's why, Widman said, she began to panic when it got dark. "I was thinking, what if they never find her?"

Widman said she pays about $3,000 a month to keep her mother at Castle.

Nadine Fox, Castle's executive director, said the facility, which opened in 1999, has camera surveillance, and that its dementia unit is locked with a keypad.

Unit residents are allowed to walk out into the courtyard without supervision, she said, because the gate is always locked. In this instance, Fox said, a contracted workman left it unlocked. Now, she says, the center has changed the lock and employees are the only ones allowed to have a key.

Serial wanderers

In some cases, deaths and other injuries befell residents who had wandered previously, sometimes several times, Newsday found.

Many families said they didn't understand how this could happen. Once a resident wanders, they said, there should be additional security or surveillance that focuses on them specifically.

For instance, both Marie Bond and Patricia O'Connor were identified as wanderers before they were found lying dead near their respective centers.

Both instances occurred in 1996. In O'Connor's case, a police report noted that she "had a habit of roaming, she was classified by staff as a 'wanderer.'" Bond's grandniece, Jodie Kochman, said she had wandered before, and that she had been "reassured" that the staff was "going to keep a watch on her because they knew that she had gotten out before."

But both elderly women were able to leave unnoticed, with fatal consequences.

O'Connor was found nine days after her 85th birthday, lying five feet from the door of Senior Quarters in East Northport, now called Atria East Northport. Atria didn't operate it at the time. Wearing nothing but a pajama top and a bra, she died of exposure during an unexpected April snowstorm.

Marie Bond was found lying about 100 feet from the entrance of what was then Senior Plaza in Hauppauge, her shoes 15 feet away. Her death certificate listed hypothermia as a contributing factor to her death.

Medical experts say that once a person with dementia has wandered, it can become a pattern in their lives.

"It becomes like a way of being," said Sheryl Zimmerman, co-director of the Program on Aging, Disability and Long-Term Care at the University of North Carolina. "Anyone familiar with the disease process is aware of that."

She says facilities need to do more than just stop wandering, they need to "create an environment where people can wander safely" by building "a circle somewhere" indoors or a controlled area outdoors.

But some question whether regulators understand the size of the wandering problem.

Wayne Osten, director of the state health department's office of health systems management, seemed surprised by the large numbers Newsday found using police reports. Currently, he said, the department has no concrete numbers and "can't quantify" the problem either generally, or on an individual basis.

Reporting all incidents

He said that was "a concern," but suggested issues could be better addressed by improving how residents are assessed when they enter and reside in assisted living.

Some families also suggest forcing facilities to immediately report every incident of wandering to the state might mean that centers keep more specific records. In several instances, including the case involving Marie Bond, families and managers had different memories of what actually occurred.

Kochman, for instance, said staff acknowledged that Marie Bond had wandered previously, and promised to keep a closer eye on her. But Stephanie Woods, administrator of Senior Plaza, disputed that, saying she knew of no other time when Bond was missing.

"It was terrible what happened to Marie, but it wasn't because we weren't taking care of her," Woods said.

Danzker's daughters say they believe their mother wandered from the dining room, not the secure unit, as staffers at Birchwood have said.

Like many family members interviewed by Newsday, Sheila Shaw, Danzker's daughter, said she believes the number of residents who wander is much higher than reported. In her mother's case, there was no missing person's report filed with police when she disappeared. But other records obtained by Newsday revealed a disturbing pattern at Birchwood, where Danzker was. In the six months prior to her disappearance, there were three other wanderers reported to police from Birchwood, a fact Shaw said she was unaware of. Since then, there have been six incidents reported.

When asked about the Danzker case, Steffens, who said he's worked at Birchwood for 23 years, said, "Our staff didn't do anything inappropriate. . . . It was a freak thing." The state ultimately cited Birchwood for poor supervision.

When asked about the nine other incidents in which police were called to help find wanderers, he said, "I don't remember that. We have a secured area," he said. "As society is becoming more aware of dementia, we recognize the need for dementia services. . . ."

Steffens said his facility tries "to keep up with modern technology." They hold regular monthly training sessions for workers, he said, as well as "whole seminars on dementia behavior as part of our orientation process."

Calls for legislation

Shaw, whose family filed a lawsuit against Birchwood and settled in 2001, said she's concerned that company-by-company efforts, such as those described by Steffens, are simply not enough.

The story identifies possible solutions at the macrolevel

The reporters point out long-term systemic solutions that can be implemented in order to affect a larger portion of the problem.

She believes the whole system needs to be overhauled, including the creation of updated rules on training and increased staffing levels. "I hope nobody else ever has to go through what we did," she said.

Fred Griesbach of AARP would also like to see changes. "These are people who are essentially entrusting themselves to the care of these facilities that call themselves assisted living," Griesbach said. "If you say you're going to provide monitoring and people are able to walk out the front door, there is something seriously amiss.

"The reality is we don't have a definition, oversight, or regulation of what we call assisted living. And until we get it, this is going to continue."

And the lack of oversight of this frail and confused population concerns some experts. "Clearly we have laws that say you can't leave a two- to five-year-old alone," says Dr. Barry Reisberg, of the dementia center at New York University Medical Center. "But we don't have those laws for Alzheimer's patients, and the care needs are really the same."

BIG STORY COMPONENTS

News organizations publish stories like "A Tragic Vulnerability" after extensive research and careful planning.

Now that you have read "A Tragic Vulnerability," go back and scan the paragraphs. Note how much information the reporters included in the story, the different types of people they interviewed, the data they used and how they managed to tie it all together into a compelling and convincing story.

Only with fiction can you write something from nothing. A nonfiction story is only as good as the information the writer gathers. It is only as believable as the data and anecdotes incorporated in it. It is only as gripping as the people in it. To write a great story you must gather great information. That takes time, thought and effort. To see what goes into a good investigative story, let's break "A Tragic Vulnerability" into its components (refer back to Exhibit 7.1, page 154).

Something important is at stake

In doing a big story, you ask many people many questions. You ask them to provide information, knowledge, opinions, analysis, memories and emotions. You expect your readers to invest a significant part of their time reading and thinking about your story or stories. Sometimes you may ask your readers to learn something they would rather not know. Who wants bad news? Most people don't really want to know their government representatives are crooks, or the food they buy is unsafe, or the air they breathe is unhealthy, unless you can convince them that it is personally important. The reason sources help you with an investigative story and the reason readers stay with you is because something is at stake that needs to be disclosed and learned.

It might be the death of one person. It might be the aesthetics or culture of a neighborhood. It might be money that is lost, stolen or misspent. It might be a death or an injury waiting to happen. It might be one person wrongfully convicted or hundreds of people wrongfully hassled by police. Newsday discovered a pattern of preventable deaths of elderly people with dementia and wanted to make sure others knew about the problem and could take steps to fix it.

The problem affects people

It isn't enough to lay out a problem. To convince readers of the importance of a problem you must show how it affects real people. You need to bring it to life with vivid details.

For a political or economic story to resonate with a reader, the reader has to connect to the people at the heart of the story. You must show readers how the issue or problem either affects them or you must get them to care about the people the problem affects. The Newsday team didn't focus on the bureaucracy that regulates or fails to regulate assisted living centers or the system that lumps together mentally able and mentally disabled old people. They focused on Ethel Danzker, Emmy Eriksson, Dorothy Rausch and their families.

"We were all dealing with horrific stories," MacKeen said about the eight months she spent on the story. "As we were interviewing everyone, we had photos and we started putting them on this little wall. To other people who came into the room it seemed morbid but it gave face to the people we were trying to give a voice to."[10]

The writers of the story used vivid details to bring to life people about whom the reader might otherwise not care. They brought Ethel Danzker to life in the story. The reader sees Danzker wearing a thin polyester dress, stockings and sneakers as she walks out of Birchwood Assisted Living on a night when the temperature dropped to 37 degrees. She's not just some old lady, but a mother who was once mentally sharp, and who was known for soft hugs and stuffed cabbage. Those are details you can see, smell and feel.

MacKeen said many of those details came out of interviews with family members and documents filed as part of lawsuits against the assisted living centers.[11] They used the details to hammer home the importance of this story. It's not a story about legislation, government failure or corporate greed. It is a story about Sheila Shaw of Northport, still grieving from the death of her mother. It is about Kevin Steiger, who is angry over the death of his grandmother. It is about what happens to the grandmothers and grandsons in the world when regulators fail to take action, when assisted living facilities are mismanaged and when neglect occurs.

The emotions the writers captured came from interviews with family members that were difficult to get and difficult to do.

"Hearing their stories was hard," MacKeen said. "Getting their trust [was difficult]. It was hard going back to the families over and over again. You had to continually go back. Some people would talk to you once but then they didn't want to talk again. But your questions change over time."[12]

The story uncovers information that is not widely known

Your readers will invest a significant amount of time reading your article, and they expect they will learn something new out of it. That doesn't mean that you need to uncover top secret information. You might focus on a problem that only a small segment of society knows about. It could be a problem invisible to all but the people hurt by it. When muckraker Jacob Riis took his camera through dilapidated New York tenements in the late 1880s, what he documented wasn't secret. But because it was a world that wealthier people did not inhabit, society had been able to ignore the problems of the poor until they were brought to light.

It could be a series of well-known events that, together, form a troubling pattern or trend that you are the first to spot. It was no secret that Ethel Danzker died wandering out of a nursing home one winter night. Health reporter

Dawn MacKeen originally intended to spend one to two days reporting on one death at one nursing home. But when she and the other reporters found additional cases and pored through them, they began to connect them to multiple missing person reports out of one nursing home after another.[13] From there, they discovered a problem of preventable deaths that few people knew about. The Newsday team even managed to surprise Wayne Osten, director of the state health department's Office of Health Systems Management, with the number of elderly people they found through police reports. His department had been unable to quantify the problem.

Sometimes a story explores something everyone knows occurs, but it lays out for the first time why or how it occurs, who is responsible or possible alternatives. In reporting the story, the Newsday team looked into everything from the systems for medicating patients to what locks the facilities had on their doors, staffing shortages, the high cost of care, the soaring numbers of patients with dementia and the lack of care alternatives. Sometimes what is new is that you provide an overall view of a problem when most people see only a tiny part and have limited perspectives on it. This story provides that overall view as it discloses a greater understanding of the scope and ramifications of a problem. By connecting many dots in a story, then the people most affected by the problem, the people causing the problem, and even the so-called experts gain a greater understanding and learn something new.

The story identifies the cause of the problem

Once we get people to understand that something important is at stake, we must determine the causes of the problem or problems we identified. Newsday made us care about people with dementia who wandered out of assisted living facilities. Next they had to determine the cause—the parties responsible and the reasons for it.

In the story, we find out that outdated laws didn't require assisted living facilities to provide specific security measures. It didn't even allow them to unless they set up a special ward for patients with dementia. We learn in at least one case, it wasn't until an elderly patient had wandered off that the assisted living facility installed any special security equipment or hired special staff.

In trying to explain why and how something could have happened, don't shirk from laying blame if the evidence points to a culprit. Things don't just happen; they are made to happen or allowed to happen. That means that someone made it happen or allowed it to happen. In some cases, many people share responsibility. In other cases, one person is ultimately responsible. The best stories make clear exactly who is responsible and for what. The Newsday story identified two culprits: Sunrise Senior Living, Inc., a large operator of assisted living centers, and the New York State Department of Health, which failed to update regulations to address changing demographics.

The story identifies possible solutions and obstacles to those solutions

Whenever you do a story that focuses on a problem, you need to provide a solution or solutions, even if the solutions seem unrealistic. Look for two sets of solutions:

- Short-term changes at the microlevel that individuals or individual organizations could adopt to help prevent the problem or alleviate it.
- Long-term systemic reforms at the industry, municipal, state or national levels.

The Newsday story points to a series of short-term actions that could be taken to prevent elderly people from wandering out of the care facilities: locked units, alarm bracelets, camera surveillance, lower staff to patient ratios, and better trained staff. One expert suggested that assisted care centers establish protected places where their patients could safely wander. Newsday also explored systemic changes such as outdated laws that had failed to keep up with a changing industry.

Investigative stories should spur people to act. With the Internet, more readers will find your story when they search for solutions to the problems you highlight or to similar problems happening elsewhere. In pointing out possible solutions, you will show your readers actions they can take. One month after Newsday published its series then-New York Governor George Pataki introduced a bill to force unlicensed facilities to register with the state health department and allow for the licensing of other types of adult care facilities so that they can care for seniors with Alzheimer's and dementia. It passed later that year.[14]

You can also point out why solutions that exist aren't in place. The obstacles could be contradictory laws, prohibitive costs, or a Catch-22 situation whereby the solution to this particular set of problems results in other problems. Political barriers could prevent solutions from taking place if the solutions will benefit one group of players versus another. Or they could be related to current or historical discrimination, and for the solutions to be adopted, some people with the power or money to solve the problem would have to rise above discriminatory attitudes or behaviors. The Newsday story shows how one solution would be to force care facilities to diagnose elderly patients and require that those with dementia be put into special facilities, but that would significantly raise the cost for many families who already struggle to pay for the assisted living care. As a result, many more families might resign themselves to caring for their family member at home even though they don't have the emotional or professional skills to handle the task.

The evidence backs up the case

When you report and write an investigative story, you will make the most convincing case when you back it up with a combination of anecdotal evidence, informed opinions, documents and data. The Newsday reporters interviewed about 100 family members of nursing home residents. They also talked to doctors, nurses and researchers who specialize in gerontology and who care for elderly patients, a former industry administrator who now counsels families on placements, government regulators and police. Finally, they made a point to also include directors and spokespeople from assisted living centers and companies that operate them.

MacKeen said it took a long time to find people who worked in assisted living centers or in the industry and who could talk to them about conditions. "That was really, really hard," she said. "It took old fashioned reporting—one person leads to another and another. We found a couple of people who were really frank about what they witnessed."[15]

They also examined court and police records, and reports from the National Alzheimer's Association and the American Association of Retired Persons. They also reviewed thousands of pages of state health documents and four years' worth of legal and police records.

MacKeen said they compiled the information they collected and entered it into databases that allowed them to cross-reference and find patterns between cases involving individuals and the different care centers and the corporate owners. For instance, they could connect incidents of beaten people, missing people or health violations. That gave them hard numbers. "You can't just say something is happening, you have to back it up," MacKeen said. "All of a sudden you start to see a problem. The numbers really pop out."[16]

The story provides context

Context enables the reader to fully understand a problem or situation. To convey context, a story needs to provide the problem's scope and history, and compare what happens or has happened in other places or at other times.

Scope

To understand the seriousness of a problem, the reader needs to understand its scope. You don't want readers to think that a problem is limited to the examples you cite in the story when it is much more widespread. On the other hand, you don't want them to fear that it is more widespread when it is just limited to cases you cite. You want readers to get a handle on what's really going on.

You can detail the scope in different ways. Sometimes scope is an aggregate number of cases, sometimes it is geographic distance, sometimes it is a percentage or per-capita figure. It could be a time element such as showing how long a problem has occurred. It could be the number of people affected, or bodies of water polluted, or miles of roadway in danger. It could be how many animal species face extinction, the percentage of schools that will lose money, or the amount of money they will lose. Newsday detailed the scope through the following facts:

- At the time of the Newsday story, more than half of all residents of assisted living centers in the nation had dementia — as many as 3,500 on Long Island alone.

- Long Island police responded to reports of missing people from assisted living centers more than 100 times in one year, even though few of those reports were in state regulatory records.
- According to the national Alzheimer's Association, as many as 60 percent of people with the disease will wander and become lost at some point.

An effective way to communicate the scope of a problem is to combine data and expert opinions — the aggregate dollars combined with percentage of people affected as explained by an economist who tells you the bottom line.

History

To understand why something is happening we need to know how it got to that point. To frame the story in a historical context, you need to ask yourself a series of questions. Let's see them in the context of "A Tragic Vulnerability":

Was it always like this?   The Newsday story notes that in the 1980s when the industry began, it focused on people who didn't require nursing home care.

How did it change?   In the 1990s, a big growth occurred in the 85-plus population, and many of the assisted care facilities began attracting those needing nursing home care in order to fill empty beds. More and more, companies offered services to people with dementia without doing what it takes to adequately provide the care needed.

What decisions led to the change, and who made those decisions?   After the 1990 U.S. Census showed a jump in the population of people age 85 and over, new facilities owners joined industry pioneers to build new centers for elderly care and facilities that had cared for younger people re-invented themselves to care for older people.

Comparisons

You can also achieve context by comparing the same problem in two different places or on two different levels. You can compare your city against another city or your city against the rest of the state or nation. You can make comparisons with a place that is very similar to the area you are covering or very different. Or you can do both.

The Newsday story, for example, refers to two studies conducted in Florida of 718 people with dementia that found that 93 had died from wandering out of private homes, nursing homes and assisted care centers and that those who had died were overrepresented in assisted care centers.

Another story in the series included this paragraph as well:

Some states have begun to recognize the toxic consequences of violence and dementia. For instance, in December, Oregon lawmakers introduced new rules to ban firearms at all senior care facilities, after a resident with dementia at one facility shot and killed two others and then himself in November.[17]

This paragraph serves two purposes. First, readers learn that the problem of violence in assisted care facilities is not limited to homes in New York State, and second, readers become more aware of the need for legislation when the article contrasts the inaction of New York legislators against the action taking place elsewhere.

CONCLUSION

F our months after Newsday published the series on assisted living centers, Lauren Terrazzano was diagnosed with lung cancer, and she died in 2007. But she had devoted her professional life to helping people by telling their stories and putting the spotlight on problems that needed to be addressed. She and Dawn MacKeen were beat reporters when they teamed up to investigate assisted living centers. Their story is a great example of the components that make up a good investigation. And their work shows how to take a complicated subject in which some people may not be interested and create a story that will make people care.

EXERCISES

1. Find an investigative story listed in the Extra!Extra! section of the IRE Web site, http://ire.org, that interests you. In that story or set of stories, try to identify examples of the components detailed in this chapter:
   a. What's at stake?
   b. How does the problem affect people?
   c. Does the story uncover information that is not widely known?
   d. Does the story point to the cause of the problem?
   e. Does it identify possible solutions?
   f. What is the evidence that backs up the case?
   g. How does the story provide context?

2. Think about something you might want to investigate.
   a. Is anything important at stake?
   b. Will you be able to find "real people" and bring them to life for the reader through vivid details?
   c. What might be the causes of the problem?
   d. Can you think of possible solutions?
   e. What diverse sources can you turn to to make a case and back it up with anecdotal evidence, documents and data?
   f. How will you be able to put the problem into context for the reader?

Based on what you have found so far in your preliminary research and in your interviews, see if you can answer the following questions:

a. What is the particular problem that is central to the story?

b. Who are the people most affected, and have you talked to them or will you talk to them?

c. Who do you think is responsible, and how will you document and quantify it?

d. How might your story uncover information that is not widely known or that some powerful person would wish to keep secret?

e. Can you identify possible solutions to the problem?

f. What is the history and scope of the problem?

g. Could legislative changes or enforcement actions solve or alleviate the problem?

h. Do you have someone who can serve as a narrative thread for your story, i.e., who you can center the story around and who will help you tell it and bring it to life?

i. What vivid details can you find that will make the reader feel as if they are experiencing the problem firsthand?

NOTES

1. Lauren Terrazzano and Eden Laikin, Dawn Mac-Keen and Amanda Harris. "A tragic vulnerability: Special report; Assisted-living facilities on Long Island having trouble handling larger number of seniors with dementia." *Newsday*, April 18, 2004.

2. Dawn MacKeen. Phone interview, April 4, 2008.

3. Eden Laikin. Phone interview, Feb. 7, 2008.

4. Ibid.

5. Dawn MacKeen. Phone interviews, April 4 and Dec. 4, 2008.

6. Eden Laikin. Phone interviews, Feb. 7 and Dec. 3, 2008.

7. Dawn MacKeen. Phone interviews, April 4 and Dec. 4, 2008.

8. Eden Laikin. Phone interviews, Feb. 7 and Dec. 3, 2008.

9. Ibid.

10. Dawn MacKeen. Phone interviews, April 4 and Dec. 4, 2008.

11. Ibid.

12. Ibid.

13. Ibid.

14. Lauren Terrazzano and Dawn MacKeen. "Stricter guidelines: Pataki to offer an assisted living bill." Eden Laikin contributed to this story. *Newsday*, May 24, 2004, p. A02.

15. Dawn MacKeen. Phone interviews, April 4 and Dec. 4, 2008.

16. Ibid.

17. Eden Laikin and Lauren Terrazzano. "Voiceless amid violence, SPECIAL REPORT: Assaults against residents with dementia, some reported, some not, occur too often." *Newsday*, April 20, 2004, p. A06.

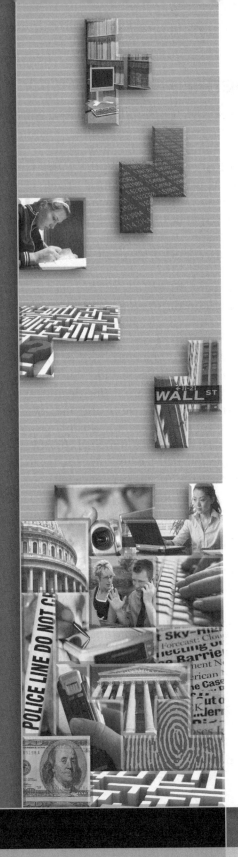

Documenting the Story

CHAPTER PREVIEW No matter how many people you interview for your story and how diverse and expert they are, you will find it hard to prove your premise without documentation. Documents include the forms, papers and correspondence that can leave a trail of evidence. They come in many forms, and to find them you need to understand how people communicate and the different ways information is created, distributed and stored. You will discover where to look for different types of documents over the Internet and learn why you need to look offline as well.

8

CHAPTER

DOCUMENTATION IN THE DIGITAL AGE

W e live in a documented world. The world we reside in is intricately connected to government and business. Think about how many times in your life someone handed you a form to fill out. We must fill out forms when we rent an apartment, buy a house, apply for loans, enter college, apply for jobs, pay taxes, get professional licenses, learn to drive, register a car, become a citizen, get a passport, get a credit card, or get electricity and water to a home or business. You even have to fill out a form to get a newspaper or magazine delivered to your house. Every 10 years, the government requires you to fill out a U.S. Census form that asks you a host of personal questions. A doctor filled out a form when you were born and will do so when you die.

Corporations and governments are document driven as well. No decisions are made without someone recording the decision on some form of electronic paper. It could be the go-ahead a manager e-mails to an employer, or a policy memo a director sends to managers or a purchase order from a department head to a supplier. This e-correspondence creates a record, which means that for every question you might have about something involving individuals, businesses or government, you may be able to find the answer in an electronic document. The advantage of an electronic document is that once someone creates and saves it, which must be done to send it, the person can't un-create it and can't easily destroy it. Meanwhile, it can be duplicated, distributed and searched. In other words, it's a beautiful electronic world for the journalist who knows what information to search for, and knows what to do with information when she gets hold of it. The truth is not only out there, it's searchable.

THE NEED TO NAIL DOWN THE STORY

I n February 2008, the New York Times ran a story about Arizona Senator John McCain, while he was running for the Republican presidential nomination. It included revelations that he had had an affair with a telecommunications industry lobbyist during the time he chaired the U.S. Senate Commerce Committee.[1] As a result of the story, McCain's popularity, as measured by opinion polls, actually increased. Why? The story relied solely on anecdotes from former McCain staffers, most of them anonymous. Many readers didn't believe it. Instead they thought it proved that the New York Times was out to get McCain. The problem was that the Times failed to nail the story.

To nail a story you must report it so well that the argument the story makes is difficult to refute. It requires that you back up the story with solid evidence. Anecdotes are a type of evidence, but they tend to be unconvincing on their own. If your readers don't believe the speaker, they won't believe the anecdote. Documents, however, are another matter.

Because a document is a record of something, it can be matched up against other statements or other evidence. Even though people do lie or make mistakes on documents, this ability to compare facts makes a document more credible than a statement alone. Journalists seek out documents when they need to report something that people will have difficulty believing or won't want to believe. In 2008, the Detroit Free Press proved an affair between Mayor Kwame Kilpatrick and his chief of staff and showed how it was at the heart of a $9 million payout to police whistle-blowers, by obtaining copies of text messages between the two.[2] If the Detroit Free Press had simply said that Kilpatrick was having an affair, many people would be incredulous. But by having documented evidence, the story was convincing.

When you get wind of a story that you need to prove, you want to consider all the different forms that proof might take. Exhibit 8.1 offers a list of documents you can consider for your case.

WWW.

The Detroit Free Press Story
www.freep.com/apps/
pbcs.dll/article?AID=
/20080124/NEWS05/
801240414/&imw=Y

Know what you need

Don't go off on an endless search for documents. While you can find massive amounts of documents online and off, not all will actually benefit your story. Sometimes reporters stumble on information while looking for something quite different. But generally you waste time if you seek documents without an idea of what you want. In his coverage of Watergate, Carl Bernstein flew from Washington, D.C., to Florida to look at bank records but he didn't do it as a fishing expedition; he was after proof of an illegal slush fund that he knew existed.[3] The Detroit Free Press didn't go after the mayor's text messages on a lark. The reporters had serious questions about a costly legal settlement, but the court had sealed the records.

Proof comes in many different forms. | **EXHIBIT 8.1**

Agendas	Divorce papers	Phone records
Applications	Financial disclosure forms	Photos
Appointment calendars	Financial statements	PowerPoint presentations
Audits	Flow charts	Project proposals
Autopsy reports	Handbooks	Purchase orders
Bids	Inspection reports	Receipts
Blueprints	Insurance policies	Sticky notes
Cancelled checks	Internal memos	Tax records
Congressional testimony	Licenses	Text messages
Contracts	Maps	Transcripts
Court briefs	Medical records	Videos
Depositions	Minutes	Voter registration cards

So before you begin your hunt for documents, ask yourself the following questions so that you will know which types of documents you need:

1. What do I want to know?

Return to your hypothesis and think about the problem you need to investigate. What kind of information will help you prove it? If you suspect your university is building an unnecessary parking structure, then you will want records of discussions university administrators had before making the decision to build the garage. If you want to investigate unnecessary arrests, you will want to see police reports and other arrest records.

2. What kind of documents might hold the answer?

Will the information be something an administrator would communicate via memo or letter? Maybe it is information that some agency routinely collects and so would be available in a form someone must fill out, such as a permit request or a license application.

3. Who would have created those documents?

If it is a letter you seek, who wrote it? If you want records of a meeting, you need the organization's secretary who recorded the minutes or someone who took notes while the meeting took place. Police officers create the police reports that end up in criminal case files.

4. Who might have received them?

Copies of meeting notes might be sent to all meeting attendees. Police reports might go to the chief of police or to the sergeant on duty. A letter or memo goes to the people the letter is addressed to as well as any number of people CC'd on it.

5. Who might have filed or stored them?

If an administrator sends a memo or letter, her administrative assistant likely has a copy. If a report is issued, a records clerk might have a copy. Police records are often stored in a central repository.

6. How do I get them?

This question may generate multiple answers. One answer might be to fill out a public records request and wait 20 days for a response. Or you could think of every person who probably has the same document on their desk or in their files and go to the one you think is most likely to provide a copy.

7. What do I do with them?

To answer this question, you must understand the role a document can play and the different ways the information in it could be useful to your investigation.

Know what a document can do for you

Just as important as knowing which documents you need is knowing how they will be used. Documents can be used in a variety of ways to prove your premise, including the following:

Show actuality

A document might prove that something important did in fact happen or it can show that something that should have happened did not. In Chapter 4 we discussed how Bill Dedman at MSNBC in August 2008 used internal e-mails between state and federal highway officials to show how many of the bridges in this country went without safety inspections.

Lay blame

Documents can name names or identify scope of responsibility. For example, a group of journalists from print, television and radio organizations in the San Francisco Bay Area formed a special investigative team to look into the murder of black journalist Chauncey Bailey in August 2007. They used cell phone records and records from a tracking device to pinpoint a suspect who was at Bailey's house around the time of his murder. As a result of the project's findings, the Alameda County district attorney's office launched an independent investigation into the murder, looking at the suspect that the police had ignored before. Exhibit 8.2 shows the Web site for the Chauncey Bailey Project. On it, readers can track the investigation and see and hear the evidence the group has collected.[4]

Prove a pattern of occurrences

One person who lost an insurance claim in a small fender bender is no big story, but a pattern of claim denials could add up to a multibillion-dollar crime. As we saw in Chapter 7, a pattern of missing person reports helped Eden Laikin and her Newsday colleagues prove inadequate care at assisted living centers.

Help you connect dots

Financial statements might show a public university is financially sound. But complaints filed with the school's buildings department might show that the buildings on the campus are in severe need of costly repairs, and the financial statements show no plans for repairs. Together the documents might depict a university that

EXHIBIT 8.2   Web site for the Chauncey Bailey Project.

Using video, audio and text stories, reporters Thomas Peele and Bob Butler led a team of reporters from a multitude of Bay Area news organizations to bring to justice the murderer of journalist Chauncey Bailey and continue the reporting that led to his death.

From chaunceybaileyproject.org. Reprinted with permission of the Center for Investigative Reporting, www.cironline.org.

will either financially or structurally collapse. Or take Clery Act reports, which colleges and universities must keep and disclose about crimes on campus. They might show few reports of sexual assaults. But records kept by the campus rape crisis counselors might show a high number of people coming in reporting sexual assaults. Together the reports show that either the police aren't maintaining truthful records or that people are afraid to report sexual crimes to the campus police.

Web sites such as Security on Campus provide both information about Clery act compliance and provide searches of universities' crime reports. You can search for your own university's report, search by factors such as campus enrollment, location and programs offered, or create an aggregated report for a region to help you connect the dots.

Campus Crime Reports

www.securityon
campus.org/index.php?
option=com_wrapper
&view=wrapper&Item
id=68

Quantify a problem

Documents can show you how much an action or inaction ends up costing. Or it can establish exactly how often a problem occurs or how bad it is. In November 2008, for example, the investigative team at television station CBS4 in Miami pored through 10,425 state inspection records of 1,358 day care centers over a two-year period and found some 150 centers with 20 or more citations for failure to comply with the state's minimal standards for day care operations.[5]

Establish causality

Documents can provide dates and times so that you can understand history and precedence and how one action or event led to another.

DOCUMENTS THAT ARE AVAILABLE ONLINE

C ommunicating via electronic print — text messages, e-mail, text documents, PDFs — can be more convenient than talking on the phone. Whenever we communicate through text or image in any way, we create a document of our communication. These documents record the decisions people make or actions people take and create a trail that a journalist can find. Online archives and search boxes give a reporter fast and easy access to much of the information he or she needs.

Let's say you want to investigate immigration busts in your county by the U.S. Immigration and Customs Enforcement agency. The Federal Register is one place you can start a search for public documents.

The Federal Register

Anytime a federal agency considers a new regulation or a change to a regulation, it must make an announcement in the Federal Register and give the public an opportunity and time to comment. You can search the Federal Register online through GPO Access. It provides a summary of a proposed rule change as well as the agency that proposed it. You will also get the name and phone number of the person at the agency who is the contact person for information about the rule. Exhibit 8.3 shows where you can enter "immigration arrests" as the search term on GPO.

The Federal Register
http://GPOaccess.gov

Exhibit 8.4 shows an example of what the results of your search may look like. These are all government documents that you can view and use.

The Federal Register offers the full files in HTML format, as a Web page, as a PDF document, or as a summary. If you click on the summary of the first result, you can read about a proposed change to federal laws that details what steps a business owner must take after the federal government informs it that one or more of its employees submitted incorrect or false social security numbers. You learn that when the federal government discovers that employees gave incorrect social security numbers, it sends employers a "no-match letter." You can see what an actual summary looks like in Exhibit 8.5. This information may be useful if the immigration arrests in your area concerned businesses that employed workers with questionable documentation.

If you download the document as a PDF, you can view the actual pages of the Federal Register. This section of the Federal Register available online is 12 pages long and among its useful information are the docket number, which will allow you to search for all kinds of documents concerning this rule change, and a contact such as the following:

EXHIBIT 8.3   GPO Access allows for electronic searches of the Federal Register.

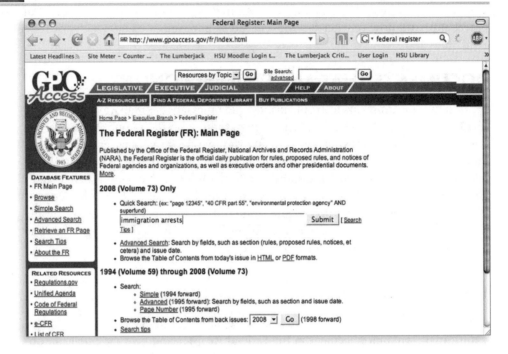

EXHIBIT 8.4   Search results yielded through the Federal Register.

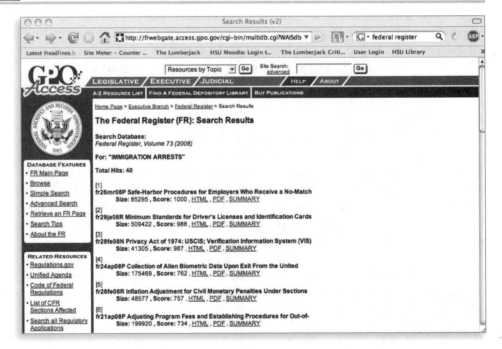

"For further information contact: Marissa Hernandez, U.S. Immigration and Customs Enforcement, 425 I St., NW., Suite 1000, Washington, DC 20536. Telephone: 202-307-0071"[6]

You now have a contact within the bureaucracy of the ICE agency. The section also reveals that ICE invites public comment on the rule change before its final adoption. This invitation is required under federal law and can lead you to people affected by a problem or who fear they will be affected by changes in the law, and possibly other knowledgeable people to interview. To find the public comments, go to the site Regulations.gov and enter the docket number. If you do this for the previous example, you will see that ICE had received more than 1,000 public comments. That's 1,000 possible sources for information; they all had enough interest in the issue to write an e-mail or letter to the federal government. Most of the letters provide contact information. With one click, you can download a letter as a PDF and find it is from a woman in Elon, N.C., who opposes the rule change because she fears that law-abiding workers will risk losing their jobs because of inaccuracies in the social security database. If you plug that woman's name with the city of Elon into Google, the search will provide her phone number. You can

Sample summary page of a proposed rule change from U.S. Immigration and Customs Enforcement.

EXHIBIT 8.5

```
DEPARTMENT OF HOMELAND SECURITY

8 CFR Part 274a

[DHS Docket No. ICEB-2006-0004; ICE 2377-06]
[RIN 1653-AA50]

Safe-Harbor Procedures for Employers Who Receive a No-Match
Letter: Clarification; Initial Regulatory Flexibility Analysis

AGENCY: U.S. Immigration and Customs Enforcement, DHS

ACTION: Supplemental proposed rule.

-------------------------------------------------------------------

SUMMARY: The Department of Homeland Security (DHS) is proposing to
amend its regulations that provide a "safe harbor" from liability
under section 274A of the Immigration and Nationality Act for employers
who follow certain procedures after receiving a notice--from the Social
Security Administration (SSA), called a "no-match letter," or from
DHS, called a "notice of suspect document"--that casts doubt on the
employment eligibility of their employees. The prior final rule was
published on August 15, 2007 (the August 2007 Final Rule).
    Implementation of that rule was preliminarily enjoined by the
United States District Court for the Northern District of California on
October 10, 2007. The district court based its preliminary injunction
on three findings. This supplemental proposed rule clarifies certain
aspects of the August 2007 Final Rule and responds to the three
findings underlying the district court's injunction.
```

Search Public Comments

www.regulations.gov/
search/index.jsp

also discover that she is a professor at Elon University. In other words, you can pick up the phone and ask to talk to her for a story. You can use this type of search to find human sources even if your story isn't about the proposed rule. Each of the 1,000 people who commented on this rule is interested in or affected by the issue of employment and immigration. Many of these people will be representatives of businesses, lobby groups, trade groups, unions and nonprofit social service and advocacy organizations. You can fill your story with them.

Congressional testimony

U.S. House and Senate Hearings

www.gpoaccess.gov/
chearings

Once you know that a change to an important federal regulation occurred or was proposed or if you learn that Congress proposes new legislation or has passed a law, you can find transcripts of congressional hearings. A search of the term "congressional hearings" on Google's U.S. Government Search gives you a main page at GPO Access, which was where you searched the Federal Register. The address Google now sends you to is the GPO Access hearings search page, displayed below as Exhibit 8.6.

To find out if there are any hearings that involved incorrect social security numbers and "no-match" letters, you can do a search for the term "no-match

---

EXHIBIT 8.6   The GPO Access congressional hearings search page.

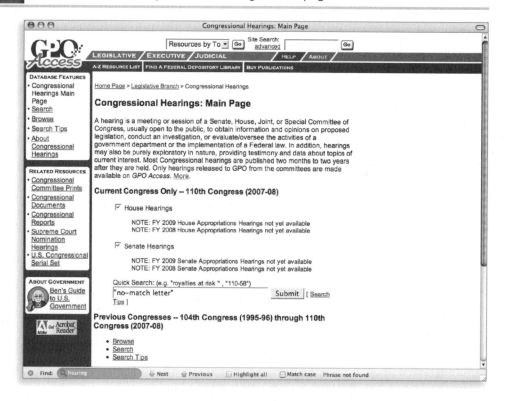

letter." The search yields eight returns, five of which appear in Exhibit 8.7. Six are the records of hearings held in the House of Representatives or the Senate, and two are reports on how many times the term you searched for appeared in the documents. You can pull up the records of the six hearings.

If you click on one of the hearings listed, "SECURITY THROUGH REGU-LARIZED IMMIGRATION AND A VIBRANT ECONOMY ACT OF 2007," you pull up the record seen in Exhibit 8.8. In this record, you will find the testimony from witnesses called before the Subcommittee on Immigration, Citizenship, Refugees, Border Security and International Law of the Committee of the Judiciary in the House of Representatives on Sept. 6, 2007.

Further in the document you can read the testimonies. That will likely give you information you could use in your story. Often good information is buried within congressional hearings that has not come out because few publications cover them unless they focus on a scandalous issue or a famous person. By reading through the testimonies you will find, for example, the story of Tony

List of legislative hearings that include the term "no-match letter."   **EXHIBIT 8.7**

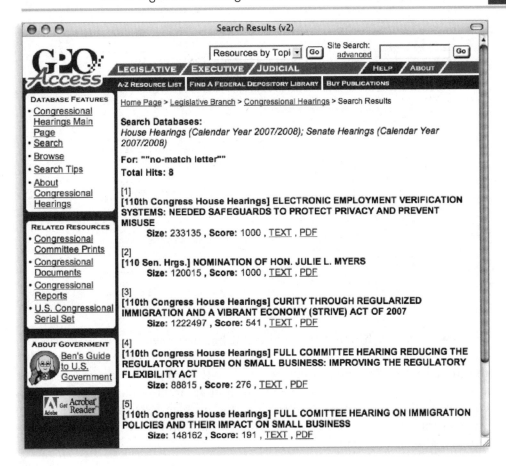

EXHIBIT 8.8   Record of testimony for a hearing regarding the Security Through Regularized Immigration and a Vibrant Economy Act of 2007.

```
◉◎◎          http://frwebgate3.access.gpo.gov - Mozilla Firefox            ◯
                              WITNESSES

The Honorable Jeff Flake, a Representative in Congress from the
  State of Arizona
    Oral Testimony...............................................  189
    Prepared Statement..........................................  191
The Honorable Joe Baca, a Representative in Congress from the
  State of California
    Oral Testimony...............................................  193
    Prepared Statement..........................................  195
The Honorable Ray LaHood, a Representative in Congress from the
  State of Illinois
    Oral Testimony...............................................  196
    Prepared Statement..........................................  197
The Honorable Brian Bilbray, a Representative in Congress from
  the State of California
    Oral Testimony...............................................  199
    Prepared Statement..........................................  201
Mr. Tony Wasilewski, Small Business Owner, Schiller Park, IL
    Oral Testimony...............................................  215
    Prepared Statement..........................................  216
Petty Officer Second Class Eduardo Gonzalez, U.S. Navy,
  Jacksonville, FL
    Oral Testimony...............................................  217
    Prepared Statement..........................................  219
Reverend Luis Cortes, Jr., President, Esperanza USA
    Oral Testimony...............................................  220
    Prepared Statement..........................................  222
Mr. Joshua Hoyt, Executive Director, Illinois Coalition for
  Immigrant and Refugee Rights
    Oral Testimony...............................................  231
    Prepared Statement..........................................  232
Ms. Cassandra Q. Butts, Senior Vice President for Domestic
  Policy, Center for American Progress
    Oral Testimony...............................................  274
    Prepared Statement..........................................  276
Mr. Michael L. Barrera, President and CEO, United States Hispanic
  Chamber of Commerce, on behalf of Mr. David Lizarraga, Chairman
  of the Board of Directors, United States Hispanic Chamber of
  Commerce
    Oral Testimony...............................................  280
    Prepared Statement..........................................  281
Ms. Julie Kirchner, Director of Government Relations, Federation
  for American Immigration Reform
    Oral Testimony...............................................  283
    Prepared Statement..........................................  285
The Honorable Corey Stewart, Chairman at-Large, Prince William
  County Board of Supervisors
    Oral Testimony...............................................  302
    Prepared Statement..........................................  303

 ⊗ Find: 🔍 wasilewski       ⬇ Next  ⬆ Previous  ▦ Highlight all  ☐ Match case
```

Wasilewski, a polish immigrant and small business owner in the suburbs of Chicago whose wife was deported back to Poland after 18 years of living in the United States. You might want to check with immigration rights groups in your area to see if they know of people in similar circumstances. You can also cite his story in your article to show how the problem affects people in other parts of the country. In other words, you can find information that will help you globalize your story.

State documents

Most state governments maintain and make available the same types of documents that you can get from the federal government. Often they are easier to find and obtain. A great source is the state auditor, whose job it is to make sure that state agencies do their jobs without wasting taxpayer money. In South Carolina, for example, two agencies are responsible for audits: the Legislative Audit Council, which performs audits of state agencies on behalf of the state General Assembly, and the Office of the State Auditor, which also audits all state agencies as well as county offices that collect or spend public funds. In June 2008, the Legislative Audit Council released a report of cell phone use by public workers that found that changes in how the state managed cell phone and pager use could save taxpayers $800,000 a year.[7]

You can download the reports from both audit agencies on their Web sites, which you can find by plugging the name of the state and the word "auditor" into a search engine. A search of the site for the "California state auditor" in July 2008 turned up a report on California's "Safely Surrendered Baby Law," which since 2001 allowed for birth mothers to surrender unwanted babies to hospitals rather than abandon them in the streets or garbage. The audit found inconsistent implementation, publicity and record keeping across counties. It also found that because of poor record keeping, 77 babies would grow up unable to learn information about their birth parents although the law entitles them to that information.

Environmental Impact Reports

EIRs provide a wealth of information and data about effects a proposed project could have on such things as transportation, housing, existing businesses and farms, population growth, demands on public services, whether any plants or animals would be harmed, any possible changes to air and water quality, and any geological risks or risks from exposure to hazardous materials.

In 1970, President Richard Nixon signed into law the National Environmental Policy Act. NEPA required federal agencies to study and consider the environmental effects before they take important actions. The act still applies whenever agencies adopt new regulations, change rules, issue permits to private companies or organizations, fund private actions, make federal land management decisions or build public facilities. Often major infrastructure projects require some federal funds or federal permits, which would require the NEPA process.[8]

The law requires developers of all such projects, whether they are the agencies themselves or an organization that needs federal funding or a federal permit, to file an environmental impact report. The EIR process also gives the public an opportunity to comment, and just as we saw in the Federal Register search above, that's a way to find those affected by a potential problem.

Environmental Impact Reports tend to be long, detailed documents. Consider this 2006 EIR for an expansion project of a gas pipeline project proposed by the Gulf South Pipeline Company, LP. You can find and download the entire document from the Internet at the Federal Energy Regulatory Commission's Web site. Buried in a section called "Alternatives" is this paragraph:

> Based on a comment provided by the NRCS, we also evaluated whether or not it could be feasible for the Tallulah Compressor Station to be sited in an area where prime farmland could be avoided. (. . .)Given the prevalence of prime farmland in Madison Parish, the unsuitability of the few available non-prime farmland areas, and engineering and hydraulic constraints associated with the positioning of compressor stations, it does not appear feasible that the compressor station could be moved to an area where prime farmland would not be affected.[9]

Statements such as this one raise a number of questions: How many farmers are affected? Are these small subsistence farms that families depend on or big corporate farms that might employ many people? Are these farms on Native American land, or have they been farmed by generations of the same families? Will this project benefit the communities the pipeline crosses or will it result in a siphoning off of needed funds? Careful reading of an Environmental Impact Report can reveal all kinds of potential problems.

Exhibit 8.9 is a list of agencies that had projects in 2007 that required an environmental impact report. From it, you can get a sense of the scope of information that is available.

Some states also have their own laws that require impact reports. They are listed in Exhibit 8.10. In some of those states, such as California, the law obligates counties and municipalities to conduct environmental assessments of publicly funded projects or any major project that requires public permits, as well. Regardless of the location of the project or government action that you are interested in, always ask whether an environmental impact report was or will be required, obtain a copy of it, and read it.

Corporate records

**U.S. Securities and
Exchange Commission**
www.sec.gov

Many corporations are publicly owned, which means that they sell at least a portion of their shares to the public. But to sell shares to the public, a corporation must abide by strict disclosure rules dictated by the U.S. Securities and Exchange Commission. They must periodically file documents with the SEC about their management structure, their business strategies, their risks of doing business and data concerning their financial health. All of these documents are available electronically through the SEC's database Edgar, which you access through the SEC's Web site.

The SEC requires companies to file many types of forms, but Exhibit 8.11 includes a few that business reporters rely on routinely.

Federal agencies and the number of their 2007 projects requiring an EIR. **EXHIBIT 8.9**

Agency	Number	Agency	Number
Forest Service	139	Rural Utilities Service	3
Federal Highway Administration	79	U.S. Air Force	3
Bureau of Land Management	52	U.S. Coast Guard	3
U.S. Army Corps of Engineers	40	Department of Housing & Urban Development	3
Federal Energy Regulatory Commission	32	Bureau of Indian Affairs	2
National Park Service	26	Community Development Block Grant	2
National Oceanic & Atmospheric Admin.	23	Federal Railroad Administration	2
U.S. Army	20	National Guard Bureau	2
Fish and Wildlife Service	16	Natural Resource Conservation Service	2
Bureau of Reclamation	13	Department of Homeland Security	2
Department of Energy	12	Department of Justice	2
Federal Transit Administration	9	Bureau of Prisons	1
Nuclear Regulatory Commission	9	Office of Surfacing Mining	1
U.S. Navy	8	Surface Transportation Board	1
General Services Administration	8	Department of Defense	1
Minerals Management Service	7	Department of State	1
Federal Aviation Administration	6	Department of Veterans Affairs	1
Tennessee Valley Authority	6	National Aeronautics & Space Administration	1
Western Area Power Administration	5	National Capital Planning Commission	1
Animal & Plant Health Inspection Service	4	National Indian Gaming Commission	1
Bonneville Power Administration	4	National Science Foundation	1
International Boundary & Water Com.	3	Total	557

States that require their own Environmental Impact Reports. **EXHIBIT 8.10**

Arkansas	Indiana	New York	Washington
California	Maryland	North Carolina	Wisconsin
Connecticut	Massachusetts	Puerto Rico	District of Columbia
Florida	Minnesota	South Dakota	
Hawaii	Montana	Virginia	

| EXHIBIT 8.11 | Short list of financial documents packed with information and easy to obtain. | |

NAME OF DOCUMENT	SEC CODE	WHAT YOU CAN FIND IN IT
Annual report	10k	Competitors, financial data, business strategy, lawsuits, problems in the retail or wholesale market.
Proxy	Def A14A	Directors and managers and how much they earn. Disgruntled investors.
Prospectus	S1	Competitors, early investors, business strategy, history.

Annual reports

To research a public corporation, first read the annual report. To see how much information is in such a document, also known by the SEC code "10k," look at the table of contents in Exhibit 8.12 for Yahoo! Inc.'s 2007 Annual Report.

Following are descriptions of what you'll find under some of the headings seen in the table of contents of Yahoo's Form 10k on the SEC Web site:

Risk factors.   The company must disclose significant risks it faces that could harm its profitability and growth. Under this heading, the company discusses threats from major competitors. Competitors are great sources for information about a company. They might tell about problems with the safety of the products produced by the company you are investigating or management problems they've noticed. In Yahoo!'s 10k, we learn that Google, Microsoft and AOL are its top competition. You could also find here whether a company is too dependent on one product line. If you were investigating the safety of a consumer product, for example, it would be relevant to know if the company was entirely dependent on sales of that product; in that case, it would likely avoid taking the product off the market.

Properties.   Under this heading in the table of contents, Yahoo! discloses that it has offices all over the world as well as in more than a dozen cities in the United States. You could find out here whether a company that is supposed to be local does business elsewhere. When you find that a company has property or leases offices in surprising locations, it may point to an activity the company doesn't want to publicize. You could also try to contact local journalists in the different regions where a big company does business. They might have interesting information about the company's activities that has not become widespread knowledge.

Legal proceedings.   Don't skip this little section, particularly if it isn't so little. The SEC requires companies to disclose in their annual reports any lawsuits they have faced. Under this heading, we learn that Yahoo! successfully fought off a

Table of contents for the 2008 Annual Report of Yahoo! Inc., as seen on sec.gov.   **EXHIBIT 8.12**

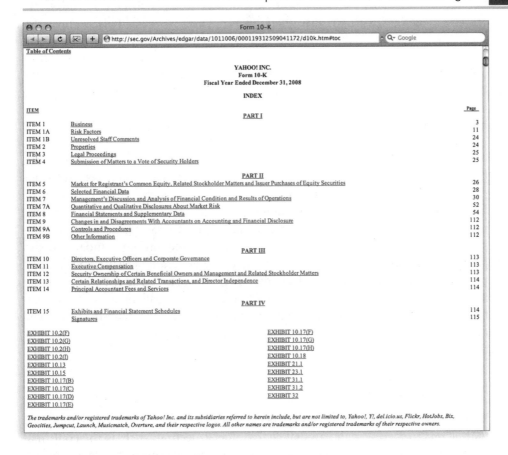

copyright lawsuit filed against one of its subsidiaries and that it was fighting shareholder class action lawsuits. These are suits that accuse companies of taking actions that aren't in the best interest of investors or misleading investors in such a way that they ended up losing money. Many such lawsuits are commonly filed against publicly held companies. You can get good information by contacting the lawyers in those suits to ask about records obtained during the discovery process. *Discovery* is an investigation process, during which one or both sides has to turn over documents to the other side (such as from the plaintiff to the defendant). It generates all sorts of documentation that the company would otherwise keep private. However, once a lawsuit ends, settlements often come with gag orders. When a gag order is imposed, you will no longer be able to get information that was part of the public record while the lawsuit was pending. Don't let corporate officials convince you that a lawsuit isn't important. Instead, watch out for what others shrug off as routine because companies, government organizations and some nonprofits often try to pass off questionable activities as everyday activities.

Financial statements.   Under this heading, the company reports its assets and liabilities and its income and losses. A company might tell its low-paid workers that it can't afford to raise their hourly wages while it tells its investors how much profit it makes. Or it might want a county government to give it low-interest loans to build a new plant and tell the county that it will be a great investment, but its financial reports might disclose that the company is on the brink of bankruptcy. A garbage hauler might tell garbage customers that it can't afford to offer free curbside collection of recycling, but its financial statements might show that it makes money by reselling the recyclable garbage.

Accountant reports.   Yahoo! disclosed no disagreements with its accountants, but always check out this section under the heading "Changes in and Disagreements With Accountants on Accounting and Financial Disclosure." When a company fires its accounting firm or an accounting firm decides it doesn't need the business, it could be a sign of financial mismanagement. Reputable accounting firms are held to standards set by the SEC, the Financial Accounting Standards Board and other agencies and are expected to abide by generally accepted accounting principles. A rift between the independent accounting firm and the client company could mean that the company wants to make creative changes to its finances that the accounting firm feels uncomfortable about. The accountant's report will disclose any change in accounting methods or anything unusual about the way the accounts were kept.

Proxy statement

This document is sent to shareholders each year to inform them of matters that will be put to a vote at the annual shareholders meeting, such as the confirmation or rejection of new directors or votes on compensation packages for top managers. Sometimes unhappy shareholders launch proxy fights to try to oust a CEO or chairman and in that way force the company to change its strategies or business practices.

These documents can lead you to the unhappy shareholders, who tend to know about all aspects of a company. The proxy statement also lists the members of the boards of directors as well as the top investors in the company and explains who they are. Often companies have interconnecting boards and investors. To visualize these interrelationships, a nifty Web site called They Rule allows you to plug in the names of any two corporations that were publicly held in 2004 (when They Rule was created) and find the interlocking connections.

They Rule
www.theyrule.net

The prospectus

Also known as a public offering, the prospectus is an often lengthy document a company must file every time it offers new shares to the public. This document will have some of the information found in the annual report but much more.

The prospectus will have a more detailed discussion of risk factors, and it also will often discuss the history of the company and explain how it was founded. It will give you historical financial figures. When a company goes public for the first time, the prospectus is often the first public disclosure of the company's profits and losses. It will disclose any business alliances the company has. It will discuss what the company expects to do with the money it raises from the offering. If the company wants to use the money to buy other companies, the prospectus will say so, or it might disclose plans to expand into new geographic markets or into new product lines.

The prospectus, known by the SEC code "S1," will also list top shareholders as well as any stockholders who sell shares in the offering. This activity can raise a red flag. The company might try to lure new investors by convincing them that the company will continue to grow and be profitable, yet the prospectus shows that some shareholders plan to cash in all or a portion of their investments. You might want to find out why. If many early shareholders cash out a significant part of their holdings, it might be a sign that they don't believe the rosy picture the prospectus paints.

Charitable organizations

Too many journalists make the mistake of thinking that just because an organization is nonprofit, no one gains profits from it. In 2007, San Diego Union-Tribune reporter Brent Schrotenboer showed his readers how that isn't the case. Box 8.1 shows the beginning of his story, "Bowling for Dollars."

Schrotenboer analyzed IRS filings to discover that while college football students who play in bowl games don't make any money, executives who work for the nonprofit bowl system make plenty.

Many nonprofits pay people high salaries. The Chronicle of Philanthropy reported in 2008 that Glenn Lowry, who heads the Museum of Modern Art in New York City, earned $1.7 million the previous year.[10]

Scams also masquerade as charitable enterprises, and charities may be run so incompetently that they spend more money on administration than on charitable endeavors. Others spend almost as much on the costs of fund-raising events as the events raise.

Uncovering scam charities and those that are inefficiently run can make great stories. In 2004, news reporter Walt Kane of cable news TV station 12 in New Jersey investigated a group that collected canned food for the poor and found fund-raisers that were tied to the Mafia and significant amounts of money unaccounted for.[11] In 2006, Darren Barbee of the Fort Worth Star-Telegram found that millions of dollars raised through charity bingo games were going only to the people running the games.[12] In 2007, Lee Rood of The Des Moines Register found that the nonprofit ACT Inc., which runs the college entrance exams accepted by many colleges and universities, pays the people who sit on its board of directors over half a million dollars each.[13]

Brent Schrotenboer's look into the "nonprofit" college bowl system[14]   BOX 8.1

"On New Year's Eve 2002, Bay Area businessman Gary Cavalli gave the college football world just what it needed — or maybe not.

He introduced another new postseason bowl game, this one called the San Francisco Bowl, to be played at AT&T Park.

It didn't go so well at first. The game, now called the Emerald Bowl, drew about 25,000 fans and had almost $112,000 more expenses than revenues. But in five years since, it's had success. As a result, Cavalli has been compensated accordingly.

In 2002, he earned $90,000.

In 2006, his compensation package was $362,018.

'Frankly, my compensation package is none of your business,' said Cavalli, the game's executive director. 'But we had a good year, so the board of directors was gracious enough to give me a nice bonus, plus some commissions.'

Such is life these days in the bowl business. While many fans and media continue to cry out for a postseason playoff format to replace it, the bowl system and its overseers just keep padding their pockets.

From 2001-05, compensation packages for bowl game executives have increased about 70 percent, with many of them more than doubling, according to an examination of the bowls' Internal Revenue Service records by The San Diego Union-Tribune. The highest-paid bowl executive in the study is the Outback Bowl's Jim McVay, who earns about $490,000, more than double the salary for the CEO of the oldest bowl, the Rose Bowl ($239,807)."

Read the complete story at www.signonsandiego.com/sports/college_football/ 20071212-9999-1s12bowls.html. Reprinted with permission of the author.

GuideStar
www.guidestar.org

Even though the U.S. government makes nonprofit organizations exempt from taxes, they must file financial statements with the Internal Revenue Service. Called Form 990, it applies to most nonprofit groups that raise more than $25,000 a year. Nonprofits' financial statements are available online from a nonprofit organization called GuideStar. To search for and view information about charities, you must register with GuideStar, but the registration is free. It is amazing how much information a Form 990 contains. It describes the purpose the organization is supposed to serve and details the organization's expenses. From this form, you can find the names of all the directors of the organization, its top employees and the salaries paid to them. You also can find out how and how much the organization raised.

Exhibit 8.13 shows two sections from a Form 990 for the San Francisco Bowl Game, which can be downloaded from GuideStar. Note that its executive director earned more than $300,000 that year even though the organization is nonprofit.

2006 Form 990 for the San Francisco Bowl (which became the Emerald Bowl).   **EXHIBIT 8.13**

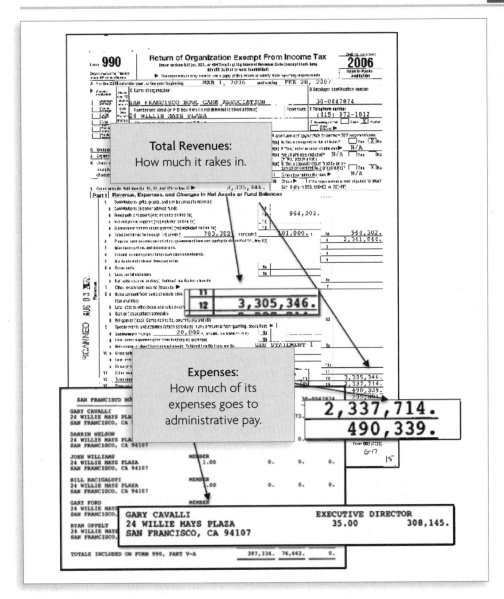

DOCUMENTS THAT ARE FOUND OFFLINE

S o much is available online that you can forget how much is only available offline. To get a sense of what you can find, go down to your county courthouse and you'll find wills, criminal and court files, birth and death certificates, voter registration cards, divorce records, and all kinds of real estate and property records. If your investigation involves anything that involves criminal complaints or civil law, head down to the courthouse. Most county clerks can be enormously helpful. Dress nice and act nicer. Recall that Newsday's "A Tragic Vulnerability" began with court files.

Other documents that you might not be able to find online are bids that companies submit to do business with the government, receipts public administrators file to get paid back for expenses while on public business and all kinds of other financial information that the government might not post online. For example, the Uniform Commercial Code is a set of laws that regulate transactions between businesses. The UCC requires businesses or individuals to file a form with the state for any transaction that involves putting up security to obtain goods or services. It is commonly used when a person wants to buy material from a supplier but won't have the cash to pay for it until the project is complete. In the form, the buyer guarantees that he will pay back the loan by putting something of value up as collateral — a pickup truck or a backhoe, for example. The form can give you a picture of the type of business someone is doing or how much money someone owes. It can show you connections between businesses and individuals, and it can document how much one business owes another.

OBTAINING DOCUMENTS FROM INDIRECT SOURCES

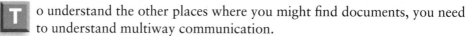 o understand the other places where you might find documents, you need to understand multiway communication.

Before the Internet, people kept their intimate thoughts and the miscellany of their lives in diaries — books that no one but the writer would see. Nowadays, people post their diaries every day on blogs using sites such as blogger.com. That means that the last bastion of solo communication has all but disappeared. Now pretty much everything entered on a digital page is meant for at least two sets of eyes.

Why is that concept important? Because if the author of the communication doesn't want to give you a copy, and you don't have a right to get it under public records legislation, you can go to the receiver of the message, who might be more willing or under a different obligation to turn it over. If multiple receivers exist, then multiple ways to get a copy also exist. Consider communication between a congressman and the head of a state agency. Congress, when it passed the Freedom of Information Act, gave itself a waiver; the public does not have a right to get congressional correspondence. But in most states, the public does have a right to get the correspondence of the heads of state agencies. Therefore, you may obtain congressional correspondence if you consider where the correspondence went.

Reports are written for multiple eyes and filed in multiple places. So are copies of most other forms of documentation. After you figure out what you need, think about all people who might have it and where they might be: federal, state or local government Web sites or offices; lawyers of plaintiffs or defendants in lawsuits; court files; police agencies; and corporations and corporate customers.

Don't think just about the present. Look back in time to find former employees, lawyers, government officials, bureaucrats and customers. Computerization allows people to store documents for a very long time in a very small space. Remember three things:

1. People make records of important decisions and actions.

2. People keep those records when those records are important.

3. When sued, people have to turn over those records to the plaintiff's lawyers during the process of discovery.

An interesting point is that people don't always recognize the importance of a document and sometimes disclose information because it seems harmless.

DOUBT THE DOCUMENTS

Investigative reporters need to be as skeptical when dealing with documents as they are with information gleaned from interviews. Consider what happened at two prestigious news organizations, CBS in 2004 and the Los Angeles Times in 2008.

On Sept. 8, 2004, the CBS Anchor Dan Rather reported on the program "60 Minutes II" that new documents provided by a retired Texas National Guard officer proved that President George W. Bush had received preferential treatment when he served in the National Guard during the Vietnam War. Less than two weeks later, Rather apologized on the air, saying that the documents turned out to be fake. CBS took him off the evening news in March 2005 and refused to renew his contract a year later. Not only were the documents forged, but experts had expressed doubts about the authenticity of the documents before CBS aired the show.[15]

In March 2008, the Los Angeles Times ran a story that revealed new details about a 1994 shooting of rap star Tupac Shakur. Investigative reporter Chuck Philips had based the story, which linked the shooting to rap star Sean Combs, on FBI documents that suggested that the attack was set up by Combs' associates. But William Bastone, an editor for smokinggun.com, a Web site that collects and posts public documents, wondered about the story. Bastone didn't believe the documents were authentic and called Philips. Philips looked into it and the next day, the newspaper retracted the story and ran an apology. Combs threatened to sue the LA Times for defamation.

Some legal experts argued that it was unlikely Combs would carry through with his threat, but the publication of the article was still a fiasco for the paper. It turned out that the fake documents were the creation of a con man, someone who was in prison at the time and who was known for having fabricated documents in the past.[16]

With these cautionary tales in mind, Box 8.2 provides some tips for ensuring that a document you acquire is authentic.

Document authenticity checklist

BOX 8.2

Howard L. Rosenberg, a producer at ABC News, says that reporters need to determine if documents they use for a story are authentic. That means that the origin of the document can't be questioned. He came up with a checklist for helping to assure yourself that a document isn't a fake.[17]

☐ **Be wary of copies.** Always try to get the original of the document, straight from an official, such as a sheriff's deputy or a court official.

☐ **Trace and maintain a "chain of custody."** From the time a document leaves the hands of the person who created it, you can chronicle every other person who handled it and determine whether any changes were made to the document and who made them.

☐ **Find an independent expert.** Certain professionals specialize in authenticating documents, usually on behalf of a plaintiff or defendant in a lawsuit. They do what's known as a *forensic analysis of a document.* They conduct tests on handwriting, typefaces, paper, ink, and so on. But Rosenberg cautions that you shouldn't confuse scientific tests with an expert's opinion, which is not as conclusive. Three organizations can refer you to an expert who can help you authenticate documents: the American Society of Questioned Document Examiners, the American Board of Forensic Document Examiners and the National Association of Document Examiners.

☐ **Know the source.** Make sure you know who created the document, how the person who is providing it to you obtained it and how that source knows who created it, and when, why and under what circumstances it was created.

☐ **Check for inconsistencies.** Look for things that don't make sense, such as facts that aren't consistent with what your sources say the document proves or names, and dates or locations that wouldn't have existed at the time the document was supposed to have been created.

☐ **Timing is everything.** Question why your source is giving you the document now, and why it hasn't appeared before.

☐ **Don't rely solely on your document.** Check out the information on it with other credible sources.

☐ **Don't be selective.** If parts of a report, for example, bolster the case you hope to make, but other parts refute it, don't ignore the parts that you don't like.

☐ **Be transparent.** When you are ready to publish your story, don't be secretive about how you got the document or where it is from and be prepared to offer it up for inspection to other publications or inform others how they can get their own copy.

Jack Shafer, a media analyst for online publication Slate.com, noted that some of the smartest people in the world fall victim to con artists. Scientists publish fake findings in prestigious journals, crooks rip off sophisticated investors, and unscrupulous police and prosecutors have hoodwinked juries into convicting innocent people. He warned against giving documents more credit than they deserve. Public agencies and public officials have been known to include untruthful information in reports and other documents. Just because something is on a piece of paper and comes from an official agency doesn't mean the information on it is true. Some reporters complain that media lawyers and cowardly editors often pressure investigative reporters to come up with documents, particularly when the human sourcing involves people with less than stellar pedigrees. The case Chuck Philips had been building for years depended in large part on testimony from people from the streets, some of whom were in jail or had criminal backgrounds. He may have been ready to believe the document because it simply confirmed what he had found through interviews.[18]

CONCLUSION

Documents can bolster your investigation. To find them, you should consider what kinds of information are collected and how the information is collected, stored and distributed. You can use documents to back up information people tell you in interviews or to prove information wrong. As with any source, you don't want to rely too much on a single document. Just because something is written on paper doesn't mean that it is true or that the document is genuine. But when used with multiple interviews and data, as discussed in the next chapter, documents can help you make a convincing case.

EXERCISES

1. Go to sec.gov and click on the link to EDGAR at "Search for Company Filings." Find the latest proxy statement for the Walt Disney Co. In it find the table for compensation paid to top executives. Who is the CEO of the Walt Disney Co., and how much did this executive receive for one year's total compensation?

2. Go to guidestar.org and register so that you can search nonprofit documents and 990 Forms for free. Search for the Form 990 for the Make a Wish Foundation of America. Read through the form and find out how much the organization paid its top officer in salary for the year covered in the form. What was its top expense outside of salaries?

3. Go to regulations.gov. Under "Search" type in the term "immigration." Find a proposed rule or rule change that interests you. Pull up the docket and see if you can find a public comment letter. Who wrote the letter, and what stand was the person taking? What issues did the person want the government to address?

4. Go to google.com/unclesam. Enter the terms "toy safety" and "congressional testimony." Find the transcript for someone who testified before a congressional committee on the issue of toy safety. What did the hearing

investigate? What argument did the person make in his or her testimony? Now see if you can find other testimony that came out of the same hearing.

5. Using an Internet search engine, find the home page for your state government and find the Web site for your state auditor. Does your state auditor post audit reports online? If so, look for a list and find a recent audit report. What did it investigate? What did it find? If you wanted to take the investigation further, what would you look into?

THE BIG STORY Project · THE BIG STORY Project · STEP 8

8.1   Now is the time to check on those public records requests you made as part of Project Story Step 3.

a. Read any material you obtained and summarize any relevant information in your Interviews spreadsheet. To do that, treat each document as a person interviewed.

b. Follow up on requests that have not yielded information. If your request was too broad, narrow it and resend to the agency. If it was rejected, file a letter of appeal to the head of the agency.

c. In light of the interviews you have done so far and material you have read, consider other public documents you might need and file those public record requests.

8.2   Brainstorm what kinds of documents might be easily available through your local and state governments and at the federal level.

a. Do laws regulate your topic?

b. Try to come up with a list of professionals who could point you to the right documentation: a professor who studies the issue, a lawyer who sues companies over the issue, an independent consultant who works with government agencies or corporate clients on it.

c. Divide up your team and assign the following areas in which to search for documents.

Local government

State government

Federal agencies

Academia

Independent consultants

NOTES

1. Jim Rutenberg, Marilyn W. Thompson, David D. Kirkpatrick and Stephen Labaton. "For McCain, self-confidence on ethics poses its own risk." *New York Times,* Feb. 21, 2008.

2. Jim Schaefer and M.L. Elrick. "Mayor Kilpatrick, chief of staff lied under oath, text messages show romantic exchanges undercut denials." *The Detroit Free Press,* Jan. 24, 2008.

3. Woodward and Bernstein. *All the President's Men.* Simon & Schuster, 1994, pp. 37–44.

4. Thomas Peele, with Bob Butler and Mary Fricker. "Evidence ignored." The Chauncey Bailey Project. See the project's full investigation at Chaunceybaileyproject.org.

5. "I-Team: How safe is your daycare? Digging into daycare safety." CBS4-Miami, Nov. 20, 2008.

6. Federal Register. March 26, 2008 (Vol. 73, No. 59).

7. South Carolina Legislative Audit Council. "Review of state use of cell phones, pagers, and satellite phones," June 2008. Available online at: http://www.lac.sc.gov/Reports/2008/Cells_Pagers_Satellites.htm.

8. Council on Environmental Quality, Executive Office of the President. *A Citizen's Guide to the NEPA: Having Your Voice Heard.* December 2007. Available online at http://ceq.hss.doe.gov/nepa/Citizens_Guide_Dec07.pdf.

9. Federal Energy Regulatory Commission. Final Environmental Impact Statement regarding Gulf South Pipeline Company, LP's East Texas to Mississippi Expansion Project under CP06-446 et al. Office of Energy Projects, May 2007, p. 4–34.

10. Patrick Cole. "MoMA chief made $1.7 million in 2007, tops for arts executives." Bloomberg newswire, Sept. 29, 2008.

11. Walt Kane. "Tin Can Charities." News 12 New Jersey broadcast, July 19–24, 2004.

12. Darren Barbee. "Bingo haul: Some landlords hit the jackpot while charities get consolation prizes." *Fort Worth Star-Telegram,* June 17, 2006.

13. Lee Rood. "Nonprofit ACT board's pay near top in U.S." *Des Moines Register,* Nov. 11, 2007.

14. Brent Schrotenboer. "Bowling for dollars." *San Diego Union-Tribune,* Dec. 12, 2007.

15. Sidney Blumenthal. "Dan Rather stands by his story." *Salon,* Sept. 27, 2007.

16. James Rainy. "The Times apologizes over article on rapper." *The Los Angeles Times,* March 27, 2008. Also see: "Big phat liar: How a federal inmate duped the Los Angeles Times, fabricated FBI reports, and linked Sean "Diddy" Combs to 1994 ambush of Tupac Shakur." thesmokinggun.com, March 26, 2008.

17. Howard L. Rosenberg. "A journalist's tips on authenticating documents." Presented at the 2005 IRE Conference. Available through the IRE Resource Center, Tipsheet 2479. Used with the author's permission.

18. Jack Shafer. "Biggie mistake: How Chuck Philips and the L.A. Times could have dodged the Tupac hoaxer." slate.com, March 27, 2008.

Available online at: https://elibrary.ferc.gov/idmws/File_list.asp?document_id=13509229.

Finding and Using Data

CHAPTER PREVIEW Now it's time to turn your attention to the numbers contained in the documents you have obtained. Through examples of several important stories that are based on numbers, you will learn how to use data in a story. You will acquire the skills to find data on the Internet as well as the knowledge to navigate government bureaucracies and negotiate with them for data. Finally, you will gain an understanding of what to do with the data you acquire — how to use data accurately to quantify an issue for your readers.

9

C H A P T E R

GETTING COMFORTABLE WITH NUMBERS

S ome journalists consider themselves to be math-challenged. That's too bad, because reporters who seek out numbers rather than run away from them can turn a good story into one that's eye-popping. Just as documents help reporters nail down the story, the data they collect help convince readers that the size and scope of the problem is something they can no longer ignore. Here are a few examples of how reporters used numbers in their big stories:

- Minneapolis Star Tribune reporters Matt McKinney and Glenn Howatt discovered that millions of dollars in farm subsidies were going to people who live in big cities and who don't do the farming of land they own. Some 2,000 people in Minneapolis and St. Paul received subsidies over an 18-month period, including a former state senator who lived in St. Paul and received $113,350.54.[1]

- Reporters at the Dallas Morning News looked at murder convictions over a seven-year period, and by cross-referencing information from a database they obtained from the Texas Department of Criminal Justice against court and police records, they found that twice the number of convicted murderers received probation as received the death penalty. Among the information they found: The system sentenced 120 killers to probation from 2000 to 2006; of those, 47 were in Dallas, which gave that county the highest percentage of murderers put on probation; three of the killers had previously killed before, 10 were later sentenced to prison for new crimes; and probation officers lost track of 15 of the killers put on probation.[2]

- Rochester Democrat and Chronicle reporter Gary Craig found that in 2006, 457 foster children, or almost half of all kids in foster care in his state, were prescribed one or more common psychotropic drugs.[3] You can see Craig's methodology for the story in Box 9.1.

Numbers can make a story stand out

Numbers can quantify and document a truth people want to deny or ignore. Perhaps some students on your campus complain that police seem to target them. The police deny this. But a database of arrests and arraignments could show a disproportionate number of arrests for things like disturbing the peace and loitering for students of a certain racial classification.

In November 2008, students at New York University found that the school was making it seem as if students who live in the campus dorms are safe, a big concern for people who consider going to the school as it is located in the heart of Greenwich Village. But they discovered that the school classified only three of the 21 dorms "on-campus." And since the other 18 were technically "off-campus," it did not have to list the crimes there in its Clery Act reports. The Washington Square News found that officially, the school ranked No. 61 out of

How the Rochester Democrat and Chronicle researched the "Potent Pills" story[4]

BOX 9.1

The idea for the story. Court reporter Michael Zeigler wrote a daily story about a ruling by a judge prohibiting the prescription of a psychotropic drug to a two-year-old child in foster care. Zeigler, Gary Craig and Editor Sebby Wilson Jacobson wondered how often that type of drug was prescribed to foster children that young.

The documents and data. Craig sent a Freedom of Information request to the N.Y. State comptroller's office for Medicaid expenditures for specific psychotropic drugs for foster children in every county. Attorneys for the state said that some counties had so few children in foster care that releasing the information might violate privacy laws by inadvertently identifying children. Craig reduced the request to three large counties. He sent out a second request expanding the types of drugs to include medications prescribed for depression and some other medications he left out in the first request. He found, to begin with, that the paper's home county had a much higher Medicaid expenditure rate of prescribing psychotropic drugs to foster children than did the rest of the state. He requested similar data from the county to cross-check the state data and try to explain the high rate. He interviewed county officials, who helped him understand the information.

Finding those affected by the problem. Craig tried to get sources in Family Court to hook him up with foster parents or the parents of foster children treated with the drugs. But that wasn't very successful. Then he discovered, through research, that while Family Court records are sealed, the hearings are open. He argued to the court for release of hearing transcripts assuring the judge that no families would be identified in articles without their permission. He used the hearing transcripts to locate and interview families.

Finding experts. He found and interviewed psychiatrists and scientists. Some he found through transcripts of congressional hearings on foster care.

Supplemental research. He read research reports that included studies done by the Government Accountability Office on the health effects of off-label medications, drugs used to treat a condition for which they have not been officially approved, on young children.

Read the complete story at www. democratandchronicle.com/apps/pbcs.dll/ article?AID=/20071209/news01/71206023.

---

the 180 largest universities for substance abuse violations. But if the 18 other dorms were included, the school shot up to No. 2.[5]

When you stumble over interesting data — someone cites a statistic in the course of a conversation, or you find it in a tangential footnote in some report — consider that a starting point. That number or set of numbers prompts questions that investigative reporters ask:

- Is it really this bad?
- Why is this happening?

- What are the ramifications of this?
- If this numerical trend continues, what effect will that have?
- Is this the tip of the iceberg?

The story "Bowling for Dollars" that Brent Schrotenboer did on college bowl games for the San Diego Union-Tribune, discussed in Chapter 8, came about when he asked these questions: "Why are there so many college bowls?" and "Why are the people who run college bowls paid so much?"

By analyzing numbers, you can discover things that weren't immediately apparent: connections between gender and income, for instance, or suicides and war veterans. Or it can show disconnects. Voting statistics could reveal how one group of people doesn't vote, for example. It can quantify inequities and reveal anomalies. The San Francisco Chronicle story on infant mortalities showed that buried within low mortality rates statewide were disturbingly high infant mortality rates in particular zip codes. Data can document the long-standing nature of a problem or reveal a trend that shows that the problem is getting worse.

Numbers can't stand alone

By itself, a number can be impersonal and cold. Newsday's "A Tragic Vulnerability" reported the cold facts that 126 elderly people went missing from assisted living centers on Long Island and that seven died. But what made the statistic especially heartbreaking was the anecdote that preceded it: the death of Ethel Danzker. The beginning of the story told readers that Ethel Danzker was someone's mother. The data that followed told them that what happened to Danzker could happen to anyone's mother or grandmother.

The Newsday story was strong because it contained convincing data. But it also had extensive interviews and numerous documents as support. It is dangerous when a journalist relies too much on numbers or suggests that numbers show more than they do. Washington Post database editor Sarah Cohen, in her book "Numbers in the Newsroom," said that a number is both a summary and a guess and that while some numbers paint accurate portraits of the world they represent, others don't.[6]

Although numbers can appear to be solid evidence of a truth, they can mislead. In January 2007, the New York Times published a story with the bold headline: "51% of Women Are Now Living Without Spouse."[7] Other newspapers, as well as magazines and TV news shows, used the Times' analysis of census data as evidence that women were swearing off men. Critics soon attacked the story because the data included females as young as 15. As a result, New York Times editor Bill Keller held a special staff meeting to discuss use of statistics in news stories.[8]

Without proper context, a number might seem to be evidence of a wide-scale phenomenon, when really it just reports a one-time occurrence. It can also make something seem better than it really is. Consider home prices. You could find a small city with an average home price twice the national average, leading you to hypothesize that it is an expensive place to live. But if you looked at all the actual sales of homes, it may turn out that while nearly all homes sold for *less* than the national average, one home sold for 10 times the national average, and so the sale of that home skewed the average. Instead of a well-off community, it's a poor community that just happens to be the place one very wealthy person calls home. That's why it's important to seek out data to back up what you find elsewhere through personal observation, anecdotal accounts, news briefs or to supplement reports or other documents.

COLLECTING DATA

Numbers help convince a skeptical readership by answering this basic request: *Tell me exactly.* But before you go fishing for data, get a good sense of what you want. If you fail to do that first, you'll end up wasting time plowing through irrelevant data. A great deal of data exist, so you need to narrow your search from the beginning. Just look at the Web site FedStats, shown in Exhibit 9.1, which is a

The amount of information you can find through easily accessible federal databases is staggering.

EXHIBIT 9.1

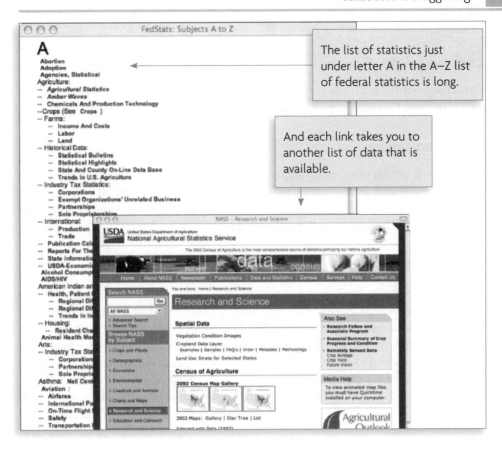

The list of statistics just under letter A in the A–Z list of federal statistics is long.

And each link takes you to another list of data that is available.

FedStats
www.fedstats.gov

portal for government databases of publicly accessible information. If you click on the "Topics A to Z" link, you will get a long list of topics, each a link to another long list of possible data downloads. And that's just one site for government data. All kinds of data are collected and disseminated by nonprofit organizations, industry groups and independent research companies.

The following guidelines will break down the data-gathering process to help you understand what to look for. Keep your story premise in mind throughout the process to keep your search on track and to serve as a reminder of your ultimate goal.

Brainstorm what you will need

Think of all the possible ways you can quantify a problem. For example, ask yourself these questions:

- How many people are affected?
- How many different *types* of people are affected?
- How dangerous is the problem?
- How widespread is the problem?
- How much will it cost to fix the problem?

Locating data

Once you come up with a list of data you need, you have to determine who can provide it or where you can find it. Following are some guidelines for locating data.

Find organizations

Ask yourself which government agencies or regulatory body would interact with the people affected by the problem, or what persons, company or organization would likely be responsible for it. Make a list. Again, try fedstats.gov if you need an overview of the agencies that are out there.

Find relevant forms

As previously mentioned, it seems as if everything that happens in our society comes with a form attached. This time you are interested in what the forms are keeping track of and what databases the forms can lead you to.

All government forms are public records, although some filings are protected by privacy laws and national security restrictions. But privacy restrictions usually disappear if you are interested in aggregate amounts instead of an individual's information. For instance, the names of gun permit holders might be protected, but public agencies can redact (delete or white-out) identifying information and give you the rest of the data. Using a search engine, search for "forms and guns" and you may find Form BF 041, the application form required for a permit to carry a machine gun in California, shown in Exhibit 9.2.

By finding and reviewing this form, you know that the California attorney general's office keeps track of who is legally able to own or manufacture a machine gun in the state, how many there are and what happens to them when they are disposed. You also now know that they must keep a database of information collected through Form BF 041. That's something you can ask for through a phone call or a records request. Every line on that form likely is a column in a database. If you are a reporter on a beat, consider every government agency that would regulate the people and organizations on your beat and request from each agency a list of their forms. Then you will get a sense of what information they collect and how you can get it.

California application for a machine gun permit.   **EXHIBIT 9.2**

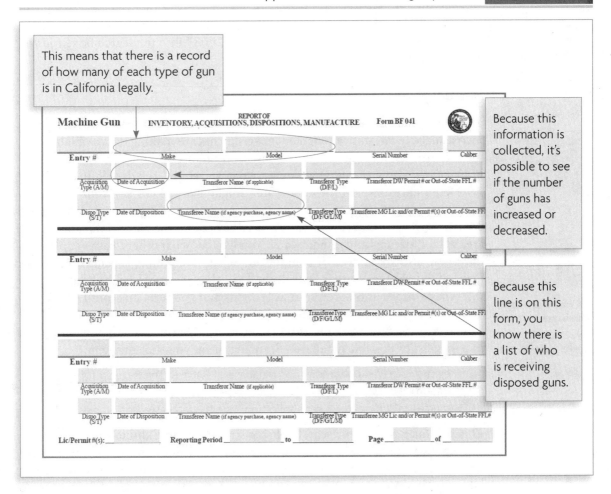

This means that there is a record of how many of each type of gun is in California legally.

Because this information is collected, it's possible to see if the number of guns has increased or decreased.

Because this line is on this form, you know there is a list of who is receiving disposed guns.

Find spreadsheets

The advanced searching capabilities of Google and other engines allow you to look specifically for Excel spreadsheets, and to limit the search to a particular domain. To see how these would work together, go to Google and click on "Advanced Search." Keep the search terms box empty but under the drop-down menu labeled "File Type" choose "Microsoft Excel," and under "Search Within a Site or Domain," plug in "ucla.edu," the domain of the University of California at Los Angeles. You'll find page after page of spreadsheet listings. Back at the top of the page, you can enter a search term relevant to your research, such as "proposal," and that will narrow it down quite a bit. One spreadsheet that shows up is a five-year listing of every professor who received an instructional improvement grant, how much they received and what the money was supposed to cover.

Or perhaps you are a student at the University of Portland who is interested in student clubs. If you return to the "Advanced Search" page and type "up.edu" into the domain box and "clubs" into the search term box you will get yearly budgets for the Associated Students of the University of Portland. You might notice that most of the links begin with "orgs.up.edu." If you plug that into the domain box, search for Excel files and plug "2008" into the search box, you will find the 2008 clubs budget.

Find databases

You can search on government Web sites for the terms "database" or "datasets." Increasingly, local, state and federal governments are making data available over the Internet. Even if the actual database isn't online, you may find references to it. Once you know the database exists, you can request the data in it.

Here's an example of how a search might work. Let's say your local government plans to improve its wastewater treatment plant using federal funds. Someone tells you that the upgrade is needed because the plant is threatening the area's lakes, streams and groundwater. You wonder what other treatment plants in the region also are in need of upgrade and what, if anything, is being done about them. If federal funds are involved, the federal government might keep track of this type of information. You start at FedStats and you see a link for "Data Access Tools." This site takes you to a list of federal agencies and the datasets you can get from them. You find a link for "EPA Databases and Software." That site takes you to a long list of possible databases. Scanning them, you spot this item:

> "Registry for EPA Applications and Databases (READ) — The Registry for EPA Applications and Databases (READ) is a catalogue of the Agency's diverse information resources, including computer application systems, databases, and models."

EPA Envirofacts Data Warehouse

www.epa.gov/enviro/
html/ef_overview.html

This link takes you to the searchable registry shown in Exhibit 9.3.

Now you plug in the term "wastewater" and find another list of possible databases. One of them is the Clean Watershed Needs Survey. You aren't just interested in watersheds, but the term "needs" piques your interest. It gets you to

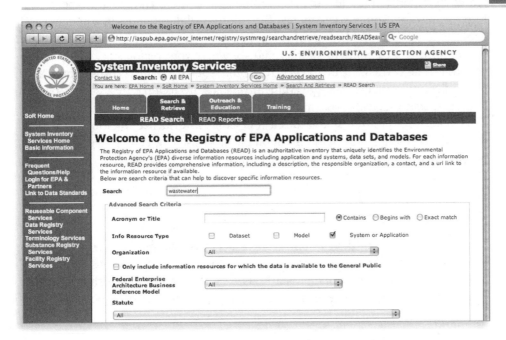

a page that seems to be a dead end, until you scroll down and notice a reference to "Access" and an Internet address, www.epa.gov/cwns.

This address leads you to a useful link called "Where you live." By following the directions for this searchable database, you get a table of wastewater treatment plants in your region deemed in need of replacement and repair. You also get a full report on how bad they are. If you want to do some comparisons, you can look at the same information for other regions to see if the needs are greater or lesser there. You might discover that your state has allowed localities to put off repairs and upgrades to sewage plants for so long that the problem is now at dangerous levels.

Find database maps

In your preliminary research, you may have used the U.S. Census Bureau to get some basic information. Now you may want to use the data in a more advanced way using database mapping tools. Let's take a look at one of them — Social Explorer.

Social Explorer gives you free access to the most recent census information (the census is taken every 10 years, i.e., 2000, 2010). All other census data going back to 1790 require a fee. That means that you could get great trend data if you are willing to pay. But let's focus on the current census. With Social Explorer, you can find information by mapping the data, which creates a visual tool that lets you spot locations. Let's say you want to know what regions of your state have the highest high school dropout rates. Using the mapping tool, you can visually spot the areas with the highest rates faster than you could get it by downloading the data into

Social Explorer
http://social
explorer.com

charts. Social Explorer also lets you search the data in a report form. When you search by reports, you select the geographic region and then the data type. Social Explorer also lets you mix and match. By choosing all the counties in your state and choosing the high school dropout category under "Education," you can compare the rates from one county to another and see where your region stacks up.

You could correlate data you get from other sources against census data to spot contradictions. Perhaps your government officials are touting great school performance so that they can avoid pouring more money into the educational system. They point to a jump in standardized test scores as evidence. By looking at high school dropout rates you could zero in on the inconsistency. Perhaps test scores rose because students with lower scores got pushed out. As Exhibit 9.4 shows, you can visually compare dropout rates in various counties in Texas using this site.

Know your rights to data

Most states specify in their public records acts that the public is entitled to information in the electronic form in which it is entered and kept. Exhibit 9.5 includes sections from two such state laws. Some states require the agency to convert the data into whatever form the requester wants, if at all possible.

EXHIBIT 9.4   A comparison of dropout rates in various Texas counties.

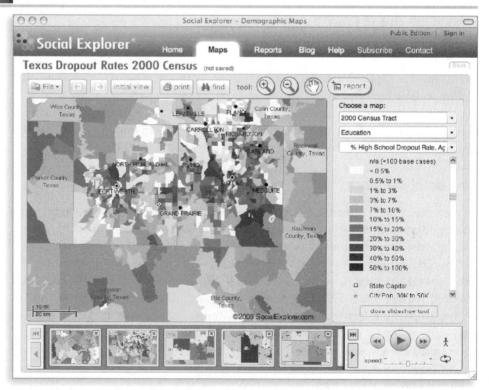

Two state laws covering the availability of data.

EXHIBIT 9.5

IDAHO PUBLIC RECORDS LAW, IDAHO CODE §§9-339 SECTION (11)

Nothing contained herein shall prevent a public agency or independent public body corporate and politic from providing a copy of a public record in electronic form if the record is available in electronic form and if the person specifically requests an electronic copy. A request for a public record and delivery of the public record may be conducted by electronic mail.

COMMONWEALTH OF PENNSYLVANIA, RIGHT TO KNOW LAW
ACT 3 OF 2008, SECTION 701: ACCESS

(a) General rule — Unless otherwise provided by law, a public record, legislative record or financial record shall be accessible for inspection and duplication in accordance with this act. A record being provided to a requester shall be provided in the medium requested if it exists in that medium; otherwise, it shall be provided in the medium in which it exists. Public records, legislative records or financial records shall be available for access during the regular business hours of an agency.

Negotiating for data

Getting data from government bureaucracies involves negotiation. You need to negotiate for how much you can get, how much it will cost and what form it will come in.

Ziva Branstetter of the Tulsa World offers a step-by-step plan in Box 9.2 to help you find and obtain data.

USING THE DATA YOU HAVE

Finding data is one thing. Working with the information is quite another. To analyze your data, you will want to use Excel or a spreadsheet equivalent. A simple spreadsheet can save you hours of time. It will give you reporting power you wouldn't otherwise have. By having all your information in one place, you can search and sort information. You can perform simple and complex formulas, clean, sort and filter data to create rankings, aggregate data and groupings by criteria. You can also join different databases to show connections and correlations. Comparing a database of people issued hunting licenses against lists of convicted felons, for example, could yield a list of convicted felons issued hunting licenses. With a database you can manage data over time to see historical trends.

Data you find through the Google Excel finder will come packaged in an Excel spreadsheet. Other data you might find on the Web often can be downloaded into Excel by cutting and pasting the data into an Excel spreadsheet. If you do that, you might need to clean up the data by *parsing* — separating different types of data into separate rows and columns. You will find instructions on how to do that in an Excel primer in Appendix C of this book.

Ziva Branstetter's steps to finding and obtaining data[9]   BOX 9.2

STEP 1: DEVELOP A DATA FRAME OF MIND

Look for paper documents with information in neat columns and rows. If the information looks like it came from a computer, it exists somewhere in a computer. The trick is to find it. Think about what kind of information an agency or official would want in a computer. Payrolls, case files, budgets, test scores, inspections and so forth are too often difficult to manage in paper form only. Don't be put off by the lingo: Excel, Access, text files, comma delimited, tab delimited, Oracle, SQL server. It's all data you can use. Collections of archived PDF files can be turned into manageable data within a few steps.

STEP 2: INTERVIEW THE DATA USERS

Find everyone on your beat who asks for and uses reports created with computerized data — these are the end users. What kinds of routine reports does your agency create? How often? What specific information is contained in these reports? What is the purpose of these reports? Ask how do you get these reports and who creates them? Try to get more than "Our Information Technology department." Get the names of the people in information technology (IT) responsible for key reports you would want.

STEP 3: INTERVIEW THE DATA KEEPERS

Get to know the people in IT, the computer geeks who control your access. Be fascinated by what they do, what information they keep. Meet them in person when you don't need anything. Don't just be another person demanding data from them. If the department is large, learn the different roles each person plays. Often different programmers are responsible for different data sets and only know about their own data. Ask what data they keep. Other data sources that the end users are not aware of may be available.

STEP 4: FIGURE OUT WHAT DATA YOU WANT

Don't ask for everything at once. Ask for something small you can start with. Example: Ask for a file of all pets licensed in your city. What are the most common dog and cat names? Who owns the most dogs or cats? Do your city officials have their pets licensed? Get fresh data. Ask the data keepers how often the data is updated and when. If the database is two years old, it's not worth asking for until they update it. Make a data schedule. Consider an annual calendar marked with the approximate dates when new sources of data will be available.

STEP 5: DO YOUR HOMEWORK

Know the law in your state. Most states allow access to electronic data. The devil is in the details. Pay attention to the section about allowable fees. Reporters Committee for Freedom of the Press, www.rcfp.org, has a great online guide to state-by-state laws and general tips about issues you will encounter. Also read court cases and attorney general opinions in your state regarding electronic records.

STEP 6: BYPASS THE PIO FOR IT

Go first to the IT department, *before* you go to the public information officer (PIO). Sometimes the IT department will feel it has the authority to give you the data directly. Even if it doesn't and you get bounced up to the PIO, the IT person will already be prepared to find the information for you. The IT person may even tell you exactly what to request from the information officer. If it isn't possible to get to the IT department, say that you need "computerized data." This way the PIO won't waste your time hunting in file cabinets for reports when you know that the information sits on a network computer. Offer to speak directly with the IT department. Make sure to put your request in writing and quote your state's law regarding electronic records if it specifically requires the release of electronic records upon request. If your state doesn't, emphasize the savings in time and resources for getting the data electronically rather than converting it to some printable form and then printing it all out. Even vast records on databases can be copied to a disk, a flash drive or even an MP3 player within minutes.

If the agency or IT department tells you it can't get the requested data out of the computer or that it can't put the data into one of the formats you request, find out what software they use. Then do a computer search for the software, call the company that makes it and find out how to export a file. Or, once you know the software, go to a forum related to that software and post a question. Chances are you'll find someone who will give you step-by-step directions that you can take back to the government agency. Also remind the PIO that since the public records act requires the agency to give you the data in the form in which it is held, it would violate the act to have a system incapable of exporting the data.

If you are told that the data are going to be expensive, examine the agency's rationale for computing the costs. While some states allow fees for programming, some agencies try to charge excessive fees. If an agency charges $100 an hour, ask how much its programmer makes an hour. If he makes that much, that's a story in itself. If the agency tries to charge you for the time it takes for the computer to spit out the information, note that regardless of how much information your request, it shouldn't take very long.

Make sure that if the agency is helpful and gets you the data quickly, you credit them in your story for that. That might help you get data as quickly the next time you submit a request.

Request a lot of data so that you can see patterns. You want several years' worth of data so that you can see patterns and changes. Don't be intimidated by large quantities, as programs such as Excel can calculate thousands of lines of information as easily as it can five lines. But know your software program's limitations; if the database keeps information for every student who has ever been enrolled at your university, it may have more data than your software can handle. In that case, you want to limit your request, to say, the last decade. In order to make potentially large amounts of data easier to examine, ask for the file formats described in Step 7.

STEP 7: KNOW THE LINGO

Make sure the agencies don't think you want their software. You don't. You only want the data to be in a usable form. That means that you want the data in an Excel or other spreadsheet file, a text file (.txt), a tab- or comma-delimited file or a fixed-width file. In a tab- or comma-delimited file, a tab or comma separates the columns. In a fixed-width file, a space separates the columns. This is important to know because Excel will ask you what format the information is in when you try to import it, although the Excel Import Wizard is so smart it can often figure it out for you once the file is opened.

Always ask for a code sheet that will tell you what is in coded data. For example, a code could be

1 = male and 2 = female

Ask for a data map, showing how long each field is and what type of data, numeric or text, is in the field. Find out whether the file is a "flat file" or relational data. Flat files have all the data in one easy table. Relational databases split it up into several tables that you have to piece together.

Adapted from "Five steps to finding and obtaining data" by Ziva Branstetter. Used with permission.

But much of the data you might gather might not come in a form that you can easily paste into a spreadsheet. In that case you will need to build one from scratch. It will be worth the effort.

What to consider when building your own database

Before you start creating your database, define its purpose. Databases can save you significant time, but they can also consume enormous amounts of it if you don't know what you are doing or why you are doing it. Think about the following:

- Try to estimate the size and scope of your project and measure that up against your resources. If you are going to have to enter all the data in yourself, you might want to start with a small sample and test it to see if it shows any patterns that will warrant more time and effort.

- If you can get some help plugging in the data, consider whether you will need the data enterer to have experience and know-how in working with data.

- Choose what software you will need and whether you have it or can get access to it. Can you do it in Excel alone, which most university computers come equipped with? Or will you need a more sophisticated program like Microsoft Access, which can show complicated relationships between people and organizations? If you don't have those programs, look elsewhere. Professors in the social sciences often use relational databases and might be able to help you out or let you use their software.

You might want to map your data geographically, but you have to consider whether you can teach yourself how to do a simple Google mashup, whether you know how to use more sophisticated Geographic Information Systems software or whether you can find someone who has access to such programs and knows how to use them. You can find GIS user groups in just about every city, and they might be able to help you turn your data into visual maps.

Setting up your database

The spreadsheet program gives you a seemingly endless number of rows and columns. If you can imagine each row as belonging to an individual person and each column a different piece of information about the person, then you can imagine a database of thousands of people with just about everything you would want to know about them.

Create logical columns and fields

If you build your own database, make sure that you don't include more than one type of information per column. This even pertains to names. Don't put both the first and last name of a person in the same column. Give the first name its own column. If there is a middle name or middle initial, give each its own column. This is important if you want to be able to sort your list easily.

Each type of information that you put into a separate column is called a "field." Don't be stingy with your fields. If there is any kind of a geographic location attached to your document or data, list it in a column for location. That will come in handy if you want to create an interactive or mashup map or if you have access to geographic analysis software.

Include in your spreadsheet any data that's possibly relevant, no matter how detailed. Sheila and Steven Steinberg, experts on mapping social science data, warn that you can always simplify detailed data, but you cannot get a more detailed analysis once you generalize the data. "Data of greater detail are fine, but data of lesser detail will simply decrease the final quality of your analysis results," they write.[10]

Code the data

If you have a relatively short list and a manageable number of fields or columns, you probably don't need to code your data. If you create a database that might grow in size and scope, however, it is a good idea to enter your information using a coding system. It allows you to keep breaking a set of information into subsets and subsets and more subsets without losing the thread of the groupings. Suppose you want to investigate religious discrimination. You first have to ascertain religious affiliations. You discover that on admission forms the university asks students to voluntarily state their religious affiliation for research purposes. You decide to put the information into a database and start with six categories: Christian, Jewish, Muslim, Buddhist, Hindu and Atheist. But then you decide you can't combine Catholics and Protestants together, yet you still want to keep them identified under Christian. You want to account for the difference between an Orthodox Jew and one who is Reformed or Conservative and the difference between a Shiite Muslim and one who is Sunni.

Here is how you might code them for clarity:

- 1 = Christian; 2 = Jewish; 3 = Muslim, 4 = Buddhist, 5 = Hindu, 6 = Atheist.
- For Christians, you add a letter tag: Catholic = 1a, Protestant = 1b.
- For Jewish students, you also add a letter tag: Reform = 2a, Conservative = 2b, Orthodox = 2c.
- Under Muslim you designate 3a = Shiite and 3b = Sunni.
- If you want to further distinguish Protestants, you could do this: Episcopalians = 1ba, Methodists = 1bb, Baptists = 1bc, Presbyterians = 1bd.

In this way, you can identify someone as Christian when you want to aggregate all the Christians together, but you can still differentiate between Protestant and Catholic and between Methodists and Baptists.

Give each row a unique identifier

When building your own databases, make sure to give each individual or entity its own unique identifier, a number that is unique to them. An example of a unique identifier is our social security numbers.

An identifier will help you distinguish between different people who have some similar information, such as names. With unique identifiers, you won't confuse the John Smith born on April 7, 1979, with the John Smith born on January 17, 1985. It also allows you to join different databases later. You could obtain a database of every faculty member in your state's public university system and a separate database of every wanted felon in the state. If you join the two databases, you could see if there are any wanted felons teaching in your university. But to join databases you need to be able to match up the same individuals from one database to the next and the easiest way to do that is if both databases rely on the same unique identifiers, such as the final four digits of a social security number. You don't want to accuse Professor Smith of being a wanted felon, just because he shares his name with one. So instead of entering "Smith" in one row and then another "Smith" in another row, you could use "9874" for the first Smith and "6783" for the second.

Check your data with a small sample

Do some early analysis to make sure your data aren't flawed. With the religious affiliations database, you might plan to plug in all 7,000 students. But first, plug in 35 and then sort the list. If your test turns up a surprisingly high percentage of Buddhists, perhaps your data are flawed and you might want to check the source of the information. It could turn out that the reason a high percentage offered their religious affiliation as Buddhist was that those students didn't bother reading the form carefully. Buddhist was the first choice they could check off and after filling out form after form they mechanically checked off the first box. You don't want to discover that your data are bad only after you plugged in all 7,000 names.

What to do with the data

Now that you have your database set up, you need to put your data and time spent to good use. Sometimes, the thing that is new in your story is a different way of looking at existing information. Even when you look at a problem that has existed a long time, you can bring fresh insight to it simply by analyzing the data to show people something they didn't realize. Following are different calculations you can do in a spreadsheet that can put your problem in perspective. To perform the calculations, you can create the formulas yourself or use the functions built into Excel, such as SUM, AVERAGE, MEDIAN, MODE, MAX and MIN.

Aggregates

It might be common knowledge that a problem occurs, but what isn't known is how many times it occurs, the number of places where it happens, the size of the cost, or the number affected, regardless of whether the number refers to people, homes, animals and so on. An *aggregate number* is the sum total and that can show the extent of the problem.

Median and Average

The *median* is the middle value in a distribution of numbers. When referring to home prices, it marks the number under which half the homes are valued and above which the other half are valued. Don't confuse that number with an *average,* which is the aggregate divided by the number of items in the count. Using the average number could mask an *anomaly* — an unusual occurrence that's way off the norm — whereas the anomaly will likely stand out when you compare it against the median.

Mode

The *mode* is the most common type of something in a list (for example, in the set 1, 1, 2, 3, 4 — 1 is the mode). It could be the most common level of pay or the most common home value. There can be multiple modes if there are multiple values that tie for occurring the most number of times (for example, if a set of numbers included 1, 1, 2, 2, 3, both 1 and 2 would be the modes). Mode is most useful when the number of items that match it accounts for a high percentage of the items in the list. Let's say you are looking at a survey that asked 100 people which age group they belong to. If you find that the mode is the age group 65–75 and there are 80 people who checked this box, you know that the group is mostly older people. A high number of people who match the mode will tell you the norm. But beware. A very low percentage of the total number of items in the list could match the mode, and if you rely on it, you could make the problem seem worse or better than it is.

Percentages and ratios

By comparing percentages for some characteristic, you could measure inequity. Let's say you know that a city spends $10 million a year on road repairs. An expert tells you that bad roads are in every part of the city and no one area has roads that are worse than in other areas. Then you find that the city spends $8 million, or 80 percent, of the total funds in a section of the city that accounts for only 10 percent of the land area. That would tell you that the city is focusing only on one small area and neglecting the rest.

Per capita

The *per capita* is a sum total divided by a total population. It can help you understand the seriousness of a problem. Say you know that a city had 20 homicides last year. If you live in a small city that's a big problem, but if you live in a metropolis that number is small. The per capita is useful for comparing two or more groups of data, where each group differs in size. If you know that a city of 1 million people had 100 homicides last year, then you know the per capita is one homicide for every 10,000 people. You can now compare that rate to neighboring cities even if they are much smaller or larger. A problem you initially think is big may turn out to be small, or vice versa, when you look at the per capita.

Percent change

When it is important to see changes over time, you need to calculate the percent change. You might discover that your college caught 280 people cheating on exams last year, but the school insists that's a small number considering there are 4,000 students enrolled. But if you find out that the school caught only 70 people last year, well that's a 400 percent increase. You calculate percent change with this formula:

percent change = new number − old number/old number * 100

Biggest and smallest

In a list, these numbers can help you spot who benefits the most versus who loses the most. It could help you find the person responsible and the people most affected by the problem.

Patterns and trends

If the percent change stays constant over a period of 10 years, you can see how long something has been a problem. Or say you've got data on campaign contributions from one lobbyist over a period of 10 election cycles. For each cycle you find the politician who received the highest contributions from the lobbyist for that year, but it's a different politician each year. Then you measure the percent of the vote each of the politicians captured in the last election and you find that each one won by more than 80 percent of the vote. The pattern could suggest that the lobbyist routinely gives the most money to candidates in safe seats.

Anomalies

Per capita, percent change, median and mode can all help you spot an *anomaly*. That can help you spot or prove something that's wrong — such as someone earning an unusually high salary, a police officer who gives an unusually high number of tickets or a criminal defendant who receives an unusually long sentence.

Think outside the cell

A database may be built in other ways. Tisha Thompson, an investigative television reporter in Washington, D.C., likes to create interactive maps of data using locations. It would work if you were doing a story on crime in your city, or the most dangerous intersections in town, or the most neglected sidewalks. This type of story used to be difficult to do, requiring expensive geographic mapping programs that are difficult to use. But mashups make it easy. Every year, the capabilities of mashups get better even as they get easier to use and as people build new tools for them.

You need to register an e-mail address with Google in order to use it, but you can create a free Gmail address in Google for that purpose. Once you do that, you can go into google.com/maps and click "My Maps." That will allow you to create a map, like the one in Exhibit 9.6. Make sure you make it unlisted, or it will be a public map, which means that people can find it and view it. Now that you've created a map you can add addresses to it. You can do this by entering an address or by having Google find it for you. Try typing in your university and Google will locate it for you. Then you will see a box on the map that allows you to save it to your map.

Once you save a location to your map, click on the address indicator on the map and a box will appear. In it you can type in information, or a bulleted list, or you can insert a link to a Web page, to a photo, or an image such as a timeline or graph stored on a photo-hosting site such as Flickr or your blog. Thompson says that she includes so much information in these boxes that when Web readers click on different places in her maps, they pull up mini-articles, such as the one shown in Exhibit 9.6.

Using a map as a database.   **EXHIBIT 9.6**

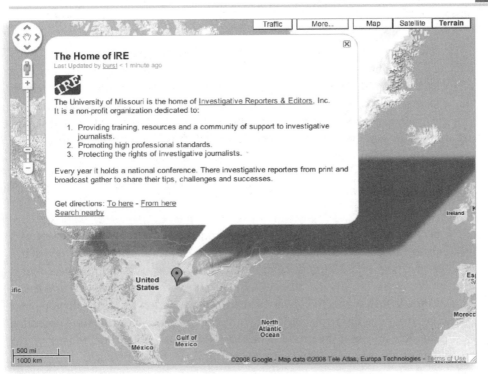

EXHIBIT 9.7   The Sunlight Foundation's mashup of a congressman's meetings.

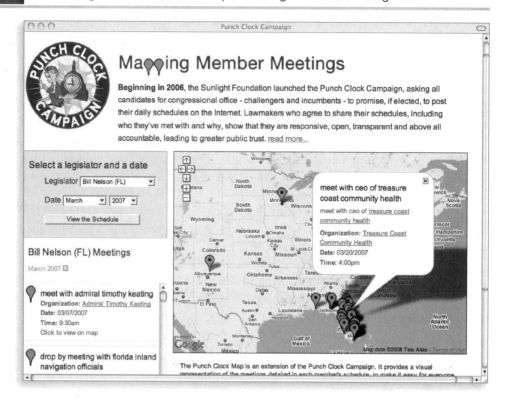

Remember that interactive maps can also become part of your final story package. The Sunlight Foundation, mentioned in Chapter 5, asked members of Congress to make public their appointment calendars. Sunlight then enters the information from those calendars, for the few legislators who agree, into a Google mashup map so that members of the public can see what their legislators are doing and with whom they meet. Exhibit 9.7 is the map for Florida Congressman Bill Nelson and his meetings in March 2007.

Punch Clock Campaign
http://punchclockmap.
sunlightprojects.org

CONCLUSION

D ata can help you quantify a problem and show the scope or intensity of a problem. Like documents, data can help convince a skeptical reader that a problem needs to be addressed. Many journalists shy away from numbers, but if you know how to find them and know what to do with them once you find them, data can show who stands to benefit or lose from a situation and can help you place blame. By analyzing data you could tell your readers, viewers or listeners something they didn't know even if the problem has been going on a long time. Mastering the art of data analysis sets an investigative reporter apart from the pack.

1. Go online to socialexplorer.com and search the U.S. Census database for data for three counties in your state. Select the categories "Median Household Income" and "Median Household Rent." How do the three counties compare? If people should be paying no more than half their household income for rent, how economically healthy are the residents in each county? Copy the charts that Social Explorer has made for you and paste them into a spreadsheet.

2. Go to www.securityoncampus.org/crimestats/index.html, the site for statistics on campus crimes compiled as required by the Jeanne Clery Act federal legislation. Plug in your school's name and find and record the crime statistics for your campus for murders, sexual offenses, and burglaries. Then do the same for three other universities of varying sizes. Take each of the figures and divide them by the number of students enrolled on the campus to find per-capita information. Which is the most dangerous according to the per-capita findings. Is it a different ranking from the aggregate numbers? Are the larger schools more or less safe than the smaller ones?

3. Using Google's advanced search functions, search in your university's domain for an Excel spreadsheet. Download it to you computer and see if you can do the following calculations using the data:

   a. An aggregate amount

   b. A median value

   c. A mode

   d. A percent change

   e. A highest or lowest amount

THE BIG STORY Project   ·   THE BIG STORY Project   ·   STEP 9

Go through all the interview notes collected so far and all the reports and documentation that you have found. What relevant data have you found or have people alluded to? This is the time to figure out how you might be able to quantify your problem.

   a. Is there a way to use numbers or other data to demonstrate inequity?

   b. Can you show an increasing or decreasing trend?

   c. Is it relevant to show a median or average value and compare it with another locality or a larger area — comparing local numbers to state or national figures, for example?

   d. Can you rank your data to show the best- or worst-case examples?

   e. Can you do a comparison with a previous time period — five years ago, for example — and show the percent change for better or worse?

NOTES

1. Matt Mckinney and Glenn Howatt. "Farm bill beneficiaries include urban dwellers." *Minneapolis Star-Tribune*, Oct. 28, 2007.

2. *Dallas Morning News*. "Unequal justice" series, Nov. 9, 2007.

3. Gary Craig. "Potent pills: More foster kids getting mood-altering drugs." *Rochester Democrat and Chronicle*, Dec. 9, 2007.

4. Gary Craig. "Foster care Rx : Medicaid data, court records show growth of off-label psych meds." *IRE Journal* (March/April 2008). And e-mail correspondence with Craig.

5. Marc Beja and Adam Playford. "Crime stats mislead on incidents in dorms." *Washington Square News*, Nov. 18, 2008.

6. Sarah Cohen. *Numbers in the Newsroom: Using Math and Statistics in News*. IRE, 2001.

7. Sam Roberts and Ariel Sabar, Brenda Goodman, Maujreen Balleza. "51% of women are now living without spouse." *The New York Times*, Jan. 16, 2007.

8. Byron Calame. "Can a 15-year-old be a 'woman without a spouse'?" *The New York Times*, Feb. 11, 2007.

9. Ziva Branstetter. "Five steps to finding and obtaining data." Tipsheet submitted to Investigative Reporters & Editors, Inc. For the 2006 IRE Annual Conference, Ft. Worth, Texas. Reprinted with permission from Ziva Branstetter.

10. Steven J. Steinberg and Sheila L. Steinberg. *Geographic Information Systems for the Social Sciences: Investigating Space and Place*. Sage Publications, 2006, p. 27.

Writing and Publishing the Story

Shaping the Story

CHAPTER PREVIEW You will learn why it is important to outline a story, particularly a big story, at every stage of your investigation. And you will find out how to connect seemingly disconnected elements in your story and how to differentiate between essential and tangential points. The benefits of using a spreadsheet program to outline your notes will be demonstrated. You also will be shown how to visualize your story by diagramming the information you gathered. Finally, a sample story will take you step-by-step through the outlining process.

10

C H A P T E R

ORGANIZING YOUR NOTES

I n a straightforward investigative story, you have a problem and a likely cause or culprit. The evidence you gather focuses around one target. But many investigations are more complicated. The cause of the problem isn't immediately clear and one target alone is not likely. To figure out how the problem arose and to find possible solutions, you talked to many different types of people about a range of subtopics. That produced a number of tangential issues. You pieced together isolated elements to uncover a big systemic problem. Remember that investigations start with a question that can't be answered without significant reporting. But what happens if everyone answers the question in a different way?

Let's consider the interviews with the fictional Joe Resident and Holly Homeowner from Chapter 6. You started out with a simple premise:

Is a resident suing the city over a pothole indicative of a bigger problem?

Then you interviewed Resident because he is the one who crashed his car and is suing the city. He thinks that if the city had fixed the pothole in time, the accident wouldn't have happened. He also told you that Homeowner had previously complained to the city. So you interviewed her. Right now it's a pretty straightforward story. But the more people you interview, the more complicated it will get.

That's because each person you interview raises new points that intersect in different ways with what everyone else says. Some people agree with each other on some points and disagree on others. Others sort of agree and sort of disagree. Then experts say, "Well, under circumstance X that is true, but when you get circumstance Y it is a whole other story." If you don't use an outline and you try to diagram how the statements, data and documents all relate to each other, the product might look like Exhibit 10.1.

With only a diagram, you would find it difficult to stay focused around a central premise and a central question. Equally important but only thinly connected pieces will begin to pull your project apart. Without a good system for organizing your notes, the center will not hold. Let's see what will happen if you try to diagram and then outline your story.

Cleaning up the mess

When you entered each piece of information in your notes into your computer, you noted whether the information suggested a major point for your story. But when you make a list of them, you may have 20 major points, and it is difficult to find a story thread in them. If you write them on a whiteboard, they could look like Exhibit 10.2.

Now let's see what it looks like if you can consolidate those major points. From 20 major points, try to consolidate them to 10. That means you combine

What a diagram of your notes may look like without any organization.   **EXHIBIT 10.1**

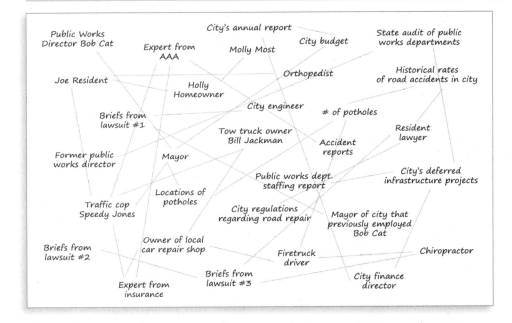

Public Works
Director Bob Cat
Expert from
AAA
City's annual report
Molly Most
City budget
State audit of public
works departments

Joe Resident
Orthopedist
Historical rates
of road accidents in city

Holly
Homeowner
City engineer
# of potholes

Briefs from
lawsuit #1
Tow truck owner
Bill Jackman
Resident
lawyer

Former public
works director
Mayor
Accident
reports

Public works dept.
staffing report
City's deferred
infrastructure projects

Traffic cop
Speedy Jones
Locations of
potholes

City regulations
regarding road repair
Mayor of city that
previously employed
Bob Cat

Briefs from
lawsuit #2
Owner of local
car repair shop
Firetruck
driver
Chiropractor

Expert from
insurance
Briefs from
lawsuit #3
City finance
director

Looking at major points to find a story thread.   **EXHIBIT 10.2**

Speed of repairs
not according to
pothole size

Car accidents
cause medical
problems

Potholes cause
car accidents

Lawsuits
costs city
money

Car insurance
rates higher
than elsewhere

School busses
ride over
potholes

Public works
director approves
repair schedule

Car accidents
spur lawsuits

City council
determines
PW budget

Bad streets
affect emergency
services

What's the
story?

Budget problems
result in cuts to
city services

PW says it follows
set guidelines
for repairs

New public
works director

City government
doesn't respond to
resident complaints

PW guidelines
differ from
other cities

Repairs particularly
bad on south side
of town

Potholes spur
complaints by
residents

Records show public
works department
busy with repairs

Repairs not so
bad on north
side of town

Other cities
don't have the
pothole problem

EXHIBIT 10.3   A story diagram answers the question "What have I got?"

What's the Story?

City Staffing		Budget Cuts
Repairs quicker in some sections of the city	Lawsuits	Complaints by residents
New public works director	System for street repairs	Car Accidents
Other cities don't have the same problem		Unresponsive city government

them into more generalized points. You might leave one alone, but connect three others together. Now you have a diagram that looks something like Exhibit 10.3.

Visually, it seems less of a mess. But you still don't have a focus for your story. It will be difficult to write a first draft from that diagram. You need to group your information by some kind of progression. If you do, you will find that complaints from city residents don't match up with information you get from the public works department. Residents say the city doesn't respond to complaints and doesn't repair the roads, but data show that the repair crews have been busy. The lawsuit says the city should have repaired the roads in a certain amount of time according to standard protocols, and you find that the public works department isn't following those guidelines. The change in guidelines seems to coincide with a slash to the public works budget. Let's now try to put these points into some order with a flow chart, or "connection map."

By making a connection map like the one shown in Exhibit 10.4, you start to see that all the information leads to the public works department and budget cuts. When you start to poke around there, you see some curious connections: a new public works director, a different way of managing repairs than you see in other cities and inequity in the locations and the speed of repairs connected in some ways to the budget cuts.

The diagram finally gives your story a focus and leads you to tighten your premise:

> In response to budget cuts, the public works department is neglecting the roads in sections of our city, which puts residents there at risk.

You have a much clearer focus, but it will still be difficult to write the story draft. The diagram helps you understand your story better, but it doesn't give you a lead or a story structure. To move from your focus to a workable story, you need to turn to an outline.

A connection map of your pothole story notes.   **EXHIBIT 10.4**

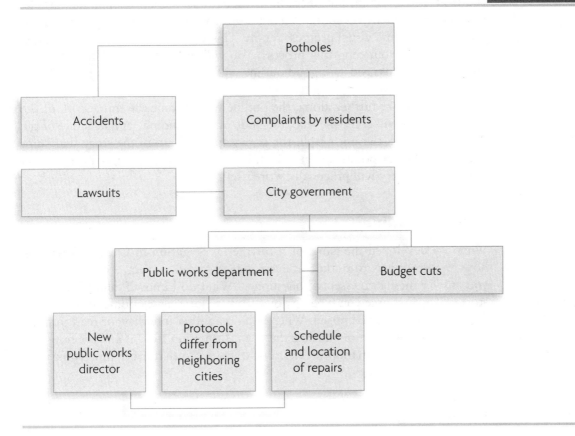

THE STORY OUTLINE

In the beginning of an investigative story, the outline serves to clarify what little you know. Later, it helps you focus your project and keep you from veering off on time-wasting tangents by organizing your accumulating knowledge into the most important points. Toward the end, it becomes an outline of the actual story, which makes writing easier.

The frustrating aspect of an investigative project is that you will gather a great deal of information and then toss 95 percent of it when you sit down to write the story. But you won't know what part of your information makes up that important 5 percent until you gather enough information to spot patterns and contradictions. Organization helps you make those connections.

An outline will keep you focused. It will help you understand how each new interview fits into the storyline and how to figure out when the story needs to be changed because of new information. With an outline, you will be able to differentiate between the essential and the tangential.

Outlines also enable you to see the progress you make, which will help keep you from becoming disillusioned. In investigations, sometimes maintaining the passion with which you started becomes difficult. An outline can keep you going by giving you a visual progress report. This also helps you plan out the next logical steps in your reporting process. You will see how much you now know and what you still need — a good outline will reveal holes in the story before it is too late to fill them.

When you are further along, the outline will become the framework of the story. Out of it will come the lead, the body and the ending. The structure of the outline will form the nut graph, the paragraph high up in the story that summarizes all the key points for the reader. If you put enough thought into the final outline, your story will practically write itself.

When to outline

When we developed the game plan for the investigation in Chapter 5 we saw how important it is to outline at every stage of your project. An outline helps you answer these two essential questions: "What do I know?" and "What's the story?" The first time you type up notes from an interview, outline the points the person you interviewed raised. When you do another interview or read through a piece of documentation, outline the key information from it and see how that fits in with the information previously gathered. Do that every time you gather a piece of relevant data.

What to use

You can outline on a piece of notebook paper, sticky notes, in a word processing document, on a whiteboard or blackboard. Later in this chapter, I will show you how to outline using a spreadsheet.

How to outline

Regardless of what medium you use, you need to begin with a basic outline. The following sections will guide you through the outlining process using the pothole story as an example. Notice how the premise and the main question change as you get further into the investigation. The pothole investigation expands depending on the information you find. It will take numerous outlines for you to see your story emerge, to spot your lead and to create a structure with all the pieces in the proper order.

Outline 1

You look at your interview with Joe Resident and summarize your notes. Exhibit 10.5 is the summary you create.

1. The pothole was big.
2. It had opened up sometime in October, at least four weeks before the filing of the suit.
3. Joe Resident crashed his car November 20.
4. He called the city three times before his crash to ask that the pothole be fixed.
5. This wasn't the first pothole he called to complain about. Each time his calls were ignored.
6. He's suing for $100,000 to replace his car, to compensate him for pain and suffering and to have the pothole fixed.

To outline, try to consolidate the information as you did in the story chart earlier in this chapter. From six points you come up with three. Your first outline would look like Exhibit 10.6.

The first outline.   **EXHIBIT 10.6**

Outline 1

1. Potholes cause accidents.
   - At least one person crashed his car because of a big pothole.

2. People have complained to the city.
   - Residents say the city doesn't respond.

3. People are suing.
   - If successful, lawsuits could be costly to taxpayers.

From the first outline comes this premise:

The city's failure to repair potholes puts the lives of residents at risk and could cost the city financially.

Outline 2

You now ask: What's the scope of the problem? Now let's consider the Holly Homeowner interview. You interviewed her because Joe Resident said she complained to the city. She tells you that she would watch cars plunge into the hole every day and think to herself that it was going to kill someone one day. She called the city twice herself to complain. She also said her friend Molly Most has a bigger one near her house seven blocks away. Molly's really worried because the school bus that her two children ride on has to go over that hole every day. Exhibit 10.7 shows your new outline in light of Homeowner's interview. This second outline doesn't change the story premise.

EXHIBIT 10.7   The second outline.

Outline 2

1. Potholes are becoming a big problem
   - Joe Resident crashed his car.
   - Holly Homeowner worries someone will get killed.
   - Molly Most worries about her children on the bus.

2. The city doesn't respond to calls.
   - Resident and Homeowner both complained.
   - Nothing happened as a result of complaints.

3. Lawsuits
   - If this and possibly other lawsuits are successful, they will be costly to taxpayers.

Outline 3

This time you ask: How dangerous are the city streets, and is it a result of the city's failure to maintain them? Then you file a public records request for reports of complaints about potholes and for all applications from residents for street repairs. You discover that 75 people complained about 27 different potholes over a one-year period, that on average each of those potholes received five complaints and that the time period from the first complaint to the last complaint per pothole was two weeks. Ten of the potholes are still unrepaired. The oldest complaint for a pothole that remains unrepaired is 10 months old.

Exhibit 10.8 shows how this new information can be integrated into your third outline. Even though you are adding information, the third outline gives the story more focus.

Outline 3

1. Potholes are becoming a big problem.
   A. 75 people complained about 27 potholes.
   B. Holly Homeowner has one so big she calls it the Grand Canyon.
   C. Molly Most worries about the school bus.
   D. Joe Resident crashed his car and sued over one.

2. How the city responds.
   A. Poor record of responding to complaints.
   B. Some potholes fixed promptly but not all.

The scope of the problem emerges in the third outline and changes the premise:

The city seems to be neglecting some roads. That puts residents in those areas at risk and could subject the city to hefty legal costs.

Outline 4

You now have a handle on the scope, but you still want to know how dangerous the potholes are and you have some new questions to ask: Why is the city failing to adequately maintain its streets considering how many people file complaints? As previously discussed, the answer to one set of questions often leads to another set.

You request data on the staffing levels of the city public works department, its budget and all records regarding repair and maintenance of city streets for the past year. You find out that the department has only half the personnel it would have if fully staffed. You discover that the city has slashed the public works budget 5 percent for each of the past five years and has plans to cut it again. You speak to an expert, an economist, and learn that with cost-of-living wage increases and the rising cost of construction material, the cuts are effectively equal to a 10 percent cut.

Exhibit 10.9 is your fourth outline. You can now see the story taking shape.

EXHIBIT 10.9   The fourth outline.

Outline 4

1. Potholes are becoming a big problem
    A. At least 27 potholes over a one-year period concerned people enough to file complaints.
    B. At least one car crash as a result.
    C. City records show 75 people complained in the past year.
    D. Some residents feel the situation remains dangerous:
        • Holly Homeowner worries someone will get killed.
        • Molly Most worries about her children on the bus.

2. The city doesn't respond to calls.
    A. Lawsuits
        • At least one person crashed car because of a big pothole.
        • If successful, lawsuits could cost city financially.
    B. At least one person complained of city's failure to respond to complaints.

3. Public Works Department.
    A. Budget slashed.
    B. Understaffed.
    C. Some potholes fixed faster than others.

In the fourth outline, new information changes your premise:

> Because of budget cuts, the city appears to be neglecting roads in some parts of the city, leaving residents there at risk and spurring lawsuits over accidents.

Outline 5

At this point, you have enough information that you can think about the overall shape of your story. While you are between interviews or waiting for documents, you look through your notes to find a possible lead. Exhibit 10.10 is the fifth outline you write in preparation for your first story draft.

The fifth outline.   **EXHIBIT 10.10**

Outline 5

1. Tentative lead: Every time a car would drive down Holly Homeowner's street last year, she would hold her breath. One of these days, she knew, a car would hit the pothole at the end of the street and spin out of control. That's what finally happened to Joe Resident.

2. City streets are filled with dangerous potholes.
   A. In the past year 75 people complained of 27 potholes.

3. Some potholes were repaired faster than others.
   A. The city's public works department has been underfunded for at least five years.
   B. It now operates at half its full staffing level.
   C. That means that not all streets can get adequate attention.

4. People like Joe Resident are turning to the courts for relief.
   A. This might cost taxpayers more in the long run.

Outline 6

Now you start to track down all 75 of the people who filed complaints with the city. You set up interviews with the head of the public works department and the mayor. You go to the court to get the full case file of the Joe Resident lawsuit. You do a LexisNexis search of all suits filed against the city for the past year. You call two cities that have a population roughly the size of yours and that have the same general climate conditions and find out their public works staffing levels, the size of their budgets and, anecdotally, whether they have pothole problems. You want to see if staffing in your city is less than or greater than staffing levels at comparable cities. You map out the potholes that people complained about. In addition, you get the addresses for every member of the city council and plot them against the potholes to see if a correlation exists between the ones that were repaired quickly and the ones that were ignored. You include the address of the director of public works, and it turns out that the closer the pothole is to the public works director's house, the faster the pothole got repaired.

Exhibit 10.11 shows your new outline. As you can see, it is looking more like a full story.

EXHIBIT 10.11   The sixth outline.

Outline 6

1. Tentative lead: City residents who don't live near Public Works Director Bob Cat better watch out for potholes on the road home. There seem to be more of them the farther away they live from his house. Joe Resident didn't know that when his car hit a pothole and crashed last November. Nor did Holly Homeowner, who held her breath each time she saw someone drive over a big pothole on her street. She knew that someday someone would crash their car when they hit it too fast. She called the city to make sure they fixed it. They didn't. She called again and again.

2. Repairing of potholes
    A. Some potholes get filled faster than others.
    B. There seems to be a pattern related to the location of the home of Public Works Director Bob Cat.

3. Residents have complained and been ignored.
    A. Homeowner and Most are just two of 75 people.

4. Spending on public works
    A. Budget cuts.
    B. Department is underfunded.
    C. Department operates at half its full staffing level.

5. Courts intervene
    A. Who is suing the city.
    B. What it could cost taxpayers in the long run.

Your premise changes once again:

The city's public works department is prioritizing road repairs in a way that benefits the department's chief. And that's contributing to the dangerous condition of some roads, putting the lives of residents at risk.

In the beginning, you might be able to jot an outline quickly on a whiteboard, in a page of your notebook or in a word processing document. But in a sizable investigation you will gather a significant amount of information from many different sources. Much of it will be tangential or contradictory. You won't be sure if and how it connects. Most investigations aren't as neat as the one shaping up against the public works director. The best stories aren't black and white; they are much more complicated than that. To stay on top of a more complicated story, let's see what a spreadsheet can do for you.

USING A SPREADSHEET TO OUTLINE YOUR STORY

Remember the spreadsheet you created in Chapter 6 to organize your interviews? If you entered your interviews into a spreadsheet in the first place, you won't have to re-enter them repeatedly as your investigation and your outlines progress. Instead you can note the major points and tangential issues each piece of information suggests and then sort them in order to consolidate them according to the points or tangents they represent. Your outline will emerge out of this sorting process.

Even if you did not use a spreadsheet to organize your interviews, it can still be used to outline. The benefit of letting a spreadsheet help you outline your information is that it becomes a living document that grows and changes as your project progresses. In it you can organize and reorganize your information each time you add to it. It also helps you pull out pieces of information without losing track of where the information came from.

In Chapter 6, I showed you how to enter into a spreadsheet the notes from the Joe Resident and Holly Homeowner interviews and to add a column called "Major Points." Now you can see why using a few key words can help you spot patterns. When you sort the spreadsheet by the "Major Points" column, your spreadsheet program will group together all the statements that suggest that potholes cause accidents. It will be a visual status report of how thoroughly you proved that point in your investigation. It might crystallize for you the importance of information that you might otherwise have understated. Recall from Chapter 7 that it was only toward the end of their investigation that the Newsday reporters realized that elderly people who were allowed to wander out of assisted living centers were the most compelling part of their story. An outline created in a spreadsheet program could get you to recognize the most convincing aspect of your story earlier in your investigation.

You may have already entered interview notes into your spreadsheet. But you also want to add to your project spreadsheet any relevant information that you obtained from documents, data and other information sources. Treat each document and piece of data as information you gleaned from an interview. What questions did you ask of it and what information did it give you? If you do this, you can start connecting the dots in your story by sorting the information in your spreadsheet. Enter the information from your data and documents using the same steps you used for the interviews.

Sorting the findings

To stay organized, you'll want to do any sorting or manipulating of your findings on a separate sheet rather than on the one that you entered your interviews, documents and data into. To do this, highlight all the cells in your spreadsheet. An easy way is to click the icon in the upper left-hand corner of your spreadsheet. Then open a new sheet in the same workbook and paste the cells there. Because you created different names for the cells in each interview and anchored the notes in the "Answer" column with a hyperlink, you won't forget where the information came from and you can easily refer to your original documents.

Appreciating the power of a spreadsheet program such as Excel for outlining is difficult until you consider a project that involves as many as a hundred interviews, pages and pages of documents and reams of data spread over dozens of notebooks. An essential piece of information might be buried in an otherwise long, tedious and useless interview. But if you noted that piece of information under "Major Points," Excel will find it for you and group it with the rest of the essential information from the other interviews when you sort by "Major Points."

To see how that would work, let's return to the first interview. If you entered Joe Resident's information in Excel and then sorted the spreadsheet by the "Major Points" column, you will see the initial outline in Exhibit 10.12.

Now we add the Homeowner interview to the spreadsheet. If we sort it again, Exhibit 10.13 shows how the outline in the "Major Points" column now

EXHIBIT 10.12 The Joe Resident interview sorted by "Major Points."

Joe Resident and Holly Homeowner interviews sorted by "Major Points."   **EXHIBIT 10.13**

	Person Interviewe	Question	Answer	Major Points
	A	C	D	E
2	**Joe Resident**	So why sue the city?	He thinks it might be the only way to get the city to take care of the roads.	People are suing
3	**Holly Homeowner**	Did you call anyone about it?	She complained to the city three times. "Once I went down and filled out a form they had. But nothing happened."	People have complained to the city
4	**Joe Resident**	Why do you think the city is responsible?	"A woman down the road said she had called the city three times to warn them about the pothole and get them to fix it."	People have complained to the city
5	**Joe Resident**	Why are you suing the city?	"I crashed my car because I hit a pothole the city should have fixed."	Potholes cause accidents
6	**Joe Resident**	What happened?	"I was driving along, hit the hole and my car popped up. I lost control of it and hit a telephone pole."	Potholes cause accidents
7	**Holly Homeowner**	Has it caused problems?	Joe Resident crashed his car. "But every time I saw someone drive down the street I would hold my breath. I just knew someone would hit it going a little too fast."	Potholes cause accidents
8	**Holly Homeowner**	Do you know how fast Joe went when he hit it?	"It doesn't really matter because any faster than a crawl over that hole is too dangerous. But you don't see it until you are on top of it. Anyone who knows drives over it like you would a speed bump, but the speed limit is 25 here. And if you drove over that hole at 25, well... "	Potholes cause accidents
9	**Holly Homeowner**	How long has it been like that?	Since the fall, at least. "Long enough for my kids to name it."	The problem has existed for some time
10	**Holly Homeowner**	Have potholes been a problem.	"Well, there is that one that you can see right here from my front door. We call it the Grand Canyon."	The problem is serious
11	**Joe Resident**	How bad was the accident?	"My car was totaled. The front just accordioned in. My back has been killing me ever since."	The problem is serious

Sheet1   Sheet2   Sheet3   Sheet4   +

looks. For this example, I drew a border around the groups of "Major Points," which you can do using the border tool on the formatting toolbar.

If you color-coded your information by interview source, then you will see, in the "Major Points" sort, whenever many different sources back a major point. Add notes from a third interview and resort by "Major Points" to see how the new information fits into your outline and when new major points come up, as shown in Exhibit 10.14.

Another way to visualize your story is to leave certain columns visible while making the rest invisible (using "Format > Columns > Hide" commands) and then "Merge" the visible boxes that share the same major points ("Format > Cells > Merge"). You will want to do this on a new worksheet, however, because Excel doesn't allow you to sort a worksheet after you have merged cells.

After having merged the visible boxes that share the same major points, we will see in Exhibit 10.15 that the outline has become clearer. It now shows

EXHIBIT 10.14 Joe Resident, Holly Homeowner and Molly Most interviews sorted by "Major Points."

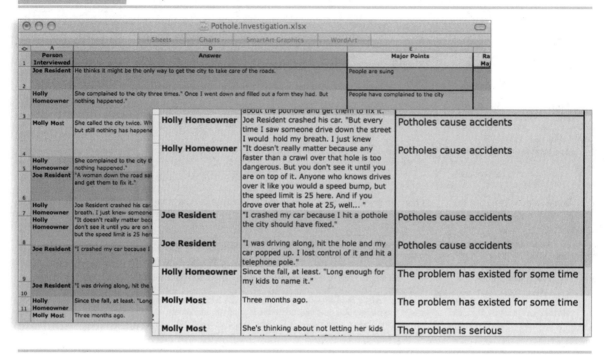

EXHIBIT 10.15 Merged "Major Points" on a separate sheet.

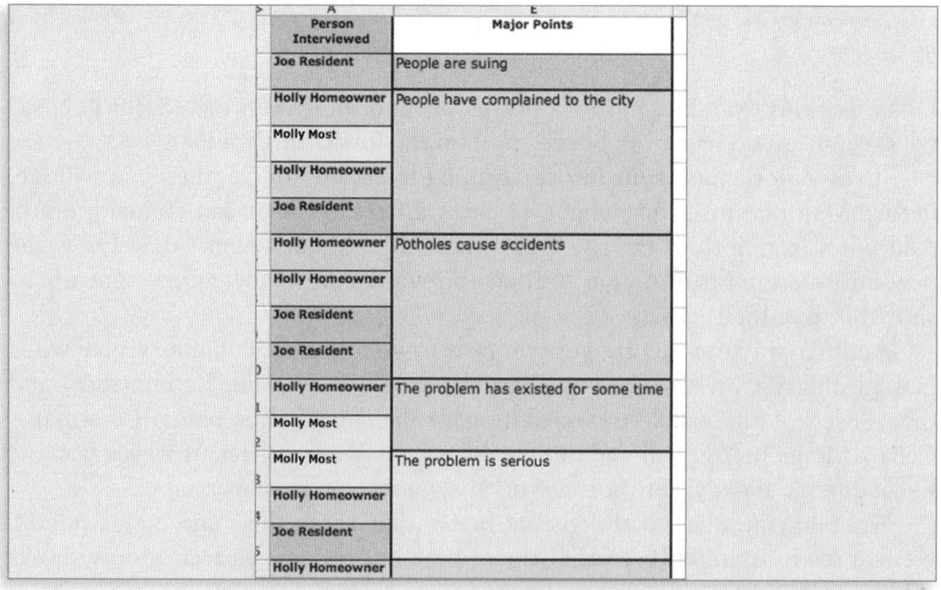

the different people who supported the different points. Again, this ability becomes more valuable the more interviews you do and the more data and documents you sift through.

Ranking the findings to create an outline

Excel can't measure the importance of one text entry over another, it can only sort your major points alphabetically. So add another column and call it "Major Points Ranked." You will find this works best if done before you merge any cells together. Go through each of the points and rank them according to your own measurement of their importance. When you sort, the "Answer" and "Major Points" columns will look more like the outline for a first draft. Exhibit 10.16 shows how ranking and sorting the major points yields information on how much support you have for each point and gives you a strong story outline.

Many investigative reporters take the time to master a sophisticated spreadsheet program because it is a powerful tool for analyzing massive amounts of information. If you write the right formula structure (in Excel called a "Function") using one of a myriad of possible formulas (in Excel through the "Formula Builder"), it will search through your data, find information you seek and compare it. Box 10.1 walks you through one example, creating a formula that will fill in the "Rankings" column for you, based on what is entered as a major point.

Full interview notes with "Major Points" ranked and sorted.   **EXHIBIT 10.16**

	A Person Interviewed	D Answer	E Major Points	F Rank
2	Holly Homeowner	Joe Resident crashed his car. "But every time I saw someone drive down the street I would hold my breath. I just knew someone would hit it going a little too fast."	Potholes cause accidents	1
3		"It doesn't really matter because any faster than a crawl over that hole is too dangerous. But you don't see it until you are on top of it. Anyone who knows drives over it like you would a speed bump, but the speed		1
4	Joe Resident	"I crashed my car because I hit a pothole the city should have fixed."		1
5		"I was driving along, hit the hole and my car popped up. I lost control of it and hit a telephone pole."		1
6	Molly Most	She's thinking about not letting her kids take the bus to school. But that means that she will have to drive them and she won't be able to make it to work on time that way.	The problem is serious	2
7	Holly Homeowner	"Well, there is that one that you can see right here from my front door. We call it the Grand Canyon."		2
8	Joe Resident	"My car was totaled. The front just accordioned in. My back has been killing me ever since."		2
9	Holly Homeowner	She complained to the city three times. "Once I went down and filled out a form they had. But nothing happened."	People have complained to the city	3
10	Molly Most	She called the city twice. When nothing happened she went to city hall. A man said it would be fixed but still nothing has happened.		3
11	Public Works Records	75 complaints about 27 different potholes over the past year.		3
12	Joe Resident	"A woman down the road said she had called the city three times to warn them about the pothole and get them to fix it."		3
13	Holly Homeowner	Since the fall, at least. "Long enough for my kids to name it."	The problem has existed for some time	4
14	Molly Most	Three months ago.		4
15	Joe Resident	He thinks it might be the only way to get the city to take care of the roads.	People are suing	5
	Holly	"I gave up back in June."		

Using the IF function to automatically rank data   BOX 10.1

magine the project with 100 sources of information — interviews, data, documents, and so on. You entered into Excel all the information that you deemed possibly relevant to your investigation. You noted the different major points that each belonged to. Now you want to rank them, but you are looking at the prospect of assigning rankings to hundreds of rows of materials. Instead, you can tell Excel to do it for you as long as you tell it which major points get which ranking. For that you need an **IF function.**

Let's see how it handles the simple but laborious task of assigning rankings. Here is the list of major points with the rank we want to assign to them:

Potholes cause accidents.	1
The problem is serious.	2
People have complained to the city.	3
The problem has existed for some time.	4
People are suing.	5

We want to tell Excel to assign the number 1 if it finds that a cell in the "Major Points" column contains the phrase "Potholes cause accidents," to assign the number 2 if it finds the phrase "The problem is serious," and so on.

The **IF function** works like this:

IF(logical_test,value_if_true,value_if_false)

A logical test could be equal to, or greater or less than. Our logical test is whether the information in the "Major Points" column is equal to a particular phrase. This is the formula we write and we type it in the first cell of the "Rank" column. Let's say that the "Major Points" column is D and the first cell is 2. We type:

=IF(D2="Potholes cause accidents","1",IF(D2="The problem is serious","2",IF(D2="People have complained to the city","3",IF(D2="The problem has existed for some time","4",IF(D2="People are suing","5")))))

It will then choose what number to put into the accompanying cells in the "Rank" column, according to your instructions. If the information in a cell doesn't match any of those, it will enter FALSE.

Copy the formula that you wrote in cell D2 into every other cell in the D column. To do that you just need to right-click on the cell, select "Copy," then click on the cell again and drag down the column as far as you want to apply the formula. Then right-click and select "Paste." Excel will assign rankings to every cell according your instructions, whether you have 10 rows or 10,000.

Now you just have to sort the "Rank" column and you have a rough outline for your first draft. If you decide to change rankings, you just do it once in the formula in the first cell of the column and then recopy the changed formula to the rest of the boxes. Excel will automatically reassign the rankings, and you can sort again to reorganize the outline. The "Major Points" and "Rank" columns will look something like Exhibit 10.17.

Using a spreadsheet may seem like a tedious process for a simple story, but when you have a complicated story that involves lots of pieces of information from many different sources, this process can help you sort through it all very quickly. The trick is entering the information into Excel in the first place and making notes in different columns of the major points that each piece of information suggests. You can also make notes in a separate "Leads" column when any piece of information suggests a possible lead for your story; then after you've done dozens of interviews, you can bring those possible leads to the top by sorting the spreadsheet by the "Leads" column as you did with the "Major Points" column.

CONCLUSION

Many reporters can handle the information-gathering process. They know how to write. But when it comes to organization, they have difficulty. It takes work to make sense out of a mess of information and turn an assortment of facts, anecdotes and details into a compelling read. In a big, complicated story, you can't go straight from gathering the information to writing the story. You will lose your reader. You will need to take your reader slowly through the story because you want your reader to fully understand the problem. But to do that you must fully understand it yourself. Outlines help you work through your story, prioritize the information you collected and string it together into a structure that makes sense.

EXHIBIT 10.17

The sorted "Major Points" and "Rank" columns.

E Major Points	F Rank
Potholes cause accidents	1
	1
	1
	1
The problem is serious	2
	2
	2
People have complained to the city	3
	3
	3
	3
	3
The problem has existed for some time	4
	4
People are suing	5

EXERCISES

1. Do five person-on-street interviews with students on your campus about crime on or around the campus. After the first interview, create an outline of the information you gathered from it. From it, develop a premise as if this interview were an investigation into campus crime. Re-outline after each subsequent interview and see if your premise changes. Finally, find the Clery Act crime data for your campus and pull out of it relevant information about crimes. Re-outline your story with that data.

2. As a class, each student should write on a piece of paper the top three problems facing this country and try to be as specific as possible. On a whiteboard list all the answers. Now try to consolidate those problems to five broader issues. Now rank those issues according to the number of students who named that issue as a problem. From that list come up with a story premise. If you had to turn this into a story, what would be your lead?

THE BIG STORY Project • THE BIG STORY Project • STEP 10

10.1 Go through every interview and jot down the major points on a blackboard or on a wiki spreadsheet. Do the same for the data you collected and the documents and reports you gathered. Try to consolidate the points into five major groupings. How do they relate to your premise? Now is the time to change your premise if you need to.

10.2 Look for contradictions or shades of gray to explore in a sidebar. Try to order the groupings by level of importance.

10.3 See if you can find one interviewee who connects all the points and who can serve as a narrative thread.

10.4 Write up a tentative lead and a nut graph that summarizes all the major points in the story.

10.5 Brainstorm ways to end the story.

10.6 What are the holes in your story that you still need to fill? Who can answer the questions the holes raise, or where might you find the data that will fill the holes?

10.7 Write up a new To Do list to fill in the holes.

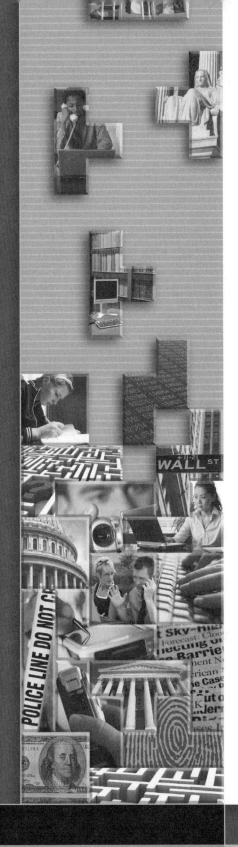

Writing the Story

CHAPTER PREVIEW You will be writing your story using a simplified process of multiple drafts. You will learn how to conquer the fear of the blank page to create a cohesive story or set of stories that are complete, clear, convincing and compelling. Following a four-stage process, you will concentrate on one of those goals in each draft. You will acquire the skill of breaking up long stories using sidebars, boxes and bullets. Finally, you will get an overview of writing as part of a team investigation.

11

CONQUERING THE BLANK SCREEN

S ometimes it seems as if the blank page is more intimidating than the most fearsome person you have ever interviewed. Publication never seems so far off as when you sit down to actually write the story. By this time, your head will be so clogged with information that it might seem to be one big mess. Even though you worked through an outline and reworked it over and over to the point where it seemed just right, when you sit down to write the story the outline is just your starting point.

Writing the story may be the most difficult part of the investigative process. To write the story you must feel comfortable enough with your conclusions to publish them. But chances are, you will want more time. You may fear that you need to get more information and interview more people before you can be sure. Some investigative projects never get completed simply because the journalist can't break off the process.

Know that you won't exhaust all possible sources; the number of possible sources or documents is almost infinite. Instead, start writing as soon as you have some evidence to support your hypothesis.

THE DRAFTING PROCESS

I n guiding you through the process of carrying out an investigative story from premise to publication, I am going to simplify the writing stage. In reality, reporters work through many versions before they feel it is good enough to go to print. Instead, I am going to take you through a shorter process to serve as a jumping off point.

For starters, you can't default to an inverted pyramid structure. To hold your readers through a big story to the end, you can't stuff the most important information at the top. You need to weave it throughout the story. Just as their attention begins to flag, you shake them and say, "Wait! There's this too!" Just when they think they've got it all down, you tell them something else that gets them to say, "Wow! I had no idea!"

Over time you will develop your own system, but for now you can start by following the 4Cs system. It involves four drafts, based on the four Cs, or criteria, your story must meet:

1. Complete
2. Clear
3. Convincing
4. Compelling

First draft: Making it complete

For the first go, try to write a story that has as few holes as possible. Concentrate on presenting the problem and giving the reader more than enough information to understand what is going on. If you lay blame, now is the time to make sure your evidence is solid while you still have plenty of time to go back for added support, if needed.

Think about the central characters

Take time before you start tossing the information on the screen to identify the individuals at the heart of your story. The story about inadequate inspections of elevators isn't about elevators or regulations. It is about the people who ride the elevators and expect them to work. The story on potholes is a story about the people who must drive on bad roads and residents who worry about safety.

Identify the problem

After you identify the people in the story, identify the problem at the heart of the story. Is it potholes or budget cuts to a needed service? Is it wasted taxpayer resources? Is it a corrupt government? Go back to your premise. Now scan your notes and remind yourself why the problem exists and how it works. Clay Felker, the legendary founder of New York Magazine, used to tell writers to give readers a situation. The two things people want to know, he would say, are why things are the way they are and how things work.[1] In the course of laying out the what, why and how, you will detail the when and where and explain the possible solutions that exist. You should be able to go back to the major points you identified in your last outline and assign them to five different sections:

1. What the problem is.
2. Why it is happening.
3. How it works.
4. How we got here.
5. What solutions could solve it or lessen the harm.

If you are working with a spreadsheet, add a column next to the one for "Major Points" and call it "Sections." Then try assigning one major point to each of the above sections. If you have 10 major points, it will force you to consolidate them. The more complicated your story, the more simply you need to tell it so that you won't lose your reader.

Put in everything that makes your case

From your notes use everything you think the reader should know. Don't worry about the perfect lead or the perfect kicker. For now, don't worry about the length. Later, you will think about length and how to present the story under space constraints.

Now toss everything to the screen one section at a time. But be prepared. It will seem like a mess. First drafts are ugly. They tend to be disorganized, tedious and boring. You may doubt whether anyone will care. Have faith.

Make your case as airtight as possible. When you find holes, you know you've got some reporting left to do. Make those calls now. It is common to find holes when you do your first draft, and often you may not fully understand the story yourself until you sit down to write. When you attempt to write the first draft, questions may pop into your head that become obvious only at this stage.

Second draft: Making it clear

Now take the disorganized first draft and give it clarity, which means that you don't want to confuse your readers. Making your story clear is a challenge with a complicated story. For many reporters this stage may be the most tedious part of the writing process. Once you master clarity, then you can concentrate on making the story compelling and convincing, which many reporters find more enjoyable.

Write for the reader. The danger at this point in your project is that you are too immersed in your story. You interviewed so many people, you read so many reports and you stuffed your head with so many facts and figures, that you can't think like someone new to the topic. You now understand terms and concepts that you didn't at the start of your investigation. Mentally you need to revert to that time. Anything that you had to learn along the way, any concepts you needed explained to you, you now have to explain to your readers. Don't underestimate the importance of this task. Your goal is to inform people of something important that is not widely known. But people will stop reading what they don't understand. And all your effort will be wasted if no one reads it.

So take a deep breath. Do yoga or take a walk. Have a cup of coffee or a snack. You need to clear your head of all the information crowded in it. If you fail to clear your head before you start this second draft, you could end up with one that is tedious and convoluted.

Achieving clarity is a four-step process:

1. Eliminate the nonessentials.
2. Add back information.
3. Give the story scale.
4. Set up a structure.

1. Eliminate the nonessentials

The central question right now is this: What does your reader need to know? In the framework of your second draft, include only that information needed to identify the problem, explain why it exists and how it can be solved.

As you write, you will find that you need to eliminate much of the information that you have gathered. Pioneering muckraker Lincoln Steffens once said, "I never tell all of the truth. I don't have to — one-tenth is sufficient to make any decent man rise feeling outraged."[2]

While you needed to gather the information in order to understand the problem, the reader doesn't need to know all of it and telling the story doesn't demand that every detail be included. What gets left behind? Interviews you had to wrangle for, information from reports tedious to read, data difficult to analyze and wonderful anecdotes and killer quotes that aren't relevant. Here, the Cut command is your friend. But save the deletions in a separate file. Some of them may end up back in the story.

2. Add back information

Read through what you have, and, at the end of every paragraph, ask yourself this question: Will the reader be confused? After you strip your story to its essentials, return to the cut material and add back enough background information or details so that the reader *easily* understands what you say. Just because you worked hard getting the story doesn't mean that the reader should work hard reading it. The opposite is true. The *reason* you worked hard is so that the reader won't have to.

As you write, imagine that you are telling your story out loud to a person you know. He's at your side, listening intently. But just as you gather steam, he pokes you in the arm and says: "Hold on. I don't get it." So you stop and explain. You don't get back to the next part of your story until he nods and says: "Oh, now I get it, go on." He keeps doing that as you try to tell your story. With all those explanations, your text will seem choppy. But it doesn't have to be elegant on the second draft. It just has to be complete and clear.

3. Give the story scale

When you cite statistics or data, bring them down to a scale the reader can understand. You might write that the city spends $15 million to repair potholes. The problem with such a large sum is that it doesn't mean much to the reader. But it will if you say that the number represents $75 per resident or $5,000 a pothole, or if you add that most cities half the size spend $20 million, or if you say that an average-sized pothole typically costs no more than $1,500 to fix.

So do the math. Don't make your reader calculate. If you cannot put your numbers into perspective without additional reporting, this is the time to do that extra reporting.

4. Set up a structure

This step will transition you to your third draft. For your reader to follow the story, it must be organized. You need a solid structure. You should choose a format that seems to work best for the story you want to tell and for the information that you gathered. You can be creative with your structure. But you cannot write a story as stream of consciousness or unplanned prose.

The five structures discussed below will provide a starting point from which you can build your subsequent drafts.

The Focus Structure.   From the Missouri Group's book, "Beyond the Inverted Pyramid," this structure focuses on one person who can illustrate the problem. You can start with a descriptive or anecdotal lead and then transition to a theme paragraph that tells the reader what the story is about.[3] This is what is known as the *nut graph;* it gets at the nut or the gist of the story. In the Internet age, readers have an endless choice of stories they can read. They will skim headlines and the first few graphs that appear on a Web page to pick the ones they think will interest them. If you want them to read your story you *must* tell them in advance what they will get. They won't read anything on faith.

"A Tragic Vulnerability," discussed in Chapter 7, is written in this style. The first seven paragraphs are an anecdotal lead: How Ethel Danzker froze to death when she wandered out of Birchwood Assisted Living and how that affected her daughter. The next four make up the nut graph. It explains how big the problem is and how bad it is.

After the theme, give the readers just enough material to whet their appetite for more. The Missouri Group calls this a *teaser graph,* or *foreshadowing.* In "A Tragic Vulnerability," the teaser graph tells the reader that some centers have increased their security but that the problem continues.

Then the body of the story is the evidence to support the theme. To end it, you bring back the person you focused on in the lead. Finally, the Newsday story brings Danzker's daughter back at the end.

The Chronological Structure.   In the second structure suggested by the Missouri Group, you organize your information chronologically. This type of structure works well when you recreate the events that led up to a problem. The culmination should be something dramatic. You don't have to go from beginning to end. You could start at the culmination and then flash back to the beginning. Think of the movie "Gandhi," which opens with the assassination of Mahatma Gandhi, then goes to South Africa where he started out as a young lawyer. Or you can start in the middle of the story at a particularly exciting point. Think of the beginning of "The Lord of the Rings," which starts at the birthday disappearance of Bilbo Baggins. The reader learns later that a lot happened before that point. The story "Nobody's Fault" (found in Appendix A.3) follows that structure. It begins with a suicide of James Lee Peters in a county jail and then takes readers through his life from birth. It returns to the suicide near the end, where it presents the details of how he managed to hang himself.

The chronological structure also works if the story centers on something about which the reader is already familiar. In this case, the general knowledge of the event is what threads the narrative and what keeps the reader grounded.

The Converging Narrative Structure.   In this structure you tell a story by the different perspectives of the people in it. For it to work, you first need to figure out the essential elements, and then find the different people who can take the readers through each element. This works well for going step-by-step through a natural disaster or an epidemic. Former San Francisco Chronicle reporter Randy Shilts used converging narrative to map out the beginning of the AIDS epidemic in his now classic book "And the Band Played On." Shilts let the reader see the beginnings of the spread of HIV through the eyes of an early carrier of the disease, and of the doctors and nurses who start seeing the patients come through their offices and emergency rooms.[4]

The MacGuffin Structure.   You might have your readers follow someone or something through a meandering story. It could be something that everyone wants or that people fight over — a piece of property, a legislative bill, water rights, and so on. The term "MacGuffin" was used by film director Alfred Hitchcock to describe something that is central to the plot — in the movie "39 Steps" it was plans for a bomb, in "Foreign Correspondent" it was a missing diplomat and in the "Trouble With Harry" it was a dead body. Author Michael Pollan used this approach in 2002 when he wanted to explain to readers of the New York Times Magazine the ins and outs of the cattle industry. His story "Power Steer" begins with an 8-month-old calf he bought for $598 and tracks the calf to slaughter. Along the way, Pollan tells readers more than they ever expected to learn about the meat industry.[5]

The ABCDE Structure.   Writer Anne Lamott, in her book on writing, "Bird by Bird: Some Instructions and Writing on Life," suggested an ABCDE outline for fictional stories. But it also works well for nonfiction: Action, Background, Conflict, Development, End.[6] Here is an example of how it works with the pothole story:

- **Action:** Molly Most watches as the school bus approaches her house and says a silent prayer each time it drives over that massive pothole on her street.

- **Background:** Her fears are justified. Joe Resident crashed his car on a pothole. He, Most, and other residents say the city neglects the roads and puts peoples lives at risk.

- **Conflict:** City budget cuts mean that any money for road repairs has to come from other services. The skeleton crew in the public works department is scrambling to keep up with the problem.

- **Development:** Moving the story forward. Lawsuits against the city could cost it even more money.

- **End:** Back to Molly Most and her kids.

Third draft: Making it convincing

To convince readers of your premise, you need to give them evidence in the form of examples, data and confirmation by documents and experts. So while in the first draft you stripped out anything that reeked of repetition, in the third draft you may add some back. You need to be able to say to your readers, "Here is what is happening and we know that because of this evidence." You might recall that trend stories are built on the idea of three. If you find just one of something, it could be a freak occurrence. Two could be a coincidence. But if you find three examples, it probably means that even more exist. Three is a convincing number. If you give readers three examples or a combination of examples, evidential data and a confirmation by an expert, you will convince them that there is a big problem. Box 11.1 shows a Focus Structure based on sets of three. You can work the other story structures around sets of three as well.

Don't overload your story with examples. You don't want the reader to say, "Enough, already! I get it!" It is about quality, not quantity. Include only your most telling examples and only as many as you need to be convincing. That means that you will have to abandon some good anecdotes, quotes and examples. But they still serve an important purpose. Louise Kiernan, the writing coach at the

---

Using sets of threes with the Focus Structure   BOX 11.1

LEAD: An anecdote or scene setter that pulls the reader in.

NUT GRAPH: Summary of your five sections: What the problem is; why it is happening; how it works; how we got here; solutions that could solve it or lessen the harm.

QUOTE THAT ILLUSTRATES THE PROBLEM AND WHETS THE READER'S APPETITE FOR MORE.

A. What the problem is:

- Example A1
- Example A2
- Example A3

QUOTE OR ANECDOTE TO SUMMARIZE THE PROBLEM AND TRANSITION TO NEXT SECTION.

B. Why the problem is happening:

- Example B1
- Evidential data B2
- Comment from expert B3

Transition to next section.

C. How it all works:

- Explanation from expert C1
- Anecdote from stakeholder C2
- Personal observation C3

Transition to next section.

D. How we got here:

- Anecdote D1
- Trendline data D2
- Expert quote D3 that transitions to next section

E. Solutions:

- Statement from expert E1
- Example of how it's done elsewhere.
- Example of how it's done elsewhere.

END: Quote that brings you back to the start or summarizes the frustration of the people affected.

Chicago Tribune said what doesn't make it into the story serves to strengthen *your* confidence in the story and that makes the story itself stronger.[7]

Fourth draft: Making it compelling

Don't put your readers to sleep. Instead shake them awake. A history of horse racing in the United States might bore most readers, but the book "Seabiscuit" by Laura Hillenbrand is a gripping read and became a best-selling sensation in 2000 because she wove together thrilling anecdotes filled with vivid details, action and tension. The book is part converging narrative (the story is about a horse trainer, a jockey and Seabiscuit's owner, Charles Howard) and part MacGuffin (Seabiscuit serves as the central object that the story revolves around).[8]

You wove into your story all the information you needed to inform your readers about a problem, explained how it happened and what should be done about it, and convinced them that the problem is important. But you also need it to be a story that draws them in and forces them to stay from beginning to end. It needs to be written in such a way that once they are done reading, they can't stop thinking about it. You can add these qualities to your story in two ways: Weave in gripping details and control the pace of the narrative through the story.

Compelling details

In this last draft, you want to make your readers care. That's why you need to include key elements that carry the reader through each paragraph and compel them to the end. Earlier I suggested that you clear your head with yoga or a cup of coffee. Now you need to clear your head by putting aside — momentarily — that third draft you worked so hard on. That's because in going for clarity, and concentrating on making it complete and convincing, you likely left out powerful details and startling facts. So reread your notes and see if there is anything in them that would help make your reader care.

In Brady Averill's story, "If These Walls Could Talk," it wasn't essential to add that a student's dirty closet could be the breeding ground for mice, but it's enough to shock the reader into staying with the story to find out what's going on.

Story movement

Tom French, a Pulitzer Prize-winning writer at the St. Petersburg Times and a guru of narrative writing, said that to make your writing powerful you need to understand how to use action, tension and pace. Each paragraph should drive the reader to read the paragraph that follows.[9]

Rising action.   One way you do that is through rising action. Consider the section of text in Box 11.2, which is from the collaborative story "A Stunning Toll."

Rising action in "A Stunning Toll"   BOX 11.2

"While others in his age group might have been bar-hopping and ducking into alleys to puke, Goodchild — a vegetarian for 11 years who walks with a limp left from a run-in with a truck when he was a teen-ager — chose a spot on that evening in February 2005 and began to play in celebration of his birthday a couple of days earlier.

"That's when the cops came up — three or four, he recalls — and one offered what Goodchild first thought was just free and friendly advice: You need a permit to play live music on an Austin street.

"Goodchild said he asked where and how he could get one.

"'If you don't have a permit,' he recalled one officer saying, 'we're going to send you to jail.'

"'You can't send me to jail for playing guitar.'

"'I bet I can.'

"He thought it was a joke, Goodchild said, until an officer grabbed his guitar, saying it could be used — think of El Kabong cartoons — as a weapon. Goodchild held onto his cherished instrument, but the officers jerked him to his feet, he said, and two played tug-of-war with his arms. One jumped onto his left side and slammed him to the concrete on his right arm, busting open his right cheek.

"The officers ordered him to get his right arm behind his back, he said, but it was pinned under him, and they wouldn't let him up. That's when he felt electricity throttling his nervous system, 'like touching a live wire or putting my hand in a socket.'"

You can read the full story in Appendix A.6.

The story starts with one man playing guitar. Then it brings in several police officers who offer what seems to be simple advice. A bit of dialog ends with the idea of Goodchild going to jail. Then the police officers grab the guitar and use it as a weapon. One slams him against the concrete, injuring him. Finally, the officers zap Goodchild with electricity.

Rising action is the *opposite* of inverted pyramid, where you start with your most important information. Instead you build up to that. You start with something small, slow or quiet. Then you add to it little by little, each time making it more: bigger, faster, louder. Rising action doesn't have to focus on something bad. You could build up to beauty or elation. When done by a master, the reader is left breathless.

Tension.   Another technique is to use tension. All good stories center around conflict and tension comes out of conflict. You identified the conflict in your story when you identified the people responsible for a problem and the people the problem affects. You have conflict when you have people who will benefit from the status quo and people who want change or when one person's solution is another person's problem. In "A Stunning Toll," the conflict is the perceived need for police to control the people they arrest versus a person's right not to have police inflict pain. You will have tension when you adequately represent the perspectives of all sides in your conflict.

Pace. The speed at which you tell different parts of your story is its pace. It's a counterintuitive process, French said. The faster or more powerful the action, the slower you should relate it. The slower and more tedious your information, the faster you should take the reader through it.[10] In "A Stunning Toll," the authors devote 106 words to explaining the circumstances under which guards in the McLennan County Jail tase inmates. The information came out of incident reports and have to do with jail procedure, which could make for dull reading. So the writers give us just the relevant information and move on. They took much more time, which translates to more space, in the story of guitarist Trevor Goodchild.

Adding the final pieces

To add the final pieces, go back to your third draft and try to match up each paragraph of necessary information with the compelling elements you highlighted in your notes. Paragraph by paragraph, ask yourself these questions:

- Is there someone in my notes who can help me say this better?
- Do I have any anecdotes that can illustrate this?
- Are there any facts that will drive this point home?

Don't try to work a story around a great quote or an anecdote, and don't try to force in someone whose story you so want to tell but who takes the reader to a place that isn't necessary to the story. This process can be painful, because often the great interviews arise out of empathy. You connect with some of the people you interview and leaving them out of the story might feel heartless.

If you really feel you need to add these extra stories in, go back to those people. Run by them some or all the information that the story centers around. See what they think. When you first interviewed them, you didn't know where your story would end up. Now you do. Does it, and how does it, pertain to their experience? Do they agree or disagree? Can they recall a moment where they were in that exact or similar situation? Are they worried that it might happen again? The new comments they give you will be more relevant to your story.

USING STORY ELEMENTS EFFECTIVELY

The information you collect in the form of anecdotes, examples, data and expert commentary are the ingredients that make up your story. But use them appropriately. Otherwise, like the wrong spice in a recipe, they could overpower your story and change its flavor.

Quotes

Quotes may be the single most-effective storytelling device. But don't overuse them. A story told only through quotes is just as tedious a read as one with no quotes. As a writer, you can generally say something better than most people can speak it. But sometimes no one can quite describe something like the person affected.

Here's what you might write:

> Some voters think that City Councilman John Law is a hypocrite. He accepted political action campaign money from the Democratic Central Committee for the general election and this violates a promise he made to voters early in the campaign.

Here is how Raúl Resident describes it:

> "When John Law took that money he slapped us in the face," Raúl Resident said. "We nominated him because he said he would break the Democratic machine."

You also use quotes like Raúl Resident's when you need something said in a strong way, but you don't feel comfortable saying it yourself. But don't hide behind other people's quotes. Take the advice of Miami Herald editor Manny Garcia, who said, "Write without apology."[11] When you are done with a big story, it should be so thoroughly reported that you should be able to say things with confidence. If you can't, you need to make at least one more call. Never go to press with a story you aren't sure of. But once you are sure, don't couch your words.

Leads and kickers

You can start your story in innumerable ways, which is why crafting a good lead is so difficult. You want to grab the reader's attention and capture the essence of your story, and to do that you need to go beyond the simple 5Ws lead. Many people start with anecdotes because they do all of those things. Consider the following lead from a story about teenagers who work dangerous jobs:

> Four months after turning 15, Lucero Gayton began work on the night shift at a House of Raeford Farms chicken plant. Starting at 11 each night, when most girls her age were asleep, the shy teenager with brown eyes was working 10-hour shifts, wielding a sharp knife, cutting muscles from thousands of freshly killed chickens.[12]

But anecdotes aren't the only way to start a story. You could start with something surprising such as a fact or a description that the reader wouldn't expect or something that doesn't seem right.

USA Today reporters Blake Morrison and Brad Heath started their story about poor air quality this way:

> The growl of air-monitoring equipment has replaced the chatter of children at Meredith Hitchens Elementary School in this Cincinnati suburb along the Ohio River. School district officials pulled all students from Hitchens three years ago, after

Blake Morrison and Brad Heath's Story

www.usatoday.com/news/nation/environment/school-air1.htm

air samples outside the building showed high levels of chemicals coming from the plastics plant across the street. The levels were so dangerous that the Ohio EPA concluded the risk of getting cancer there was 50 times higher than what the state considers acceptable.[13]

James Sandler started this 2007 story, which appeared on Salon.org, like this:

> If there is any doubt about how the Bush administration treats government whistle-blowers, consider the case of Teresa Chambers. She was hired in early 2002, with impeccable law enforcement credentials, to become chief of the United States Park Police. But after Chambers raised concerns publicly that crime was up in the nation's parks, she was rebuked by superiors and fired. When Chambers fought to regain her job through the legal system meant to protect whistle-blowers, government lawyers fought back, and associated her with terrorists. Despite a multiyear legal struggle, she is still fighting for her job.[14]

James Sandler's Story
www.salon.com/
news/feature/2007/
11/01/whistleblowers

The trick to crafting a good lead is finding the idea in your notes. You need to search for a lead, rather than make one up. If you did enough investigating, it will be there in a story someone told you, a shocking fact or a piece of irony.

Put as much thought into your ending as into your lead. Tom French, the writing guru, likened writing to music and said that you need to build up to a crescendo so that you end on something quiet and beautiful or sad and painful. By the time you reach the end, the reader has stuck with you for a long time and through a lot of information. You can offer the reward of closure, of an ending you put significant thought into.[15]

If you end with a quote, you can give the last word to someone central to the story. It's a way of reminding the readers that even though your byline is on the story, it's not your story. You are just the one telling it. It's also a way of reminding the reader that the story isn't about a building or a piece of land or legislation or some notion of something. It's about real people.

You can use also end with a quote to underline an important concept. Consider the quote that Associated Press reporter Jean Heller used to end a story that broke open the Tuskegee study scandal. In 1972, she reported that the U.S. Public Health Service had been using black men as guinea pigs, withholding penicillin from them to study the effects of syphilis on the human body. Instead of ending with a quote from one of the people in the study or the family of someone who had participated in the study and died of syphilis, she ended with a Public Health Service official who argued that withholding penicillin didn't mean the people in the experiment didn't receive good care:

> "We see to it that they get a complete physical at least every two years," he said. "We can't treat them for syphilis but we can treat them for hernias and arthritis and any other problem they have. I guess you'd say we're doing all we can."[16]

That quote serves to emphasize the disconnect between the doctors and the people they treated and the tragic irony of the situation.

You can end a story in other ways. You could, for example, end with a startling conclusion. In 1977, Mother Jones writer Mark Dowie showed how Ford Motor Company knew for seven years that its Pinto automobile was designed in such a way that people would likely burn to death in low-speed rear-end collisions. He ended the piece this way:

> The original draft of the Motor Vehicle Safety Act provided for criminal sanction against a manufacturer who willfully placed an unsafe car on the market. Early in the proceedings the auto industry lobbied the provision out of the bill. Since then, there have been those damage settlements, of course, but the only government punishment meted out to auto companies for noncompliance to standards has been a minuscule fine, usually $5,000 to $10,000. One wonders how long the Ford Motor Company would continue to market lethal cars were Henry Ford II and Lee Iacocca serving 20-year terms in Leavenworth for consumer homicide.[17]

Mark Dowie's Story
www.motherjones.
com/news/feature/
1977/09/dowie.html

The story is more than 7,000 words long, but that was the only time in it that Dowie used the word "homicide." The whole story built up to that word. He ends telling the reader exactly what the point of the story was — that Mother Jones was accusing one of the biggest companies in the world of murder.

PREPPING FOR PUBLICATION

After your fourth draft, you should feel pretty good. But the story isn't ready for publication yet. Now you must consider presentation and format. Will you have space to run it straight? Where will you break the pages for the Web? You might want to cut it into a main piece and sidebars. Remember the visual elements you considered in Chapter 5 when you first laid out the game plan for your investigation. You need to plan how to incorporate the photos you took into your story package. Perhaps you want to break some of the information out into slide shows or photo essays. Now is when you take length into consideration.

Cut it down to size

You don't want to send your story to an editor who will take a pair of digital scissors to it. You worked too hard selecting the information, figuring out your structure and weaving through it the details and compelling elements for someone else to cut it down. When someone commissions you to do a story or you work as a staff reporter and writer, your editor tells you from the start how much space or time you will have to work with. You need to tailor your reporting to the editor's space. Even when you aren't constrained from the beginning, when you gear your story for publication, you will have to meet someone else's space restrictions.

Let's consider that your story is in one gigantic block of 4,000 words and it will appear online. Your editor might want it broken up. One page on the Web will contain about 750 words, and she might not want readers to have to click through too many jumps. Thus, she may want a main bar of about 750 words, with the rest broken up into sidebars, or perhaps she will want separate pieces for different days of the week. In either case, you will need to figure out what to put into the main bar, and then how to take the remaining 3,000 words and spread them among four or more stories.

As you gain investigative journalism experience, you will begin designing your set of stories early in the reporting process.

The art of the sidebar

Some papers won't let you jump front page stories to the inside of the paper, and some Web sites won't make readers click through to a continuation. For reporters and writers that means you have to keep your story short or make it a main bar that pairs with one or more sidebars. You could do that in a number of ways:

Summary and main points.   Make your main bar a summary story. It hits all the main points, but it leaves out most of the evidence. Then you separate each major point from the rest and convert it into a short article.

5Ws stories.   Design five stories to represent the five Ws by doing the following:

- For the main bar, you focus on the who and the what, looking at just one person affected by the problem, but you include a small section that expands it to all the people affected.
- Another story looks at the why and concentrates on the people who benefit from the status quo and the power structure that protects it.
- For the when, you could run a timeline that takes the reader from the origin of the problem to the present and explores future solutions.
- For the where, you could run a map with informative boxes pointing to different key places.
- For the how, you could design a simple flow chart.

Individual experiences.   If you wrote according to a converging narrative structure, you could break out the different experiences or perspectives of the people affected. Instead of stringing them together in one piece, you separate each one so that each experience is a stand-alone story tied to an explanatory main story.

Chronological.   You can break up a chronologic format into past, present and future. One story would deal with the present problem, one with how we got here (the past) and one would move the story forward.

Boxes and bullets

Editors love bullets. By putting information in bullet form, you can cut repetitious transitions that take up space. If you start with a summary main bar, you could include each major point in bullets. Online, each bulleted point can be a hyperlink to another page or sidebar that explores an issue.

You can also take out the facts that you used to make your story compelling and break them out into their own fact boxes. The downside to removing interesting facts from the body of your story is that they helped shake up readers just when attention might start to flag. But that's less important if you size your stories into more digestible pieces.

Kill the widows

That's the phrase used to describe a process of editing by eliminating the words hanging at the end of a paragraph. When one or two words take up an entire line at the end of a paragraph, they are called *widows.* You can usually get rid of widows if you connect two paragraphs, but that can create paragraphs that are too long. Instead, see if you can eliminate each widow by tightening up the wording within the paragraph until the single word or pair of words moves up. Change passive verbs and delete unnecessary adjectives and adverbs. This editing process will force you to consider the value of the text to the story. You start to tighten and end up taking out whole paragraphs. Once you work your way through the story, change the margins in your word processing program. That will create new widows. Keep repeating this exercise. Each time, look for ways to kill the widows by tightening and deleting. You will end up with copy that's clean and lean.

Another way to tighten your copy is to force yourself to take out 15 percent of your word count without losing any substance. Most inexperienced writers overwrite. Probably your copy has repetition you didn't spot, and you won't unless you force yourself to take the scissors to your words.

WRITING FOR THE TEAM PROJECT

These writing processes work well on an individual level, but what if you are part of a team? The team writing process can be handled in a number of ways, as we'll discuss now. See also Box 11.3.

Designate a writer.   If this method is chosen, the head writer should be selected at the outset of the project. If the story involves the investigation of a target person, the head writer should interview or be part of the team that interviews the target.

Divide it up.   This will work if you outline the stories into a mainbar and sidebars. Different people can each take a chunk. Or you can decide to write the piece as one long story, but different people take a different chunk within it. If you do it that way, you should designate one key writer to concentrate on consistency, flow and the narrative thread.

Bob Greene's method for team writing[18]

BOX 11.3

Longtime Newsday editor Bob Greene is considered the father of team reporting. He presented this list at a journalism conference in 1988, before the Internet changed the way team members can communicate. Still it is useful to see how one of the most successful investigative reporting teams in the industry handled the writing process.

1. Draft outline.
2. Hold conferences to discuss the story and graphics.
3. Write the first draft.
4. The team reads the first draft.
5. The top editor reads the first draft.
6. Write the second draft.
7. The team reads the second draft.
8. The top editor reads the second draft.
9. Fix the draft to include all suggestions and fill all holes.
10. The copy editor reads the draft.
11. The team rereads the draft.
12. The lawyer reads the draft.
13. Fix the copy according to suggestions from the team and lawyer.
14. Check proofs, headlines, subheads, jump heads, taglines, captions, etc., for accuracy and possible libel.

Structure like a pyramid. If the project originates out of a class project, each person could write a version of the first draft. The writers of the most thorough versions write the second draft. The authors of the clearest second draft write the third draft. And finally the best writer takes the third draft (a vote can be taken if needed to elect the writer). As a team, polish the final draft. All team members provide input in terms of what information should be included and eliminated and in the organizational structure.

Use a wiki. This is a messy approach but it can work for the right group of reporters and writers. Here are two ways you can handle the drafts as wiki:

1. *Paint by numbers.* You start out with an outline on a wiki page and team members fill it in according to assignments. It is *essential* that you start with a strong outline and that everyone sticks with it.
2. *Round robin.* One person starts the wiki, who passes it off to another member, etc. In this method, only one person works on the wiki at a time, although everyone can see what is being written and can offer suggestions.

VERIFYING THE STORY

Checking your story for accuracy is the single most-important step in the entire investigative project, regardless of whether you spent a few days or many years reporting the story. You need to doubt your information. Now is the time to triple check *everything*. Do it paragraph by paragraph. Where did you get that information? Who said it? What document did it come from? Have someone else redo your math and make sure your numbers add up. On team projects, team members need to call every person quoted or paraphrased. It's a good idea to have members of the team call people that others interviewed and read the quotes or paraphrases to the interviewees. Call your experts again and review your premise one more time. You can run a correction after the fact, but you can't take it back. In investigative reporting, you will likely be accusing somebody of something and so you must be right.

Consider the following thought process that Carl Bernstein went through, after months of interviewing person after person about the Watergate burglary and despite having as a key source one of the top officials in the FBI:

> Bernstein had spent most of the previous night unable to sleep, thinking about the implications of what they had written and what they were about to write. What if they were being unfair to the President of the United States, damaging not just the man but the institution? And, by extension, the country? Suppose the reporters' assumptions were wrong. That somehow they had been horribly misled. What happened to a couple of punk reporters who took the country on a roller-coaster ride? Could it be that the wads of cash in Stans' safe had been merely discretionary funds that had been misspent by a few overzealous underlings? Or that the reporters and their sources had fed on one another's suspicions and speculations? No less awful, suppose the reporters were being set up. What if the White House had seen its chance to finish off the Washington Post and further undermine the credibility of the press? What if Haldeman had never asked for authority over the money, or had never exercised his authority?[19]

Recall what happened to Dan Rather and Los Angeles Times Reporter Chuck Philips in our discussion of fake documents in Chapter 8. Both failed to do adequate due diligence. If your project took a significant amount of time, someone you interviewed early in your investigation may no longer feel the same way about the topic. You may have misunderstood something someone told you. Someone you talked to might have given you wrong information, and if you ask them again, they will realize the mistake. Something might have changed between the time that you interviewed someone and the time you are ready to publish.

You won't know until you call back your sources. This should not be a time-consuming process. People who are difficult to get the first time around are usually easier to contact once you already talked with them. Plus, even the most reluctant sources want to make sure that they won't be misquoted or that their quotes won't be taken out of context. You will find that when you call someone to verify a quote, they won't take long to call you back.

CONCLUSION

our story will emerge out of your notes. But a long story based on many interviews, data and documents doesn't write itself. Writing an in-depth investigative story can be a painful process. You will need to leave in your notes people you connected to and who helped you out. You may need to leave for a future project a tangent that some people you interviewed felt was important, and you know that they will be disappointed and upset when they read, see or hear your story.

To master the writing process, you need to start with a strong outline and then write multiple drafts. A thorough, clear, compelling and convincing story will not happen on your first draft or even your second. With each draft you will gain confidence and that confidence will give power to your writing.

As you outline and write, fill in any holes in the story by making phone calls to find the information missing from the story. Think about how and where to use emotional quotes, telling anecdotes and startling facts. Look in your notes for your lead and put as much thought into your ending as you did for the beginning. Consider ways to shorten your story and break it up into pieces easy for an online reader or broadcast audience to digest. Finally, make sure you verify every word in your story, paragraph by paragraph.

EXERCISES

1. Go to the Web site of the nonprofit investigative reporting group Propublic at http://propublica.org. Select a story and analyze how the writer structured the narrative.

   a. Why do you think the writer or writers chose to lead the story the way they did?

   b. How did they handle the organization of all the information included in the story?

   c. What evidence did the writers cite to make the story convincing?

   d. Is the story compelling, and what do you think makes it so?

2. Go to the Web site for Mother Jones magazine at http://motherjones.org, search for and read the story "Pinto Madness."

   a. What makes the story so convincing?

   b. If publishing it today, how might you break it into parts to go into a print package or Web site?

THE BIG STORY Project · THE BIG STORY Project · STEP 11

11.1 Write the first draft of your story from the outline you developed in Chapter 10. Try to make it as complete as possible:

   a. Identify the central characters.

   b. Identify the problem.

c. Explain how the problem works.

d. Explain why the problem occurs.

e. Show how we got to this point.

f. Point out possible solutions.

11.2 If you are working as a team, you could write a first draft in a number of ways:

a. Put the outline on a wiki and assign each member of the team a different section of the story to write. One person should take on the task of connecting all the pieces together and giving the story shape, consistency and flow.

b. Each person in the class could write a version of the first draft. Then the team leader will take the best version and distribute it to the rest of the team. You will write the second draft from that version of the first draft.

c. Together, rewrite the lead, the nut graph and the ending. One person is assigned to write the first draft using the outline, and the lead, nut graph and ending composed by the class.

NOTES

1. John Koblin and Spencer Morgan. "Clay Felker: Made New York into a magazine." *New York Observer,* July 1, 2008.

2. Justin Kaplan. *Lincoln Steffens: A Biography.* Simon and Schuster, 2004, p. 131.

3. George Kennedy, Daryl R. Moen and Don Ranly. *Beyond the Inverted Pyramid: Effective Writing for Newspapers, Magazines, and Specialized Publications.* St. Martin's Press, 2002.

4. Randy Shilts. *And the Band Played On.*

5. Michael Pollan. "Power streer" *New York Times Magazine,* March 31, 2002.

6. Anne Lamott. *Bird by Bird: Some Instructions on and Writing on Life.* Anchor Books 1995, p. 62.

7. Louise Kiernan. "Writing complicated stories." In *Telling True Stories: A Nonfiction Writer's Guide.* Edited by Mark Kramer and Wendy Call. Plume, 2007.

8. Laura Hillenbrand. *Seabiscuit: An American Legend.* Random House, 2003.

9. Tom French. "Sequencing text as line." In *Telling True Stories: A Nonfiction Writer's Guide.* Edited by Mark Kramer and Wendy Call. Plume, 2007, pp. 141–144.

10. Ibid.

11. Manny Garcia. Comment made at a workshop entitled "Bulletproofing the Investigation." IRE National Convention, Miami, June 2008.

12. Franco Ordoñez and Ames Alexander. "Hard labor at a tender age: Raid at poultry plant reveals problem beyond illegal immigration. Workers as young as 15 were found on the line." *Charlotte Observer,* Nov. 9, 2008.

13. Blake Morrison and Brad Heath. "Possible air hazards rarely considered in plans for schools." *USA Today,* Dec. 8, 2008.

14. James Sandler. "The war on whistleblowers." *Salon,* Nov. 1, 2007.

15. Tom French.

16. Jean Heller. "Syphilis victims in U.S. study went untreated for 40 years." Associated Press, July 26, 1972.

17. Mark Dowie. "Pinto madness." *Mother Jones* (Sept./Oct. 1977).

18. Bob Greene. "Organizing the Investigative Project." Distributed at the IRE National Conference, Minneapolis, 1988. Tipsheet 578 available at the IRE Resource Center.

19. Bernstein and Woodward, *All the President's Men,* p. 178.

Legal and Ethical Considerations

CHAPTER PREVIEW In this chapter you will explore the legal and ethical problems that you may encounter when you launch, carry out and publish an investigation. Your story might depend on gaining access to government meetings or records. You must be aware of any state or federal laws that affect whether and how you can gather this information. You need to consider whether you will be subject to a subpoena, how you could protect your sources and how far you should go in doing so. You will become acquainted with the criteria the courts have used to determine libel and issues of privacy. And investigative editors will give you advice on ways to make your investigation airtight.

12

CHAPTER

WHAT YOU ARE UP AGAINST

Throughout this book we've discussed the many different ways you can successfully carry out an investigation. But you must also consider your limitations, and these will be defined in part by laws and ethical considerations. You may decide that the problem you need to investigate is so terrible it overrides the privacy rights of the people involved. The law might say you don't have rights to access. Or the government might have the right to the information you gather, whether or not it ends up in a published or broadcast story. Even if you think the story is such that you can justify crossing some ethical boundaries, can you afford to cross legal ones? To make those kinds of decisions, first you need to be grounded in the laws and ethical guidelines.

ACCESSING THE COURT SYSTEM

Recall that the Newsday investigation that resulted in "A Tragic Vulnerability" began with court cases. So did Gary Craig's "Potent Pills" story about foster kids prescribed mood-altering drugs, and "Nobody's Fault" about the suicide in a county jail relied on court records.

Lawsuits, criminal files, records of divorce proceedings and probate hearings, and other matters that end up before judges are often an essential part of many investigative reporting projects. But you aren't always entitled to sit in on court hearings or gain access to records. You can watch most court proceedings, for example, but not family court matters in many states. You can get most court records, but not settlement records if they were closed as part of the settlement agreement. So investigative reporters need to know what they have rights to and what they don't, because sometimes the judge in whose courtroom a session is held or who has the ability to impose a gag order on records isn't well versed on laws governing access and the public's right to information. Sometimes the investigative reporter has to educate people who are supposed to be legal experts.

Public access

While every state has some guarantees of open access to government meetings and actions, some states have laws that are more restrictive than others. As of 2008, the Reporters Committee for the Freedom of the Press reported that while Vermont had few limitations to the public's right of access, the laws in Washington, D.C., were much more restrictive.[1] If your investigation will require getting copies of trial records or sitting in on court sessions or government meetings, you should check your state open access and public records acts. You don't want to find out after you've gotten the green light for an investigation of Family Court that all family court sessions and records in your state are off limits to you. The Reporters Committee for Freedom of the Press has a handy guide online for each state at their Web site.

Open Government Guide

www.rcfp.org/ogg

What you need to know about the public access laws in your state	BOX 12.1

- What government bodies are covered?

- How does the law define a "meeting," and what meetings will I not be entitled to attend?

- What kind of notice and how much notice is a governmental body required to issue before holding a meeting or taking an action?

- On what grounds can a judicial or governmental body close a hearing to me?

- If a meeting or a hearing is closed under the law, what information about it am I entitled to?

- What kind of private organizations, if any, fall under the state's public access laws, and to what extent are they covered by the same rules?

- What are the government agency's policies regarding public access?

- Are the policies discriminatory, and do they single out members of the media?

- How can I appeal a denial of access under my state's laws?

Local officials are often uninformed about rights to access. They may tell you that you aren't permitted to attend certain meetings or sit in on certain court sessions, when the law says that you are entitled to do so. Only by knowing and citing the law in your state will you gain the access that is your legal right.

Box 12.1 offers questions that you need to be able to answer in regard to your state's public access laws.

The courts have held that the First Amendment does not guarantee the public or the press access to all public facilities, although access might be granted through government policy or statute. Restrictions that limit press access to jails, public schools and government buildings have generally been upheld in court.

Access to court proceedings

The U.S. Supreme Court has repeatedly ruled that to protect the public's confidence in the judicial process, court proceedings are presumed to be open to the public, although it makes an exception for juvenile proceedings. To close a court hearing, a judge must do so on a case-by-case basis. The Supreme Court has held that judges can't close the voir dire process. That's when attorneys on both sides of a case pick the jury. And judges can't close preliminary hearings.

To close all or a portion of a court proceeding to the public, a judge must give the public notice and allow people to challenge that decision. The party who wants the hearing closed must prove that a compelling interest exists: They must show, for example, that opening the court to the public would harm the defendant's constitutional right to a fair trial. The decision must also be "narrowly tailored." If the defendant's rights can be protected by closing off one person's testimony, for example, or having one discussion between attorneys held in a judge's chamber, then the judge can't close the entire trial to the public or press.

Finally, the judge must put on the record any rationale for closing the proceedings or portion of the proceedings. That means that the judge can't just announce in court that a hearing is closed and leave it at that.

Juvenile hearings

While there is no constitutional right to attend juvenile hearings, check your state laws. Under California law, for example, you may gain access to juvenile proceedings at the request of the juvenile and parents or guardians. The law might also give the judge the authority to allow the press access under certain conditions, such as if you could legitimately argue that the name of the juvenile had already been well publicized in connection with the alleged crime. Similarly, check to see what kind of access you might be permitted if your story involves family court hearings involving children. Depending on your state law, you might also have rights to information about juvenile convictions and incarcerations.[2]

Access to jurors

The press does not have a right to contact jurors during a court proceeding, and you need to know in advance the penalties for doing so. You could be subject to fines or even jail for violating this rule. After a trial ends, jurors do have the right to talk to the press at their own discretion.

Grand jury proceedings

A grand jury is a panel of citizens whose job it is to investigate allegations of crimes and issue indictments, which charge someone or a group of people with a crime. The U.S. Constitution requires grand juries for capital crimes on the federal level. Some states allow for grand juries for both criminal and civil cases. In California, for example, a grand jury is formed each year in every county and the panel acts as a county auditor.

Grand jury proceedings are closed to the press and public. You don't have a presumptive right to the documents or witness statements that the jurors read or heard during the proceedings, even after the hearings end. Sometimes, a grand jury issues a report to the public at the end of its session. Check your state law to see exactly what the restrictions to access are, and what information you might be able to get. The repercussions for violating laws regarding grand jury secrecy can be stiff. Remember that when reporter Mark Fainaru-Wada and his colleague Lance Williams used grand jury testimony of baseball players Barry Bonds and Jason Giambi in a series of stories, they spent the next two years fighting subpoenas and a prison sentence. At one point in the case, the San Francisco Chronicle, which published the stories, was hit with fines of $1,000 a day.[3]

Gag orders

The First Amendment prohibits prior restraint of publication, meaning that a reporter or publication cannot be legally barred from making a story public. The problem comes when publication will interfere with someone else's constitutional right. If a judge can't close off hearings to the press, he can issue a gag order to prohibit lawyers or witnesses involved in a case from speaking to the press about it. But before judges can issue gag orders they must issue notice and allow the press to challenge the decision.

The Student Press Law Center suggests that if a judge tries to issue a gag order, a reporter should research previous court cases that went forward in that court that had greater publicity and carried no gag order. Also, inform the court how much publicity the case or crime has already received. You want to be able to argue that a gag order would not protect or change the defendant's right to a fair trial. Research and point out whether viable alternatives to a gag order exist, such as a change in venue, which would move the trial location to a place where the potential jurors would not be influenced by press coverage.[4]

A court can, and commonly does, seal court records after a civil case is over in order to protect trade secrets. Court settlements, too, often prevent the parties involved in the case from disclosing the terms of the settlement. Note that if you investigate an ongoing case, make sure to access as many records and documents as you can *before* the case ends. Once it ends, documents that you can get during the proceedings may end up off limits.

Judges might be able to close other types of civil court proceedings, such as mental health hearings. In addition, more and more civil disputes are settled by private mediators, and the press is not entitled access to these types of proceedings or their records.

ACCESSING PRIVATE PLACES AND INFORMATION

Sometimes the information you need is behind the doors of a private corporation, organization or home. That can be a major obstacle because you don't have rights of access to those places. Even if you can get in, you don't have the right to photograph, videotape or record what goes on there without the permission of everyone whose picture you take or voice you record. If you fail to get permission you could be subject to criminal penalties. State laws generally define a *private place* as any location in which the people in it can reasonably expect privacy. The Student Press Law Center says that if an event occurs on private property, such as someone's house or business, you should find out if members of the public are invited. If so, you should be able to argue that the press has the same right as the public.[5]

Reacting to police restrictions

Know the guidelines the police use to manage press access, says Geanne Rosenberg, an attorney and professor of journalism at Baruch College. If the police department issues press passes and grants access only to reporters who have them, obtain a pass. You and your news organization should also develop a policy for reacting to orders that you leave a property or stay away from it. Decide whether and when you should stand your ground and risk arrest or a lawsuit, or when you should leave.[6]

Consider what happened to Kelly Campbell in 2001. A reporter for the Potomac News and Manassas Journal in Virginia at the time, she was interviewing a principal in a local high school about an experiment in a science class that involved making newborn ducklings believe that the children in the class were mother ducks. When she asked about some people calling the experiment inhumane, the principal abruptly ended the interview and told her to leave. A police officer on the school grounds escorted Campbell out and charged her with trespassing, a misdemeanor. She received a sentence of 50 hours of community service, was ordered to pay a $50 fine and serve a year's probation in which she was to stay away from the school.[7] Know what you and your organization would do in this situation.

If you are ordered by officials to leave the scene of an event, try to determine whether it is taking place in a public forum, a nonpublic forum or on private property. Also, determine whether any restrictions have been placed on general public access to the area and whether the event involves a significant threat to public safety. If such a threat exists, police may argue later that they ordered you to leave for your own or the public's protection. Find out how long the restrictions are expected to stay in place. A court is more likely to rule that access limitations were reasonable if they were of short duration.[8]

Recording phone conversations

Depending on where you are calling from and the location of the person you call, it could be illegal to tape the conversation without the person's explicit permission. The laws vary from one state to another. Federal law and some 38 states plus Washington, D.C., require only one person on the call to be aware that it is taped; that means that if you tape it yourself, you don't have to tell the other person. Things get a little complicated when you call interstate. Although federal law might apply, so might the law of the state in which the person is located. How that applies when you call someone who has a California phone number but is talking on a cell phone while in Colorado isn't clear. It also isn't clear what law the courts would apply should the taping be done of a voice over an Internet phone system such as Skype or Vonage. Because of the lack of clarity it is a good idea, as well as good ethical practice, to inform anyone in any conversation you wish to tape of your intention to tape the call or interview. While consent is presumed if your tape recorder or camera is in full view, it is good protocol to ask for consent even under those conditions. You may not be able to tell, for example, that someone you are interviewing is legally blind and can't make out the camera or tape recorder you hold or simply does not understand what the device is.

Finally, you may find yourself in a situation where someone provides you with the tape of a conversation or videotape of some event that occurred on private property. In 2001, the U.S. Supreme Court ruled that reporters and media organizations could *not* be held liable for or prevented from publishing or broadcasting a tape or photograph that was illegally recorded or taken as long as they did not take part in the illegal taping or photographing.

The bottom line is that if you believe your project needs or would benefit from the photographing or recording of activities that occur on private property, you should research your state's laws and the laws for the state in which the interviewee or activity is located. Ask yourself these questions:

- Do the laws require the consent of all parties? If so make sure that all parties agree to the recording before you record them or film them.
- Are there criminal penalties? If so, consider other ways of obtaining the information that do not violate the law. Or consider whether you can do your story without the information.
- Can I face a civil suit? If yes, seek out ways to protect yourself such as getting consent in writing.
- Is there a specific hidden camera law? If yes, make sure you follow its guidelines and talk to a lawyer before using a hidden camera in your reporting.
- Are there additional penalties for disclosing or publishing information? If yes, you should talk to a lawyer before publishing.

Box 12.2 contains additional advice regarding privacy issues from the Student Press Law Center, a nonprofit organization headquartered in Arlington, Va.

States' Laws on Taping Conversations
www.rcfp.org/taping/states.html

PROTECTING YOUR SOURCES AND NOTES

A s important as access to a story are the legal ramifications that could result from doing the story, so you must take them into account. Find out your organization's policies or talk with your editor if you foresee even the slight possibility of a problem. Think about how far you would go to protect your sources. You should make a decision on how you will respond to subpoenas, search warrants and other legal action that may come as a result of speaking with certain sources.

Shield laws

Laws that protect a journalist from having to reveal confidential sources to police, a prosecutor or in a court of law are called shield laws. But not all states have them and they differ from state to state. At the end of 2008, the U.S. Senate

A legal brief on invasion of privacy law from the Student Press Law Center[9]   BOX 12.2

The legal right of privacy has been defined as the right to be let alone, the right of a person "to withhold himself and his property from public scrutiny if he so chooses." *Federal Trade Commission v. American Tobacco Co.,* 262 U.S. 276 (1923). However, unlike the First Amendment right to free speech, privacy (in the media context) is not a right explicitly guaranteed by the Constitution. Instead, privacy law has developed over the last 100 years. During that time, four separate kinds of privacy invasion have emerged: (1) Public Disclosure of Private and Embarrassing Facts, (2) False Light, (3) Intrusion and (4) Misappropriation.

1. PUBLIC DISCLOSURE OF PRIVATE AND EMBARRASSING FACTS

Courts have recognized that certain intimate details about people, even though true, may be "off limits" to the press and public. For example, publishing detailed information about a private person's sexual conduct, medical condition or educational records might result in legal trouble. To succeed in this kind of lawsuit, the person suing must show that the information was

(1) sufficiently private or not already in the public domain,

(2) sufficiently intimate, and

(3) highly offensive to a reasonable person.

The "Newsworthiness" Defense

A news organization will be protected from a private facts privacy claim if it can show that the material published was "newsworthy." Almost any information about a well-known public figure or a public official will be considered newsworthy. Furthermore, reports of recent involvement in criminal behavior will be considered newsworthy for anyone.

Printing the Names of Minors

In the unanimous 1979 decision, *Smith v. Daily Mail,* 443 U.S. 97 (1979), the U.S. Supreme Court ruled that the First Amendment protects the right of journalists to use the names of minors in newsworthy stories as long as the information is "lawfully obtained" and "truthfully" reported.

2. FALSE LIGHT

A false light claim can arise anytime you unflatteringly portray — in words or pictures — a person as something that he or she is not. A typical "false light" problem can arise where a misleading caption is published with a photo (for example, a caption describes a bystander at an unlawful demonstration as a "participant"). The elements of false light, found in the Restatement (Second) of Torts, Sec. 652E are "(1) the portrayal must be found to be 'highly offensive to a reasonable person' and (2) the actor had knowledge of or acted in reckless disregard as to the falsity of the publicized matter and the false light in which the other would be placed."

The same legal standards that apply to libel apply to false light. The distinction between false light and libel is that in false light claims one need not prove injury or damage to reputation, but only that the statement was highly offensive. Courts in some states have refused to recognize false light claims because of their similarity to libel.

3. INTRUSION UPON SECLUSION

Intrusion is a claim often based on the act of news gathering. A reporter can be sued even when the information obtained is never published. It occurs when a reporter gathers information about a person in a place where that person has a reasonable right to expect privacy. However, newsworthiness can also be a defense to this kind of privacy invasion. As a general rule, reporters are allowed to enter privately owned public places, for example, private school campuses or malls. However, also as a general rule, they must leave when they are asked.

The three most common types of intrusion are

(1) **Trespass:** going onto private property without the owner's consent.

(2) **Secret Surveillance:** using bugging equipment or hidden cameras. The laws vary by state, but as a general rule reporters can legally photograph or record anything from a public area, such as a sidewalk, but they cannot use technology to improve upon what an unaided person would be able to see or hear from that public place.

(3) **Misrepresentation:** invalid or exceeded consent. Undercover reporting is not necessarily an invasion of privacy as long as the disguise is not used as a means to trespass or engage in an activity that would not otherwise be allowed. For example, it would not be an intrusion for a minority student reporter to pose as a potential pledge to investigate a story about racial discrimination inside a fraternity. The reporter has a right to pledge whether he is serious about it or not.

4. MISAPPROPRIATION OF NAME OR LIKENESS

Misappropriation is the unauthorized use of a person's name, photograph, likeness, voice or endorsement to promote the sale of a commercial product or service. (For example, using a photo of your school's star athlete for a pizza restaurant without her permission.) To avoid problems, publications should routinely have subjects sign a model release form written in simple, straightforward language when using their name or likeness

in a commercial. Regardless of whether or not a release form has been signed, however, courts have generally allowed the media to reuse editorial photos or clips in its own self-promotion provided there is no suggestion that the person actually endorsed the publication.

Consent as a Defense

With all four forms of invasion of privacy, consent is a valid defense. However, if you intend to rely on consent as your defense to a privacy claim, you must make sure that you obtain the consent from someone with a legal right to give it and be candid with your subject about what information you want to use and how you intend to use it. While not necessary to be valid, consent is always easiest to prove when it is in writing.

Can a Minor Give Valid Consent?

Consent is and should be effective if a minor is "capable of appreciating the nature, extent and probable consequences of the conduct (to which he consents)," even if parental consent is not obtained or expressly refused. Restatement of Torts (Second), Sec. 892A. This reasoning is in line with what courts have said when determining whether a child is responsible for the injuries he causes, his crimes and confessions to crimes. When obtaining consent from a minor, it is essential that a student journalist take extra precautions to insure that the minor is fully informed of what is taking place. While most minor high school students probably can provide valid consent, most elementary-aged children, because of their immaturity, probably cannot.

© 2001 Student Press Law Center. Reprinted with permission from the Student Press Law Center.

had failed to pass a federal shield law, known as the Free Flow of Information Act. That means that were you to interview a source about a matter that interested the police or an investigating agency, you could be subject to a subpoena and possibly jail time. It is important that before you agree to grant a source anonymity or confidentiality, you understand your rights and responsibilities. A number of journalists have served jail time rather than divulge their sources, and you need to consider whether you would be willing to do so as well.

Subpoenas

A survey of television and print news organizations by University of Arizona law professor Ron Nell Andersen Jones found that 781 respondents in 23 states had been hit with more than 3,000 subpoenas in 2006. He told the American Journalism Review that television broadcasters in every market and all daily newspapers with a circulation of more than 10,000 said they'd been hit. Some of the subpoenas demanded that reporters reveal confidential sources and others demanded notes or other information obtained in the news-gathering process. The subject matters of the stories were varied: immigration, employment discrimination, federal crimes, the Federal Communications Commission, and civil rights actions.[10]

In 2008, a federal judge threatened a former USA Today reporter with fines of $5,000 a day for seven days for refusing to testify about stories she did about an anthrax scare. The judge held her personally responsible for paying those fines and said he wouldn't allow her former employer or anyone else to cover them for her.[11]

In 2007, Josh Wolf, an independent videographer, spent more than seven months in federal prison for refusing to testify before a federal grand jury about a videotape he had taken in San Francisco at a protest against the G-8 conference. The grand jury was investigating allegations of arson. Although it was a city police car that had been set on fire, the car was funded with federal money, hence the federal grand jury investigation. Wolf was finally released after he agreed to turn over the videotape and answer two questions in writing. Although California has a shield law that protects journalists from having to reveal sources to prosecutors or before a judge or jury, there was no corresponding federal law.[12]

In 2002, Vanessa Leggett, a legal researcher who was working on a book about a murder-for-hire spent more than five months in federal prison after federal prosecutors subpoenaed all her notes and tapes and ordered her to give them not only a copy but the originals as well.[13]

The Reporters Committee for Freedom of the Press says that "under no circumstances" should you comply with a subpoena for material concerning a published story or the gathering of information for a story. If you work for a news organization, it is likely that your organization has a lawyer. But most freelance journalists do not have lawyers on retainer, nor do many student publications. That means that if you are served with a subpoena, you must find one. If you can't find one who will handle your case for free, hiring a lawyer could be expensive. The Student Press Law Center maintains a referral network of lawyers throughout the country who are willing to represent student journalists on a pro bono basis, which means that they will charge no fees. If you are a college student, and you need legal advice, the SPLC can be a great resource.[14]

SPLC Legal Help
www.splc.org/
legalhelp.asp

Search warrants

Although the U.S. Supreme Court has held that the First Amendment does not exempt reporters from search warrants that meet the probable cause requirements of the Fourth Amendment, the federal Privacy Protection Act of 1980 does prevent police from getting warrants for a reporter's notes, files, photographs or video. The law says that if police feel they need the material a reporter or a press organization holds, then they need to get a judge to issue a subpoena. Note that the law does not prevent police from getting a search warrant if they have probable cause to believe the reporter committed a crime or aided and abetted in a crime.

If you investigate something that is deemed to be illegal, you could open yourself up to charges of criminal activity. Journalists have been subject to search warrants and jailed for possession of child pornography even after they argued that it was part of an investigative reporting project.

As part of the news-gathering process, some reporters need to contact lawbreakers or whistle-blowers who might be violating federal or state law if they disclose secret information as part of a story. Sometimes, these reporters make sure that they don't include identifying information in their notes or they try to code or otherwise disguise it.

LIBEL

If you anticipate that your project will make any accusations against people or organizations, you also have to worry about libel and consider ways to protect yourself and your news organization from the start. With investigative stories, you need to be especially sensitive to libel implications; it is more likely that your story is long and filled with data and complicated information. This can increase the possibility that the information you get may be wrong, that your analysis might be flawed or that you might misunderstand legal or scientific terminology. These things have happened to the best and most experienced of reporters. Box 12.3 reviews the four elements that must be proven to charge someone with libel.

In the United States, truth is an absolute defense against claims of libel or slander. The problem is that truth is often difficult to prove. Many reporters

The four elements of libel

BOX 12.3

1. PUBLICATION

The material must have been published or broadcast. But note that publication does not necessarily begin when your story comes out in a newspaper or magazine, is aired on television or the radio or goes live on the Web.

Consider the case of the Alton Telegraph. In 1969, two investigative reporters for a small Illinois community newspaper were looking into connections between a local bank and organized crime. A tip led them to believe that a criminal organization was funneling money through the bank to a local real estate developer, and they wondered if a recently formed federal task force that was investigating the criminal organization was also looking into it. They wrote a confidential memo to the task force, but then ended up dropping the story. While they never published a story on the developer, the task force sent the reporters' information to the Federal Home Loan Bank Board, which notified the bank, which cut off the developer's financing. Years later, the developer discovered the memo, traced his financial troubles back to the reporters and sued the paper. A jury in 1980 — more than 10 years after the reporters first sent their memo to federal investigators — awarded the developer $9.2 million. This was the largest libel award at the time in the history of the United States, almost four times what the newspaper was worth. The plaintiff in that case argued successfully that the reporters had been lazy and that they had tried to get the federal investigators to do their work for them.[15]

In determining your risk of libel, note how many different forms publication can now take in the age of the Internet. Electronic communication is so convenient now that people regularly use e-mail or text messaging in place of phone calls or in-person conversations. But by putting comments about somebody down electronically and transmitting them to a third party, you are publishing them.

2. IDENTIFICATION

Someone can't successfully sue for libel if they aren't identified in the published material. But just as you have to accept an expansive definition of the term *published,* you have to understand that people can be identified even if you don't specifically name them. Referring to "a member of the Green Party" in a small community where everyone is a Republican, for example, might effectively identify someone you don't name. Or referring to "a high-level female executive" effectively identifies someone who works in a company where all other executives are male. You could identify an unnamed person if you say he often panhandles at a particular intersection, if he is the only person known for doing that. People can be identified by their political preference, by an unusual car they drive, by where they live or by unusual physical features or attire. Attorney and writer John Zelezny cautions that you need to ask yourself whether a reader, viewer or listener would reasonably be able to identify the person, not whether you as a content producer intended to identify him.[16]

3. HARM

To sue for libel, a person generally needs to show that the published material caused harm to his reputation. But this is not always the case. For some accusations, such as committing a crime or committing fraud, the courts will presume that the person's reputation is harmed. On the other hand the Supreme Court has found that someone whose reputation was already tarnished cannot argue that a publication caused further harm.

4. FAULT

In 1964 in *New York Times Co. v. Sullivan*, the U.S. Supreme Court held that journalists cannot be held liable for making honest mistakes in reporting about public officials. To prove fault regarding someone deemed a public official, it must be proved that you acted with "actual malice" or "reckless disregard" of the truth. That means that for a jury to find that you libeled a public official, you either had to know the published statement was false or did nothing to ascertain whether it was true. But consider how unpredictable a jury can be. If you end up in court, you have to trust that the jury will believe you when you say you didn't know. The best protection against this accusation is to triple-check all your facts and don't rely on a single source for information.

confuse truth and accuracy. Just because you accurately cite from a document or quote a source doesn't ensure that the information is truthful. Often, stories are based at least partly on people's recollections and opinions and those could be faulty or biased. Your editor will likely question where you got the information on which you based your premise. It should be based on facts that can be verified. If it is based on information that can't be verified, such as one person's recollections of an event of which there is no written or taped record, the evidence probably isn't enough to base a story around. Don't rely solely on one person or document for the truth.

Know public versus private figures

If you anticipate that your project will make accusations against a person or an organization, understand the different risks of libel and the different levels of scrutiny the courts expect from journalists, depending on the type of person or organization the accusations are leveled against. Ask yourself: What do you seek to report, and who does it involve? Exhibit 12.1 indicates the basic differences between public officials, public figures and private individuals.

The courts have ruled that news organizations must take greater care when reporting about private individuals than they do public officials or public figures. As stated previously, to prove libel, a public figure must show that the reporter or news organization acted negligently or with malice or made accusations they knew were false or did little to ascertain whether the information was true. However, private individuals need only prove that:

- the information is false,
- it identified them,

EXHIBIT 12.1   When is a person a public official, a public figure or a private individual?

Public official.   Someone who, at the least, has substantial control and responsibility over governmental affairs.

Public figure.   Someone who has achieved enough fame or notoriety to have become commonly known, has voluntarily taken a leading role in a public controversy or who has been thrust into the public spotlight because of a public controversy.

Private individual.   Someone who does not have control over a community, is not famous or is not in the public spotlight.

- it damaged their reputation, or
- the reporter or news organization did something wrong or failed to do something they should have done.

Although reporters should know the difference between public and private figures, the Student Press Law Center says not to get caught up trying to figure out whether anyone mentioned in a story is a public figure or private individual. Some people, such as teachers or businesspeople, fit somewhere in between. Instead, treat all your subjects and sources as private individuals. To protect yourself, your news organization and your story, hold your reporting up to the *highest* standards of proof.

Keep research diverse and thorough

Thoroughly research your subject and rely on numerous and diverse sources, both credible people and documents. That's the best way to protect yourself in advance. Understand that some people lie to reporters, others fervently believe incorrect information, and others rewrite history of past events in their own minds in the way they wish things had occurred. People have selective eyesight and hearing and that shapes their memories. They tend to see what they want to see and fail to see or hear things that are unpleasant or which won't help their cause.

That's why you need to seek out diverse types of sources. Interview people affected by the problem you investigate, people apparently responsible, and independent experts with no axes to grind. When sources and documents disagree, try to explain rather than ignore the differences. Zero in on contradictions and watch for anything that sounds implausible. If you find that facts don't add up, check with multiple sources of information that you get elsewhere.

Because of the need for a variety of sources, avoid rushing your story. You should be able to give subjects of stories sufficient time to respond to any accusations. Finally, be transparent and disclose to your editors, your sources and your readers, viewers or listeners the manner in which you obtained all your information.

Beware of conspiracy theories

If you look hard enough, you can piece together enough "facts" to support any case you want to make. In the book "Foucault's Pendulum," author Umberto Eco created three characters who, for a lark, decide to contrive the ultimate conspiracy, which involves a secret organization called the Knights Templar. His three characters cobble together assorted bits of "evidence" for their preposterous conspiracy until they begin to believe the story themselves. They convince themselves that even though they originally thought they fabricated the plot, perhaps they had simply stumbled upon it. They tell themselves that the proof is undeniable.[17] Don't find yourself getting caught up in your premise, trying to seek out only the facts that seem to prove it. If you go about your investigation scientifically and try to disprove rather than prove your hypothesis, you will be less likely to fall into the conspiracy theory trap.

ETHICAL CONSIDERATIONS

Investigative reporters often face ethical dilemmas in their reporting. They try to uncover a truth someone doesn't want exposed. That means the subject of the investigation will often go to great lengths to keep facts hidden. A journalist might feel the truth will be revealed only if she commits some act of deception. That might involve sneaking into a military hospital as the Washington Post's Dana Priest and Anne Hull did in 2007 to expose the government's neglect and mistreatment of injured war veterans. They believed that they needed to do so to expose the mistreatment of injured soldiers.

Ethics involves the weighing of bad options to find the one that will result in the greatest good and the least harm. But to act ethically, transgressions can only be considered as last resorts. The length to which some reporters have gone in an attempt to prove their cases has gotten them and their news organizations in trouble.

Consider what happened at the Cincinnati Enquirer in 1998. Two experienced investigative reporters, Cameron McWhirter and Mike Gallagher spent a year investigating Chiquita Brands, the worldwide seller of bananas that had headquarters in Cincinnati. Among other things, the reporters looked into allegations that the company sprayed its fields with toxic pesticides well above levels acceptable in the United States, that it operated a string of subsidiaries disguised as independent local companies, that its ships had been used to transport cocaine and that it had closed plantations in order to bust local unions. Their investigation, based on numerous interviews as well as leaked corporate documents, resulted in an 18-page investigative package. But two months later, the Gannett newspaper printed a front-page apology. It ran the apology three times and announced it would pay Chiquita more than $10 million.[18]

What happened? In the course of reporting the story, Gallagher had gained access to the company's internal voice mails and had based at least one of his allegations on information from them. In accessing the voice mails, Chiquita charged, the reporter had broken into the company and stolen proprietary information, even after his editor and a lawyer for the newspaper told him not to do so. The newspaper fired him and a grand jury indicted him. To avoid a jail sentence, Gallagher exposed a confidential source, violating an ethical rule that most reporters consider sacred.

The firing of Gallagher, the payment to Chiquita and the apology received far more widespread and sustained news coverage than did the original series of articles. That was the real shame of the fiasco, argued Bruce Shapiro, who taught investigative reporting at Yale University at the time. He noted that none of the stories that reported the Enquirer's apology bothered to look into the allegations about Chiquita, and that no one seemed disturbed that a reporter faced jail time for the publication of a story that no one had shown to be false. But perhaps the greatest shame of the case was that Gallagher overstepped bounds when he didn't have to. He didn't need the voice mails to prove the bulk of the allegations in his story. The story would have been just as damning against Chiquita without the only allegation that needed the voice mail substantiation, which was that Chiquita had committed bribery.[19]

Another case study in what can go wrong if you cross an ethical line involved the ABC news show Primetime Live. In 1992, the show's producers sought to prove that a supermarket chain called Food Lion sold rotten meat to the public. To achieve this, they applied for jobs at Food Lion and, as employees, used hidden cameras to film their evidence.

The story they aired accused Food Lion of selling rotten meat, bleaching fish to cover up smells and changing expiration dates to sell old meat. Food Lion sued ABC, not for libel, but for fraud and trespass. A jury found ABC guilty and fined it $5 million in punitive damages. Most of the news coverage of the lawsuit, which can still be read on the Web and through news archives, suggests that Food Lion chose not to sue for libel because it knew it couldn't prove the story false. Ergo, the stories suggest, the allegations were true.

But unlike the Chiquita investigative story, which was substantiated by later independent investigations and developments, examinations of ABC's practices revealed a shoddy investigation that was problematic from the get-go. To begin with, the producers were prodded into doing the story by the disgruntled United Food and Commercial Workers Union. That in itself isn't bad; many stories originate from disgruntled workers, jealous competitors, frustrated customers, even angry former spouses. But ABC's producers worked closely with the union to get the jobs at Food Lion; the producers were coached on how to act and given fraudulent referrals and recommendations. They aired unsupported claims from union workers and heavily edited footage to create the impression that the supermarket was forcing its workers to sell bad meat and to eliminate any comments that would repudiate the union's allegations.[20]

In 1999, the U.S. Circuit Court of Appeals for the 4th District threw out all but $2 of the verdict, ruling that the plaintiff's arguments for fraud were insupportable. But it did agree that ABC had committed trespass.[21] Regardless, under accepted rules of ethics, they should only have gone in undercover and lied about their roles as journalists as a last resort after trying to get the story through other means — through state food inspection records, for example, or by buying meat from the supermarket and having it independently tested.

In contrast, reporters from the Chicago Tribune bought and tested fish in 2005 to show high levels of mercury in fish sold by Chicago-area supermarkets. For the story "The Mercury Menace: Toxic Risk on Your Plate," the Tribune bought 144 samples of eight kinds of fresh and canned fish and paid to have the fish tested by an independent laboratory. They found high levels of mercury in swordfish as well as in two types of fish for which the government had not issued warnings: orange roughy and walleye.[22] Sam Roe and Michael Hawthorne, the reporters involved in the story, produced a strong piece of investigative journalism and did not have to face trials, fines, jail time or shame.

While the laws change and ethical dilemmas involve gray areas, news editors, journalism scholars and legal advisers have developed some guidelines that can help you anticipate and avoid problems.

Sam Roe and Michael Hawthorne's Story
www.chicagotribune.
com/news/specials/
chi-mercury-3-story,
0,4192281.story

Always double-check

Understand that just because you accurately cite from a document doesn't mean the information is correct. When you check your facts, check them against a different source and don't ignore documents that contradict anecdotal evidence or anecdotal evidence that contradicts the written record. Mark Katches, assistant managing editor for projects and investigations at the Milwaukee Journal-Sentinel, says you should consider bringing in outside experts who can act as guides. He notes that Dave Umhoefer, a reporter for the Journal-Sentinel, built a database of pension data and found through his own calculations that county workers had amassed $50 million in illegal pension benefits. "That wasn't good enough," Katches said. To bolster the findings, the paper hired two actuaries to analyze the data at a cost of about $1,000. "That gave the story a heck of a lot more authority," he said. The story, "Pension twist costs county millions," won the Pulitzer Prize for local reporting in 2008.[23]

George Papajohn, assistant managing editor for projects at the Chicago Tribune, says that to prevent problems after publication, you need to involve any

Dave Umhoefer's Story
www.pulitzer.org/
archives/7718

editors who will be reading and making changes to your story early in the writing process. "Make sure you can get feedback from them early. You don't want them making major edits at the last minute." Before the story goes to publication, read through it carefully, take a pen and actually put a checkmark over every word, not just every fact, Papajohn advises.[24]

Keep an objective mind

Don't set out to "get" someone. Instead of centering your story around blaming someone for a problem, center it around the problem. Let blame arise out of your honest attempt to explain a problem and find solutions for it. If you are convinced from the start that someone is guilty, you will find enough "facts" to support the premise. Don't be blind to facts that will contradict your assumptions.

Understand and respect the law

You should always try to obey the law, but sometimes that's easier said than done. Some journalists think they are entitled to all information and anything that obstructs their path to it is a violation of their First Amendment rights. Others think it is important to obey the law, but that some stories involve problems so serious that the good that comes from breaking the law to gather proof and publish a story necessitates the legal risks.

Bob Steele, director of the ethics program at the Poynter Institute, wrote that respect for the law doesn't mean blind obedience. Governments change unfair or discriminatory laws or policies at times but sometimes only after people use civil disobedience — they intentionally break the bad law or policy. Sometimes a news organization must "test the legal line" to expose a government's violation of the public trust or wrongdoing by people in power. Steele developed a list of six criteria that a journalist should meet to justify breaking the law.[25]

1. The information must be of "vital public interest" or "necessary to prevent profound harm to individuals."
2. You have exhausted all other means of obtaining the information.
3. You must be willing to disclose what you did and why.
4. You aren't going after your story in a sloppy manner but instead are putting into it adequate time, care and resources to do it "fully and fairly."
5. Everyone involved in the project weighs all the positive and negative ramifications to all people possibly affected by the story and thinks through the ethical and legal considerations in a thoughtful, collaborative decision-making process.
6. You are willing to pay the price — including public criticism and attacks against your reputation and the reputation of the industry. That price might also include going to jail or paying fines or other penalties.

Weigh promises

Geanne Rosenberg warns that any promises you make to sources could limit or restrict your ability to publish and could create legal problems if you do publish. He says think twice before making any commitments, whether via e-mail, over the phone, in person or by a written agreement.[26]

New York Times reporter Judith Miller spent almost three months in federal prison for refusing to reveal her source in the Bush administration who violated national security laws by identifying CIA spy Valerie Plame. While her fellow journalists applauded her for protecting her source, they criticized her at the same time for having granted anonymity to her source, I. Lewis Libby, the chief of staff to Vice President Dick Cheney. Anonymity should be granted rarely, and only to protect a source who provides needed information at great risk to himself. Libby apparently had used Miller to leak the information as part of a coordinated strategy to discredit Joseph Wilson, the husband of Plame.[27]

Reveal trade secrets selectively

You can also get into trouble if you expose corporate trade secrets. Both the Chiquita and Food Lion cases demonstrate that truth and accuracy won't always protect you against charges that you broke the law or used deceptive practices to get information.

A commonly held belief is that people who leak stolen or secret documents to the press can get fired or worse, but that journalists are protected under the First Amendment to publish. But bear in mind what happened to Internet site wikileaks.org, which seeks to create the world's largest public database of leaked secret documents. In February 2008, Federal District Court judge Jeffrey White issued an injunction that forced Wikileaks' ISP to shut down the site and block use of its domain name. A Cayman Islands bank had argued that the site had unlawfully published confidential and proprietary information. But almost immediately mirror sites sprung up and people discovered other ways to reach Wikileaks. Two weeks later, the judge reversed his decision and acknowledged that the First Amendment did not permit prior restraint; in other words, while the government can punish someone when publication of information violates the law, it can't prevent publication.[28]

Still, Rosenberg advises journalists against using deceptive tactics to obtain a trade secret.[29] Keep records of how you acquired the secret company information that might fall under the broad trade-secret umbrella, he says. He also suggests that if you don't ask, you can't tell — it may be best to not know where the information came from. However, if you don't know the sources of key documents you may have difficulty authenticating them.

The bottom line? Talk to a lawyer or a law professor before publishing material you suspect might have been obtained improperly or before taking any action that might violate the law. Again, as a student, you might be able to get legal help from the Student Press Law Center.

Don't ambush your targets

When setting up a case against someone, make sure you give the person adequate time to comment and defend his actions or position. Many reporters and editors go further. They lay out all the facts and data, even going so far as to provide a copy of the database used to derive the information. George Papajohn, the Chicago Tribune editor, said that his paper does a virtual readback and goes over with targets the major points in the story, fact by fact. "They will be completely prepared for what will happen," he said. Go to great lengths to get more than a "no comment," he said.[30]

Waiting won't cost you the scoop. For a story about a design flaw in cribs that resulted in infant deaths, the paper decided to hold the story an entire week while the corporation that made the cribs dragged its feet on commenting. But when it did comment, it told the reporter that as a result of the newspaper's findings, it would recall a million cribs and that it did not want a single baby sleeping in those cribs.

"It gave much more teeth to the story," Papajohn said of the story "Hidden Hazards," which won a Pulitzer Prize for investigative reporting. "The company didn't acknowledge that we prompted the recall, but we were able to say in the story that the recall came after our inquiries and the implication was clear to our readers. The story still was very powerful. In laying out the chronology, we could show how nothing happened for years until we started investigating and how we found a defective crib that the federal investigator had been unable to track down." Papajohn also advises that when you include the comments from the target, make sure you present his side high up, before the jump.[31]

Getting interviews from the person or organization you accuse is advantageous for other reasons. You will end up with a more three-dimensional characterization of your target. That will make your story more convincing. If you spend all your time with the people affected but only do one or two interviews with your target, you may unintentionally slant the story. From your stakeholders you will get and present vivid details of their recollections and you will be able to effectively recreate history from their perspective, but you will not be able to do the same from the target's perspective.

Source everything

However you organize and store the information you gather, source it from the moment you collect it. Get in the habit of jotting down in your notepad the time, date and location as well as the name of the person or the document the informa-

Hidden Hazards Continuing Investigation

www.chicagotribune.
com/news/chi-safety-
child-hazards-main,0,
7129923.special

tion comes from. When you transfer your notes to the computer do the same. Review Chapter 6 to see how you can create a hyperlink in a word processing file or spreadsheet, so that the information is anchored to the source of it until you are ready to publish. You will thank yourself at the fact-checking stage if you meticulously source the information you gather. You will only be as certain of the finished story as you are of the sources of the information you relied on in your analysis.

Give everyone a heads-up

Papajohn says that you need to make certain that *everyone* cited or photographed in your story knows they will be in it and how they will be portrayed. "Who wants to be the person at the Saturday picnic and their neighbor comes up to them and shows them a picture of them on the front page when it is about poisoned fish that you are buying to feed your children?" he asks.[32]

Write what you know

While doubt is healthy, don't start second-guessing yourself when you sit down to write the story. If you do that, you might water down your language or make it vague and that could present worse problems. If you thoroughly reported the story, and your sources are reliable and varied, write it.

CONCLUSION

Investigative projects take time, effort and thought. You don't want all that wasted because the way you gathered your information or presented it makes people question your conclusions or question your ethics. Don't take shortcuts when it comes to the law and ethical dilemmas. Even if your intentions are honorable, even if all you want is to expose a problem that needs to be exposed or prove that someone or something is causing harm, your project will likely do no good if your methodology is shown to be shoddy, your reporting sloppy and that you broke laws when you didn't have to. The Society of Professional Journalists goes by this credo: Minimize harm.

If you are unsure about whether your actions will present legal risks, seek legal advice. Try to gain information through less problematic means first. Only consider options that involve legal or ethical risks after you pursue other options first. Consider whether the story you want to do requires information that you can't get through legal or ethical means. And finally, consider whether the story needs to be done at all. Only after you consider all the legal and ethical risks, all the possible methods of getting the information, and weigh these factors against the benefits that you think your reporting will do, should you proceed.

EXERCISES

1. For each of the four possible scenarios for investigative stories that follow, decide on a method of investigation and explore the ethical or legal problems you might face. Ask yourself the following questions:

   - What are the benefits of carrying out the investigation and publishing a story?
   - What are the risks?
   - How can I minimize the risks to me and my organization and minimize harm to my sources or story subjects?

     a. Your university is planning on building a new recreation center and has hired a big company from out of the area to build it. A local contractor who lost out on the project told you the company the school hired had a history of using substandard material in its construction projects that makes the buildings unsafe.

     b. You overheard that the people who work in the maintenance department trade off sick days and overtime in a complicated schedule system in order to get overtime even though they worked only 40-hour weeks. It is allegedly costing the school more than $100,000 a year in wages.

     c. You suspect that freshmen in the athletic program are being steered to majors where the professors are known for easy As and are allowed to substitute easy courses for some difficult ones required of the rest of the freshman class.

     d. To find sources and background information for a story you are working on, you join a listserv, an e-mail discussion group in which people who are interested in the same topic post letters that are sent to all members. You learn through the listserv of the firing of a company official because of some scandal that occurred within the company. One of the e-mails that you receive as a member of the listserv appears to be a smoking gun document.

2. Research your state's open access and public records laws and answer the questions in Box 12.1. Then sit in on a court session, attend a public meeting or ask for public records.

THE BIG STORY Project • THE BIG STORY Project • STEP 12

12.1 Write a second draft of your story with a focus on clarity.
   a. Eliminate what's not essential.

b. Add back information needed for reader comprehension.

c. Bring the story down to scale.

d. Set up a structure.

12.2 Either individually or as a group, reexamine the methods you used to gather information in your project. What legal or ethical problems, including issues involving access and privacy, did you encounter?

12.3 If your story has geographic elements, create a mashup map (see the discussion in Chapter 9).

NOTES

1. Reporters Committee for the Freedom of the Press. You may compare the access laws of each state with the Open Government Guide of the Reporters Committee for Freedom of the Press at http://rcfp.org/ogg.

2. California Newspaper Publishers Association and the California First Amendment Coalition. *The Right to Know: A Guide to Public Access and Media Law.* Chapter 5.

3. Reporters Committee for the Freedom of the Press. "Balco Grand Jury investigation." Part of a special report titled "Shields and Subpoenas." You can find it at http://www.rcfp.org/shields_and_subpoenas.html#balco.

4. Student Press Law Center. "Student media guide to news gathering: Gathering news, legally," http://splc.org. The full Web address for the media guide is: https://www.splc.org/legalresearch.asp?id=21.

5. Ibid.

6. Geanne Rosenberg. "Top 10 rules for limiting legal risk." Knight Citizen News Network, http://www.kcnn.org/legal_risk.

7. Reporters Committee for the Freedom of the Press. "Reporter accepts probation after interview arrest." Sept. 25, 2001.

8. Reporters Committee for the Freedom of the Press. "Attacking access problems," rcfp.org.

9. Student Press Law Center. The SPLC brief can also be viewed online at: http://www.splc.org/legal research.asp?id=29.

10. Kevin Rector. "A flurry of subpoenas." *American Journalism Review* online exclusive. (April/May 2008), http://www.ajr.org/Article.asp?id=4511.

11. National Lawyers Guild. "National Lawyers Guild condemns jailing of journalist blogger." Aug. 1, 2006, http://nlgsf.org. Also Ken Paulson. "The real cost of fining a reporter." *USA Today,* March 12, 2008, p. 11A.

12. Bob Egelko and Jim Herron Zamora. "The Josh Wolf case: Blogger freed after giving video to feds." *San Francisco Chronicle,* April 4, 2007, p. B1, http://www.sfgate.com/cgi-bin/article.cgi?f=/c/a/2007/04/04/WOLF.TMP.

13. Ross Milloy. "Writer who was jailed in notes dispute is freed." *The New York Times,* Jan. 5, 2002, http://query.nytimes.com/gst/fullpage.html?res=9C04E6D81F30F936A35752C0A9649C8B63.

14. See also Student Press Law Center. "Legal brief on libel law." 2001. You can find it at http://www.splc.org/legalresearch. asp?id=27.

15. Much has been written about this case. Those who want to read more about it should see Thomas B. Littlewood, *Coals of Fire: The Alton Telegraph Libel Case,* Southern Illinois University Press, 1988.

16. John Zelezny. *Communications Law: Liberties, Restraints and the Modern Media.* Wadsworth Publishing, 2006.

17. Umberto Eco. *Foucault's Pendulum.* Harcourt Brace Jovanovich, 1988.

18. Bruce Shapiro. "Rotten bananas: While the media race to condemn the Cincinnati reporter who broke into Chiquita's voice mail, they're forgetting who the real villain is." *Salon,* July 8, 1998, http://www.salon.com/media/1998/07/08media.html.

19. Ibid.

20. Marc Gunther and Henry Goldblatt. "Yikes, Diane Sawyer's downstairs! When ABC's Primetime Live burned Food Lion in a TV expose about rotten food, the supermarket chain mishandled the crisis and made matters worse." *Fortune Magazine*, Dec. 23, 1996.

21. Felicity Barringer. "Appeals court rejects damages against ABC in Food Lion case." *The New York Times,* Oct. 21, 1999.

22. Sam Roe and Michael Hawthorne. "The mercury menace: Toxic risk on your plate." *The Chicago Tribune,* Dec. 11, 2005.

23. Mark Katches. "Bulletproofing your investigation." You can read "Pension twist" at http://www.js online.com/story/index.aspx?id=639331.

24. George Papajohn. Comments made at a workshop on "Bulletproofing the investigation." IRE National Convention, Miami, June 2008.

25. Bob Steele. "Can ethics trump law: Six criteria to help you decide when it's OK to break the law." Sept. 14, 2003, http://www.poynter.org/column. asp?id=36&aid=47873.

26. G. Rosenberg. "Top 10 Rules."

27. Jim Naureckas. "Defending Judith Miller's indefensible choice: How do you expose corruption by protecting the corrupt?" *Extra!* (Sept./Oct. 2005).

28. Bob Elgo. "Swiss bank drops suit against Wikileaks site." *San Francisco Chronicle,* March 6, 2008, p. A4.

29. G. Rosenberg. "Top Ten Rules."

30. Papajohn. "Bulletproofing."

31. Papajohn. "Bulletproofing." And e-mail correspondence, Dec. 29, 2008.

32. Papajohn. "Bulletproofing."

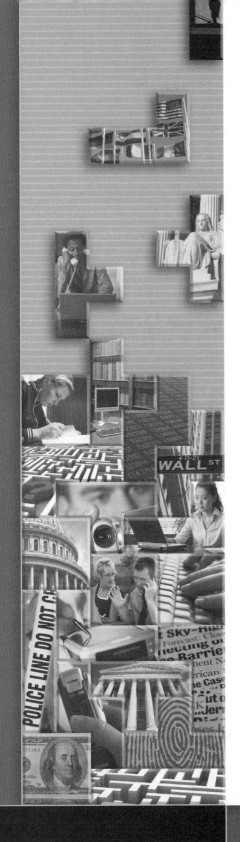

Advanced Reporting Methods

CHAPTER PREVIEW Investigative reporters employ various methods to carry out their investigations, depending on the size of the project and the subject they want to investigate. In this chapter you will learn about several different advanced methods: undercover reporting, submersion journalism, distributed reporting, crowdsourcing, investigating an individual versus an institution, computer-assisted reporting, and the running investigation. Finally, you will get an overview of methods for keeping your information secure, including noteworthy examples and tips from the experts.

13

INVESTIGATING A CLOSED INSTITUTION

Regardless of how much experience or know-how an investigative reporter may have, sometimes the techniques discussed in the previous chapters are not enough to break through an institution's wall. Some institutions are so closed that investigating their activities seems impossible. These include the following:

- Private corporations exempt from most Securities and Exchange Commission disclosure rules
- Public corporations that effectively gag their employees
- Large educational and charitable institutions
- Uncooperative governments

Public access laws don't always apply and using them effectively often requires that you know what to look for. That's difficult if an organization is run like a fortress, and the employees inside it try to obstruct your path rather than help you navigate the maze they work in.

To find your way through the maze, you need to understand three basic tactics large organizations use to obstruct, misdirect and confuse journalists.

1. *The CIA approach.* With this tactic, a company gives out no information. Call and ask for the location to their main office, and their public relations people will neither confirm nor deny the corporation exists.

2. *The ever-helpful approach.* This tactic was mastered by semiconductor giant Intel Corp. When I covered it during the Internet boom of the '90s, it had some 95 public relations people. They would return your calls immediately, hook you up with corporate executives, send you all kinds of material and answer all your questions. Only after that process was complete did you realize that they never actually gave you the information you sought.

3. *The scavenger hunt.* That's where you might get the information you seek, but it will come only after you go through so many people who point you in so many different directions that you might forget what it was you were looking for in the first place.

Now you need two things to start your investigation: a map and a key.

A map

The map is a chart of the organization or institution. Exhibit 13.1 is a map of a typical corporation. All institutions and organizations have organizational charts that lay out the chain of command. These charts are not always available to the public, but they are almost always distributed to new employees, to investors and to regulators. Often the map is posted somewhere deep within the organization's Web site, and you can find it with the right combination of Internet search engine and terms.

Chain of command for a large corporation.   **EXHIBIT 13.1**

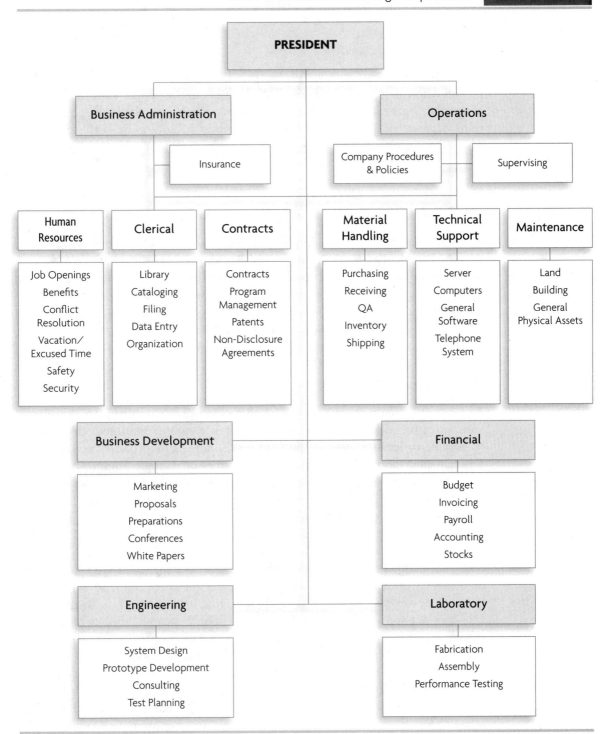

People within the organization often don't understand the value of the map, so if you simply ask for an organizational chart they usually will give it to you.

A key

Once you have a map, you can look for a key that will let you in. The key is a person who can get you through all the barriers to the people with the answers. When the organization operates as a fortress, the front door is the public relations department. But you won't likely get past it. So you need the side door. These three people can serve as your keys to the side door:

1. The person at the top.
2. The person at the bottom.
3. The person on the outside who has connections to the inside.

When you can't find the key person, don't assume that no one will talk. In "All the President's Men," Bernstein and Woodward explained how they wanted to talk to someone on the grand jury investigating the Watergate break-in but found out that the names of jurors were kept secret. Knowing that 90 people worked in the clerk's office, Woodward went there and systematically questioned every employee he could find until he found one who let him rifle through the files where the names were stored.[1]

1. The person at the top

To reach the person at the top, you need a direct phone number. An executive's administrative assistant will likely direct you to public relations, so you need to be able to leave a message directly on the CEO's or president's voice mail. You can find the names of most top executives on Google Finance or Yahoo! Finance. Then search the Internet for any mention that lists the contact information. Sometimes it will be listed when she appears at industry gatherings or when she speaks to her local Rotary Club.

Once you have the number, try calling it in the evening after the assistant has gone home for the day, early in the morning before she arrives or on the weekend when she is off. People at the top often work long hours, and after hours they tend to answer their own phones. Often the person at the top is so confident of her own power and authority that she feels that a "Do Not Talk to the Press" rule does not apply to her. If you have done enough research, know what you are talking about and what you are looking for, and if your questions interest her, she might grant you an interview or give you the access you need to reach someone else in the organization. Never be intimidated by people just because of the position they hold. Don't think someone won't talk to you just because you don't have the prestige of The New York Times. The CEO might not want the publicity a New York Times story will generate, but you might seem more benign.

You might also get to the person at the top by doing a story she wants done. You might have little interest in writing about a new product line the company is launching or a new public awareness campaign a government agency is planning, but offering to do so could be your key to the inside. The soft story could lead to the hard one.

Finally, look them up using an electronic phone directory such as switchboard.com or zabasearch.com. If they are listed, call them at home. Lips that are zipped tight at work may open up at home. Follow two rules when calling people at home:

1. Never hesitate to do it.
2. Apologize when you do. Be respectful when you "invade" a private home.

2. The person at the bottom

Investigative journalists tend to make up a name for this person. He or she might be Fred or Karen. "He" works in a windowless office and only comes out for industry conferences, which is where you can find him. While the person at the top may feel the rules don't apply to her, the person at the bottom may not know the rules he is supposed to follow. No one expects you to find him, so no one told him not to talk. The people at the bottom know what goes on above them. They can tell you how things work in the company or institution, how things are going and what problems people might be worried about. He can point you to the right people to talk to and the right questions you should ask.

If you look again at the organizational chart in Exhibit 13.1 you can see that the Operations division includes a section for Material Handling. Within that is a department for QA, or Quality Assurance. A clerk in the quality assurance department would be a good example of a person at the bottom who would likely have great information to share. He would know the quality control processes within the company, how problems are spotted and what happens when the company discovers problems with the product.

Understanding the role the person at the bottom can play for you is important. Don't base your story solely on him. You can't be sure how much he really understands, so you have to confirm elsewhere everything he tells you. You also don't want to reward his help and his possible naivety by getting him in trouble. Ten years from now he might be at the top of the company. If you treat him fairly, you might end up with a key source later on.

3. The person on the outside

Companies, organizations and institutions don't operate in a vacuum. They must interact with other companies and organizations. They buy things from each other and collaborate on projects. Employees at one place often complain or brag about their organization to their counterparts who work elsewhere. That means that you might be able to find someone knowledgeable about Organization A in Organization B, if the two work together.

If you are interested in investigating a university that operates under a cloak of secrecy, try finding someone at a rival university or one that partners with it. You might try talking to competing companies or customers of a corporation that interests you or to an independent consultant who advises the company and its competitors on product development issues, sales strategies, mergers and alliances, or legal issues. While these people aren't likely to break confidentiality agreements, they might be able to point you in the right direction, introduce you to the right people on the inside, and suggest some questions that you should ask.

When you can't find the key

If no one inside or outside the company is willing to cooperate, go to the regulators who watch over industry. Private corporations might be exempt from most securities laws, but they aren't exempt from environmental regulations. They have to register with whatever state they are based in. They must file taxes and adhere to commerce regulations, which means that there is a paper trail to follow. There may be a nongovernmental body that regulates the industry as well. The Financial Accounting Standards Board, for example, is a private body that sets standards for financial reporting that companies are expected to follow.

You can also try the company's exes, or ex-employees. They can be wonderful sources of information. They know how things work, who is in charge, what the problems are and where you should turn to for more information. They can tell you about the regulations and the funny business. But just as you must be cautious when getting information from a low-level employee, you need to be careful when using information from ex-employees. The information they give you may be tainted by bitter feelings or resentment they feel toward their former employer. You don't want to base an entire story around one ex-employee. But if you get information from one or more ex-employees that jibes with information from current employees and from outside sources who work with the organization you are investigating, then each piece strengthens the investigation.

INVESTIGATING AN INDIVIDUAL

When your target is one person rather than a group or an institution, you still need a key to the inside. You need to find out not only what this person does but what makes him tick. You will need to talk to business acquaintances, friends, families, rivals and enemies. You want to find the paper trail the person leaves. Think forms and documentation from business and professional licenses, to driving licenses and voter registration cards. Sometimes an event in someone's life opens the person up to wide public disclosure of personal information, for example, the sale or purchase of real estate, a divorce, a battle over child custody, or a suit against an employer for breach of contract or against a neighbor for building too high a fence. Here, too, are exes you can turn to: former spouses, partners, colleagues, bosses, employees, professors, classmates, teammates, neighbors, childhood friends. You might even find ex-family — sons, daughters, nephews or nieces — who are willing to share information about the person. As with ex-employers, understand that the information these people might offer might be tainted by resentment. But as a component to an investigation, as one of many sources you rely on, an ex-partner, ex-spouse, or an estranged relative could prove invaluable.

INVESTIGATING A CONSPIRACY

Sometimes the problem involves a group of people or organizations — an oligarchy of big pharmaceutical companies *and* the regulators who let them bend the rules; a group of construction companies *and* the organized crime families who control them. What you might need to prove is the connection between these players. You will likely need someone on the inside, very close to the inside, or who was previously on the inside and has gotten out.

Deep Throat advised Bob Woodward to go after the people at the bottom first, then work his way up the ladder. Once you can show people the evidence you have, Deep Throat said, they will turn over more evidence that will help you convict the people above them:

> (. . .) the rope has to tighten slowly around everyone's neck. You build convincingly from the outer edges in, you get ten times the evidence you need against the Hunts and Liddys. They feel hopelessly finished — they may not talk right away, but the grip is on them. Then you move up and do the same thing at the next level. If you shoot too high and miss, then everybody feels more secure.[2]

ALTERNATIVE INVESTIGATIVE TECHNIQUES

Sometimes you may come up with a premise that can't be proved through interviews alone, and documentation or data appears to be lacking. Perhaps an organization managed to gag its employees and avoid leaving any paper trail. Maybe someone in the community holds enormous power but no official position, and how he wields that power isn't clear. Maybe you suspect a wide inequity in the distribution of resources, but you seem to be the only one who acknowledges it. For situations like these, reporters can turn to advanced techniques. Some, like undercover reporting, come with ethical risks. Others, such as submersion journalism, could come with physical or psychological sacrifices. Yet others require specialized knowledge, such as the ability to write simple computer programs or know how to use sophisticated software. But these risks and efforts can pay off. The journalists who successfully carry out these types of investigations are able to report stories reported nowhere else.

Undercover Reporting

"I've decided to call myself Marie Catherine Ochs. It is, may my ancestors forgive me, a family name. I have some claim to it, and I'm well versed in its European origins. Besides, it sounds much too square to be phony."[3]

That's how famed feminist Gloria Steinem explained how she entered the world of the Playboy Bunny in 1963 to investigate the treatment of women at Hugh Hefner's Playboy Club. It was one of a number of landmark investigations over the past century conducted by women undercover. In the 1950s, Marvel Cooke stood on a street corner to peddle herself off as one of the many black day laborers who hired themselves out as housecleaners. She wanted to document the low wages and humiliating treatment these women received. In 2001, Barbara Ehrenreich published "Nickel and Dimed: On (Not) Getting By in America," after going undercover as a minimum-wage worker to expose a system that pays people too little to live on. Going back to 1887, Nellie Bly got herself committed to Blackwell's Island Insane Asylum in New York to expose the abusive treatment of patients who were mentally ill. Box 13.1 offers an excerpt from her story.

These stories show the successes of undercover reporting, but going under-cover can present problems. It is deceptive, which violates the number one rule of journalism — honesty. You may risk a lawsuit. In Chapter 12, we saw what happened to ABC News when it had reporters work undercover as employees of a supermarket suspected of selling bad meat. Although undercover work is risky, a problem might be so bad you can't ignore it and won't be able to prove the problem and lay blame where it belongs without going undercover. It might be warranted if you need to investigate an organization in which people are too afraid to talk. Or it might be necessary when you investigate a place or person with a reputation so golden that no one would believe a whistle-blower without first-hand documented evidence. This was the case for reporter J. David McSwane.

In 2005, the Colorado high school senior wanted to know how far an army recruiter would go to get someone to enlist. McSwane went to his local army recruitment center and posed as a drug- and alcohol-addicted high school drop-out. These problems should have disqualified him for the Army. Instead, as he reported in his high school's newspaper, an army recruiter showed him how to temporarily detox his body in preparation for a drug test and how to get a forged diploma and create a phony high school transcript. McSwane taped phone conversations with army recruiters and had a friend film a trip he made to a local tobacco shop to buy a detox kit in the company of and at the suggestion of a recruiter. After the story was published, KCNC, a CBS station in Denver, covered his story and investigated his assertions.[4] Newspapers and magazines across the country picked up the story and did their own investigations into local recruiting centers. Finally, the Army conducted its own investigation into recruitment practices and in May 2005 ordered the more than 7,000 recruiters around the country to "stand down" for a day of retraining.[5]

"On the 22d of September I was asked by the World if I could have myself committed to one of the asylums for the insane in New York, with a view to writing a plain and unvarnished narrative of the treatment of the patients therein and the methods of management, etc. Did I think I had the courage to go through such an ordeal as the mission would demand? Could I assume the characteristics of insanity to such a degree that I could pass the doctors, live for a week among the insane without the authorities there finding out that I was only a 'chiel amang 'em takin' notes?' I said I believed I could. I had some faith in my own ability as an actress and thought I could assume insanity long enough to accomplish any mission entrusted to me. Could I pass a week in the insane ward at Blackwell's Island? I said I could and I would. And I did.

"(. . .)I succeeded in getting committed to the insane ward at Blackwell's Island, where I spent ten days and nights and had an experience which I shall never forget. I took upon myself to enact the part of a poor, unfortunate crazy girl, and felt it my duty not to shirk any of the disagreeable results that should follow. I became one of the city's insane wards for that length of time, experienced much, and saw and heard more of the treatment accorded to this helpless class of our population, and when I had seen and heard enough, my release was promptly secured. I left the insane ward with pleasure and regret — pleasure that I was once more able to enjoy the free breath of heaven; regret that I could not have brought with me some of the unfortunate women who lived and suffered with me, and who, I am convinced, are just as sane as I was and am now myself.

"But here let me say one thing: From the moment I entered the insane ward on the Island, I made no attempt to keep up the assumed role of insanity. I talked and acted just as I do in ordinary life. Yet strange to say, the more sanely I talked and acted the crazier I was thought to be by all except one physician, whose kindness and gentle ways I shall not soon forget."

Read the entire story at http://digital.library.upenn. edu/women/bly/madhouse/madhouse.html

While this particular story was duplicated by newspaper and stations around the country, undercover reporters risk admonishment from other media outlets and even from the readers they hope to inform. Even journalists are split on whether going undercover is an appropriate reporting choice.

Consider what happened to Ken Silverstein in 2007. The writer and editor for *Harper's Magazine* posed as an executive of a natural gas exporter that did business with the government of Turkmenistan, a country with a terrible human rights reputation. He wanted to see if Washington, D.C., lobbying firms would be willing to help polish up the country's reputation. He was able to show what lobbyists did for repressive regimes to help them secure favor with the U.S. government.[7]

Some journalists took exception to the way he did the story. Washington Post media critic Howard Kurtz noted that most media organizations avoid undercover reporting because "no matter how good the story, lying to get it raises as many questions about journalists as their subjects."[8] Others say that some stories can't be done without it. Jacqueline McLean, an investigative reporter with Fox-9 News in Minneapolis, sent two employees from her station undercover to an army recruiting station in May 2008 and found that the recruiters were as manipulative as they were with McSwane three years earlier.[9] She's a proponent of undercover reporting when done right and has a number of tips for reporters who want to try it.

McLean explains that you don't need sophisticated equipment if you can film or take pictures out in the open in public places. A digital video or still camera works fine. When going after someone, study them to see how they operate and do as much research as possible before you go in undercover. Make sure that you fit in and practice every possible scenario. That includes working out how you will ask your questions, what you should say if you are questioned and what you should do if you are caught.

McLean also says that you should not base your whole story on the hidden camera video or audio. In addition, make sure that the video is as factual as the story — don't distort through selective editing. Notify your target after you shoot the hidden camera footage and offer to sit down with them, show them the recordings and let them respond. It's a good idea to have a lawyer view your photos or footage before you publish or broadcast to ensure you haven't violated any laws and will not be at risk of a lawsuit.[10]

For a good discussion on the ethics and necessities of undercover reporting, check out an Oct. 17, 2008, broadcast of On the Media, available on its Web site. Called "Cover Ups," it is produced by WNYC for National Public Radio.

"Cover Ups" Audio and Transcript

www.onthemedia.org/transcripts/2008/10/17/04

Submersion journalism

This type of journalism used to be called *participatory journalism,* until people began using that term for journalism projects that include participation by the public in the reporting process. *Submersion journalism* is undercover reporting without the deception; a journalist submerses herself in the thing she reports on with the knowledge of the people or organization targeted. Author Ted Conover wanted to do a story in 2000 about a prison guard, but the New York department of corrections prison refused him entry to a training facility. So he applied for the officer training program himself. When he got accepted, he went through the training and spent a year as a prison guard before publishing his experiences in the book "New Jack: Guarding Sing Sing."[11]

Submersion reporting is a great method for a journalist who is just starting out, particularly if, as with Conover's project, your investigation requires you to get a paying job. The downside is that it can be lonely. You don't get the camaraderie that comes with working in a newsroom with other reporters and it can be a painful experience. You also want to make sure you can get out. It would be a terrible idea to enlist in the Army, for example, to investigate boot camp conditions, if you don't wish to serve a full tour of duty. Taking a dangerous job would not be a good idea if you don't have the stomach to handle it. Many jobs require employees to sign confidentiality agreements, and you shouldn't sign one if you know you will have to break it.

To take on a participatory reporting project, make sure you fully document your experience. Keep a daily journal. Or better yet, blog as frequently as you can. You might try creating a Twitter account and send updates to yourself. Twitter is a popular online service that allows you to constantly send text messages (tweets) to anyone who signs up to your Twitter feeds. Each tweet is limited to 140 characters and that's just twice the length of this sentence. By opening a Twitter account and tweeting to yourself, you wouldn't need to pull out a conspicuous notepad and you wouldn't have to trust your memory.

Twitter
http://twitter.com

Documenting your journey using all five senses is the important thing. Record what you see, hear, touch, smell and taste as well as what you think in the moment.

For more examples of this kind of reporting, check out the book "Submersion Journalism: Reporting in the Radical First Person," edited by Bill Wasik and Roger D. Hodge.[12]

Distributed reporting

In the age of skeletal budgets, this method is gaining in popularity. It stems from the notion that news organizations that don't compete with one another can collaborate. In *distributed reporting,* a number of different news outlets team up to report on the same subject in their separate newsrooms. As long as all the participating organizations are equally enthusiastic about the project, it can produce great results. It can give small publications the resources and power of a national news organization. In a national newsweekly, for example, an editor would assign a national story, and reporters in bureaus throughout the country would report in their separate locations and send the information to a national writer who would put it together into one big story. It is a bit like team reporting on a larger scale.

Distributed reporting works in much of the same way. Many college newspapers are located throughout the country, but by themselves they have minimal resources. A handful of college newspapers in five states could partner to investigate how recent changes to the federal student loan program affect college students. Each participating newspaper could look into a subtopic and pool the information collected. In 2006, a distributed reporting project in Texas coordinated by the Mayborn Graduate School of Journalism at the University of North Texas investigated how police around the state used tasers. Students from UNT, the University of Texas at Arlington and Tarleton State University filed more than 500 public records requests with hundreds of police agencies. The stories that resulted spurred Fort Worth legislator Ron Burnam to propose a bill that would restrict taser use. One of the stories that resulted was the piece "A Stunning Toll," which depicted the guitarist Trevor Goodchild who was tasered by police.[13]

The running investigation

This kind of investigation is done bit by bit, usually as part of a beat. It has some advantages, especially if you work a beat or work for an organization that doesn't normally do large investigative projects. It benefits the organization because it provides a steady stream of copy to fill the Web site, airtime or print pages over time and doesn't require a costly special section. You start with a small, focused story and then follow it over time with your stories serving as updates. If you cover a story where sources are few or closed off, the initial story will encourage people to come forward. The former employees you couldn't find and the rivals you didn't know about might contact you to point out the aspects of the story or tangents you missed.

You may end up with as many or more stories than a single investigative project, but because it doesn't have the "special report" tag on it, it may seem more manageable. Try planning a running investigation the same way you would a one-time investigative project. In Chapter 5 we discussed how you might plan for a main bar and sidebars, graphic elements and multimedia. You would do the same with a running investigation, but then parcel them out over a longer period of time. Your investigation will build as you publish each story.

In a massive running investigation, the Detroit Free Press began with this story that ran Jan. 24, 2008, this way:

> Detroit Mayor Kwame Kilpatrick and his chief of staff lied about their relationship last summer at a police whistle-blower trial that has cost the cash-strapped city more than $9 million, according to records obtained by the Free Press.
>
> The false testimony potentially exposes them to felony perjury charges, legal experts say.
>
> Kilpatrick and chief of staff Christine Beatty denied during testimony in August that they had a sexual relationship. But the records, a series of text messages, show them engaged in romantic banter as well as planning and recounting sexual liaisons.[14]

Reporters Jim Schaefer and M.L. Elrick used the Michigan Freedom of Information Act to obtain the text messages between Kilpatrick and his chief of staff. Kilpatrick ended up pleading guilty to felony charges, was sentenced to 120 days in jail and five years' probation, had to pay $1 million in restitution and lost his license to practice law. The paper published more than 600 stories on the scandal over the next year. It posted all kinds of documents, such as the legal decision that ordered the text messages made public, the text messages themselves, and Kilpatrick's resignation letter.[15] Exhibit 13.2 shows how the Free Press displayed the smoking gun text messages on its Web site.

Kwame Kilpatrick's text messages as they appeared in the Free Press investigation.   **EXHIBIT 13.2**

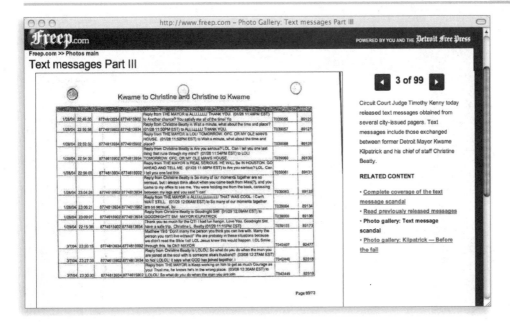

In what may prove to be the ultimate running investigation, reporters Bill Allison and Anupama Narayanswamy of the Sunlight Foundation began blogging their efforts to track the actions of senators and representatives of the U.S. Congress. They tell readers about the calls they make, the FOIA letters they send out, the data and reports they get and the questions they ask. They write about problems they have in their investigations and how they work them out. You can read an archive of their blog at the Sunlight Foundation's Web site.

Real Time Investigations
http://realtime.
sunlightprojects.org

Crowdsourcing

In a *crowdsourcing* investigation, you send out a question to your readers in your newspaper, online or as part of a news broadcast and ask them to participate in the investigation. So instead of introducing the readers to the investigation with your findings, your first story is just an announcement that you plan to investigate the topic along with an explanation of what it is you want to know and how you think your readers, viewers or listeners might help.

This announcement turns the reporter's or organization's Web site into a massive wiki. Jeff Howe, a contributing editor to Wired Magazine, was one of the first journalists to spot the trend. He says its foundations are the principles of open source software community-building through shared rather than proprietary knowledge.[16] Like distributed reporting, it can give organizations with little resources the power to investigate big stories.

EXHIBIT 13.3	A crowdsourcing letter posted by the News-Press, asking for input on a city investigation.[17]

Exhibit 13.3 is the letter to readers that the News-Press of Ft. Myers, Fla., posted on its Web site in 2006.

The News-Press posted the letter, along with the reporters' contact information, in response to reader complaints that the city charged them tens of thousands of dollars to hook up new homes to water and sewer lines. The readers wanted to know why the fees were so high. The response to the newspaper's letter was overwhelming. Readers formed themselves into investigative groups. Over the next few weeks, a special online forum received more than 6,000 postings. Some readers created their own discussion threads and people with specialized knowledge offered their expertise. As a result, within weeks the city cut hookup fees by 30 percent. The paper kept the investigation going; it had raised all kinds of issues, such as the discovery that hookups were a result of a massive expansion that was going to cost an enormous amount of taxpayer funds.

After the success of that story and others that relied on reader participation, Gannett restructured the newsrooms in all its nearly 90 papers to incorporate and expand on crowdsourcing techniques.

Crowdsourcing is especially popular with Web-based news organizations. Consider the following:

- In February 2008, Talking Points Memo, a blog on national politics founded by Joshua Marshall, became the first Internet-only news site to win a prestigious George Polk Award for its coverage of the firing of eight U.S. attorneys.[18] While it has a small paid staff that includes some full-time reporters, it also relies on tips from readers. When it wants to conduct a big investigation or wade through big reports, it will ask its readers to help out.

- In OffTheBus, a crowdsourcing project of the Huffington Post and a nonprofit site called newassignment.net, some 12,000 people participated, gathering information, providing video footage and conducting interviews. At one point, the Huffington Post asked OffTheBus participants to help it profile every superdelegate to the 2008 Democratic Primary. Hundreds of people contributed information and with it, the site was able to produce an interactive map that allowed people to learn about the superdelegates in their states.[19] The resulting map is shown in Exhibit 13.4.

An interactive map from the OffTheBus project shows profiles of 2008 Democratic superdelegates that were submitted by readers.   **EXHIBIT 13.4**

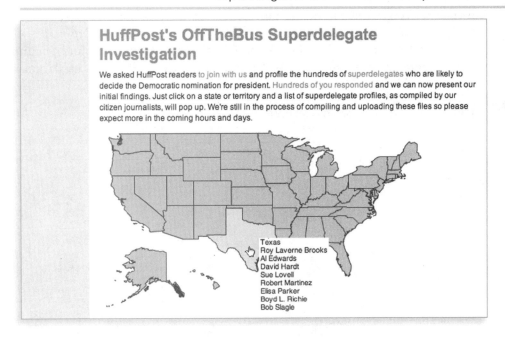

HuffPost's OffTheBus Superdelegate Investigation

We asked HuffPost readers to join with us and profile the hundreds of superdelegates who are likely to decide the Democratic nomination for president. Hundreds of you responded and we can now present our initial findings. Just click on a state or territory and a list of superdelegate profiles, as compiled by our citizen journalists, will pop up. We're still in the process of compiling and uploading these files so please expect more in the coming hours and days.

Texas
Roy Laverne Brooks
Al Edwards
David Hardt
Sue Lovell
Robert Martinez
Elisa Parker
Boyd L. Richie
Bob Slagle

COMPUTER-ASSISTED REPORTING

A nother advanced reporting method used by investigative journalists is computer-assisted reporting, also known as CAR. It is a bit like the term *investigative reporting:* Just as many reporters incorporate some investigative techniques into daily reporting, many reporters incorporate some aspects of CAR into their investigative projects. This may be as basic as using Excel to do data analysis, or using Google maps to plot out the geographic distribution of a problem. But some reporters become CAR specialists and do sophisticated data collection and analysis, such as social networking analysis, data scraping and mapping.

Social network analysis

A relatively new tool that enables journalists to explore patterns of interactions is called *social network analysis*. It relies on relational database software such as MySQL, Microsoft Access or FileMaker Pro. Some journalists use an open source program called UCINET to do their social data mapping.

In social networking analysis, you link up tables of information to create a social map. For example, you might connect these tables:

- A list of state legislators that includes the high school they graduated from
- A list of state contractors that includes their high school as well
- A list of lobbyists that includes the state legislators they had lunch with

By performing the analysis, you can quickly see connections between contractors, legislators and lobbyists. The more tables you add and the more information you can connect, the more complex the relationships become. A visual representation of these connections is called a *social relationship map*.

Exhibit 13.5 contains a network map that Robert Hanneman and Shaun Bowler created at the University of California at Riverside. They used cam-

---

EXHIBIT 13.5   Network map of campaign contributions in California.

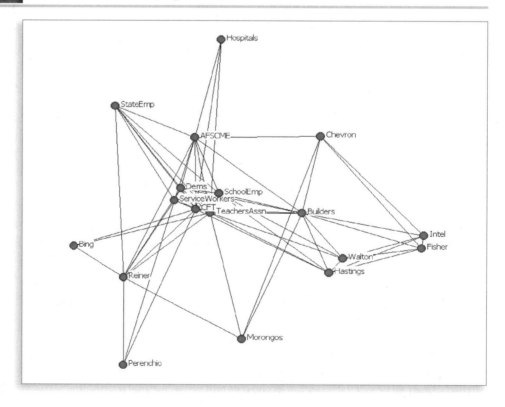

paign contribution data from an online database maintained by the California secretary of state to explore the intersection of interests between groups and individuals who were major donors of multiple statewide ballot propositions between 2002 and 2005.[20]

Sometimes a social relationship map will make hidden relationships visible and will show you the importance of relationships that you might have otherwise underestimated. Perhaps a local man holds no official position in the government, and his name never appears on official documents. But through a social relationship map, you might see that he had lunch with a number of important figures in your city, and each one of those people were connected to a particular and obscure piece of legislation.

IRE's Social Network Analysis Links
www.ire.org/sna

Data scraping

Endless amounts of information are stored on the Internet. Unfortunately, it may be difficult to find a path to that information. The databases that store it show you only one record at a time and only when you make a specific record request for it. To get at all the information in a database, CAR reporters "scrape" the database. They do this by learning an open source computer language known as Python and using a software program called Django, also available for free. A number of free tutorials and online manuals are available to help you learn Python, such as How to Think Like a Computer Scientist: Learning with Python.[21] Reporters can then analyze the information they've obtained using a spreadsheet or a database program based on a computer language called Structured Query Language, or SQL.

Free Python Tutorial
http://openbook
project.net/thinkC
Spy/index.xhtml

Download Django
www.djangoproject.
com

Official Python site
http://python.org

Reporters have learned that by spending a little time learning data-scraping programs, they can save a lot of time that would otherwise be spent searching through data. In 2008, Hank Sims, editor of the North Coast Journal, a community weekly in Arcata, Calif., wanted to find out if the Department of Defense spent any money in his rural outpost and, if so, what the money bought. He wanted to use the database USAspending.gov, shown in Exhibit 13.6, which allows visitors to search a database of all contracts given out by federal agencies by state or congressional district. However, it cannot be searched by city or zip code. So Sims wrote a computer script using Django to instruct the program that underlies the USAspending.gov Web site to return the data in a format that would allow him to enter it into his own database program.

"I got a list of zip codes in the county," Sims said. "I wrote a script that said give me every federal contract for each of these zip codes. It went out and returned it in XML. Then I could use a SQL database to get at that further."[22]

Sims was able to localize military spending and make his readers understand that even in a county in California, far away from Washington, D.C., changes in the U.S. military budget could affect the local economy. You can read an excerpt of the story in Box 13.2 (page 309).

EXHIBIT 13.6   Sample search results for federal contracts performed in California.

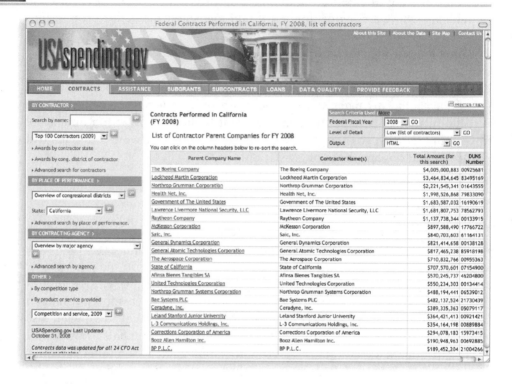

Mapping

In Chapters 5 and 9 you learned how you can use maps to organize and display your data. However, some CAR stories rely on sophisticated geographic mapping techniques that go beyond the capabilities of Google or other online mapping programs. This type of computer-assisted reporting involves the use of a geographic information system (GIS). Geographers and other social scientists have used GIS for years to map out social and environmental problems.

This type of software takes data from publicly available databases such as the U.S. Census, university or government research, data you collect yourself and that you compile into a spreadsheet program, or information collected with a global-positioning system monitor and plots it out according to geographic location. In this way you can find connections between crime rates and government expenditures on public safety, housing patterns, industrial development and children's health.

Using GIS software and data they collect or find, journalists can prove inequities that the government or society ignores or denies. In 2006, the Washington Post mapped out crime data in the District of Columbia and found that the areas where the most robberies occurred were some of the most economically vibrant neighborhoods while the poorer neighborhoods suffered more from homicides.[23]

An excerpt from Hank Sims' "Humboldt at War: Local military contractors feed and clothe soldiers, keep birds and bats safe"[24]   BOX 13.2

"The United States of America has now spent upwards $500 billion on the war and subsequent occupation of Iraq. In the same time (since government fiscal year 2002–2003) the U.S. Department of Defense has spent almost $1.5 trillion on contracts with private companies — not all of it directly related to the war, but all of it required to maintain the Pentagon and the branches of the service in one way or another. That figure — $1.5 trillion — is taken from USAspending.gov, the government's online data clearinghouse on federal spending. The site also shows that $20 million has been spent with contractors based in Humboldt County. It's a pittance by national standards, but for some local businesses and researchers it's made all the difference.

"There's a few conclusions that can be drawn by looking at the list of 24 Humboldt County companies and other contractors that have done business with the military since 2000. For one, it shows that Humboldt County's principal value to the federal government lies principally in its relationship with the outdoors. The vast majority of money the military spends here goes to one of two business sectors: consultants with specialties in the ecological sciences and firms that got their start by catering to outdoor enthusiasts. If military spending is any guide — and it's probably as good a guide as any — our niche in the world economy stems from our relationship with the natural world.

"The other thing that the list makes obvious is that that niche is overwhelmingly dominated by the county's second city. Over three-quarters of the military contracts that go to Humboldt County go to Arcata. A portion of this is due to the scientific community centered around Humboldt State University. (Humboldt State itself has done over $700,000 worth of business with the Dept. of Defense, which helps fund research and development through the university's Sponsored Programs Foundation.) But by far the larger part goes to Arcata's vibrant manufacturing scene, which has supplied branches of the Pentagon with boats, clothing, refrigerators, furniture and musical instruments.

"At the same time, of course, Arcata is also the spiritual home of the local antiwar movement, at times making national headlines for the anti-Bush, anti-military items that have popped up on its City Council agenda. But the contradiction is not as great as it might seem. In the first place, by national standards military spending in the city is miniscule. In fiscal year 2006 (September 2005 through August 2006), the Dept. of Defense spent almost $300 billion on contracts — just about $1,000 for every resident of the United States. Meanwhile, it spent only $1.48 million in Arcata, or about $86 per resident."

Read the full story at www.northcoastjournal.com/ issues/2008/03/13/humboldt-war

Reprinted with permission from the North Coast Journal.

Exhibit 13.7 shows how Humboldt State University natural resources and sociology professors Steven and Sheila Steinberg mapped out pesticide use in the Central Valley in California against locations of elementary schools.

If you don't have the desire or time to learn how to use sophisticated database programming or GIS software, but you have an idea for an important story

EXHIBIT 13.7   An ArcView GIS rendering of pesticide use on farms in the Central Valley in California layered on top of the location of elementary schools.

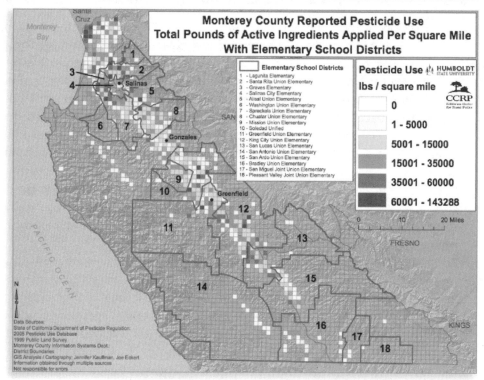

Monterey County Reported Pesticide Use
Total Pounds of Active Ingredients Applied Per Square Mile
With Elementary School Districts

Elementary School Districts
1 - Lagunita Elementary
2 - Santa Rita Union Elementary
3 - Graves Elementary
4 - Salinas City Elementary
5 - Alisal Union Elementary
6 - Washington Union Elementary
7 - Spreckels Union Elementary
8 - Chualar Union Elementary
9 - Mission Union Elementary
10 - Soledad Unified
11 - Greenfield Union Elementary
12 - King City Union Elementary
13 - San Lucas Union Elementary
14 - San Antonio Union Elementary
15 - San Ardo Union Elementary
16 - Bradley Union Elementary
17 - San Miguel Joint Union Elementary
18 - Pleasant Valley Joint Union Elementary

Pesticide Use   HUMBOLDT STATE UNIVERSITY
lbs / square mile   CCRP
0
1 - 5000
5001 - 15000
15001 - 35000
35001 - 60000
60001 - 143288

Data Sources:
State of California Department of Pesticide Regulation:
2005 Pesticide Use Database
1999 Public Land Survey
Monterey County Information Systems Dept.:
District Boundaries
GIS Analysis / Cartography: Jennifer Kauffman, Joe Eckert
Information obtained through multiple sources
Not responsible for errors

Source: Map created by Steven J. and Sheila L. Steinberg. Reprinted with their permission.

that would depend on that kind of knowledge, you might be able to find someone who can do that analysis for you. Universities house social scientists who use GIS software and work with relational databases. The National Institute for Computer-Assisted Reporting at the University of Missouri will also work with students on databases and mapping. You might also partner with a large news organization or a nonprofit research group that would be interested in the results of your investigation, and which might be able to team you up with a database expert or a reporter experienced in mapping technology or data analysis. People who can bridge data analysis programming and journalism are highly sought after in the industry.

NICAR
http://data.nicar.org

ADVANCED METHODS FOR KEEPING INFORMATION SECURE

B e aware of the threat to privacy and security when gathering and working with sensitive information. In 2006, three disturbing events occurred that are worth noting:

- In January 2006, the U.S. Department of Justice issued subpoenas to four search engines to gather information on possible child molesters. It sought a random sample of 1 million Web pages that people could search through Google. While Google fought the subpoenas, AOL, Yahoo! and Microsoft provided at least some information the government wanted.[25]

- In August 2006, AOL released some 20 million search records of some 650,000 users, identifying each user by number. With that number and the search information, reporters from the New York Times were able to track down a 62-year-old woman in the state of Georgia who searched for landscapers and ideas on how to deal with urinating dogs.[26]

- Throughout the year, the technology corporation Hewlett-Packard hired private investigators to spy on reporters from seven news organizations. This included reporter Dawn Kawamoto, from the online technology news service CNET, whose phone records HP illegally obtained and pored through.[27]

These events prove that if you store information on the Web, you risk it getting into the hands of other people. You might also need to be aware that packet sniffers are becoming more prevalent. Information on the Internet travels in packets on a network. *Sniffers* are software tools on a network that allow someone at the network to see all the information that travels on it. Sniffers can be programmed to look for certain types of information or forms of activity. That means that someone at a company or organization you investigate could watch you as you poke around on the company's Web site.[28]

When you store information on a site like blogger.com, which is owned by Google, or MySpace, which is owned by the News Corporation, you effectively turn over that data to a large corporation. Regardless of their privacy policies, you lose control over it. If you delete the information from your site, it does not necessarily get deleted off the server it is stored on. If you want to see how that works in practice, take a look at the Wayback Machine, a site maintained by a nonprofit organization called the Internet Archive, which captures and stores Web sites for future retrieval by researchers. Exhibit 13.8 shows how the Wayback Machine can be used to view early incarnations of Facebook.

Internet Archive
www.archive.org

Or you can go into Google and pull up pages using the "Cached" link, located at the end of any search result like the one in Exhibit 13.9. It allows you to pull up a snapshot of a site even after the person who maintains the site has pulled that information off the Web.[29]

If your project involves the collecting of information from people or about people who are at risk of losing their jobs or who might be in trouble with the law or criminal entities, you might want to find a more secure method of storing and sharing your information whether you are working alone or with team members. You could set up code names for people and organizations when entering them into electronic documents that you share over the Internet. That way, even if your documents became searchable over the Web, a search engine couldn't find them by name. You could also store your information on personal

EXHIBIT 13.8   Archival images of the original Facebook domain, www.thefacebook.com, from the Wayback Machine.

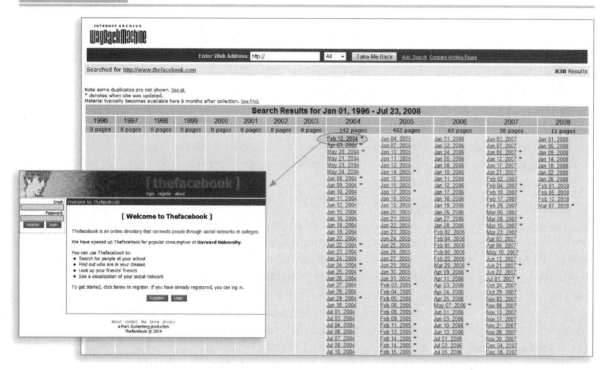

hard drives and share it through the use of flash drives, keeping it off shared networks altogether.

Another thing to consider is how noticeable your own searches for information might be. In 2007, the Lumberjack student newspaper at Humboldt State University in California signed onto a free Web site tracking service called Site Meter. It gives you statistics on the people who click on the site. Not only does it tell you aggregate page views, but it lists the domain address of each viewer and the geographic location of the domain. Exhibit 13.10 shows Site Meter's listing of visitors to the newspaper's site.

EXHIBIT 13.9   Even after someone takes down an older version of a Web page, it remains available in a cache version, which can be accessed through Google's "Cached" link.

Site Meter's listing of visitors to a site.   **EXHIBIT 13.10**

	The Lumberjack Recent Visitors by Visit Details			
Detail	Domain Name	Visit Time	Page Views	Visit Length
1	207.183.244.#			
2	98.98.238.#			
3	comcast.net			
4	humboldt.edu			
5	clarku.edu			
6	clarku.edu			
7	humboldt.edu			
8	suddenlink.net			
9	aol.com			
10	pa.net			
11	suddenlink.net			
12	ddsteel.com			
13	comcast.net			
14	comcast.net			
15	orangehomedsl.co.u			
16	bluewin.ch			
17	humboldt.edu			
18	comcast.net			
19	artistuntied.com			
20	suddenlink.net			

	The Lumberjack Recent Visitors by Referrals
Detail	Referring URL
61	unknown
62	unknown
63	http://www.google.com/search?q...UTF-8&sourceid=ie7&rlz=1I7TSHA
64	http://www.google.com/search?h...matli band members&btnG=Search
65	http://forum.nin.com/bb/read.php?21,34913,page=7
66	unknown
67	http://news.google.com/news?hl...ancisco gay parade&btnG=Search
68	http://www.google.com/search?h...cd=1&q=aurora odelberg&spell=1
69	http://www.google.com/search?q...n-US:official&client=firefox-a
70	http://www.google.com/search?c... lumberjack&btnG=Google Search
71	unknown
72	http://www.google.com/search?h...umberjack humboldt&btnG=Search
73	http://www.google.com/search?h...ro&btnG=Google Search&aq=f&oq=
74	http://images.google.com/imgre...=345&w=230&sz=19&hl=en&start=2
75	http://www.google.com/search?h...pray, activists&start=120&sa=N
76	http://www.google.com.au/searc...and hero comes to stores&meta=
77	http://mailcenter.comcast.net/...=Show&no=399&uid=248192&sid=c0
78	http://www.google.com/search?h...er&btnG=Google Search&aq=f&oq=
79	http://www.google.com/search?h...q=all pets humboldt pa&spell=1
80	http://www.google.com/search?q...n-US:official&client=firefox-a

1 2 3 [4] 5

In one chart Site Meter tells us that someone with an e-mail address from Clark University, which has only about 3,000 students, visited the Lumberjack Web site at least twice. In another, it allows us to see the referral pages. That means that we can see the Google search and search term that took the person to the Lumberjack site.

While some domain names tell you little, such as verizon.net, for instance, other domains tell you something about the user. A university domain, for example, lets you know that the person who came onto the site is a faculty, student, administrator or staff of that university. It also tells the newspaper how the user got to the Web site. If the user came via Google, not only does that info show, but the actual Google search page shows. That means that the newspaper can see the exact search terms the user used that took him to the site.

Consider this scenario: You are investigating an obscure corporation. As part of your investigation, you surf through the corporation's Web site. Because it is not a well-known organization, likely it doesn't get a lot of Web traffic. You, meanwhile, are doing your surfing off a college computer and your college has only 1,500 students. The corporation will be able to see that you are collecting information about it, and they will be able to see exactly what information you collect. If you use a search engine to find them, they will be able to see the search terms you used. This can tip the company off to a possible investigation, leading them to close off easy means of access. They also can potentially use this information to find out who you are.

Site Meter
www.sitemeter.com

Security privacy expert Greg Conti, a professor of computer science at the U.S. Military Academy at West Point, suggested that you mask your identity by doing Internet searches on different computers and devices; each individual computer and Internet device has a different IP address and that is the main way a search engine tags you as a user. The problem gets complicated if you want to use some of the free tools offered by Google and other information companies, because to do so they make you register with them and they can then tag you across computing platforms.[30]

A scene in the movie "All the President's Men" depicts Washington Post editor Ben Bradlee, played by Jason Robards, standing on his front lawn in his bathrobe talking to reporters Bob Woodward and Carl Bernstein, played by Robert Redford and Dustin Hoffman. They tell him they can't talk inside the house because Deep Throat said it was probably wiretapped. Bradlee says: "We're under a lot of pressure, you know, and you put us there. Nothing's riding on this except the, uh, First Amendment to the Constitution, freedom of the press, and maybe the future of the country. Not that any of that matters, but if you guys fuck up again, I'm going to get mad. Goodnight."[31]

Keep track of your information and also keep track of who may be tracking you.

CONCLUSION

Investigative reporters often incorporate different methods for getting hard-to-get information. Some strategize ways to penetrate a closed organization. Others use hidden cameras to go undercover. Mapping programs help reporters find geographic correlations, and new computer programs let reporters search out and grab information buried in databases on the Web. News organizations are experimenting with ways to involve readers in the information-gathering process. What methods you employ will depend on what you want to investigate and how difficult it will be to get the information you need to prove or disprove your premise. But always consider the legal and ethical issues involved in the different reporting methods and take the steps necessary to protect yourself, your sources and your information.

EXERCISES

1. As a simple crowdsourcing project, select someone in the class who is a member of Facebook. In the person's status box, post this question:

   "I am trying to collect examples of bad housing conditions. Does anyone out there have a story to tell me about their current housing situation or know of anyone with a good story?"

   See how many anecdotes and examples you can collect as a result.

2. Come up with five questions that could be put to a readership as part of a hypothetical crowdsourcing project in your local area. If you were the editor of your local newspaper, how would you go about getting your readers involved in an investigation into those questions?

3. How would you go about investigating the questions you came up with in Exercise 2 through submersion reporting? How difficult would that be to do?

4. Try to think of a story that would only work through undercover reporting. Why would other methods not work? How can you minimize possible ethical problems regarding deception, privacy and trespass?

THE BIG STORY Project • THE BIG STORY Project • STEP 13

13.1 Write a third draft of your story that focuses on making your story as convincing as possible.

13.2 Create a timeline for your story, either as a print graphic or multimedia. Remember, sites like dipity.com provide free timelines.

13.3 Go to the Web sites of the Student Press Law Center (splc.org) and the Reporters Committee for Freedom of the Press (rcfp.org) and see if you can find advice from legal experts to guide you in dealing with those legal and ethical problems.

13.4 Assign someone to be a devil's advocate. That person should try to punch holes in your project from a legal and ethical standpoint. The rest of the group must be able to respond to the devil's advocate's arguments. If you can't, try to come up with an alternate method for investigating the problem.

NOTES

1. Carl Bernstein and Bob Woodward. *All the President's Men.* Simon & Schuster, 1974, p. 208.

2. Ibid., p. 196.

3. Gloria Steinem. *Outrageous Acts and Everyday Rebellions.* Second Edition. Henry Holt, 1983, p. 33.

4. Brian Dakss. "Army recruiters face investigation." CBS News. May 2, 2005. http://www.cbsnews.com/stories/2005/05/02/earlyshow/main692361.shtml.

5. Gerry J. Gilmore. "Army recruiters stand down to refocus on values." American Forces Press Service, May 20, 2005.

6. Nellie Bly [Elizabeth Jane Cochrane Seaman]. *Ten Days in a Mad-House.* Ian L. Munro, 1887.

7. Ken Silverstein. "Their men in Washington: Undercover with D.C.'s lobbyists for hire." *Harper's,* July 2007.

8. Howard Kurtz. "Stung by Harper's in a web of deceit." *Washington Post,* June 25, 2007, p. C01.

9. Jacqueline McLean. "Investigators: Recruiting wrongs?" MyFoxTwinCities.com. Broadcast May 13, 2008.

10. Jacqueline McLean. "Tricks of the trade: Hidden cameras to getting in the door." Presented at the IRE Conference, Atlanta, 2004. Available through the IRE Resource Center, Tipsheet 2173.

11. Ted Conover. *New Jack: Guarding Sing Sing*. Random House, 2000.

12. B. Wasik and R.D. Hodge (eds.). *Submersion Journalism: Reporting in the Radical First Person*. New Press, 2008.

13. "A stunning toll: Taser related deaths and questionable uses of the weapon are mounting in Texas." *Ft. Worth Weekly*, March 8, 2006. You can find out more about the Mayborn Institute's distributed reporting program at http://themayborn. unt.edu/dist_rep.htm.

14. Jim Schaefer and M.L. Elrick. "Mayor Kilpatrick, chief of staff lied under oath, text messages show: Romantic exchanges undercut denials." *Detroit Free Press*, Jan. 24, 2008.

15. See the Free Press' entire coverage at http://freep. com/kwamekilpatrick.

16. Jeff Howe. "The rise of crowdsourcing." *Wired*, June 2006.

17. Tom Hayden. "Help investigate controversial project." http://www.news-press.com/apps/ pbcs.dll/article?AID=/20060714/CAPEWATER/ 307140001/1075. Also see Jeff Howe, "Gannett to crowdsource news," *Wired News*, Nov. 3, 2006.

18. Noam Cohen. "Blogger, sans pajamas, rakes muck and a prize." *The New York Times*, Feb. 25, 2008.

19. You can find the Off the Bus Project at http:// www.huffingtonpost.com/p/huffposts-offthebus- superdeleg.html.

20. Reprinted with permission from Robert Hanneman.

21. A.B. Downey, J. Elkner and C. Meyers. *How to Think Like a Computer Scientist: Learning with Python*. Green Tea Press, 2002.

22. Interview with Hank Sims, Dec. 12, 2008.

23. Allison Klein and Dan Keating. "Liveliest D.C. neighborhoods also jumping with robberies." *Washington Post*, Oct. 13, 2006, p. A1.

24. Hank Sims. "Humboldt at war." *North Coast Journal*, March 13, 2008.

25. Arshad Mohammed. "Google refuses demand for search information." *Washington Post*, Jan. 20, 2006, p. A01, http://www.washington post.com/wp-dyn/content/article/2006/01/19/ AR2006011903331.html.

26. Michael Barbaro and Tom Zeller, Jr. "A face is exposed for AOL searcher no. 4417749." *The New York Times*, Aug. 9, 2006, http://query.ny- times.com/gst/fullpage.htmlres=9E0CE3DD1F3FF 93AA3575BC0A9609C8B63.

27. Damon Darlin. "Deeper spying is seen in Hewlett review." *The New York Times*, Sept. 18, 2006, http://www.nytimes.com/2006/09/18/technology/ 18hp.html?scp=5&sq=dawn+kawamoto&st=nyt.

28. Theresa Carey. "Phighting phishes and pharmers." *Barron's*, June 2, 2007.

29. http://www.archive.org/index.php

30. Gregory Conti. "Googling considered harmful." Paper presented at the New Security Paradigms Workshop, Dagstuhl, Germany, October 2006.

31. *All the President's Men*. Warner Brothers, 1976.

Pitching the Story

CHAPTER PREVIEW In this chapter, you'll learn how to pitch your story proposal to an editor. You will see how important it is to focus your proposal around criteria an editor will consider when deciding whether to okay an investigative project. Specifically, you will understand the importance of relevance, methodology and execution to your story proposal. You will acquire the skills to draft a preliminary outline for your story, to create a visual diagram of your methodology and to storyboard it. Finally, you will receive advice on how to get the time and resources you will need to carry out your project and start earning your credibility.

14

C H A P T E R

KNOW WHAT EDITORS WANT

"What else you got going?"

T hose are the five words that crush many a good investigative idea before the reporter even has time to flesh out the story. Unless you plan to publish your investigation on your own blog or in your own newsletter, you need to convince a skeptical publisher, editor or producer to green-light the story. Otherwise you might spend time, energy and money on research and interviews for nothing. Or you won't ever find the time to work on it, because no one will clear you of your other responsibilities.

But if you put serious time and thought into developing your story pitch as well as your game plan for action, you might find support for your proposal even from an editor or publisher who hasn't shown any interest in investigative work. Most editors want to publish good, serious, hard-hitting journalism but they don't want to waste valuable time and resources on a story that won't happen. They are often skeptical that their reporters can handle complicated subjects and turn them into compelling reads. They must deal with the reality that they've got pages or airtime to fill every day, week or month. They can't take chances on a story that won't happen or that will collapse.

When Dawn MacKeen and Lauren Terrazzano decided to team up for their story "A Tragic Vulnerability," they realized they would need time off from their daily reporting beats. Newsday had a dedicated team of investigative reporters, but neither of the women were on it. They needed to make sure they would be given the time and resources necessary to properly report the story. "We met and mapped out the different areas we could cover," MacKeen said. "Then we went to talk to one of the editors. We went in with a plan. We kind of burst into his office. We presented a case for the resources."[1]

In putting together a pitch, you need to know what your editor will want.

Start with the story's focus

A reporter could lay out pages of detailed facts, but an editor will still ask: "What's the story?" Editors don't want an unclear idea or unconnected statistics. In Chapter 5, we discussed turning a vague concept into a focused premise. Do the same here. Tell your editor: "The city's failure to properly maintain city streets is putting residents at risk of accidents." You know that the premise changes as the project evolves and that your focus may shift. But you need a plan to start with, and your editor and all the members of your investigative team must agree on its initial focus.

Outline the entire project

A reluctant editor will want to know that your project won't turn into a time-consuming mess. That's why you need to show him a strong structure even before you start your interviews.

If you can show your editor a well-planned structure, it will go a long way in alleviating his fears and skepticism. Early on in the investigation of Boys Town, The Omaha Sun team framed their story in seven pieces: how the Boys Town charity created and sustained its image; how it operated as a landowner, an incorporated village, a U.S. Post Office, a school system, a tax-exempt organization and a licensed child-care service provider.[2]

A storyboard is also a good way to present the outline of your project, especially if you have multimedia elements that will go with it. You saw in Chapter 5 how a storyboard worked as a visual To Do list, and it can also serve as a visual plan for your editor.

Tell why readers, viewers or listeners will care

Visceral juices is a term for deep emotional feelings readers get when they read something that makes them care. Your editor will want to know why your readers would care about your story. An editor won't grant you time and resources to do a big project just because you find the subject interesting. And it isn't enough that you think the story will win awards. Some editors might care, but in a time of skeletal staff and tight budgets, many won't.

Longtime Newsday editor Bob Greene said you should determine whether and how the problem you want to investigate relates to the community you write for and about.[3] Will it be an important story to tell? Will it be a good story, meaning one that people feel compelled to read? Some angles that you could use to show how the story will connect with your publication's audience include the following:

- The story is about something that affects them directly.
- They can identify with the people at the heart of the story.
- They feel like they know the person at the heart of the story.
- The story deals with an issue that is inherently unfair or will spur action from the audience.

Point out the news angle

Sometimes it isn't enough to show why readers will care. Editors want to know why the publication should run the story *now*. That becomes a problem when you discover an issue that has existed a long time. Many good investigative stories lack an obvious time element. When that happens, you need to push the story forward. Consider again the proposal for a story about government contracts. The problem has existed forever, it seems. But likely a new contract for a new project is coming up sometime next year. Perhaps a new supervisor on the board or a new contractor will be involved in the bidding process. Another election is coming up and that will mean a new round of political donations. All of these can be used to justify the story. You can also move a story forward if you focus on possible solutions to the problem that have yet to be implemented. The problem may be old news, but any solutions will be new. So even to find possible solutions, however tenuous or improbable they may be, introduces a new element to the story.

You could also piggyback off some action that is expected at the state or national level and pitch your investigation as a localization. While an editor might have a difficult time understanding why you want to investigate a long-standing local problem now, he can understand why you would want to localize a state or national issue currently in the news.

Explain the methodology

Your editor will want to know how you plan to carry out your investigation. Mark Katches, the assistant managing editor for projects and investigations at the Milwaukee Journal Sentinel, said to write a *nerd box* early. That's what he calls the box that newspapers throw on top of a story that explains to the readers how the investigation was carried out.[4]

Your methods will need to be transparent as you will have to admit and explain them to the readers. But going through this process at the beginning of your investigation could help convince a reluctant editor that you know what you need to do. Write the box explaining the methodology as early as possible, in the first few weeks of reporting, he suggested. That way you will make sure you and everyone involved in the story feel good about the methodology.[5]

Box 14.1 is a nerd box from a project the nonprofit Center for Public Integrity did to find out how many privately funded trips congressional legislators accepted.

Prove you can prove it

Provide a list of sources you plan to rely on. If you intend to base your story primarily on interviews, you need to estimate how numerous, diverse and credible they will be. You need to tell your editor whether you may have to grant sources anonymity and what that will cost you in credibility. If your news organization doesn't allow the use of anonymous sources, that could be a problem. Both you and your editor need to figure out from the start how to work around that problem.

The tougher the accusation you expect to make, the more your editor will want to see documents and data to support your premise, so you need to figure out where you likely will find them. Recall again, what happened to Dan Rather and Chuck Philips. Many editors are reluctant to okay investigative projects because they fear the consequences if the investigation explodes in their faces; they've seen it happen at other news organizations. So you need to demonstrate why that won't happen in your investigation and how you will be able to get the proof you need.

These requirements mean that you need to be honest about your own abilities. In Chapter 5 we saw that you should consider the do-ability of a project before you take it on, and part of that consideration is your own abilities and preferences.

METHODOLOGY

WASHINGTON, June 5, 2006 — In a nine-month analysis of privately financed travel data based on sometimes incomplete congressional disclosure forms, the Center for Public Integrity and its partners took the following steps to ensure that the resulting data would be as true as possible to the forms filed by members of Congress and their staffers.

What we did:

- Drew up detailed templates for data entry teams at Secure Paper Solutions of Fredericksburg, Va.

- Scanned batches of trip forms by member (and, where possible, by year) into PDF files, which were transmitted electronically to servers at SPS.

- Once data entry was complete, downloaded data files from SPS and imported them into the Center's internal database server.

- Reviewed 30,000 pages of raw documents — including forms and attachments — and compared them with the data entered. Each apparent error or inconsistency was reviewed by a database editor.

- Analyzed traveler names to standardize them to 715 members and 5,945 staffers.

- Compared start dates and end dates of trips taken by people with the same or similar names to identify amendments and duplicate filings.

- Built a calendar of all trips taken by people with the same or similar names to identify travel that overlapped to identify amendments and duplicate filings.

- Analyzed start, end and signature dates and examined cases in which they were nonsequential or inconsistent, identifying additional amendments and data entry errors.

- Identified the sole sponsor reported on 23,380 forms out of 26,577 received.

- Attributed the trips to 3,208 organizations and identified an additional 265 forms listing no identifiable sponsor.

- Identified the remaining trips as having been co-sponsored by multiple organizations or sponsored by organizations that could not be identified as having financed multiple trips.

- Removed from analysis 82 forms reported to be sponsored by lawmakers' offices, Cabinet agencies or other arms of the federal government.

- Excluded from analysis all trips that did not begin between Jan. 1, 2000, and June 30, 2005 (one trip which began within that period ended outside of it, on July 1, 2005).

- Adjusted totals to account for forms on which travelers incorrectly added subtotals in the space reserved for "Other" expenses. Leaving them in could have led to double counting.

- Set to zero all totals reported in foreign currency.

- Compared trips with identical costs to identify duplicates and amendments with name variations not previously identified.

- Consulted five years of congressional directories to resolve inconsistencies in the entry of staffers' names and identify whether chiefs of staff, administrative assistants and others whose signatures appeared approving forms

(continued)

were in fact supervised by the member under whose name the forms were filed.

- Compared signature data to the name of the member under which congressional officials filed the trip. This corrected 524 forms filed under the name of someone other than the member responsible for approving them.

- Checked incomplete dates and assigned them to a year. By default, they were assigned to the year in which they were filed (in the House) and then that date was adjusted based on the signature and date stamp dates on the forms themselves.

- Reviewed trips reported as having no cost to identify "advanced authorization forms" that reported approval of a trip rather than that a trip had been taken and paid for by an outside sponsor.

- Called congressional offices about hundreds of trips that appeared to have violated ethics rules. Changes were only made to these trips when specific data entry errors were identified in the process.

- Researched reported destinations to identify whether the destination was foreign or domestic.

What we did not do:

- Attempt to determine whether committee staff members' forms were signed by the proper supervisor.

- Attempt to harmonize sponsorships (except in a few limited cases in which it was necessitated by additional reporting) when different staffers listed conflicting sponsors for what appeared to be the same trip.

- Attempt to determine the precise job titles and roles of travelers other than members.

- Attempt to modify the data based on interviews; the goal was to ensure that the data accurately reflected what was disclosed on the forms, not what legislators and staffers later said they had intended to disclose.

- Attempt to attribute sponsorship proportionally to the various sponsors of co-sponsored trips.

- Attempt to determine whether ethics rules required the filing of specific forms, such as those without substantial costs or with no travel cost listed.

Reprinted with permission from The Center for Public Integrity.

THE CENTER FOR
PUBLIC INTEGRITY

That's something you should be prepared to discuss with your editor as well. You might need to build your own database, so you have to consider whether you can figure out how to do that. And be reasonable about where you can get support. Consider how difficult it would be, for example, to do a story that required you to get medical or psychiatric or psychological records. The Health Insurance Portability and Accountability Act makes it all but impossible to get information about individual patients without the cooperation and permission from the patients themselves. If a private corporation is at the heart of your story, documents also might be difficult to get. And while you might have the right to public records, getting hold of the documents could be a bureaucratic nightmare.

Understand the ramifications

Your editor will want to know what problems your project might cause. If you can prove your hypothesis, someone or something will likely have to take the blame for the problem you pinpoint. Address that possibility before you start, because you don't want your story killed halfway through when it turns out that the party responsible is an influential citizen, a powerful politician or a big advertiser that your publisher doesn't want to confront. You need to know from the get-go that you have the full support of your editor and publisher. You also want to assess how serious the accusation might be and how difficult it might be to prove. Big differences exist between accusing someone of breaking the law versus arguing that the standards set by the law cause problems, or between accusing a company of making shoddy products versus accusing it of selling products that kill.

You can't predict what will happen after you publish your story, but you need to anticipate the possible consequences. It might be possible that someone or a group of people gets fired from a job or is forced to resign their positions. An organization you write about or a business you interview might get hit with a boycott. Someone you profile might find herself harassed by neighbors or shunned by friends. If you plan to do a story about gang activity, for example, or a story about a dangerous cult or criminal connections, then you or your sources could find themselves in danger. If you were to do a story about treatment of illegal immigrants, your sources could risk deportation. To prevent problems down the road, you need to discuss with your editor all the possibilities in advance.

GETTING THE TIME AND RESOURCES YOU NEED

You must be able to pull the story off. Even if you present the best plan with the best reasons, your investigation won't go anywhere if your editor doesn't think you have the time to produce it. Remember, she's skeptical by nature and tight with resources. You've got to convince her that you can execute under conditions that she can accept.

Negotiate for some relief from regular duties

Orlando Sentinel reporter Mary Shanklin suggests that you negotiate with your editor for how much time you will be permitted to work on the project and how much she will expect from you on a daily or weekly basis in terms of your regular beat or general assignments. If you don't get firm commitments from your editor, you risk never getting the time to work on the story. As part of this negotiation process, discuss the stories you expect to come up on your beat and how they will be covered. Try to get your editor to appoint someone as backup for when something crops up on your beat at a time when you need to work on your investigative story.[7]

You need to show how you will be able to interview people between calls on your regular assignments. And you should get your editor to agree how much of your beat you will be expected to keep up with. While you can work on two things at once, you won't be able to find time for your project if your editor expects two or three daily stories at the same time. See if you can get relief from any routine work you do, such as police logs or news briefs. Or see if you can get an agreement to only do the small stuff while a general assignment reporter handles bigger daily stories.

Bargain for time off

Calculate the total time off you will need from regular obligations. Consider how many people you will need to interview and how difficult it will be to get the data you need. Things to include in your calculations include the following:

- How difficult will it be to reach your sources? Are they extremely busy, and will you likely play phone tag with them? Are they people you will only be able to meet with or talk to at certain times of the day or certain days of the week? Will you have to travel to meet with them?
- How many documents will you need to find? Can you find them on the Internet or will you have to drive to different places for them?
- Will you need to request documents under your state records act or the federal Freedom of Information Act, and how much time will that likely take?
- Will you need to create your own spreadsheets or databases?

If you lay out too many of the tasks you need to do, you might discourage your editor. But if you can demonstrate that you thought through your plan, you will make her more confident of your ability to carry it off. Miami Herald metro editor Manny Garcia recommends that you double the time estimate. The Chicago Tribune's George Papajohn suggests that you build in time for fact-checking, conversations with lawyers for your news organization and for last-minute surprises. When you investigate corporations, they can bury you with documents as a delay tactic. You need to read through it all, and you need time to do that.[8]

Set a deadline

Editors and producers need to fill pages and airtime. If you can promise them the ability to do that on a certain date or over a certain number of days, they will show more enthusiasm for your project. Visualize your package in print, on the Web or on the air. Do you see it as one story on one day or several stories on the same day? Perhaps you see it as a series over a period of days or weeks. If you don't think your editor will give you time off your beat, perhaps you can propose it as a running investigation. Consider the different pieces to your package. You could write a main story that gets to the heart of the problem. Then you can do a sidebar or second-day profile on a key participant. A third story could focus on possible solutions. For each piece, come up with a tentative publication schedule, preferably one tied to a news angle.

Know what resources you'll need

You need to know from the start whether your publication or station will pay the costs of the research and travel you will need to do. If you need to get government documents and you anticipate that the government officials won't be very receptive to your requests for information, you might have to file public records requests. That will take time and could cost money. In California, a copy of a birth or death certificate can cost $15 alone. Court transcripts that aren't already printed out can cost $3 per page. In the worst case, some governments have tried to collect thousands of dollars from news organizations for public records. At a minimum expect copying to cost from a dime to a couple of dollars per page. You might have to travel; for example, anticipate the time it takes to travel to interviews, plus the cost of gas or train or airfare if that's necessary. You might need to take people out to lunch and that can add up as well. If your news organization doesn't cover those costs, you might have to figure out another way to get the information. When I worked for a tight-fisted organization, I would tell sources that I couldn't let them pay and couldn't pay for them, so I would suggest coffee instead, something I could afford. Interviewing sources in their homes costs nothing except the gas or bus fare to get there.

Have a backup plan ready

Since editors hate to send you off on a time-consuming, resource-heavy project without a guarantee of success, it helps to show that whether or not you prove your hypothesis, you will get a good story out of your labor. To do that, you need to come up with Plan B, the story you believe you can do if you find out that you've guessed wrong, that the tip doesn't pan out, or that the information you base your hypothesis on is actually a unique occurrence rather than a pattern of wrongdoing. If you can't show that Public Works Director Bob Cat is directing city resources toward helping his friends and connections, it is good to be able to show that city resources are being stretched dangerously thin or that lawsuits could force the city to take money from needed services and redirect them to road repairs.

Confront the déjà vu

Editors don't want you to reinvent the wheel. Make sure you do a thorough background search to see if anyone in academia or the nonprofit sector has already studied the problem or if any other publications have already attempted to investigate it. Duplication can especially be a problem if the issue has been particularly newsworthy, as the chance is greater that a similar story has already been done. Your editor will not want you to retread old ground. So be prepared to show how your story will be different or better.

WRITE EVERYTHING UP

Just about every special projects editor will demand to see your plan in writing. Even in organizations that don't have a formal process for pitching a big story, the editor will want your proposal in the form of a memo. The more thorough the memo, the more likely the project will get approved. In the memo you want to include the premise, a detailed summary, a list of sources you think you can get and will need, and the documents and data that you think will provide your evidence. Exhibit 14.1 provides a sample memo format.

EXHIBIT 14.1   Example of a proposal memo.

MEMO

To: Editor
From: Reporter
Date: 09/09/20xx
Subject: Plans for an investigative story

Dear Editor:

I am writing this memo to propose a reporting project important to our readers and that will likely drive substantial traffic to our Web site and generate reader response.

- **Focus/premise:** The city's failure to properly maintain city streets is putting residents at risk of accidents.

- **Tentative Lead:** Every time Molly Most sees the school bus turn down her block, she says a silent prayer. Then she holds her breath. Because every day that bus hits a pothole so big, she can see the front of the bus go up, and then down.

- **Detailed summary:** The city was recently hit with a lawsuit when someone crashed his car into a pothole that he says the city should have fixed. I've found at least a few residents who say they made repeated calls to the city about dangerous potholes, but nothing was done. This project would investigate what potholes get filled, how much is spent on pothole repairs, whether more lawsuits are coming.

- **Why our readers would care:** Potholes annoy everyone who must drive over them. Good roads are a basic service most people think the city should provide, and when it doesn't, that makes people angry.

- **Why we should do this story:** If we could show that there is a problem with how the city allocates resources and present solutions, we would perform a service to our readers. If it got city leaders to address the problem of bad roads, it could prevent accidents and possibly save lives.

Continued. **EXHIBIT 14.1**

- **Main sources:** Joe Resident who sued the city; Holly Homeowner and Molly Most, who filed complaints; Bob Cat who heads the public works department.

- **Other sources:** People who work in the public works department, the former head of the public works department, lawyers, transportation experts, someone from the auto insurance industry.

- **Data and documentary evidence:** City budget and public works budget. Records of street repairs. Police reports on car accidents. Legal briefs and discovery from the lawsuit. Mashup map of potholes and accidents in the city.

- **Visual presentation: Interactive map.** Video interviews with city residents. Graphs that show possible correlation between budget cuts and complaints about street repairs, if I can find the data to support it. Q&A with Bob Cat about the pothole problem.

- **Potential costs:** Unknown public records request costs. No major travel will be necessary. The court documents will cost about 20 cents a page, but we may need to photocopy hundreds of pages.

- **Previous stories:** Both we and our competition have done stories on budget cuts, but no one has focused on road repairs. One obscure academic study connected bad roads to orthopedic problems.

- **Plan B:** If I can't prove that the city is doing anything wrong, I feel confident I can do a good story about how budget cuts are stretching necessary city services thin.

I will e-mail you later in the week to see if you are interested and to set up a time to talk more about the story.

It's best to have your full outline and storyboard on hand, just in case the editor wants to see more than your memo provides. You also want to lay out the reasons you think the reader will care, why it is important to do the story and how much time and resources it will take.

The best time to approach an editor is when you've done just enough preliminary research to have a clear premise and have a good handle on your sources and methodology. If you do too much work prior to talking with your editor, it might be for nothing — your editor might not go for it and you'll have wasted significant time. Or your editor might think you kept him out of the loop. But don't go in too early. You'll want to be able to answer his questions confidently and thoroughly, so you need enough information to do so. It would help to be able to go in with several relevant interviews under your belt and some data that show that the problem exists.

START EARNING YOUR CREDIBILITY

F ormer Los Angeles Times investigative reporter Myron Levin said he was fortunate to work for years with editors who trusted him. But he earned that trust in large part by never overselling his stories. "I was always nagged by doubt," he said. "I was criticized for underplaying things."

Levin advises not going to an editor with "blue sky predictions" that could put you under pressure to do things that you might not otherwise do or that won't pan out. When you promise a story that excites your editor and you can't deliver it, you will find that you won't get a very warm welcome the next time you propose a big project.

Until you can build up enough credibility and trust to get editors to loosen the leash, try starting small, Levin suggests. Instead of a two-month story, try one that will take two days to report and write. Plan out a number of mini-projects, connected by a central theme, but just propose one at a time. Once your editor sees that the two days were well spent, he might give you a week. If that leads to a good story, you might get a month. Or it will get you more serious consideration for your next big proposal.[9]

CONCLUSION

A n investigative project takes time and effort. Put as much thought into pitching your story as you do in finding it. Even publications that do little to no investigative work like to be able to boast about having published one. You need to convince a reluctant editor that you are capable, that you thought through how you will carry out the investigation, and that it won't be a waste of time or explode in your face. A well-constructed pitch will force you to create a focused strategy that will help you once you begin the information-gathering process. And if you can convince your editor or producer that you know what you are doing, it will give you the confidence you need for negotiating with sources for information and for convincing reluctant sources to talk to you.

EXERCISES

Following are some ideas for investigative projects. Take one or more and develop a plan to pitch the story to an editor. Try to make it focused and sketch out a rough outline using the storyboard diagram shown in Exhibit 14.2. Come up with a list of reasons why your readers would care. Try to think of a news angle. Sketch out a game plan that lays out how much time and resources you will need and that anticipates all the problems you might encounter.

1. Is the training people go through before they can become local police officers adequate?

Storyboard of an investigative package.   **EXHIBIT 14.2**

OVERVIEW	**WHO IS AFFECTED**	**THE WHERE**
Text summary:	Text summary:	Text summary:
Text format:	Text format:	Text format:
Graphic/photo/ multimedia:	Graphic/photo/ multimedia:	Graphic/photo/ multimedia:
News angle:		

THE WHEN	**WHO IS RESPONSIBLE**	**SOLUTIONS**
Text summary:	Text summary:	Text summary:
Text format:	Text format:	Text format:
Graphic/photo/ multimedia:	Graphic/photo/ multimedia:	Graphic/photo/ multimedia:

SCOPE	**THE HOW**	**THE WHY**
Text summary:	Text summary:	Text summary:
Text format:	Text format:	Text format:
Graphic/photo/ multimedia:	Graphic/photo/ multimedia:	Graphic/photo/ multimedia:

2. Based on the quality and cost of education at two-year colleges versus the first two years at nearby universities, which is a better deal?

3. Heaps of junk: How much could your college or university save if it simply replaced the oldest appliances and machinery on campus with new, energy-efficient ones?

14.1   Write the fourth draft of your story to make it as compelling as possible. See if you can weave into your story structure enough examples, convincing data, illustrative anecdotes and explanations and comments from experts. See if you can control tension, action and pacing.

14.2   As a group or individually, write up a project memo that you would use to pitch your project to an editor.

14.3   Prepare the final visual and multimedia elements of your story. Try to add one more by choosing one of the following:

    a. Put together a slide show.

    b. Do a man-on-the-street story with accompanying photos, asking people to comment on the findings from your story.

    c. Put together a comparison table of two contrasting elements in your story.

    d. Prepare an audio summary as a podcast.

NOTES

1. Phone interview with Dawn MacKeen, April 4, 2008.

2. Paul Williams. *Investigative Reporting and Editing.* Prentice Hall, 1978, pp. 172–173.

3. Bob Greene. Handwritten notes on Tipsheet 578, "Organizing the investigative project." 1988. Available at the IRE Resource Center.

4. Mark Katches. Comment made at a workshop entitled "Bulletproofing the investigation." IRE Conference, Miami, June 2008.

5. Ibid.

6. Center for Public Integrity. Methodology for Power Trips series, http://projects.publicintegrity.org/powertrips/default.aspx?act=methodology.

7. Mary Shanklin. "Managing and juggling: How to cover a beat and still produce." Presented at the Better Watchdog workshop, Orlando, Fla., February, 2005. Available through the IRE Resource Center, Tipsheet 2271.

8. Manny Garcia with Mark Katches and George Papajohn. "Bulletproofing the investigation." Panel discussion, IRE Conference, Miami, June 6, 2008.

9. Myron Levin. Phone interview.

Sample Investigative Stories

The Game Plan Checklist

An Excel Cheat Sheet

A P P E N D I C E S

A

Sample Investigative Stories

When you read a book like "All the President's Men," you may feel either inspired or discouraged. Inspired, because it shows how two young reporters could bring down a presidential administration that had abused its power and overstepped its authority. Discouraged, because the two reporters had the resources of the Washington Post behind them, legendary publisher Katherine Graham backing them, and a high-ranking official of the FBI secretly helping them. I'd bet good money you won't have any of those things when you first start reporting.

Other terrific books take you through many of the great investigative stories written in this country over the past 200 years; for example, "Shaking the Foundations," edited by Bruce Shapiro, and "Muckraking! The Journalism That Changed America," edited by William and Judith Serrin. But since I intend this book to inspire a new generation of young journalists, I think it is important to show you examples of great investigative journalism done at the college level. The stories that follow are complicated, and many involve the gathering of public documents. They exposed something important and wrong and they aimed to effect change. Although the subjects vary, the stories share many characteristics, and all are excellent examples of what students can do in investigative reporting, even with limited resources and experience.

NOTE: Stories A.1 through A.8 are stories written by students, though all were published either in student or professional publications. Story A.9 is by a professional journalist. These stories are reproduced as originally published and have not been edited or changed to appear in this book. I have written introductory notes for the stories.

All of these stories are reprinted with permission.

A.1   No Room for Sex Offenders

OVERVIEW

Do you know who your neighbors are? That's the question University of Oregon student Whitney Malkin asked in 2007. She read that the University of Washington had asked its state government to relocate sex offenders living nearby. She wondered how many lived near her school. Too many, she found. The reason was that the law pushed those committed of sexual crimes away from day care centers and elementary, middle and high schools, but not colleges. Neighborhoods near a college, it turned out, were one of the few places sex offenders could reside.

No Room for Sex Offenders

Campus housing may be one of few areas available for convicts

By Whitney Malkin, The Register-Guard, December 2, 2007

EDITOR'S NOTE: In Washington, the state recently relocated 13 convicted sex offenders who were living near the University of Washington, in response to complaints from the university. In Georgia, the Supreme Court in November threw out state restrictions on where sex offenders can live, a move that has other states questioning their own restrictions. In Lane County, an inspection of public records of sex offenders' addresses shows clusters of offenders near the University of Oregon and throughout west Eugene.

Moving into her first apartment, 20-year-old Laquisha Smith had no idea five registered sex offenders were living in the building next door.

The University of Oregon junior lives just a block from campus in an area known for its abundance of student housing.

But students aren't the only ones who call the West University neighborhood home — state records show 25 registered sex offenders live in the area.

The ex-cons are clustered near campus because probation officers say, in many cases, it's the most suitable place for them.

But some area residents, including Smith, say they're concerned for their safety.

When informed of her neighbors' convictions, the Los Angeles native was shocked.

"It just doesn't seem safe," she said. "I don't know why they're allowed to live so close."

The state Department of Corrections prohibits many of Oregon's sex offenders from living near schools, playgrounds or day care centers, but the ban doesn't include universities, because most students are legal adults.

Andrea Schlesinger, Lane County's parole and probation supervisor, says her team of probation officers enforces residency requirements placed on offenders by state law.

"We're probably more likely to approve housing near the university," she said. "The majority of guys we deal with have histories of abusing minors."

But records show not all of them do.

One of Smith's neighbors was convicted of raping and sodomizing teenage and adult women.

The offender, who the Oregon State Police's sex offender registry lists as "a power rapist who grabs and threatens to kill his victims," was convicted of first-degree rape and sodomy in 1979 and sentenced to 25 years in prison.

Then, in 2003 — 12 years after his release from prison for his first conviction — the 48-year-old was convicted of attempted sodomy of a Springfield woman and served 35 months in prison.

Now, he lives at the West University Quads apartment building, a complex on East 16th Avenue.

The man is one of five sex offenders that state records show living in the ramshackle three-story building, nestled among sorority houses and student rentals.

Three of the five offenders living in the West University Quads are predatory, a label Oregon law defines as a person who has a tendency to victimize or injure others and who has been convicted of certain sex crimes such as rape, sodomy and sex abuse.

One predatory sex offender who lives in the building said offenders live at the Quads because it is the only place that would take them.

"If I get kicked out of here, I'm going to be homeless," said the man, who agreed to an interview on the condition his name not be used. "There just isn't anywhere else for me to go."

Although he committed his crimes more than 17 years ago, the offender says when he got out of prison, finding a place to live was difficult. Getting a job was even harder, he said.

"It's just one of those crimes you can't explain to people because it's such an emotional issue," he said of his first-degree sodomy conviction, which led to a seven-year prison term. "People just have a real knee-jerk reaction."

Now, the offender, who earned a master's degree in English from the University of Oregon, said he spends his nights working as a janitor in an empty bookstore and his days worrying neighbors will discover his past.

For more than a decade, he says he's been living at the Quads, where creaking stairs and dingy balconies lead to 48 cramped one-room apartments.

Few Eugene landlords rent to sex offenders, so Schlesinger said she's not surprised that when a landlord does so, a cluster of offenders develops.

"Word gets out," she says. "We've got a whole staff of (parole officers) who are trying to find these guys places to live."

Erin Johnston and his wife, Robyn, of Veneta owned the Quads building until March when they sold it to Limestone Partners LLC II, a partnership of investors from New York.

Johnston said he didn't know sex offenders were living in the building for the 12 years he owned it. But he said he was aware that many of his tenants had been in rehabilitation programs and were receiving state assistance.

"No one will rent to these people," Johnston said of tenants who were on parole or in rehabilitation programs. "Because of that, it's a huge market, but we tried to be very careful and selective."

Although he did not require applicants to list criminal histories, Johnston says he worked with the Quads' on-site manager to evict tenants if he was notified they had violated terms of their probation.

O'Malley Hayes, a managing member of the building's current owner, Limestone, did not return calls regarding this story. But examination of the building's renter's application shows applicants are not required to disclose their criminal history.

Similar to Washington rules

Washington state's laws regarding sex offender housing restrictions are similar to Oregon's, but this fall, the state's department of corrections relocated 13 offenders living near the University of Washington's Seattle campus.

Earlier this year, UW administrators contacted Gov. Christine Gregoire, telling her of the 25 offenders living in student neighborhoods.

University President Mark Emmert didn't think sex offenders should be living near students. Gregoire agreed.

Now, because of the governor's decision, the department of corrections has moved 13 offenders who are on probation and classified by the state as likely to reoffend, says Chad Lewis, a spokesman for the Washington state Department of Corrections.

Zone a bad idea, official says

In Eugene, Schlesinger says she's not surprised by the reaction of UW administrators, but thinks creating a similar campus "buffer zone" in Eugene is a bad idea.

The problem, she says, is that probation officers already have too few areas to place the more than 450 sex offenders living in Lane County.

"So many people say, 'Not in my backyard,'" Schlesinger said. "But the reality is, they have to live somewhere."

Chris Swires, a 33-year-old predatory offender and University of Oregon student, says he has faced his share of problems in finding a place to live while completing his art history degree.

Convicted of sexually abusing children in 1998, Swires says when neighbors found out about his conviction and 75-month prison sentence through the state's online sex-offender registry, they complained to the landlord.

He said he found himself on the street, evicted from his campus rental.

"You just hope everyday that no one is going to find out," he says. "It's really hard."

Swires says he has moved away from the campus area and is looking to purchase a home in west Eugene. He says he doesn't think offenders should be banned from campus neighborhoods.

"We're already under so many restrictions that we can't live near a school or a church or a playground that we're really limited in where we can live," he says. "It's not going to help the problem to create more restrictions."

Some long-term residents

A comparison of public records that list the home addresses of sex offenders in Eugene with campus apartment buildings shows five offenders living in different campus-area rentals owned by Eugene-based Stewardship Properties, and two offenders living in buildings owned by TalRay Holdings, also of Eugene.

Four of the seven men live in quads, sharing bathrooms and kitchens with other renters.

Although TalRay does not usually rent to sex offenders, Helen Macht, a property supervisor, says in some cases the company makes exceptions — only after talking to an offender's parole officer and reviewing their crimes.

She says both of the offenders living in the company's buildings have resided there for more than 10 years and have never caused problems.

Cate Wolfenbarger, the property manager for Stewardship, says her company runs as many background checks on potential renters as they can, but don't always screen everyone.

She says she was unaware offenders were living in Stewardship's buildings.

But Eugene police officers who work in the campus area say they know of the population of offenders living in and near buildings housing students.

"The fact that you have registered and non-registered sex offenders living on or near campus with students is concerning," said Eugene police public information officer Kerry Delf, adding that some sex offenders violate terms of their parole and do not register with the parole and probation office.

University of Oregon Director of Public Safety Kevin Williams says the University of Washington's model merits research and investigation.

"I think that's a unique case," he said of the work done by Seattle area law enforcement and campus administration.

"It's one we should look at and see if it would work here."

But Phil Weiler, senior director of public and media relations, says it is not something the university is actively pursuing.

But some students, such as university sophomore Jessica Williams, say they think it should be. "I don't think that's fair at all that they're just allowed to live here and we have no idea," said Williams, who lives in the neighborhood and walks by the Quads building each morning on her way to class. "Is that safe?"

Neighbors such as Smith, the UO junior from Los Angeles, say they want something done.

Smith says the idea of not having to look over her shoulder on the way to class is appealing, and she has made plans to move at the end of the university's fall term.

"As much as I'd like to say they've served their time and should have the freedom to live where they're going to live, I'm not sure how safe I feel," she said. "It's really creepy, knowing they're right there."

A.2   Running On Borrowed Time

OVERVIEW

How safe is that elevator? Oliver Symonds was going about his day when he noticed something that made him a little uncomfortable. The elevator he was riding in had a permit that had long since expired. That meant that students were riding every day in elevators that had not been inspected in months, and that their safety could be at risk. Symonds started to wonder just how many elevators on campus had gone uninspected and what that meant for his campus community.

Running On Borrowed Time

*HSU elevators operating
on expired permits*

By Oliver Symonds, The Lumberjack, Humboldt State University, 2006

If you rely on elevators to maneuver around campus, be warned, they have been operating on expired permits for more than four months.

Permits inside campus elevators have posted expirations dating back to at least April, meaning they have not been inspected for operation by the Department of Industrial Relations' Division of Occupational Safety and Health in almost a year and a half.

Louis Okin, a history professor at HSU, depends on the elevator in Founder's Hall every day to get to class. Until last Thursday, Okin was unaware the permit in that elevator expired 133 days ago.

"Now it makes me nervous to ride in them," he said. Unfortunately, he, unlike others, doesn't have much choice because he is disabled.

Kevin O'Brien, the new director of the Student Disability Resource Center, was also unaware the elevator permits had expired. Although he recognized elevators are sometimes necessary for people with a disability, he feels the issue is broader than the Student Disability Resource Center since elevators are meant for everyone.

While outdated permits raise concern for some, Director of Plant Operations Tim Moxon said that state inspectors are historically late with inspections. According to Moxon, state inspectors work in geographic zones and keep track of permit expiration dates on their own.

"I've got a posted permit that is out of date," Moxon said, "but that's the government's fault."

The annual state inspections are not the only inspections the elevators undergo, however. At least once a month, Moxon said, the Otis Elevator Company performs routine inspections. There are also staff members on campus capable of maintaining elevators, but only do so in emergency situations for liability reasons.

"If Otis is in Crescent City, we're not going to wait an hour and a half if someone is trapped in an elevator," Moxon said.

Otis Elevator Company was unavailable for comment as of press time.

HSU is not the only campus to fall behind in elevator inspections. In 2005, students from UC Davis reported elevators on their campus that had expired permits including one that earned the nickname 'Death Trap' due to the 20 months that had passed since its permit expired. Other campuses that have had expired permits in recent years include Cal Poly Pomona and UCLA.

While Davis' 20 months belittle the four months that have passed since HSU's permits expired, Moxon said that in the past some of HSU's elevators have gone up to two years before being inspected by state officials.

It is common, Moxon said, for HSU to receive a lot of fix-it tickets after the DOSH inspection is conducted. Sometimes the ticket is for something minor like a misplaced ladder, sometimes not.

A.3   Nobody's Fault

OVERVIEW

Who is responsible when one man dies in jail? Every-one. In September 2007, James Lee Peters, a Native American man, killed himself in the county jail. In January, students in my investigative reporting class at Humboldt State University in Northern California decided to take a look at this case and see what it could tell them about the county's mental health and criminal justice systems. They started with these two questions: Why did he kill himself, and could the death have been prevented? In trying to get answers they ran up against a wall of silence. When mental health officials wouldn't talk to them, they pored through public records. And they found that deaths like Peters were preventable, but only if the county made major changes in the way it treats mentally ill people.

Nobody's Fault

The anatomy of a suicide in the Humboldt County Jail

By HSU Investigative Reporting students, Chris Hoff, Karina Gonzalez, Matthew Barry, Matthew Hawk, Marc Kozachenko, Tatiana Cummings, Cassandra Hoisington, Melinda Spencer, Deunn Willis, Nicole Willens, Adrian Emery and Meghannraye Sutton, The North Coast Journal, May 15, 2008

James Lee Peters spent his 25th birthday last August behind the walls of the Humboldt County Jail, waiting to be taken to a state mental hospital. He spent his previous birthday much the same way. He wouldn't live to see the next. Instead, 10 days after he turned 25, Peters took the sheet off his bed, tore it into strips, tied them together and hanged himself. He would be on life support for eight days at St. Joseph Hospital before he would die of asphyxiation.

If Peters understood what he was doing when he ended his life, it might have been the only time he fully understood his actions. Complications at birth gave him learning disabilities and a low IQ. Throughout his life he needed mental health counseling but received little. He tended to lash out when he was angry and that repeatedly put him in trouble with the law. What began as small outbursts became increasingly violent, until the criminal justice system could no longer overlook the threat he represented. Instead, as his criminal record piled up, the Humboldt County Superior Court bounced him between a variety of mental health facilities, but only to make him competent enough to stand trial.

But this story doesn't stop with Peters. Because the tragedy is that we fill our jail, and jails across the state and country, with people just like him. There are alternatives, but not in Humboldt County.

"This community treats dogs better than the mentally ill," said District Attorney Paul Gallegos. "My hope is that we [would] treat our mentally ill better than we treat a dog."

What little we know about James Lee Peters plays out through documents obtained under the California Public Records Act. Everyone he interacted with, from teachers, police officers, lawyers, doctors, counselors, probation officers and jail guards refused to speak about him or his particular case for this story. Neither would members of his family, who still grieve over his death and who intend to file suit against any party they can find responsible. As of yet, no lawsuit has been filed.

Here's what we do know. James Lee Peters, nicknamed Hans, was a Yurok Indian from Hoopa who entered the world much the same way he would leave it: gasping for air.

At birth Peters was without oxygen for several minutes. That manifested into developmental and cognitive problems. Jamie Lynn Solano gave birth to Peters at age 16; he was the first of her three children. His biological father did not acknowledge him and the first years of his life weren't easy. He suffered physical abuse and several members of his family battled with drug and alcohol problems.

Sometime in his childhood Peters saw a counselor briefly in Hoopa but stopped because the family feared he would be taken from his mother. Around age five, social workers took him from his mother and he went to live with his grandmother Joyce Croix, whom Peters credited with raising him.

If you drive east on Highway 299 and head north on Highway 96 through dense redwood forests, you will descend into the Hoopa Valley. Here a Ray's Food and the Lucky Bear Casino stand against a backdrop of jagged mountains. Nearby, the Trinity River flows past grounds where Hoopa residents still hold ancient healing and renewal ceremonies, such as the sacred Jump Dance and Boat Dance.

With about 2,600 people on 144 square miles, Hoopa is at once the state's largest Indian reservation and a small town where everyone knows everyone. The sovereign nation is separated from the rest of the county by both distance and culture. The tribal government administers health services on the reservation, including some drug, alcohol and mental health treatment, but offers no residential treatment facility. It educates students in conjunction with the Klamath-Trinity Joint Union School District.

Peters had a difficult time learning, so he was put in special education classes at Hoopa Valley Elementary. His fourth-grade yearbook picture shows a dark-haired boy with a big smile. The picture of him in fifth grade shows an 11-year-old boy standing straight and looking proud. (Few of the people who knew Peters at that age were willing to speak of him on the record. Most of what follows comes from reports written later by officials and psychologists who interacted with him at various stages in his journey through the criminal justice system.)

In the ninth grade, his grandmother died. Peters later said that that period in his life was emotionally difficult for him, and as a result he had trouble in school. He was involved in three physical fights, was caught with marijuana, and was expelled.

At 14, psychological evaluations determined that his verbal comprehension was "particularly impaired." He continued his education at Captain John Continuation High School in Hoopa,

and was shuffled between the homes of various members of his extended family. But he lacked a primary guardian.

The lack of guidance took its toll. At 16, he picked up a rock and threw it at a teacher's car, cracking the windshield. Police charged him with battery of a school employee and he served 60 days in Juvenile Hall. In throwing that rock he threw himself into the Humboldt County criminal justice system and he would never climb out of it.

The Hoopa Valley Tribal Police station has no holding cell. Each time a suspect is arrested police drive him 60 miles to the county jail in Eureka. Taking someone that far for relatively minor crimes adds a "traumatic element" to an already traumatic situation, said Graham Hill, chief of the Rio Dell police department. While Rio Dell sits at the opposite end of the county, his department also lacks a holding cell. The drive from Rio Dell to Eureka is just 25 miles, but that extra trauma, he said, can do more harm in the long run for prisoners who are mentally ill. The geographic distance also makes it difficult for family to visit prisoners in the county jail.

Peters soon added two more infractions — criminal threat of assault and battery and assault with a deadly weapon — to his juvenile record. About that time, he landed his first and only job, that of a choker setter for Three Star Logging Company, a typical entry level job in the logging business.

As a choker setter, he would likely have trudged up hillsides machines could not access, to wrap a cable under and around a log, forming a noose so that they could be pulled up to a place where they can be put on a truck. It is not an easy job, said Robert VanNatta, part owner of a 30-year-old logging business in Apiary, Ore.

While VanNatta didn't employ Peters or know of him, he could explain the type of work Peters likely had. "You cannot exaggerate the difficulty and danger of choker setting," VanNatta said. After securing the noose, the choker setter must quickly get away or risk getting crushed from rolling logs. Peters liked manual labor, but quit after he was denied a $1.25 an hour raise. That marked the end of his employment and education.

Unable to control his anger or impulses, his offenses became increasingly serious. As an adult numerous evaluations found that he suffered from Paranoid Personality Disorder, mild mental retardation and schizophrenia. At 24, his IQ was 67, which is the equivalent to that of an average 11-year-old child. Only 2.3 percent of the population possess IQs lower than 70.

His trouble deepened in 2001. Between October of that year and August 2002, he would be arrested five times. In two of those cases he assaulted women. In one he threatened a woman with great bodily injury. As a result of those arrests, he was sentenced to a 52-week batterer's program that he would never complete, and three years probation. When released, he became a statistic.

Megan Gotcher was Hans Peters' probation officer and is now a senior officer for the Humboldt County Probation Department. There are more than 50 officers in the county, but each officer is responsible for 60–100 probationers at a time.

"If you have a hundred cases, it is hard," Gotcher said. "You deal with searches, subpoenas and home contracts. Sometimes you just have to put out the fire." Probation officers work closely with Hoopa Human Services, but are not trained in mental health services.

The Humboldt County Superior Court questioned Peters' mental health in Dec. 2001 and placed him on two years of conditional release under a program run by the county's Department of Health and Family Services. It was responsible for providing Peters with treatment and supervision while he lived in his community.

But whatever supervision it gave him wasn't enough. In Aug. 2003, police arrested him for pushing his mother and assaulting a friend of hers with a shovel, sending him to the hospital. Around that time a car accident left him with major injuries. Peters would later tell a probation officer that after the accident, he more easily lost his temper and experienced suicidal feelings.

That January, police arrested him for trespassing and vandalism. A month later, they arrested him again for attacking a man with an iron. He was sentenced to three more years' probation, but this time the court ordered him to enroll with the Redwood Coast Regional Center, a private, non-profit referral agency for the treatment of people with developmental disabilities, and to participate in a counseling program run by psychologist Karl Fisher through the Hoopa Valley Tribe's Division of Human Services. While waiting for the regional center to evaluate him, he attacked an inmate and in another incident was charged with attacking a custodial officer.

Finally, in April 2004, Eureka clinical psychologist Otto Vanoni evaluated Peters and suggested that his problem was medical rather than criminal and that he belonged in a medical facility rather than a jail.

Peters was housed in isolation during the time of the evaluation, which worsened his condition, Vanoni wrote. "A failure to move him from solitary confinement and a continuation of jailing will only lead to further decomposition of functioning," Vanoni wrote. Vanoni described Peters at the time as having short brown hair, brown eyes, a mustache and "a fuzzy chin beard." At five feet, eleven inches, he weighed 155 pounds. Most important for the court, Vanoni deemed Peters mentally incapable of assisting in his own defense.

Five residential treatment facilities in California specifically treat people with developmental disabilities, but as a criminal, Peters needed to be put into a secured facility. So the Redwood Coast Regional Center sent him to the only secured facility — Porterville Developmental Center, in Tulare County, 520 miles from Hoopa.

After six months, doctors at Porterville deemed him competent and sent him to a "licensed board and care facility," according to court records. (The records don't identify the facility.) In June 2005, the regional center asked the court to terminate his commitment and release him. It argued that Peters was no longer eligible for its services as he was not developmentally disabled. In doing so it contradicted Vanoni's report a year earlier and its own subsequent finding that Peters was eligible for its services based on his diagnoses of mild mental retardation.

"It is believed now that Mr. Peters' mental status at that time of RCRC's psychological evaluation while he was incarcerated affected the results of that testing," wrote Wendy Stout, an intensive services specialist for the regional center at that time. Plus, Stout noted, Peters had not caused trouble in the eight months he'd spent in residential treatment. In layman's terms, being in jail had made Hans Peters crazy, and that tainted the psychological evaluation.

In an interview this month, San Francisco forensic psychologist Paul Good said mental retardation is a "static condition" that doesn't change and can't be cured. And as far as the courts are concerned, a competent person understands the legal process, the roles of courtroom players, legal strategies and can work with an attorney in an effective way. A person can be competent in understanding the law, but that doesn't mean they are mentally healthy.

Five months after his release, however, his anger got the best of him again. In Nov. 2005, he went to a house to talk to a woman he'd been dating. When she said she didn't want to see him, he refused to leave. Her family tried to force him out and Peters reacted by pushing a 13-year-old boy. The boy fell and injured his back against a stool. Police issued an arrest warrant, charging Peters with misdemeanor cruelty to a child.

Back in jail, things got worse. In January 2006, correctional officer Steve Christian opened the door to Peter's cell to get some janitorial items and Peters punched him in the face. When officers asked him why he did it he said, "Leave me the fuck alone. Dealing with the voices in the back of my head is hard enough, I don't need to listen to you as well."

Peters later expressed remorse and apologized for his sudden outburst at Christian. "A lot of things were messin' with my head," he said. "I feel bad. No one deserves to get punched."

Again, his lawyers questioned Peters' competency and Judge Christopher Wilson ordered another evaluation. During the two years that preceded his death, Peters, whom doctors said was mentally unable to assist in his own defense, appeared in court 25 times. Five different defense attorneys represented him and he faced 10 different deputy district attorneys and three different judges. It seemed as if Peters was the hat that everyone would pass but no one would wear.

The inability to get Peters the help he so obviously needed frustrated Judge Wilson. Over the next 18 months, Wilson would repeatedly order Peter's attorneys to get him into a local treatment program or a state hospital only to be told that no place would take him. For almost three months in the beginning of 2006, Peters sat in jail while Wilson waited for the California Department of Mental Health to determine if he qualified for conditional release. In February, Eureka clinical psychologist Michael M. Ramirez determined that Peters was still incompetent to stand trial.

But in March, the Redwood Coast Regional Center again found Peters ineligible for their services. Meanwhile Atascadero rebuffed Wilson's order and refused to take Peters.

On Nov. 6 the court acknowledged that Peters was there too long. "I'd like to know when Napa's going to come get Mr. Peters," Wilson said in court. "They said they're going to reject him because he's mentally disabled. We sent him back to the regional center. They said he's not disabled. They're just playing games with us."

Finally on Dec. 4, 2006, almost a year after his arrest, Peters was transferred to Napa State Hospital. But again, the goal was only to make him competent enough to assist in his own defense, not to silence the voices in his head. He would spend two months there and when doctors deemed him competent, he was back in the jail.

The delays Peters went through are common for the mentally ill prisoners who fill the jail, said Humboldt County Deputy District Attorney Wesley Keat, Jr. in an interview in April of this year. "Those in jail have some kind of mental illness and jailers say the jail is a mental health facility," he said. "There are a lot of people in the County Jail waiting to be transferred to a mental health facility."

The problem is that the jail is not equipped to handle such problematic prisoners, said Brenda

Godsey, public information officer for the Humboldt County Sheriffs Office. "We are not a mental health facility," she said.

Humboldt County isn't the only place with this problem. One study published in 2006 estimated that jails across the country house more than 94,000 people with severe mental illness. The Los Angeles Daily News reported in April that the psychiatric patients who fill most of the 1,000 beds in Los Angeles County's Twin Towers jail facilities have turned the jail into the largest mental institution west of the Mississippi. It cited data that show that statewide, California has just 6,285 beds for mentally ill patients or 17 for every 100,000 residents. Researchers said the state needs at least 12,200 more.

The U.S. House of Representatives passed the Mentally Ill Offender Treatment and Crime Reduction Reauthorization and Improvement Act of 2008. If passed by the Senate, it would provide grants for diversion programs and increase cooperation between the criminal justice and mental health systems.

At least 13 counties in California rely on special courts for mentally ill prisoners to ease the burden. These courts only accept criminal offenders with severe mental problems and dismiss charges after the offender commits to and completes an individualized program designed for their illness, most often one that involves a residential treatment facility. After a year of sobriety and being crime-free, the defendant attends a trial and the case is dismissed. They are then given job training and GED exam preparation.

In Gainesville, Ga., a mental health court entitled HELP (an acronym for Health, Empowerment, Linkage and Possibilities) puts prisoners on a plan for success, which includes, among other things, getting a job and taking medications. According to an article in the Gainesville Times, prosecutors, defense attorneys, case managers, treatment providers and judges work together to ensure that the prisoners stay on the right path. They review each case in weekly meetings, and determine which ones progress and which ones seem to regress.

California voters tried to address the problem back in 2004 when they passed Proposition 63, also known as the Mental Health Services Act. The statute raised an additional 1 percent tax on the 30,000 state residents (1 percent of the state population) that make an annual income of over $1 million. By 2006, the statute generated about $730 million for mental health services in California. But the law did not specifically fund mental health courts. Mental health providers across the state, and in Humboldt County in particular, complain that much more funding is needed.

A new program known as STAR (Supervised Treatment After Release) started in Humboldt County on April 1, 2007. The goal of the program is to provide evidence-based treatment in treating seriously mentally ill offenders by coordinating mental health service providers, corrections, probation, the district attorney's office, defense attorneys and community/family advocates.

The STAR program only serves 25 offenders at a time, according to its website. Regardless, Peters may have been ineligible, as it does not take inmates considered a public safety threat.

Julie Ohnemus, mental health director of the Open Door Community Health Centers said that in the past five years she has seen a jump in the number of mentally ill patients. The Arcata clinic alone sees 4,000 such patients a month, and that means that counselors can see each patient for only about 15 minutes each. That's not enough time for a doctor to properly monitor a patient. But resources are limited. The Open Door network has a total of eight counselors for both Humboldt and Del Norte counties. That's forced family practitioners to act as psychological counselors.

Hans Peters did not go to an Open Door clinic. But Ohnemus said that the clinics see people like Peters every day, released from the jail and bound to return. That's because the jail releases prisoners who suffer from severe mental conditions without any medication, and without medication they are in no condition to get themselves the help they need. "That's wrong," she said. "There's no reason not to follow up," she said.

Robynne Lute has worked as a behavior health consultant at the Humboldt Open Door since 2004. She sees about 10 patients every day. They suffer from depression, anxiety, substance abuse and chronic pain. She has lost five patients to suicide and several others to drug overdoses. One female patient hanged herself while on a waiting list for county psychiatric services.

"People are not getting what they need," she said. The county has an intensive treatment program but it only has 12 beds for three counties. There is also an emergency treatment program that can keep someone under surveillance for 72 hours. But after that it refers them to other facilities and leaves it to the patient to follow through. Meanwhile, the shortage of beds means that only people who are very sick are admitted into the two programs. "We don't have a lot of services for people that fall in between."

Perhaps Hans Peters was doomed from the start. Although suicide is taboo in the Hoopa Valley Tribe as well as many Native American cultures, rates are high and rising. The Centers for Disease Control reported in 2005 that among American Indians/Alaska Natives ages 15 to 34 years old, suicide is the second leading cause of death and the per capita rate of 21.4 per 100,000 people is 1.9 times higher than the national average for that age group. Native Americans are disproportionately represented in the Humboldt jail. On the day Peters hanged himself, the jail housed 47 Native American men accounting for 16 percent of the total jail population. Native Americans account for just six percent of the total population in Humboldt County according to a 2006 U.S. Census estimate.

If he could have been steered to an alternate fate, it would likely have had to happen early on. But deputy public defender Christina Allbright described current California law regarding minors and mental incompetency as a "huge black hole." She noted that Humboldt County has no facility to treat mentally incompetent juvenile offenders.

Some in the U.S. Congress are trying to bolster resources for Native Americans. The U.S. Senate passed the Indian Health Care Improvement Act in February. If passed by the House it would fund greater mental health services for tribes and could address the need for in-patient mental health treatment in Hoopa.

Hans Peters wanted to get treated. After Napa released him in March 2007 he told Judge Wilson that he hoped for a normal life. "I just want to go to my programs and take my medication and do good in life and get me a job, sir," he said.

His defense attorney, David Lee, argued that Peters deserved a chance at freedom. "He's served far more time in custody on all of these charges probably than anybody would have gotten at the onset," Lee told Wilson. "It's nobody's fault he was not able to handle the criminal proceedings for many, many, many, many months based on his mitigating mental condition."

Wilson was reluctant to allow Hans Peters to be released without adequate supervision. "If there's some form of decomposition, we're back to where we were," he said in court. "And that just cost Mr. Peters two years of his life."

The process took so long that Wilson released him three times during the two years to take care of personal business: Once to visit his brother, once to cash some checks and once to go to a dentist for a root canal.

In May 2007, Peters spent two days in Sempervirens Psychiatric Health Facility in Eureka, the only inpatient care facility in Humboldt County, while waiting for acceptance into a drug treatment program.

It's not clear exactly how long Peters spent outside confinement on the last go-around, but he was back in jail June 22, this time charged with false imprisonment and two counts of battery. Yet again, the court questioned his mental capability, ordered another psychological evaluation by Dr. Michael M. Ramirez, waited for a report from the mental conditional release program and ordered Peters recommitted to Napa State Hospital for recovery of trial competency.

According to a report from Deputy Coroner Charles Van Buskirk, Hans Peters did not want to return to Napa. Instead, in an attempt to prove mental competence, he had stopped taking his court-ordered medications. At 3:15 p.m. on Aug. 29, 2007, Peters fashioned a noose out of his bed sheet. Two officers found him hanging in his $7^1/_2$-by-11 foot jail cell. He had pushed the ends of the cloth strips through the small holes in a ventilation grate over his toilet, using a tool he had made by chewing on a spoon.

The officers tried to resuscitate him, but it is unclear if they were able to get a response from the body. At St. Joseph Hospital, doctors put him on life support but he never regained consciousness.

In ending his life, Peters put a stop to what had become an endless cycle: Arrest, temporary treatment, release and re-arrest. The problem is that the system expects mentally ill people like Peters, a man with the mentality of an 11-year-old boy, who suffered from paranoia and who was incapable of controlling his emotions, to get themselves the help they need.

Rebecca Porteous, a licensed clinical social worker, said she sees people come in and out of jail with recurring mental issues. When the jail releases mentally ill inmates, it instructs them to see a mental health professional. If they do that within the first two weeks, they will continue their medication. But not all do.

"It is still America," she said. "And people have free will."

A.4   An Army of Anyone

OVERVIEW

How badly does Uncle Sam want you? In 2005, Colorado high school senior J. David McSwane wanted to know how far an army recruiter would go to get someone to enlist. He donned fatigues and went to his local army recruitment center and posed as a drug and alcohol-addicted high school dropout, which should have disqualified him for the army. He was able to report how an army recruiter showed him how to temporarily detox his body in preparation for a drug test and how to get a forged diploma and create a phony high school transcript. McSwane taped phone conversations with army recruiters and had a friend film a trip he made to a local tobacco shop in the company and at the suggestion of a recruiter to buy a detox kit. His story and the stories that followed in top newspapers and magazines across the country led to an army investigation into recruitment practices. His story relied on some controversial reporting practices. In college he continued to be controversial. As editor of the Rocky Mountain Collegian at Colorado State University, he received national attention when he published an editorial on the tasering of a college student in Florida with the headline "Taser This: Fuck Bush." The board that oversees his newspaper threatened to remove him as editor, but ended up only issuing an admonishment. He made the New York Times in February 2008, when he vowed to fight a takeover of the college paper by the Gannett Corp., which had started buying up college newspapers.

An Army of Anyone

You need a high school diploma to enlist — or a recruiter willing to bend the rules.

By J. David McSwane, Denver Westword News, September 29, 2005 ■ www.westword.com/2005-09-29/news/an-army-of-anyone

For Private Kevin Shane Heitman, the completion of Army National Guard basic training last month was a day of sweet reward. After what he describes as "six months of hell," Heitman was done with basic training and advanced infantry training, ready to be a soldier. Boot camp had been the most arduous test he'd ever encountered; graduating from high school was so much easier.

He'd just faked his diploma — at his Army recruiter's suggestion.

Heitman dropped out of school in the eighth grade and doesn't have a general-equivalency diploma. For him to be a soldier in the Arkansas Army National Guard contradicts the rules and regulations that the Armed Forces set for themselves and reaffirmed this past spring.

But they didn't take into account Sergeant Lloyd Spears of the Little Rock Army recruiting office. Heitman's family says that Spears not only told Heitman a fake diploma would work, he made it for him.

The recruiter "does nothing but try to help people fix their lives," Heitman insists when asked about the faked diploma. Spears's advice, however, could ultimately cost Heitman his chance at an Army career.

Spears claims he had nothing to do with the faked diploma and has signed a sworn affidavit to that effect, according to the Arkansas Army National Guard.

Heitman's family says that Spears came into Cafe Lauren, the Little Rock restaurant where Heitman and his mother, Laurie Bennett, worked, and created the diploma using a scanner and a co-worker's high school diploma. After a few minutes of cut-and-paste with a Photoshop program, Kevin S. Heitman was a graduate of Beebe High School in Beebe, Arkansas — a feat that takes most Beebe teens four years.

"He would say, 'Get on the computer and just make up a diploma,'" remembers Bennett. "I was there."

Beebe High School confirms that Heitman was never there. The school has no record of him attending, and the date on the diploma, which was changed to 1997, isn't consistent with the signatures on the diploma. "I've been here eighteen years, and I don't know him," says Beebe principal Mike Tarkington. "[Superintendent] Marshall wasn't here in 1997. That would tell me this is fake."

The signatures on the diploma correspond to people working at the school about five years

earlier, when Nicole Goforth, Heitman's former co-worker, graduated from Beebe.

"Kevin did exactly what the recruiter said to do," says Heitman's father-in-law, Robert Edl. "I talked to the recruiter. He wanted me to make a copy of it and blow it up to 8 1/2 x 11. He made the copy here at my print shop."

The plan was for Heitman to get his GED before he left for basic training, at which point Spears would pull the fake diploma and put in the real certificate. "The recruiter said, 'As long as you get your GED, I can switch these papers to get you in there,'" Edl remembers.

But Heitman never got his GED, and the fake diploma was never pulled.

The recruiter didn't want to wait for Heitman to get a real GED before he signed him up, the family says, because Spears was trying to win a trip and a $10,000 bonus for enlisting a certain number of recruits in a specific time period. "It was his trip to Hawaii or the Bahamas or whatever," Bennett says.

"The fake-diploma thing came up because he needed him enlisted and sworn in before a certain date," Edl adds. "They can put me on a lie detector."

Bennett says Spears even promised to help cover up Heitman's drug use: "He would say, 'Kevin, go in the bathroom and pee in this cup,' and Kevin would go pee in a cup. And he would say, 'If you don't pass this, I can cover it.'"

Under military regulations, recruits are required to have graduated from high school or to have earned an equivalency diploma. They must also pass a urine analysis, physical and mental-health exams, and a criminal-background check, and receive a passing score on the Armed Services Vocational Aptitude Battery. It is the responsibility of the recruiter to make sure a potential enlistee meets those qualifications.

A photocopy of a diploma is acceptable, but the recruiter is supposed to verify its authenticity. "We don't have the manpower to check every diploma," says Christine Munn, spokeswoman for the Arkansas Army National Guard.

In his affidavit, Spears says he simply accepted a copy of what he believed to be an authentic diploma. He is still a recruiter, although the Arkansas Army National Guard says he is being investigated in connection with Heitman's enlistment.

Heitman, who is currently on duty with the National Guard in Louisiana, could lose his own $10,000 signing bonus and face a court martial.

"They're doing an investigation on me which is gonna cut off my damn bonus which I worked so goddamn hard to get," he says. "I worked so fucking hard, and you just ruined it. Your little eighteen-year-old ass just fucked me out of it. . . . Grow the fuck up, you little punk."

On March 17, my little eighteen-year-old ass published a story in The Westwind, the Arvada West High School newspaper. Titled "Army Desperation Leads to Recruiting Fraud," the article recounted my journey of deception with a few recruiters.

After seeing how military recruiters at my high school fished for students willing to fight a war, I began to wonder just how far they'd go to get one more finger on the trigger. I decided to find out for myself.

On January 20, 2005, I went to a local recruiting office with the following scenario for James David McSwane: Due to my overwhelming battle with drugs and alcohol, my incompatibility with my peers and my inability to succeed in the classroom, I gave up on my education in the eleventh grade. Although I'd dropped out of high school, I was an efficient thinker and problem-solver. I worked hard and liked to exercise. And despite my drug addiction and lack of a diploma, I aspired to serve my country and become a part of the proud legacy that is the United States Army. Now, what could the U.S. Army do for me?

I gave my spiel to a recruiter, Sergeant First Class Eric Mulero. To my surprise, he showed no interest in my addiction, saying simply, "We'll cross that bridge when we come to it."

He was adamant, however, that I set up an appointment with a GED testing facility. He said that a GED and the Armed Services Vocational Aptitude Battery were the only obstacles on my way to enlistment. But then he checked my height and weight, and said that at 6 feet 2 inches tall and 210 pounds, my body composition was not up to par with Army regulations. In order to join, I'd need to lose ten pounds and an inch off my waist.

Mulero called my house the next week. I told him I was wasting his time, because I could not stop using drugs. He should have told me that I could not join the Army with a drug addiction; instead, he said he had a solution. He would take me to this "place" to get this "stuff" that would "clean you out," and offered to pay for half the cost. What was this "stuff"? A type of detoxification drink that I could take the morning of the physical exam, he explained, and if I followed his instructions precisely, I would pass my urine test. It was no big deal, he said; he'd used it three or four times before.

On February 3, Mulero called to tell me that I'd "freakin' smoked" the ASVAB with a score of 88 out of 99 — so he was taken aback when I told him I'd failed my GED exam two days earlier.

Two weeks later, I called Mulero and told him that I could not pass the GED because of my test anxiety. The reason I'd done so well on the ASVAB, I said, was because it tested more practical skills, such as mechanics, shapes, electricity concepts and basic grammar, while the GED assessment had graphs and a writing section. Mulero should have told me that I could not get into the military without a diploma or GED; instead, he said there was the "home-school option."

He should have called it the "no-school option." A short time later, Mulero called from outside the recruiting office and explained how I could go online and forge a phony diploma, as well as fabricate a high-school transcript. He told me to use the name of a fictitious school that he'd created, "Faith Hill Baptist School."

A few clicks and $200 later, I was a graduate of Faith Hill Baptist High School. When I submitted the phony documents to Mulero, he said they looked great. He just needed to have them approved by his battalion commander.

But then Mulero was reassigned to Germany, and my enlistment packet was handed off to Sergeant Tim Pickel.

In my first conversation with Pickel, I told him that my diploma and transcripts were fakes and that I had a drug addiction. No problem, he said. On March 20 — after my first Westwind piece appeared — Pickel drove me to Pipeline, a local tobacco shop, to purchase the "black magic" detoxification kit. A friend filmed us from across the street.

I decided my investigation had gone as far as it could when Pickel asked me to sign an affidavit that I was, in fact, a graduate of Faith Hill Baptist High School. Instead, I walked out of the recruiting station without giving a reason and never returned.

In addition to the Pipeline film, I had photos and video footage of my meetings with the recruiters. I'd also taped numerous phone conversations during which the recruiters told me to lie and cheat to get into the military.

The Army says it does not condone such behavior by recruiters. "Let me sum up all of this in one word: unacceptable. Completely unacceptable," said Lieutenant Colonel Jeffrey Brodeur, the man in charge of recruiting for Colorado, when I told him what I'd found. "It appears to be a character issue. We are trained not to do that."

The recruiters were dismissed as "bad apples" and my case as an isolated incident.

But my investigation — which was picked up by KCNC-TV/Channel 4 in Denver and then went national on CBS News on April 28 — sparked other reports of recruiter misconduct. What the Army calls "recruiting improprieties" have occurred across the nation. They've ranged from ignoring medical conditions to intimidation to blatant illegalities.

On May 3, after interviewing two dozen recruiters in ten states, the New York Times reported that recruiters had concealed mental-health and police records, falsified documents and supplied cheat sheets for applicants taking the military aptitude test. Two Ohio-based Army recruiters deliberately ignored a man's bipolar disorder — a condition that would disqualify him for enlistment.

"We have to play fast and loose with the rules just to get by," another recruiter told the Times.

On May 9, KCNC reported that a recruiter had told a Grand Junction man to use a laxative just before the physical exam so that he would meet the military's weight regulations. His aptitude-test scores had also been falsified, Michael Flaherty said: "I never completed none of those tests, and my recruiter faked the documents."

On May 12, a CBS affiliate in Houston reported that a recruiter threatened to get an arrest warrant if a potential enlistee missed his meeting. Sergeant Thomas Kelt told reporters that his threat was a "marketing technique."

On May 18, a Cincinnati-based NBC affiliate caught recruiters lying about the realities of war. "You have more chance of dying here in the United States at, what is it, 36 percent die, kill rate here in the United States," one recruiter said. "People here just dying left and right, you have more chance of dying over here than you do over there."

Senator Wayne Allard sent a formal letter to Army Secretary Francis Harvey on May 12, requesting a federal investigation of questionable recruiting tactics. "According to these reports," Allard said, "the rules weren't just bent, they were broken and tossed away."

In response to growing reports of recruiting misconduct, reports that stemmed from my Westwind investigation, the Army's Recruiting Command initiated a national "Values Stand Down Day" on May 20. This one-day moratorium on recruiting would be devoted to refocusing on Army values and reviewing Army policies and procedures pertaining to recruiting.

On June 3, Army Secretary Harvey responded to Allard's request for a probe of recruiting improprieties. "The Army takes these allegations seriously, and last month initiated an investigation into the charges against certain recruiters in Colorado," he wrote. "Our overall policy is to investigate any and all allegations of wrongdoing."

Eric Mulero was scheduled for an August 30 court martial on charges of recruiting improprieties in connection with my case. I was subpoenaed to testify, but my testimony wasn't needed after he pleaded guilty to the charges. Mulero, a fifteen-year veteran, was demoted from sergeant first class to staff sergeant, and lost a grade of pay.

"I know I'm a good soldier," Mulero said after making his plea. "I used poor judgment."

Sergeant Tim Pickel received a non-judicial punishment last month, which most likely means a letter of reprimand will be on his permanent military record.

Lieutenant Colonel Brodeur, who has about 130 recruiters — including Mulero and Pickel — under his command, says his office has combed through its files, and investigators have found no evidence of any enlistee joining the Army fraudulently over the past five years in Colorado. Although Mulero and Pickel both said my fake diploma had been submitted and accepted by their battalion commander, Brodeur insists that the paperwork was not submitted.

"Your packet was never what we call 'built' and put in the system," he says. "It never went through quality-control gate number one, and there were too many glaring errors for it to pass any quality-control gate. I've got greater than 90 percent confidence in the system. It's a pretty sophisticated system. It's a very, very complicated system. It certainly has a few vulnerabilities, and that's why I say it's not 100 percent.

"For the layperson who doesn't see it work and doesn't know all of the intricacies, it would be pretty doggone difficult to identify the vulnerabilities. If all you had were the recruiters at the station on your side to get you in the Army, you still wouldn't [get in with a fake diploma]. They could not bulldoze it through."

But in Little Rock, Kevin Heitman didn't need a bulldozer to become a U.S. soldier. He just needed a recruiter willing to provide that fake diploma.

"If this is true, this is terrible," says Lieutenant Colonel Leslie Collins of the Arkansas National Guard Recruiting Battalion, the man in charge of investigating Heitman's case.

"I think it is and has always been an isolated situation," Douglas Smith, spokesman for the national Army Recruiting Command in Fort Knox, Kentucky, says of the Colorado recruiting problems. "The vast majority of all recruiters do the job of recruiting for the Army in an outstanding manner. All applicants for the service have to take a drug test; we screen all applicants for a criminal background. We check for a birth certificate, a Social Security number, look at the actual diploma."

Since Stand Down Day, "we've gone about our business of recruiting for America's army," Smith continues. "We had reports of recruiters bending the rules, violating procedures, and the General concluded it was necessary to stop the business of recruiting for a day to re-emphasize to all of us within the command the importance of maintaining America's trust in recruiters and in the institution. . . . Loyalty, duty, respect, honor, selfless service, integrity and courage — all those should apply. Making our recruiting goals is important to the Army and to the nation, but doing so with integrity is also vitally important."

The Army will not come close to meeting its goal of getting 80,000 recruits by September 30. So at the same time the military talks about raising standards for recruiters, it might want to consider lowering its standards for recruits. Plenty of young men and women with drug issues and without high school diplomas would love to serve their country; so far, they just haven't found the right recruiter.

A.5   If These Walls Could Talk . . .

OVERVIEW

Students in slums. In 2006, University of Minnesota student Brady Averill wondered why some landlords were allowed to rent out apartments to students that were barely fit for habitation. So she analyzed city building inspection records. She found that inspectors cited certain landlords repeatedly for violations, but the citations had no effect; they inspected some units owned by slumlords but ignored others, even within the same building; and that many buildings continued to suffer from the same safety problems believed to have contributed to a house fire that killed three university students earlier in the decade. After graduating, Averill (who now writes under the name, Brady Gervais) spent 12 months as an intern in the Washington, D.C., bureau of the Minnesota Star Tribune newspaper and went on to become a reporter for the Pioneer Press in St. Paul, Minn.

If These Walls Could Talk . . .

By Brady Averill, Minnesota Daily, April 17, 2006 ▪
www.mndaily.com/articles/2006/04/17/68059

Nick Vanderheyden stays out of his basement closet.

Old, crushed boxes are piled up to the ceiling. A crutch lies on top of the stack. There's an old vent in the closet somewhere. The space houses so much junk that the circuit breaker is barely reachable.

The closet is the perfect hiding place for critters, Vanderheyden said.

"There might be hazards in my house; there might be mice," he said. "I don't really know."

An inspector found eight violations at 1090 16th Ave. S.E. in early November. Violations included a need for repairs to the garage, patio, floors, plumbing, ceilings, windows, the storm door and smoke detectors.

Vanderheyden's home isn't unique. In fact, interviews and data reveal some rental property conditions are worse.

A Daily analysis of inspections data shows other rental properties in the Marcy-Holmes and Como neighborhoods have similar problems: floors that need to be replaced, smoke detectors that need to be installed, faucets and toilets that leak and electrical wiring that requires professional work.

Despite Minneapolis' efforts to inspect more rental properties and to enforce new penalties for landlords who don't comply with codes, inspectors continue to cite landlords around the University for not meeting the city's housing standards.

And some of the same violations that popped up during a 2003–2004 safety sweep — when inspectors looked for safety issues in hundreds of Marcy-Holmes and Como properties after three University students died in a house fire — remained in the top tier of violations between February 2004 and November 2005.

In the Daily's analysis of this data, findings include:

- Certain landlords are cited repeatedly for violations.

- In at least one instance, inspectors found problems in one unit, but didn't inspect the adjoining unit, owned by the same landlord, where other issues existed.

- Plumbing, smoke detector and electrical issues were top violations found during the 2003–2004 safety sweep and are among the top 20 problems since then.

- Plumbing violations are the most frequently cited problems found inside homes since the safety sweep with 107 violations. Smoke detectors are a close second with 102 violations.

Minneapolis housing inspector Sarah Maxwell finds a lot of smoke detector violations — especially in basements — which she thinks are caused by a lack of education, she said during a supervised February ride-along.

JoAnn Velde, deputy director of Minneapolis housing inspection services, attributed the violations to inspectors getting into homes and finding problems.

"It could be because we're doing a thorough license inspection," she said.

Fire Marshal Dave Dewall, who leads the Minneapolis Fire Department in its multi-unit rental property inspections, said inspectors continue to see the same violations because of "human nature."

Inspections alone won't change human behavior, but education will, he said.

Tenants are part of that education. Landlords can't always know if problems exist in properties unless tenants inform them.

In the past few years the fire department and housing inspection services have added new ways to enforce the city's housing codes.

The fire department and the housing inspections division plan to perform rental license inspections in every rental property by 2010. This is part of its five-year plan that started in January 2005. In the 17 years before the plan, inspectors had not been inside every property in the city. Instead they focused on "problem properties."

The City Council passed new ordinances in 2004, including tougher recourse for landlords who repeatedly violate the city's rental property maintenance code.

Still, tenants, advocates and neighborhood leaders question whether the city is doing enough to crack down on poorly maintained, and sometimes unsafe, housing. Many say landlord behavior has not changed enough in the past few years.

Same old story

The neighborhoods around campus are notorious for old, rundown homes. Tours of the Marcy-Holmes and Como neighborhoods show porches falling apart, slanted foundations and broken windows.

The "slummy" lifestyle is a romantic notion for college students, said Ardes Johnson, who has been a Dinkytown resident for 15 years.

Many college students said they want the freedom of off-campus living, but they also want safe, livable homes to go to after a long day of classes and work.

University alumnus Michael Huntley wanted a comfortable home. He didn't find that living at 1701 Como Ave. S.E., where the city turned off the water at least five times between fall 2003 and fall 2004. At their landlord's request, Huntley said, he and his roommates paid the property owner instead of the city directly.

Huntley remembers from day one always wearing shoes in his home because the carpet was dirty and, in some spots, smelled like urine, he said.

And when he left the duplex for good, he said he never received his damage deposit. He since has sued his former landlord Doug Doty and settled in housing conciliation court.

Between March 2002 and September 2005, inspectors found 42 violations at 1701 Como Ave. S.E. and 1703 Como Ave. S.E., which is part of the duplex. The violations ranged from broken windows to water-damaged surfaces to missing smoke detectors.

Inspectors found plumbing and smoke detector violations during the safety sweep. They again found those two problems, among others, during a fall inspection at 1703 Como Ave. S.E.

The 2003–2004 safety sweep and rental license inspections are supposed to make rental properties like the duplex safer.

That hasn't stopped the same violations from popping up at the duplex, data and interviews with current and former tenants show. Doty did not return several calls for comment and when reached at his home, he declined to comment.

"He's one of the more prominent names in our office, too," said Barb Boysen, a legal assistant in University Student Legal Service. "Probably out of proportion to what you would expect for the number of properties he owns around here."

Taking issue

Housing advocates and landlords are skeptical of the rental license inspections that have occurred at various Minneapolis rental properties.

Spencer Blaw, a housing advocate who sits on the Minnesota Tenants Union board, called the five-year plan "bullshit."

"It's just not going to happen," he said.

Blaw said the city has promised more inspections in the past.

"It's nothing new," he said.

University Concerned Landlord Association president Jason Klohs said he supports the license inspections. He criticizes the process, however.

Klohs, who owns nine rental properties, said he wanted to be involved before rental license inspections occurred at some of his rental properties this winter. Although landlords are notified, inspectors get approval from tenants and set appointments with them.

Early notification could help landlords address issues sooner rather than later, he said.

Inspectors performed a license inspection at Vanderheyden's home this fall. But as of March 9, he still saw issues in his home.

The bathroom faucet leaks. Although these issues aren't considered violations, doorknobs are located only on the interior side of the front and back doors. The garage can't be used for storage. A station wagon with 1992 license plates sits in the garage among old gas cans, boxes and other miscellanea.

Mike Murphy of RP Management, a company that manages hundreds of rental properties around the Twin Cities, said the garage isn't for tenants' use.

But Vanderheyden said he'd like to get resolved what he said are problems in the house. Ultimately he will not complain to his landlord. As a student, he said he doesn't have the time.

'Serious situation'

Vanderheyden's experience doesn't compare to what some University students endured while living at 719 13th Ave. S.E. earlier this year.

After finding six gas leaks in early March, CenterPoint Energy red-tagged and turned off the home's boiler. A red tag indicates the appliance has to be shut off because it creates unsafe conditions. The boiler previously had been yellow-tagged, which indicates a potential problem down the road.

"The red tag is a serious situation," Velde said.

City inspectors ruled the home uninhabitable and sent a letter of intent to condemn the house to Nicholas Puzak, owner of Cardinal Properties. In addition to ordering him to fix the boiler, an inspector asked that he provide a smoke detector in the basement and missing covers in the breaker box. The inspector also requested painting the garage and home's exterior, and repairing the porch.

The tenants have since moved. Puzak said he has since bought a new furnace and fixed a gas valve on the boiler.

"This was a serious, serious threat to health and safety," said Boysen, who is working on a case to help the former tenants recoup their March rent and damage deposit.

Puzak, whose only single-family property is at 719 13th Ave., said he responded when CenterPoint initially yellow-tagged the boiler.

"If it was a real emergency, they would have red-tagged it immediately," he said.

In October 2003, during the safety sweep, an inspector cited Puzak for not properly posting his license, needing to install faceplates on electrical outlets and needing to repair fixtures at that property.

'We love our landlords'

Not everyone is unhappy with their living situation.

University senior Ta Ho said he likes his 1063 12th Ave. S.E. residence. And the violations an inspector found during a license inspection this fall don't bother him because his landlords, Allison and Tim Thiesing, responded quickly.

"We love our landlords," Ho said.

When a sprinkler hose flooded the basement, the landlords hired people to replace the carpet and fix the walls. Within a week the basement was livable, Ho said.

"We've had our fair share of problems, but (our landlords) have been fast to react to them," he said.

Allison Thiesing, who rents one other property in Prospect Park, said she and her husband respond quickly for good reason.

"I look at it like I would want it to be safe enough for my kids to live in the house," she said.

Landlord watchdog

Not all landlords act like the Thiesings.

And members of neighborhood associations are plenty aware of it.

Johnson, a Dinkytown resident who sits on the Marcy-Holmes Neighborhood Revitalization Program committee, said housing inspections services had agreed to send the association a monthly list of violations. The association then would send letters to landlords about the importance of complying with city codes.

She said the association last got a list in September.

The wake-up call that changed the housing environment

These issues — the good and the bad — aren't news to Paul Zerby, a former Minneapolis City Council member. He said he knew "substandard" housing existed in University neighborhoods long before a fall 2003 fire killed three University students. He saw firsthand the problems while door-knocking in 2001.

"It was terrible stuff," he said.

Zerby advocated the safety sweep after the University students died. More than four months and hundreds of inspections later, housing officials and community leaders declared rental properties in the Marcy-Holmes and Como neighborhoods safe, according to earlier media reports.

"Did they stay safe? We don't know until we get another complaint," Velde said. "But in that moment in time, yes."

Opinions vary on the lasting impact of the safety sweep.

"There are some landlords that haven't changed at all," said James De Sota, neighborhood coordinator for the Southeast Como Improvement Association.

Melissa Bean, executive director of the Marcy-Holmes Neighborhood Association, thinks differently.

"In my mind, there have been some improvements due to the sweep," she said.

Not that there couldn't be more improvement.

"Is there a long way to go? In many instances, yes," she said.

Bill Dane, a University Student Legal Services lawyer and housing advocate, said properties in Marcy-Holmes and Como neighborhoods have shown an overall improvement.

He should know. The housing advocate lives in the Como neighborhood and works with students who experience rental problems.

But he said the houses in Marcy-Holmes and Como don't seem maintained.

"I was thinking things are looking bad again."

A.6   A Stunning Toll

OVERVIEW

Discovering how lethal "nonlethal" weapons can be. To examine how Tasers and other "nonlethal" weapons are being used by law enforcement official in Texas, journalism students around the state requested records on weapons use and prisoner deaths from hundreds of Texas law enforcement agencies.

This article, which was sponsored by the Freedom of Information Foundation of Texas' Light of Day Project, the Mayborn Graduate Institute of Journalism's Distributed Reporting Project, and Fort Worth Weekly, is based on interviews and thousands of pages of records obtained by students under the Texas Public Information Act, under the direction of Weekly staffer and Mayborn instructor Dan Malone and Weekly editor Gayle Reaves.

Students who contributed to this report include Mayborn graduate students Joel Brillant, Byrdie Franco, Reyna Gobel, Don Jones, Komla Hans Masro, Katy McDaniel, Trevor Naughton, Nicole Osei, Britney Porter, Jacob Taylor, and Rashaun Trammell; University of North Texas journalism students Crystal Adams, Crystal Barbour, Mason Canales, Sarah Eibel, Noor Elashi, Christopher Ferguson, Amy Fowler, Justin Garison, Latricia Harjes, Jessica Johnson, Rian Johnson, Michelle Mashburn, Imelda McClure, Brad McDonald, Brandon Musselman, Claudia Nwaogu, James O'Brien, Melissa Procell, Amanda Quinlan, Fatima Quiroz, Clarisa Ramirez, Rachel Routon, Sarah Seeley, Aakriti Tandon, Samuel Taylor, Erin Tritschler, Emily White, Sloan White, Lindsay Wilps and Rebekah Wolf. Joanna Cattanach, a student in Baylor University's Masters of International Journalism program and intern at the Freedom of Information Foundation of Texas, and Beth Wreford, a Texas Christian University student interning at Fort Worth Weekly, also contributed to this report.

Many of the records obtained by students can be reviewed at the Mayborn's Web site at http://may-borninstitute.unt.edu/academics/dist_rep.htm. Other news organizations are encouraged to make use of those records as long as they credit the students' reporting. To learn more about the FOIFT's Light of Day Project visit www.lightofdayproject.org.

A Stunning Toll

Taser-related deaths and questionable uses of the weapon are mounting in Texas

Ft. Worth Weekly, March 8, 2006   ■
www.fwweekly.com/content.asp?article=3743

Sitting in the back of a police cruiser, his green eyes burning and massive body convulsing, Barney Lee Green was certain that he was about to die.

Police in the Houston suburb of Pasadena had pulled Green over on that day last November for what might have been a routine traffic stop. But neither the big man's behavior nor the officers' reactions were routine. Records show that as the officer who made the stop approached Green's car, he saw that the driver was "chewing vigorously" and trying to wash down what he was chewing with a drink of water. The officer told him to spit it out; Green refused.

Pasadena police carry pepper spray and Taser stun guns, so-called non-lethal weapons that law enforcement agencies across the country have issued, to give their officers in tough situations options other than drawing their firearms.

Only a few weeks earlier, Green had been released from prison after serving a sentence for drug possession. Before that, prison officials say, the 38-year-old carpenter had also done time for aggravated assault. But nothing in the reports from that day that have been made public suggest that Green threatened the officer or had a weapon. He simply appears to have been a 6' 3," 300-pound man who wasn't following police orders.

The patrolman ordered Green to place his hands on the steering wheel. When he repeatedly refused, the officer sprayed him in the face with pepper spray, then stunned him twice in the shoulder with a Taser.

Those initial electrical jolts apparently allowed the officer to get Green out of his car and cuff him. But the officer still wanted whatever was in his mouth. As Green lay flat on his stomach beside his vehicle, the patrolman, by this time joined by another officer, ordered him to spit out whatever he was chewing. He refused, and they stunned him again. The Taser may have subdued the big man, but it couldn't make him spit.

Police eventually handcuffed and loaded Green — and whatever he still had in his mouth — into a patrol car. Then, records show, as they were driving to the jail with the situation seemingly under control, [Green] matter-of-factly announced, "I'm going to die" and began shaking and convulsing.

The officer driving told officials he was only seconds away from the jail when Green made his announcement. Instead of changing course and heading to a hospital, the officer radioed for an ambulance to meet them at the jail. By the time they arrived at the jail, Green was "slumped over the seat and became unconscious," records show. The ambulance got him to the hospital. He was placed on life support and died later that day.

Green's death fits into several disturbing patterns regarding the electrical pulse weapons that have come into wide use in this country in the last several years. Despite being labeled non-lethal, the weapons are being involved repeatedly in deaths, frequently in cases where the tasered person was on drugs. And records show that the deaths and questionable usages of the weapon are happening more frequently in Texas than in all but a couple of places on this continent. Texas is tied for third among all U.S. states as the location of the most Taser-related deaths. This state accounts for 12 of the approximately 170 known Taser-related deaths in the last five years. In three other Texas cases,

suspects died after being both tasered and shot. The locale where the largest number of those Texas deaths have occurred: Tarrant County, where four people died in Fort Worth police custody, plus a fifth death that occurred in Euless.

What's more, documents obtained under the Texas Public Information Act, along with interviews with police and those arrested, reveal that in many of the state's law enforcement agencies, officers aren't waiting for a possible life-or-death crisis before they unholster the Taser. Many law enforcement officers are using the yellow-and-black, pistol-gripped weapon as a first-choice persuader — like a high-tech baton. The president of TASER International told Fort Worth Weekly last month that the stun weapons his company manufactures are "not a disciplinary tool" and shouldn't be used that way. Nonetheless, records reveal that the weapons, marketed as an alternative to lethal force, are being used in situations where lethal force would almost never be used — as a routine way of gaining compliance from people who are offering no violence or threat.

The process of gathering records for this story also revealed another problematic statistic about Texas sheriff's departments: Many of them don't appear to be following the law regarding public records. About a fourth of the state's 254 sheriff's offices failed to respond at all to the records requests mailed by the college journalism students who helped research and report this story. Many sheriff's offices complied promptly and helpfully with the students' requests. But others said they could not find the records requested, or they demanded hundreds or thousands of dollars for records that other law enforcement officials provided free of charge.

Randy Sanders of Lubbock, president of the Freedom of Information Foundation of Texas, which helped fund the research for this story, said his understanding is that if a government agency does not respond to an open-records request, it means the records are open. "The fact that some of the counties have requested large amounts of money, on the surface, seems very inappropriate," he said. "To use a procedure that is so expensive . . . actually seals [the records] from public inspection."

In the meantime, Taser use continues to grow among the state's law enforcement agencies. Small-town deputy sheriffs are packing Tasers along with big-city cops across the state. Policies that govern the use of the weapon are all over the map — but almost all the agencies continue to maintain that the weapon is safe, as does TASER International. The company contends that the vast majority of deaths that occur after the use of one of their weapons are due totally or in large part to other factors, such as drug use.

"Police departments have stuck to the line that they're not lethal," said Debbie Russell, who runs the Taser hotline for the American Civil Liberties Union in Central Texas. "They are training them to use them liberally. One officer used it 18 times" in about 18 months, she said. "If they were using their guns half that much, people would be screaming about that."

Barney Green's family doesn't understand why Green wasn't taken straight to the hospital. And they've waited more than three month even to get a report about what, officially, caused his convulsions in the back of that patrol car and, ultimately, his death.

"The cops are trained, highly trained," said Green's sister, Bonnie Tengg. "They should know the difference between a real 'I'm going to die' and a not real 'I'm going to die'," she said. "And it's common sense to take him straight to the hospital if he looked so bad."

**

A 66-year-old in Kansas who probably had a weak heart
Was tasered for honking her horn, trying to park
By the way, in her own driveway
Such a dangerous charge —
Beware there's grannies at large.

Trevor Goodchild had just turned 22 and was feeling good about life. That was before he got tasered for playing the guitar.

Sixth Street in Austin is the live-music center of the self-described Live Music Capital of the World, so there are guitars pretty much all over the place. Most are a lot louder than Goodchild's, an unamplified classical model that had been his friend through his childhood time in foster care and his beginning adulthood.

While others in his age group might have been bar-hopping and ducking into alleys to puke, Goodchild — a vegetarian for 11 years who walks with a limp left from a run-in with a truck when he was a teen-ager — chose a spot on that evening in February 2005 and began to play in celebration of his birthday a couple of days earlier.

That's when the cops came up — three or four, he recalls — and one offered what Goodchild first thought was just free and friendly advice: You need a permit to play live music on an Austin street.

Goodchild said he asked where and how he could get one.

"If you don't have a permit," he recalled one officer saying, "we're going to send you to jail."

"You can't send me to jail for playing guitar."

"I bet I can."

He thought it was a joke, Goodchild said, until an officer grabbed his guitar, saying it could be used — think of El Kabong cartoons — as a weapon. Goodchild held onto his cherished instrument, but the officers jerked him to his feet, he said, and two played tug-of-war with his arms. One jumped onto his left side and slammed him to the concrete on his right arm, busting open his right cheek.

The officers ordered him to get his right arm behind his back, he said, but it was pinned under him, and they wouldn't let him up. That's when he felt electricity throttling his nervous system, "like touching a live wire or putting my hand in a socket."

It's not clear from records how many times the young guitarist was tasered. But Goodchild says he was hit seven to eight times, at least twice while he was on the ground, and that the shocks caused him to have convulsions due in part to an existing seizure disorder.

Asked about Goodchild's case, Austin police spokesperson Toni Chovanetz referred a reporter to the department's use-of-force policy, which says the amount of force used "must be the minimum amount which is reasonable."

Goodchild was taken to the Austin city jail, where he was charged with resisting arrest. The officers who arrested him, police records show, also accused him of violating city ordinances forbidding blocking the sidewalk and playing guitar on a city street without a permit. Goodchild said he was sentenced to six hours of community service for the ordinance violation. The resisting-arrest case has not yet been tried.

But he wonders now whether he might just as easily have wound up in the county morgue. "If Tasers are supposed to replace guns," he asked, then if the officers hadn't had the Tasers, "would I have been shot for playing classical guitar?"

A good question, it would seem, since the company line on Tasers is that they keep deranged, drug-crazed, or violent offenders from being shot dead. With a Taser, company officials say, such dangerous criminals can be rendered docile and then easily handcuffed. It's an argument that portrays the Taser as a humane, even a merciful weapon.

"Saving lives every day" is the motto on TASER International's web site. But in practice, records show that Texas law enforcement officers are routinely using Tasers against people who don't appear to represent any kind of serious threat against an officer or the public — situations in which police would almost certainly never have used a gun, but in which the perpetrators of inconsequential crimes — or no crime at all — have ended up dead or seriously harmed.

In Fort Worth, one person who died after being tasered multiple times had done nothing more serious than briefly trespass on a parking lot, then run from an officer. Another man died after being tasered because he hid in a closet and wouldn't come out when police came to arrest him for allegedly stealing electricity. A prostitute died after she approached police asking for help and then got in a tussle with an officer because he saw that she had a crack pipe and arrested her.

Trevor Goodchild found reports of many such situations when his own experience led him to research what was happening around the country with Tasers. He wrote a rap song about it, including the lines quoted above.

The lyrics also include references to pregnant women being tasered while in jail for refusing to follow jailers' order. The rap isn't far off the mark from what is happening in some Texas jails, where Tasers seem to be the latest thing in compliance equipment.

If you ever end up in Texas' Wichita County jail, watch out for the bean hole.

That's what jailers and prisoners alike call the slot in cell doors through which inmates get their meal trays. Some inmates like to stand with their arms sticking out of the slot, a violation of the rules. So they get tasered.

Last August, a woman old enough to be Goodchild's grandmother was mad because jailers had denied her phone privileges, punishment for aggressive behavior earlier that day, records show. The 63-year-old was kicking and hitting her cell door and jamming her arm through the bean hole. When she refused to remove her arm from the slot, records show she got a three-second jolt from a Taser.

In fact, Wichita County has found Tasers so useful for such purposes that it has stopped using nightsticks. "It's our opinion on the Taser that they are certainly a much safer and much preferred intermediate weapon than a baton anyway," Chief Deputy Cecil Yoder said. "We feel it protects our officer and protects the public. It's certainly uncomfortable for five seconds, but after that they can stand up and walk and talk . . . and neither one of them are hurt."

When the Taser is used in his jail to enforce a jailer's order, Yoder said, the Taser is used directly against the inmate's body "in the very same way as the old-type stun guns were used."

The difference between today's Tasers and the "old-type stun guns," however, is the current. Tasers are far more powerful. And each new generation of the weapon packs more wallop.

In the McLennan County jail in Waco, 14 inmates have gotten the treatment during the last five years, according to sheriff's office records.

McClennan County officials refused to release their use-of-force policy. But based on incident reports, it appears that Tasers are used only after an inmate repeatedly refuses to obey an order and ignores a warning that the Taser is the next step. A special detail team that transfers unruly inmates takes over: one officer with the Taser, one with the pepper-ball gun as a backup, one with the "jammer" that keeps the cell door half-closed, one with a video camera, and two with handcuffs.

Typically, after the inmate has been tasered and cuffed, he or she is moved to another cell, placed in a restraint chair, and put on a watch.

Not all the inmates who have been shocked were being violent, the reports show. Some were just refusing to comply with orders.

In one instance, an inmate was hearing voices and kicking the walls. Officers had been able to get him to sit quietly on the bed for short periods but hadn't convinced him to come to the door to be handcuffed. Rather than entering the cell during one of his quiet, lucid times, they waited until the special detail team arrived, then tasered the man and placed him in restraints, records show.

And yet, according to Tom Smith, the president of TASER International, his company's shock weapons aren't intended for such uses. A Taser "is not a disciplinary tool," he said at a recent Dallas press conference. The purpose of the event was to promote the use of a new line of Tasers to be sold to civilians.

In fact, the jail officers who use Tasers to get inmates to follow orders are not necessarily violating their own departments' guidelines. Use-of-force policies denote what level of force, from verbal commands to guns, should be used in various situations — and the place of Tasers in that ranking varies greatly from county to county.

In some places, Tasers are ranked right below firearms and are to be used only when someone's life or physical safety is threatened. In Parker County, where the sheriff's office handed out Tasers to its deputies in 2004, the stun weapons are on the same level as a baton or chemical spray. In Ector County, they are ranked even lower on the use-of-force scale. Officers there are permitted to use Tasers as the next step after verbal commands, before any kind of hand-to-hand force, if suspects fail to comply.

Journalism students used the Texas Public Information Act to request records from Texas sheriffs documenting how their departments have used non-lethal weapons such as stun guns, deaths associated with such weapons, and use-of-force policies. They also reviewed 4,100 pages of custodial death reports that sheriffs and other law enforcement agencies are required to file with the Texas attorney general when someone dies in their custody for whatever reason.

About 90 sheriff's departments released records with little fuss. Another 50 responded by saying their officers didn't use Tasers. About three dozen others asked permission from the attorney general to withhold some of the records or demanded payment that far outstripped this project's ability to pay.

Although state law requires governmental agencies to respond to such requests in writing within 10 days, students have yet to receive responses from more than 70 sheriff's departments.

Joel White, immediate past president of the Freedom of Information Foundation and an attorney who helped students draft their request for records, said he was disturbed to learn that students have not received responses from that many sheriffs.

"Those kinds of sheriff's departments are giving other sheriff's departments a bad name, because there's no excuse for not knowing the basic open-records requirement," he said. "They need to be sent to school."

Many Texas sheriffs released records for free or for a small fee. Others, however, refused to waive fees and asked for thousands of dollars in copying and research costs. For example, the Harris County Sheriff's Department refused to waive fees, failed to specify what the fees for records would be, and further stated "it is not possible to estimate when the copies sought by your request will be available."

Guadalupe County demanded a $5,000 deposit before beginning work to locate the records and said it expected to be reimbursed for the time it took a deputy to locate the documents. At the $14.71-per-hour rate for the three-month minimum period, the sheriff figured the search would require, the estimated bill topped $7,000. El Paso County similarly demanded $1,836.

The human-rights group Amnesty International, which counts prisoner treatment as a high priority, has called for a moratorium on all Taser use until experts decide if they're really safe.

But the group isn't necessarily against Tasers, spokesperson Edward Jackson noted; in fact, international human-rights laws mandate the development of nonlethal weapons.

"There are times when they need to be used," he said. "How much sense does it make to think police should use their guns instead of a nonlethal, incapacitating weapon?"

The concern, Jackson said, is whether they're used properly and whether police have all the information and guidance they need to use them wisely.

"There are a whole lot of people that are contacting us who've had seizures," he said. One person who was shocked multiple times reported having seizures for three months. Another reported going blind in one eye.

Others, including TASER International officials, say long experience has already shown Tasers to be safe. Smith said autopsies listed the Taser as a contributing factor in only 20 of the 167 deaths noted nationwide — and as the cause of death in only one case. And in many of those cases, Smith said, the stress from a violent struggle with police, heart problems, or serious drug abuse also were factors in the deaths.

"Anybody who has suffered any long-lasting or fatal effects after the use of a Taser has all been proven [to have been harmed] by some other input other than just a Taser," said Yoder, the Wichita County chief deputy.

The growing debate over the stun weapons' use hasn't helped TASER International's fortunes, which in recent months have turned downward as rapidly and dramatically as they once rose. TASER stock, which debuted in an initial public offering in 2001 at $13 a share, peaked at close to $148 in 2004 but is now selling for about $6.

The company has other problems as well. Investors and others have filed a series of lawsuits against TASER International, alleging that the company misled the public about its products' safety and the company's financial prospects and that key company officials engaged in a questionable sell-off of TASER stock for personal gain. In documents filed with the Securities and Exchange Commission, the company pledged to "defend these lawsuits vigorously." And investors weren't the only ones going to court. Nationwide, the company faces another 45 lawsuits alleging wrongful death or injuries — including some sustained by law enforcement officers during training, according to a recent filing with the Securities and Exchange Commission.

Smith predicted that the company will prevail in all the litigation. "A lot of people see TASER as a company with a lot of money and expect us to settle, but we're not that kind of company," he said.

Last year, the SEC initiated an inquiry into some of those matters. In December, SEC staffers advised the company that it wouldn't recommend enforcement proceedings on some allegations — but that its inquiry into insider trading has become a formal investigation.

If only real-life experience is going to prove or disprove the Taser's safety in the public's mind, the scale of the experiment is expanding. The company now sells a personal Taser for civilian use.

Texas legislators grappled with the issue of private Tasers last year. Police and human-rights advocates warned them that personal shocking devices were a very bad idea. Sgt. Chris Jones, a 26-year Houston Police Department veteran, testified on behalf of the Combined Law Enforcement Associations of Texas. He was worried that untrained Taser-toters would use them on innocent fellow citizens, police, or themselves.

"They're kind of a finicky device," Sgt. Jones said. "If you don't know what you're doing, you could discharge them accidentally." He classified personal Tasers with "[brass] knuckles, switchblades, or a chemical dispensing device."

Debbie Russell of the ACLU said cops could be in danger because the 2-inch electric dart could penetrate a bullet-proof vest.

The original bill, sponsored by Rep. Elvira Reyna, a Dallas Democrat, put personal Tasers on a list of banned weapons, along with machine guns, explosive weapons, short-barrel firearms, firearm silencers, armor-piercing ammunition, and zip guns.

By the time Gov. Rick Perry signed the final version into law on June 18, however, the legislation only made it illegal to try to take a cop's Taser — but left it legal for Texans to carry them on their own.

Barney Green's family said they languished for months hearing nothing more from officials about his death beyond what they were told the night he died — that he had been taken to the hospital and it "didn't look good." His sister said she's been calling the Harris County Medical Examiner, trying to learn what killed her brother. Until this week, after reporters started making inquiries, all she heard was, "No we don't have anything yet."

On Monday, more than three months after Green died, a staffer in the medical examiner's office told a reporter that Green's death had been ruled an accident due to acute cocaine toxicity. As in many other cases, it is not clear whether the Taser contributed to the death.

Pasadena police officials said they could not answer questions about the case until they received a request under the Texas Public Information Act. (Nothing under state law requires that a records request be filed before officials in a government agency can talk to reporters. The act refers to records, not to interviews.) Even after they received a request, however, they still wouldn't talk.

"I'm afraid the case is still under investigation," said Pasadena police spokesman Vance Mitchell. The department, he said, could release no information "until the case is completely closed."

That's news to Bonnie Tengg, who heard about the findings in her brother's death from a reporter. "I'm a little shocked," she said. "I didn't know the case was open. I didn't know they were still investigating."

In Trevor Goodchild's case, he suffered back pains for months from the Taser shocks he received. But the incident's effect on his life is larger even than that. He's become an anti-Taser activist, working closely with the ACLU.

"Hi, everyone," his song opens. "I'm here representing T.D.M.T.H.B.T. We're "Those Disgruntled Motherfuckers That Have Been Tased." From there on, the lyrics sound more like an Amnesty report told in cadence than a typical lament. "I'm piecing together facts that would get Mother Teresa screaming," he says. And he talks about the Florida woman, "12 weeks pregnant / wouldn't strip naked in jail / So she got jolted / with high voltage." And it goes on (and on): "Piss-poor trained two-year rookies in the field / shocking you mama / because she didn't hear them yell 'Yield.'" Then the chorus: "Disrespecting cops / non-stop / will taser all of y'all . . . we don't need no more damage."

| A.7 | **Public Payroll, Family Affairs** |

OVERVIEW

Looking into the cozy relationships in Chicago. Allison Riggio and Hunter Clauss began looking into nepotism in Chicago's local government while part of a team reporting project taught by Suzanne McBride at Columbia College in Chicago. They continued it after the class ended. In a panel discussion at the IRE national convention in 2008, Riggio and Clauss said they believed that some of the people they interviewed for the story were so forthcoming because they saw them as college students who could cause no harm.

Public Payroll, Family Affairs: Aldermen Keep It Relative

By Allison Riggio and Hunter Clauss, Beachwood Reporter, April 12, 2007 ■
www.beachwoodreporter.com/politics/post_12.php

Four of the 12 Chicago aldermen running in the April 17 runoff employ relatives or other loved ones on their publicly funded ward staffs, costing taxpayers more than $400,000 a year. While laws in other major cities prohibit this practice, Chicago politicians say there's nothing wrong with hiring people they trust and think their relatives deserve the same chance as other applicants.

"That's just something that people always have done," said Ald. Madeline L. Haithcock, who's fighting challenger Bob Fioretti to hang on to her 2nd Ward seat. "Almost everybody has a relative on their staff. I have a daughter and have my husband that is watching my back on the West Side."

Haithcock is not alone, according to a six-month investigation by creatingcommunityconnections. org, and published jointly with The Beachwood Reporter.

Ald. Dorothy J. Tillman, locked in a fierce battle with two-time opponent Pat Dowell, employs her daughter Ebony T. Tillman. Ald. Rey Colón, facing a tough challenge from former Ald. Vilma Colom, hired his fiancée Martha Ramos last year. And Ald. Bernard L. Stone, who faces opponent Naisy Dolar in the 50th Ward, has employed his daughter Ilana Feketitsch for 12 years.

Two other aldermen — Arenda Troutman in the 20th Ward and Emma M. Mitts in the 37th Ward — also employ relatives. Mitts easily won another four-year term in the Feb. 27 election. Troutman lost to Willie B. Cochran, seven weeks after federal officials charged her with bribery in connection with a land deal near her South Side ward. The outgoing alderman, appointed to office by Mayor Richard M. Daley in 1991, pays her sister, Faye E. Troutman, $67,008 a year. Both the alderman and her sister declined to discuss the issue.

Haithcock, who was appointed alderman by Mayor Daley in 1993, said she hired her husband, Gordon E. Haithcock, after he worked 41 years as a manager for the U.S. Postal Service. He's classified as an "assistant to the alderman" in city payroll records and earns $67,008 a year.

Haithcock's daughter, Tanya D. Haithcock, earns $47,388 as a staff assistant. She works with the schools and helps with anything else that needs to be done, the alderman said. Haithcock added, "She doesn't work completely all the time because she has MS."

Combined with the alderman's $98,125 annual salary, the Haithcock family is on track to gross $212,521 in taxpayer money this year. Gordon Haithcock declined to talk about his employment; repeated attempts to reach Tanya Haithcock were unsuccessful.

Fioretti, Haithcock's opponent, says others are capable of working on an alderman's staff. Elected officials putting their relatives on the public payroll creates a "lazy" staff that is "only in it for their own pockets."

"I know when I'm the alderman I'm not going to have family members on my staff," said Fioretti, who won the most number of votes in the Feb. 27

election — 28 percent compared to the alderman's 21 percent.

Other aldermen offer no apologies for hiring their loved ones.

"So I'm guilty of nepotism, how about that?" said Stone, one of the longest-serving aldermen on the 50-member Chicago City Council.

His opponent, however, doesn't view this hiring practice in the same way. Dolar says an alderman's personal staff should be regulated like any other city office, where government workers and elected officials are banned from hiring their family members. Since the mid-1980s, the city's ethics ordinance has prohibited aldermen from employing relatives on their committee staffs, but no such ban exists for their ward offices.

"It is the alderman's responsibility that we hire the most qualified people and reflect the diversity of the neighborhood," Dolar said.

Stone employs his daughter, Ilana Feketitsch, as his chief of staff. Feketitsch said her 12 years of working for her father, who's been in office since 1973, makes her qualified for the position, which earns her $63,804 annually.

Tillman, who was appointed 3rd Ward alderman by then-Mayor Harold Washington in 1983, employs her daughter Ebony at a yearly rate of $52,320. Ebony Tillman, listed as an "assistant to the alderman" in city payroll records, did not respond to repeated requests for interviews, and her mother, Ald. Tillman, declined to discuss the matter.

This is not the first time the alderman has been in the news for hiring family members. The Lakefront Outlook, a weekly newspaper on the South Side, reported last year that Tillman was involved with patronage dealings involving the non-profit Harold Washington Cultural Center. The paper reported that another daughter, Jimalita Tillman, works as executive director of the organization that manages the cultural center, while son Bemaji serves on the group's board of directors.

Dowell, Tillman's runoff opponent, pledges not to hire any of her relatives if elected. She calls the practice "inappropriate" and, along with Ald.-elect Sandi Jackson in the 7th Ward, has signed an ethics statement Dowell said could reduce the hiring of relatives.

Over on the West Side in the 35th Ward, Ald. Colón pays his fiancée, Martha Ramos, $73,968 to be his chief of staff. Before being elected four years ago, Colón believed hiring relatives created a "layer of unprofessionalism," but now that he's an alderman Colón said he needs a staff he can trust.

"First, I was outside throwing stones; now I'm inside the house," he said.

Challenger Colom, who held the seat from 1995 to 2003, thinks anyone living with an alderman — including domestic partners and children — should not be hired. Colom said she once employed her former sister-in-law on her ward staff.

"I feel that there are many people in the community and outside of the community that have the skills and talents necessary to accomplish the goals of an alderman's office," Colom said. "If they work for the city, I don't have a problem with that, but to work in the alderman's office . . . (that) just doesn't sit well with people."

She's not the only one uncomfortable about aldermen hiring their relatives.

"I've never employed anybody in my family in my staff nor do I intend on doing that," said Ald. Toni Preckwinkle of the 4th Ward.

Ald. Ariel E. Reboyras of the 30th Ward says he doesn't hire his relatives because he believes it would raise questions with his constituents.

"It's very much frowned upon," Reboyras said. "If you want to be a one-termer, sure, go ahead. But you shouldn't do it because it is the taxpayers' money."

It's up to voters whether the practice continues, said Ald. Joe Moore of the 49th Ward. He thinks if voters are satisfied with the services they receive from their alderman, then they may look the other way.

"It should be left to the voters to decide whether that's the best use of their tax dollars," he said.

That doesn't sit well with public watchdog groups and some political scientists. They warn such hiring practices cause voters to become disillusioned, leading them to stop trusting officials and participating in their government.

"Nepotism causes people to be alienated from the political process," said Dick Simpson, a political science professor at the University of Illinois at Chicago and an alderman from 1971 to 1979.

Jay Stewart, executive director of the Better Government Association, agrees but notes, "It may be stinky, lousy, but not illegal. If it's not illegal, [the aldermen] will do it."

"These positions should be posted," Stewart said. "They should be held for 'x' amount of time and available before (they're) just given out to a family member."

But ideally, aldermen should ban themselves from hiring relatives, Stewart says.

That's not how Ald. Richard F. Mell sees it. Mell, who chairs the Chicago City Council's Committee on Committees, Rules and Ethics, which monitors the behavior of the aldermen, says he doesn't employ any relatives on his ward staff. But he believes each of the 50 council members should be able to decide whether to hire family members.

"If they do it, they obviously raise the question of 'Are there other people who are in fact more deserving?'" said the 33rd Ward alderman. "Some people believe that because an alderman's staff is so integral to their lives that sometimes a relative would work harder than some other people."

Cindi Canary, director of the Illinois Campaign for Political Reform, believes the hiring process should be more transparent, with qualifications being emphasized over personal connections.

"It's ultimately a question of appearances," she said. "Even though I'm sure there are circumstances or exceptions to rules . . . it always needs to be made public."

In the private sector, hiring family members can be viewed as a conflict of interest, said Dow Scott, a professor at Loyola University Chicago's Graduate School of Business.

"The whole family connection can be real problematic and an issue that firms, even family-owned firms, put a lot of thought into," Scott said. "How can you keep talented people [on staff if they] know that son or daughter is going to be the president or vice president and people don't really have the same opportunities they might at a firm that didn't have a family leadership?"

Many companies have rules that prohibit family members from working in positions where one would report directly to the other, he added. "It's just not seen as good business."

Defenders of this practice, however, say it can work out well for taxpayers because family members feel pressure to do their jobs better.

"I think I worked harder than the other people just because that was my father and he wanted to make sure that I knew everything that was going on with this job," said Ald. Darcel A. Beavers of the 7th Ward. "And that [way], people couldn't say anything — because I was qualified for this job."

Beavers, the daughter of Cook County Commissioner William Beavers, started her political career 22 years ago working in her father's 7th Ward office. When William Beavers left his aldermanic post late last year, Mayor Daley selected Darcel Beavers to succeed him. She lost that post in the Feb. 27 municipal elections to Sandi Jackson, who will take over in May.

"I think people who talk about nepotism should look in the mirror and see if they've benefited from nepotism before they start talking," Darcel Beavers said.

There's no question, the outgoing alderman says, that she's qualified given her more than two decades of experience.

Bettye R. Pulphus feels the same way. Since 2003, Pulphus, who earns $63,804, has worked as an "assistant to the alderman" in her sister's West Side ward office. Why is she qualified? She points to her master's degree in social services from the University of Chicago and her 20 years of work as a block club president and precinct captain.

"People would rather look at the negatives rather than the positives," said Pulphus, who's planning to leave Ald. Mitts' office and has applied for civil service jobs with the city of Chicago and state of Illinois. "Rather than looking at it being challenging to work for a relative, they look at it as 'You've got it good.'"

In fact, Pulphus believes she's being penalized for having worked for her sister, saying it's taking her longer than expected to land another government job.

Ramos, Ald. Colón's chief of staff and fiancée, said her years of working for the Chicago Park District, where she met Colón, helped prepare her for her current job. Ramos said she was hired during a time when Colón needed a top deputy he didn't have to spend a lot of time training.

"You have a good day if you get home by 10 o'clock at night," Ramos said. "I came into the picture because I could just come in and start without skipping a heartbeat."

Paul Green, a professor of political science at Roosevelt University, has no problem with aldermen hiring their relatives as long as a person's qualifications are considered in the decision. Like Ald. Darcel Beavers, Green believes that relatives may be held to an even higher standard.

"They should not be discounted simply because they have the same last name," Green said.

"It's the quality of the person being appointed, not anything else that should be the key factor."

Adam Bellow, author of *In Praise of Nepotism: A Natural History,* said the practice of public officials hiring their relatives is nothing new to politics and is deeply rooted in American history.

"Just like with any other profession in which people are born into, politics has the same character," said Bellow, the son of Saul Bellow, in an interview. "What goes on in Chicago is nothing new or special. It's just that elsewhere it's been driven underground."

The fact that something has been going on for so long doesn't make it right, said Judy Nadler, former mayor of Santa Clara, Calif., and senior fellow in government ethics at Santa Clara University.

"Just because something has been done for a long time, or there's a history of it, it doesn't mean that it's a good practice," Nadler said. "When people bring that up to me as an excuse, I like to say 'Well, we try not to repeat our mistakes.'"

Jonathan Binder, James Jaworski, Rosalie Marquez, Jessica Pearce and Lisa Pietrzak contributed to this investigation.

A.8   Trustees Share the Wealth

OVERVIEW

How politically connected is your college? In 2008, University of North Carolina student Brendan Brown wondered about the political connections of the members of the university's board of trustees. He examined campaign finance records for national elections and found the answer: Very. Together, the dozen members had given more than $450,000 in national contests over the past decade.

Trustees Share the Wealth

UNC leaders give often, generously

By Brendan Brown, The Daily Tar Heel, April 8, 2008

The most politically active group on campus, by far, is the Board of Trustees.

In the last decade the board's current 12 members have given $483,500 to federal candidates, political parties and political action committees, not to mention thousands more in state-level contributions.

With this year's high-profile races for governor, senator and president, the trustees are sure to be heavily tapped for fundraising.

"I feel like somebody's calling me every day," Paul Fulton, a trustee and former CEO of Bassett Furniture Industries, said about requests for campaign contributions.

But whom the trustees support is determined less by political ideology than by personal relationships with candidates and their fundraisers.

Fulton, a self-described "lifelong Republican," gave $1,000 to Barack Obama because he said he was asked by fellow trustee Karol Mason, an Obama fundraiser.

Nine of the 12 trustees have contributed to Obama's campaign, a total of $18,500 dollars to date.

"People I respected and have done things for me" have asked for money, Fulton said. "Now, what am I going to do?"

Even giving to opposing sides in the same race is not unusual.

Fulton said he has given to both incumbent U.S. Sen. Elizabeth Dole, R-N.C., and N.C. Sen. Kay Hagan, D-Guilford, who is looking to take Dole's place.

"Kay has been such a great friend to the University."

But friendship is not the only reason trustees pay into federal-level campaigns.

Leroy Towns, a UNC political journalism professor, said it was "natural" for trustees to give to federal candidates.

"Federal legislation and appropriations have a huge impact on the University," he said.

UNC got $446 million in federal research money in fiscal year 2007.

"All of us are really interested in positioning the University the best we can," Fulton said.

Other than the trustees, few campus administrators regularly give to campaigns.

Dr. Bill Roper, CEO of UNC Health Care and dean of the School of Medicine, has given $46,600 to federal candidates and committees in the last decade. A few other administrators have given small amounts of money, but nothing on the scale of Roper and the trustees.

The trustees have contributed largely to N.C. candidates and federal committees of both parties. By far the greatest beneficiary has been UNC-system President Erskine Bowles.

Eight of 12 current trustees gave a total $150,500 to Bowles and his political action committee, N.C. Victory Fund, when he ran for U.S. senate in 2002 and 2004. More than three quarters of that money came from trustees Fulton, Russell Carter and Nelson Schwab.

Bowles lost both races, first to Dole then to Sen. Richard Burr, R-N.C., before becoming system president in 2006.

Generosity from the trustees often catches the eye of state political leaders, putting trustees in position for appointments to more prominent roles, such as a spot on the UNC-system Board of Governors, said Thad Beyle, a University political science professor.

"There's people who pay attention to the (campaign finance) reports."

But Mason, who declined to discuss further her role in Obama's campaign, insisted that giving money to federal campaigns was not for political gain.

"It's a personal decision."

DHS Reports Didn't Save 30 Children

By Ziva Branstetter, Tulsa World, Dec. 18, 2005

At least 30 children have died from abuse and neglect in Oklahoma in recent years, despite the fact that the state had previous reports they were being abused or neglected or had requests to check on them, an investigation by the Tulsa World has found.

In most cases, the Department of Human Services closed reports of abuse or neglect involving the children who later died, finding the reports unconfirmed.

In at least five cases, DHS closed investigations because the agency could not find the child. In eight, it had an open investigation when the child died.

In one case, DHS failed to check on a boy who moved from California, despite a request from officials there. The boy died within six months of arriving in Oklahoma, a case DHS acknowledges was "out of policy."

Tammy Taylor, the mother of a 2-year-old Tulsa boy scalded to death in June, believes her son fell through the gaps in the state's child welfare system.

In the weeks before Keenan Taylor's scalding death, DHS received three reports the toddler was being abused. Two were pending at the time of the 2-year-old's death, records show.

The boy died June 9, the day after being burned by hot water over more than 50 percent of his body. His father, Carlis Ball, did not seek medical treatment for Keenan until about 20 hours after the injury, reports show. Ball, who is charged with first-degree murder in the child's death, told police it was an accident, but police and doctors said there is evidence the scalding was intentional.

"It took something like this to happen to get everybody's attention that children are being abused. Some are even dying, and they are dying at the hands of their parents," Taylor said.

But DHS officials said, despite the state's best efforts, some children will die from abuse and neglect even though the state has reports they are being abused.

"Unless we live with these children 24 hours a day, there is no way we can truly protect a child," said Esther Rider-Salem, child protective services programs manager for DHS.

Rider-Salem said a DHS committee reviews all cases in which children die from abuse and neglect to determine whether the agency followed its policies and state law. The agency also moves quickly to protect any surviving siblings, she said.

Last fiscal year, 51 Oklahoma children died from abuse and neglect, the highest number in more than a decade. The number of children in foster care also soared to a record high, hitting 7,500 in October.

In a six-month investigation, the World reviewed medical examiners' reports, death certificates, court records and other public records to identify children who have died from abuse and neglect since July 1, 1999. State law allows DHS to release summaries of its prior contacts with a family if a primary caretaker is charged.

Of the 72 cases, DHS had prior reports of abuse, neglect or contact involving 26 children, the World found. DHS also released records showing the agency had prior contact with four more children whose deaths were reported in 2005.

The documents show that among the 30 cases, DHS received a total of 77 reports the children or their siblings were being abused or neglected. Some cases had as many as seven prior reports of abuse or neglect in the household while others received only a single report. In every case, the children were allowed to remain in the home and ultimately died from abuse or neglect.

'They didn't do anything'

About a year before Sheilla Shea confessed to police that she stabbed her 6-year-old son to death,

DHS received two reports alleging problems in the Shea household.

One report did not meet the criteria for investigation. The other case was closed after Patric and his siblings were not found to be in any immediate danger and their mother was referred to counseling services.

Shea's sister-in-law, Martha Quinton Shea, said she filed one of those reports as Sheilla Shea's mental health and the condition of the family's Tulsa home deteriorated. DHS workers interviewed Patric and Sheilla Shea at their home on June 6, 2004, and the home had been repaired, a report says.

Martha Shea said she did not call DHS again "because they didn't do anything the first time."

Patric Shea's siblings watched as their mother jumped on him and repeatedly stabbed him July 2. Sheilla Shea is being held on a charge of first-degree murder.

"After Patric's death, DHS told me that by law that they could not do anything until he is physically hurt. Now he is not hurt; he is dead," Martha Shea said.

In another case, an Enid victim's father said he had no idea an abuser was living in his own household, even though DHS was aware the woman had a history of prior complaints involving other children.

"If I had any clue she was abusive to her own children, I wouldn't let her around my child," Leroy Buffum said of his girlfriend.

DHS workers visited Buffum's home in July 2002 after receiving a complaint his girlfriend, Kathy M. Taylor, had abused his daughter, Karen Bell, 3.

The complaint could not be verified, but Buffum said DHS should have told him then the agency had four previous complaints Taylor had neglected her own children before the two started dating.

DHS confirmed one of those reports as neglect, a 1998 case involving Taylor's children living in inadequate and dangerous conditions. Taylor pleaded no contest to first-degree murder in Karen's 2003 death and received a life without parole sentence.

Buffum said he still regularly visits his daughter's gravesite, sometimes reading a book aloud.

"I'll talk to my daughter whenever things get stressful to me," Buffum said. "It helps me keep my sanity."

Rider-Salem said state law prevents DHS workers from telling others in the household about prior reports of abuse.

"We can only share with someone else what is public record, but if we do have concerns, we can get with the person who is the original abuser and say, 'You need to talk with this individual about what has gone on previously.'"

She couldn't save her

Robyn Brooks knew her granddaughter was in danger, but she said despite her pleas for help, she couldn't save her. Skyla Brooks, a 21-month-old from Bristow, died March 21, 2000, from head injuries caused by violent shaking or blunt force.

Evidence showed Skyla had knuckle marks on her forehead and 16 bruises beneath the scalp.

Kurt Vomberg Jr., the mother's boyfriend, pleaded no contest to second-degree murder and child abuse and received a 35-year prison term last year. Tammy Renee Brooks, the child's mother, received a 20-year sentence for child neglect.

Robyn Brooks, the paternal grandmother of Skyla Brooks, said Skyla was alert and playful on Feb. 16, 2000, the last time she saw the child. Brooks said she urged DHS to intervene before it was too late.

"I do not think DHS was involved as much as they could have been, but I also believe DHS workers have too heavy of a load," Brooks said. "Grandparents also do not have enough say-so. Those two things worked against Skyla and cost her her life."

'Underfunded, undermanned'

Tulsa Police Chief Dave Been said that he believes DHS Director Howard Hendrick "has done as much as anyone can do" with the agency.

"The problem is that it is such a huge, unwieldy state organization. It is tough. It is underfunded, undermanned. The case loads are too heavy."

Those in the child abuse prevention field agree it's unfair to place full responsibility on the state to protect children in jeopardy.

"We have a system that is reactive, not proactive, because we don't know what will happen," said Barbara Findeiss, executive director of the Child Abuse Network. Findeiss said DHS workers are not alone in making decisions. Every county is represented by a multidisciplinary team, made up of every agency investigating child abuse and neglect in that area.

Parent Child Center Executive Director Claudette Selph said DHS has been hampered by low salaries for workers, resulting in high turnover and inexperienced staff.

"It's not that we're putting resources in the wrong places; it's that we are not putting enough resources in place," Selph said.

DHS child welfare workers have an average of 15 to 20 cases each, almost twice the level recommended by the Child Welfare League of America, said DHS spokesman George Johnson. The agency has asked lawmakers for 112 additional child welfare workers next fiscal year, at a cost of $4.1 million.

The Game Plan Checklist

1. Develop the premise

■ Start with a question that can't be answered without significant reporting.

2. Gather the data

■ Gather data about the problem from media, government, academic, corporate or nonprofit organizations.

■ Interview people involved in and knowledgeable about the problem.

■ Ask yourself:

    a. What was my story to begin with and is it still the story?

    b. If my story has changed, is it because I disproved your premise?

    c. Do I need to now alter it?

    d. In order to prove it, what do I still need to find out?

    e. Who has that information and how can I reach them?

Is your story doable? Ask yourself:

1. What key pieces of information will I need, where can I get them, how difficult will they be to obtain and how long will that take?

2. Will I have access to the people essential to the story?

3. Will I need to travel far to get information?

4. Does my story depend on granting anonymity, and will that affect whether I can get the story published?

5. Do I have the nerve to ask difficult questions?

6. If my story depends on poring through reports, do I have the time and patience to do that?

7. Will I be able to analyze the data?

8. Will the story depend on someone giving me secret information?

9. Will my editors give me the space necessary to tell the story?

10. Will I have to spend time with people in a setting that makes me uncomfortable?

Set parameters. Ask yourself:

1. What is the most I want to accomplish?
2. What is the least I want to accomplish?

3. Analyze the information

- Reread and examine all of the information you've gathered.
- Draw a conclusion from the information you've gathered.
- Decide whether your hypothesis is correct or incorrect.
- Explain the cause or causes of the problem, its ramifications and possible solutions.

4. Outline the story

- Identify the major points.
- Organize the points in order of importance.
- Decide on your lead and ending.
- Find the thread that connects all your major points.

Plan out possible multimedia elements:

- An overview
- A glossary
- A case study
- Flash illustration
- Profiles
- Q&As
- Man on the street
- Information maps
- Timelines
- Information layers
- Concentric circles
- Video or slide show journey
- How-to guide
- "Where to get help" box
- Games
- Tables, charts or lists

5. Draft the story

- The first draft should be an attempt to make the story as complete as possible.
- The second draft should concentrate on clarity.
- The third draft should be a check to see if the case you are making is fully supported.
- The final draft should hone the story into a compelling read.

6. Verify the information

- Question everything.
- Run conclusions by experts and sources.
- Check every single one of your facts.

7. Publish the story

- Stop when:
    a. You have answered your central question; *and*
    b. You can present sufficient evidence to prove convincingly your conclusion; *and*
    c. You know that any more information you gather will only further prove the same point or take you in a new direction.

An Excel Cheat Sheet

GETTING STARTED

O pen up an Excel document and save it with a clear, descriptive title. Now you are ready to take a tour of the spreadsheet. Excel spreadsheets are divided into columns and rows that form a grid. Old versions of Microsoft Excel had a limit of up to 256 columns and 16,384 rows on each grid, called a worksheet. But versions from 2007 and later can handle 16,000 columns and 1 million rows. That's probably more than you will ever need, unless you wanted to know everything about every person living in the city of San Jose, Calif. If that's the case, you probably need a shrink more than you do a more powerful version of Excel.

Each block in a column or row is called a cell and has its own address: A1, B2, C3, etc. Cells can contain numbers or text.

The bar at the top of the screen is split into two sections. It is called the Formula Bar. The right side is where you enter a formula or where you can edit the contents of an individual cell. When you need to do any kind of calculation or data analysis in Excel you do it with a formula and you write that formula in any cell on the spreadsheet. Regardless of the cell you write it in, as you write it or whenever you click on it, you will see it in the Formula Bar. All formulas begin with the equal sign. Next to the equal sign is the type of calculation you want Excel to do for you: SUM, AVERAGE, MEDIAN, MODE, etc. Although the bar is called the Formula Bar, the formula itself is called a FUNCTION. You need to know that, because Excel can do so many different types of calculations (functions), you won't be able to keep track of them all. You don't have to. If you click on any cell, you can go up to the INSERT menu at the top of the screen and click on FUNCTION. That will not only give you a drop down list of every possible calculation Excel can do, but if you click on any one of them, it will give you a brief description of how it works.

FUNCTIONS AND COMMANDS

T he great thing about Excel is that once you learn to navigate, it will teach you as you go. Whenever you can't figure it out, you can go to the help menu and ask it questions. It is important to remember that when doing calculations you add, subtract, divide and multiply cell addresses or the names you give cell addresses. Don't plug the contents of a cell into the Formula Bar. By calculating by cell address rather than contents, you can change the contents of cells without having to rewrite the formulas. That means that you can tinker with your data.

Say you write up a monthly budget for yourself based on what you earn. You might want to see how much more you'd have to spend if you received a 10 percent raise or 15 percent, or 12 percent. You can keep changing the contents of the box that holds the salary figure and see how it will change the rest of the budget. Excel will recalculate as long as you used the cell addresses for your formula rather than actual numbers.

If you have a hard time thinking in terms of A2 or A5 or EE7 you can rename a cell or a group of cells. A group of cells is called a range. You do this in the left section of the Formula Bar. The window in it identifies whatever active cell you happen to be working in or a group of cells you highlighted. Once you have a cell or a range of cells identified in the Formula Bar you can type in a name for it. Here is what I mean: Suppose you just got arrested for civil disobedience and you have to come up with money for a lawyer fast. You call all your friends and find out how much each can give you. Then you do the same for your extended family. Then you do the same for all your co-workers. So you have three columns: "Friends," "Family," and "Co-workers." If you highlight the cells in the "Friends" column and go up to the first section of the Formula Bar, you can name this group of cells "Friends." Then any time you want to work with the data in that column you can calculate using the name rather than cell addresses:

=SUM (Friends)

or

=AVERAGE (Friends)

Then you do the same for your "Family" and "Co-workers" columns, each time highlighting the cells in the column, going up to the formula bar and plugging in a name for the cell range. Then you calculate how much you could raise:

=SUM (Friends+Family+Coworkers)

This is helpful when you need to keep track of different calculations involving different criteria. You can do the same thing with information in rows.

AutoSum

Excel uses the Greek letter $\sum$, or sigma, to designate a one-button function that will automatically add up a continuous column or row of numbers. It is extremely useful when you have a long column of big numbers to add. As long as there is not a blank cell in the line, the AUTOSUM function will work. You simply go to the first blank cell, either at the bottom of a column or the end of a row and hit the $\sum$ button, which is located at the top and center of the screen. When you do that, Excel will add all the numbers up the column *until* it hits a blank cell, or to the right along a row *until* it hits a blank cell. You can combine the AUTOSUM function with the Fill Handle. Say you have 50 rows and 50 columns and you want to total each of them. Just hit the blank cell at the bottom of the first column you want to total and hit AUTOSUM. Then using the Fill Handle, drag it across the row and it will automatically total the 49 other columns. Go up to first blank cell at the end of the first row you want to total and hit AUTOSUM. Click on the Fill Handle and drag it down the column, and it will automatically total every row.

Count

If you tell Excel =COUNT and then put a range of cells between the parentheses, it will count every cell in which a number is entered. Here's how it could be useful. Let's say you have a big table. Each column is a separate day in the year. There are 365 columns. Every row is an employee of a lobbying firm. Each cell contains the amount of money the employee charged to the company account for a lunch with a politician. Many of the cells are blank because on those days the employee was off or didn't take anyone out to lunch. You don't care so much how much those lunches cost, you are just interested in how many times the firm took politicians out to lunch. Excel can tell you. You find an empty cell and write =COUNT (beginning cell number:ending cell number).

Max, Min

Let's say you were interested in how much those lunches cost. Excel can zero in on the highest priced lunch or the lowest with the MAX or MIN function. You write it just like you do the COUNT function: =MAX(range) or = MIN(range). Or back to the example where you needed to raise cash to hire a lawyer, after you get out of jail you might want to take out to dinner the friend who gave you the most money, but you can't remember who that was. You tell Excel =MAX (Friends), and it will tell you. You can also find your cheapest friend that way, as well.

Countif

Better yet, Excel will count according to a criterion that you establish. If you go to INSERT and then FUNCTION and choose COUNTIF, Excel will guide you in writing the correct formula. You just have to designate the range of rows and columns where the information resides and what criteria you want. Exhibit C.1 is a snapshot of an Excel chart of crimes involving guns in New York State.

A politician insists that firearms-related crimes always amount to 9 percent of all violent crimes, and you want to find out how wrong he is. So you want to count the number of years the percentage does not equal 9. You put in =COUNTIF(D6:D20<>9). Doing formulas by complicated criteria takes some thinking, but if Excel sees you having problems constructing your formula, it offers you help with a Formula Builder.

Chart of gun crime statistics for New York.   **EXHIBIT C.1**

	2006firearmstatisticsatt5.xls				
Sheets	Charts	SmartArt Graphics	WordArt		
A	C	D	E	F	
Attachment 5					
Calendar Year 2006 Firearm Related Statistics					
Jurisdiction	Total Reported Violent Crime By Firearm	Firearm Related as a % of Total Violent Crime	GGUN Submissions (Via NYSPIN)	Stolen Gun Submissions (Via NYSPIN)	
Albany City PD	182	15.0%	93	5	
Binghamton City PD	20	9.7%	18	6	
Buffalo City PD	1,316	33.3%	592	104	
Jamestown City PD	21	12.4%	5	10	
Kingston City PD	8	9.0%	7	6	
Mount Vernon City PD	151	21.0%	35	3	
Nassau County PD	305	16.8%	307	99	
Newburgh City PD	34	8.8%	30	2	

Sumproduct

Not all data comes to you in one easy to sort data table. Perhaps you want to find out how many speeding tickets your local police issue each year. You request the data. It comes on one sheet but spread out over 100 tables, one for each officer. Each table has 12 columns, one for each month and five different rows, designating different types of vehicles ticketed. It is going to be tedious and time-consuming task to sum up every table. You go to a blank cell and type in the SUMPRODUCT formula. Between the parentheses that follow you plug in the different cell ranges for each table, each separated by a comma. Excel will give you back the total for all the columns in all the tables. If you first name the ranges in each table by the officer's name, the formula will look like something like this:

```
=SUMPRODUCT(smith,jones,oleary,mcnab,harris,lopez,chang,goldfarb,)
```

Parsing names

You might get a long Excel table of full names sorted by first name, and you need to sort by last name (there seem to be an awful lot of Johns, Barbaras, Julios and Marissas). You need to parse out the first and last name. To do that manually will be tedious and take forever. To do it with Excel will take about five steps, but if you do it for the first name, Fill Handle will copy it for the rest. Let's say the name John Smith is in cell A2. You insert four columns next to the A column.

1. In cell B2, you type =FIND (" ","A2") with a space in between the first two quote marks. Excel tells me the answer is 5 because space was in the fifth spot in the string John Smith. I copy that formula down the column.

2. Now in cell C2, you type in =LEN (A2). This tells Excel to count the number of letters in John Smith. It gives you the number 10. You copy that formula down the C column.

3. In cell D2, you type in =Right (A2,C2-B2). This tells Excel to print all the letters to the right side of the text in cell A2 starting with the fifth letter (10-5). It gives you Smith. You copy that formula down the D column.

4. Finally in cell E2, you type in =left(A2,B2). This tells Excel to give you the five letters to the left side of John Smith. It gives you John. You copy that formula down the E column.

5. Now highlight columns D and E (the last names and first names), copy it, hit PASTE SPECIAL and VALUES. That takes away the formulas and now you can delete the first three columns, leaving only the columns with the last name and the first name. Pull each of the formulas down each column using Fill Handle. When you've got a list of 100 names or more, this will save you an enormous amount of time and frustration.

Dates

Excel can add and subtract dates just as it does numbers. That means that if you subtract one date from another it will tell you the difference in days. Just make sure that the cell that holds the answer is formatted to show the answer as a number, not a date. Excel can also calculate the difference in years or months by using this formula: =DATEDIF(earlydate,olderdate,"interval") with interval being either the letter y if you want the answer to be the number of years difference, or m if you want the answer to be in months. It is handy if you have a long list of employees and their start dates, and you want to figure out the number of years they each worked.

Random numbers

Government agencies and university administrations often tell reporters that they aren't entitled to information because of privacy concerns. If they simply deleted the column with the names, it would make the data meaningless. But Excel can easily replace all the names with randomly generated identification numbers. The function works like this: =RAND(cellrange). Type that in the first box of a column, drag Fill Handle down the column and, there it is — a column of unique randomly generated numbers.

Sort

A function called AUTOFILTER under the DATA menu will give you up and down arrows on each header. If you click on these arrows, it will give you the options of sorting by ascending or descending value or by pulling the top ten values. Or, you can create your own custom filter. By doing this you can tell Excel to give you a list that includes or does not include data by criteria you establish: Equals, is greater than..., is less than..., contains..., does not contain..., ends with..., begins with... Again, this becomes very useful when trying to find individuals in a long list or the few people in a large workforce that make a certain salary range. Under the FILTER menu there is an option for ADVANCED FILTER. That allows you to designate a particular section of your worksheet you want sorted and to export it onto another worksheet.

IMPORTING AND VIEWING DATA

Most of the data you find on the Internet was inputted with Excel. Often when government agencies put data on the Web, they provide a button that allows you to download the information into an Excel chart, already formatted. If they don't there is a good chance you can simply highlight the data and copy and paste it into Excel. If that doesn't work, Excel can configure the data for you in some cases. To do this, highlight the data in a table and paste it into a word document. Save that document in HTML format. Open a blank Excel worksheet and click on the Import button if your version has one or you'll find the IMPORT function under the FILE menu. It will ask you what format your data is in: CSV, meaning that the fields (or the information that will be put into different columns) are separated by commas; FileMaker Pro (if you have a Mac) or Microsoft Access (if you have a PC; HTML; or text. If your document is in an ASCII or text format, Excel will lump all the information into one column unless the fields are separated by spaces or tabs. If that happens, you can parse it. It is much easier if you simply save it as an HTML file. Once you tell Excel what format it is in, it will take you threw a few more steps and, voilà — there it is on your spreadsheet nicely separated into columns.

Keeping values constant

When you download an Excel spreadsheet it's a good idea to examine how the agency did its calculations. Some of the formulas might be written this way: =C2/C10. The dollar signs indicate that the person who entered the information wanted Excel to keep the second value constant even as Fill Handle copied the formula down a column or across a row or to some other section of the worksheet. You might want to keep a value constant, for example, if you were calculating the percentage of a total population or calculating per capita. Anytime you want to copy a formula but keep part of it constant, put a $ in front of both the row and column designations in a cell address.

Freeze panes

Excel allows you to keep your row and column constant while scrolling down or across rows and columns that won't all fit on a computer screen. That's helpful when you are trying to look up and compare information without having to copy, move and paste columns or rows around. To do that, you simply go to the cell that's one row down and one column to the right of the column and row you want frozen. Then you go up to the WINDOW menu and select FREEZE PANES. Once you do that, you can scroll around your worksheet, but the row and column you picked will stay in place.

Split panes

You can also scroll through different sections of a very large spreadsheet at the same time by going up to the WINDOW menu and choosing SPLIT. It will break up the spreadsheet into four quadrants — actually it will create four copies of the same spreadsheet. If you bounce between the quadrants, you can scroll through each of them. Anytime you make changes to one quadrant Excel will automatically make the change to the other four copies.

Transpose

The table you download might list rows of crimes and each column is a different year. It might be easier to analyze if it were the other way around — the years as rows and the crimes as columns. To do that highlight the columns and rows you want in the table, move to a blank worksheet, go up to the EDIT menu, choose PASTE SPECIAL, then look for the Transpose button and click it. The spreadsheet should appear with the former row headings on top and the former column headings on the side.

Protect

This function is overlooked but very important, particularly if you are going to experiment with different ways of sorting your data or if you share your spreadsheets among members of a group. Make sure you keep a master copy of your spreadsheet. Under the TOOLS menu is the PROTECTION command. That will let you choose whether to protect just the one spreadsheet or every spreadsheet in that workbook. Once protected, the SORT commands disappear. To sort the data, copy the rows and columns you want and paste them into a blank spreadsheet. You will thank yourself after you have entered data haphazardly. You could sort some rows and not others by mistake or change all the formulas to values and then forget how you came up with those values. You can always unprotect a sheet or workbook, but it is easy and much better for your psyche if you protect your master sheet and keep it protected; do all your analyzing on copies.